Politics, Religion and the Song of Songs in
Seventeenth-Century England

Also by Elizabeth Clarke

THEORY AND THEOLOGY IN GEORGE HERBERT'S POETRY
'THIS DOUBLE VOICE': Gendered Writing in Early Modern England (co-edited with Danielle Clarke)

Politics, Religion and the Song of Songs in Seventeenth-Century England

By

Elizabeth Clarke
Reader in English, University of Warwick, UK

First published 2011 by
PALGRAVE MACMILLAN

Palgrave Macmillan in the UK is an imprint of Macmillan Publishers Limited, registered in England, company number 785998, of Houndmills, Basingstoke, Hampshire RG21 6XS.

Palgrave Macmillan in the US is a division of St Martin's Press LLC, 175 Fifth Avenue, New York, NY 10010.

Palgrave Macmillan is the global academic imprint of the above companies and has companies and representatives throughout the world.

Palgrave® and Macmillan® are registered trademarks in the United States, the United Kingdom, Europe and other countries.

ISBN 978–0–333–71411–9   hardback

This book is printed on paper suitable for recycling and made from fully managed and sustained forest sources. Logging, pulping and manufacturing processes are expected to conform to the environmental regulations of the country of origin.

A catalogue record for this book is available from the British Library.

A catalog record for this book is available from the Library of Congress.

10   9   8   7   6   5   4   3   2   1
20 19 18 17 16 15 14 13 12 11

Printed and bound in Great Britain by
CPI Antony Rowe, Chippenham and Eastbourne

Contents

Acknowledgements

Many thanks to the Leverhulme Trust for funding the year's research which effectively got this book started, and Thomas Docherty, Head of Department at the University of Warwick, for the term's leave without which I would never have finished it. It has taken me a long time to write this book. I am grateful for the patience of various editors at Palgrave Macmillan, and to Elisabeth Jay who originally signed me up. Conditions for this kind of authorship are significantly better now than they were when I started. The existence of electronic resources such as Early English Books Online and the new Dictionary of National Biography have transformed my life. Magisterial studies have come out recently without which this book would not have been based on such thorough scholarship.

Slowing the book up but making it much richer has been the Perdita Project and I owe so much to all those who have worked on it. Victoria Burke pointed me to a particularly interesting Scottish woman's manuscript. Sarah Ross found me another one. I owe so much to librarians: Arnold Hunt at the British Library, the unfailingly patient Bodleian librarians in Duke Humfrey, Sue Mills at the Angus Library, Regent's Park College, and David Wykes at the Dr.Williams's Library. I acknowledge the permission of the Trustees of Dr Williams's Library to publish the poem from the diary of Ollive Cooper on pp. 50–1.

As the many references to her book will demonstrate, I owe a great deal to the publications of and personal contact with Sharon Achinstein. David Norbrook and Nigel Smith have been constant encouragers and I have learned so much from them about early modern religion and politics. I am glad to have become acquainted with Tom Schwanda this year and talked about the Song of Songs with him. Sarah Poynting has helped to answer all my stupid questions. Many colleagues have read chapters of this book and commented on it for me: Lynn Robson, Jayne Archer, George Southcombe, Gillian Wright, Roger Pooley, Margaret Ezell, Elizabeth Hageman. I have given seminar papers from the material for this book at Oxford, Durham, Sussex, the London Renaissance Seminar and the American Cathedral in Paris, and am grateful for the opportunity to share research and feedback. Thanks to my postgraduate students at Warwick, Michelle DiMeo, Alice Eardley and Kate Evans in particular, who provided me with references, ideas, proofreading and much else. Thanks too to Marie-Louise Coolahan, now teaching at the University of Galway, who probably has no idea of the part she played in this book's genesis.

Thanks to my husband Matthew who has stepped in to help with numerous computer emergencies and who has printed this book out several times. I somehow seem to have acquired two beautiful daughters along the way and I want to thank Emily and Lucy for being the light of my life – and also for putting up with their mother's absence, either physically or in spirit, for some of the last few years.

Notes on reference to the text

I have throughout referred to this Biblical book as the Song of Songs, rather than the *Song of Songs* which implies that I am talking about a specific published text, or The Song of Solomon (since the text is far too late to be authored by Solomon, who was born c.1000 BC, and this designation ignores the dominant female voice in the text). When I use this designation I mean the Biblical text as transmitted through the ancient versions and as translated into English in various attempts to be faithful to the Hebrew 'original' in the early modern period. Occasionally I have used the other common early modern version of the title – Canticles – but I have not used the rather unpleasant German abbreviation (Cant) or the alarming version I have seen in some French texts (Ct). I have on the whole used a modern British edition of the Authorised Version. The references to individual verses are also those of the Authorised Version although some commentators in the seventeenth century used slight variations on chapter divisions.

The subject of this book is the use of the mystical marriage trope. This derives not only from the Song of Songs, but from the apocalyptic use of the metaphor in Revelation 21. Also included in early modern formulations of the meaning of the trope is the parable of the five wise and five foolish virgins in Matthew 25; the vivid prophecy of Hosea, who was commanded by God to marry a whore; the imagery of Romans 7: 1–6, where the soul is described as being married to the law as first husband, before the deliverance which is her marriage to Christ; and the instructions to husbands in Ephesians 5: 25–7.

Introduction

The idea for this book was conceived at Stanton Harcourt in Oxfordshire, in the room in which Alexander Pope worked on his translation of the *Iliad*. It had its origins in the bewilderment and incomprehension with which a graduate student and I tried to decipher a manuscript copy of the Earl of Shaftesbury's speech in the House of Lords, sent to Philip Harcourt in March 1679. The speech, which is treated in this book in Chapter 6, had a very important political message, of hostility to French imperial ambitions, and solidarity with European Protestants: but it was delivered entirely in the language of the biblical book of the Song of Songs. I realised that the seventeenth-century reader must have been completely familiar with that text, and understood its arcane imagery in a manner entirely divorced from a literal reading. As I found out more about the circumstances of 1679 I realised that Shaftesbury's choice of rhetoric from the Song of Songs was part of his point: it was a text loaded with political and religious significance. I began to realise how ubiquitous and influential this Biblical book was in seventeenth-century England, in sermons, commentaries and in poetry. Use of its rhetoric was prominent in many of the controversies of the period.

The use of the Song of Songs has been traced in some of the extremer movements of the seventeenth century, such as the radical mid-century prophets.[1] I wanted to explore the text's significance for more mainstream readers in the early modern period: even Quakers have been somewhat neglected in the ensuing pages, although I have dealt with some female prophets in my examination of the importance of the text for women. 'Mainstream', of course, is a very difficult category to establish, rather like the elusive term 'moderate'. Claims to moderation in the seventeenth century should rightly be treated with suspicion.[2] However, this book is concerned for the significance of the text in English history, and it tends to deal with significant politico-religious movements. For England in the early seventeenth century I define 'mainstream' as the spirituality common to many aristocrats and gentry as well as many of 'the middling sort', which can be described as Reformed in theology, and which is broadly Calvinist.

1

Anthony Milton has pointed out that this represented the spirituality of the Church of England at the start of the century, and that it was in often uneasy alliance with the ceremonial aspect of Church worship, an alliance which the activities of Archbishop Laud did much to undermine.[3] It is this large constituency for whom the vocabulary and concepts of the Song of Songs, as interpreted by earlier commentators, became particularly resonant in the political circumstances of the seventeenth century.

This book is loosely chronological in organisation, and each chapter has its roots in a particular decade of the seventeenth century. However, each chapter has a theme of its own and where necessary ranges throughout the time-scale of the book. Thus, for example, Chapter 5, 'The Seventeenth-century Woman Writer and the Bride', covers women writing from the start of the century until very near its end: however, I see the surge in authorship by women as starting in the 1650s, and this dictates the place of the study in the middle of this book, as part of a wider story about the use of the Song of Songs.

Chapter 1 deals with a Jacobean and courtly context for interpretations of the Song of Songs. The upheaval of the mid-century wars tended to divide the court from the 'godly' constituency, a division epitomised in the ejection from the Church of England of ministers who would not sign an oath of allegiance to the King in August 1662. Thus the subject-matter of this book deals with a more plebeian constituency as the century went on, and literacy and political participation became more widespread. Thus, a Calvinist consensus that dominated biblical interpretation at the start of the period fed opposition to Laudian policies in the 1630s and was the theological backbone of the Puritan opposition in the Civil War: as the court alienated so many godly readers of the Bible in the decade leading up to hostilities, the Song of Songs became an oppositional text. The suitability of this kind of spirituality for the dominant Independent denomination, and for increasing numbers of more radical sects, ensured a profound engagement with the Song of Songs in the 1640s and 1650s, and its use by women is particularly revealing (see Chapter 5). During the Interregnum, I focus on the Presbyterian/Independent theological context within which the Westminster Assembly conducted its proceedings (see Chapter 4). At the Restoration a substantial part of this population was ejected from the Church of England: nearly 2000 Nonconformist ministers. The Song of Songs became the property of radical Presbyterians and Independents, and its interpretation became a site of struggle in the 1670s (see Chapter 6). Presbyterian, Independent and Baptist denominations often co-operated under the severe persecution of the Restoration, as they did in Bristol in the 1670s, and were consciously engaged in political resistance to the ruling regime.[4] The strengthening Baptist denomination was theologically and politically at the fringes of any movement that can be deemed 'mainstream', but they were at the forefront of political action in the decade before the

Glorious Revolution, and the Song of Songs was employed by them as a key text (Epilogue).

In many ways, the struggle over the identity of the Church of England in the seventeenth century is a conflict over the meaning of the Song of Songs. Since the second century, its main protagonist, a female lover referred to somewhat euphemistically as the Bride (the love poems clearly pre-date any proposed marriage in the biblical book), had been interpreted, with support from other Scriptures such as Revelation 20, as the true Church: commentators at different times and with various theological positions used the text of the Song of Songs to support their particular ideas of her identity and constitution.[5] There were of course various understandings of the nature of the true Church abroad in seventeenth-century England, and much of the political upheaval of the century involved such disagreements. The discourses on the Song of Songs which this book treats tend not to declare their affiliations openly. In a century when censorship was often strict, treatment of a biblical text could avoid immediate and explicit label-ling as representative of a particular politico-religious position by virtue of participation in a practice that for most of the century (not all) was regarded as necessarily benign: biblical exposition. This book is a study of how one particular text accumulated a number of interpretations with a specific theological and political significance, and thus came to function as a kind of code for a politico-religious grouping. The extent of engagement with this text, and the kinds of responses to it, thus became an indirect but reliable indicator of the popularity of its ideological meanings. The fact that this book is a poem full of metaphorical devices is of importance to seventeenth-century literary history, although the story traced here is one that deals largely with non-canonical writing, except perhaps for Chapter 3, which explores courtly use of the marriage metaphor. Bibliography, history of the book and literary criticism are employed for historical and political effect: the result is a study of the reading and writing of a particular text, across as full as possible a range of readers and writers in English society.

Controversy over the Song of Songs is alive and well, although possibly with less relevance to the majority of the population now than in the early modern period, when most people knew the text and could quote from it. Some contemporary Puritans in America still offer the Song of Songs as God's instructions for married love.[6] More sceptical modern interpret-ers have tended to assume that the text was originally a love poem which has been wrested to an allegorical interpretation by religious authorities in an attempt to control the erotic content of the book. Like Paul Ricoeur, critics tend to speak of 'the obvious sense of the text' as the one that assumes it is a secular love-song.[7] In a recent volume of essays, John Barton, professor of theology at Oxford, tries to resist modern tendencies to read the text literally, as a self-evidently erotic discourse.[8] He points out that there is not one example of an ancient interpreter who produces a literal version of the text, and expresses some sympathy with the view that the text might have been actually composed in allegorical mode. Most of the volume's contributors cheerfully ignore him, however: Antonio Lopriero, asserting in defiance of Barton that the only reason the Jews allowed the text into the canon was its allegorical reading, insists on a link between Egyptian love poetry and the Song, despite the millennium that separates the two kinds of texts, a difficulty pointed out in an essay by Paul Vervus. Karl Hecker links the Song of Songs with ancient Mesopotamian cuneiform writing, whilst Richard Hunter reads it alongside Homer and Sappho. Joan B. Burton finds an assertion of female desire in her feminist reading of the text. Other recent accounts find a homosexual eroticism latent in the Song of Songs.[9]

Gendered language in the Song of Songs

It is not surprising that the text of the Song of Songs has spawned much gender criticism. A text which delineates both male and female beauty in detailed terms on several occasions is bound to lend itself to such an analysis. In the early modern period, the fact that three-fifths of the writing in what is regarded as a sacred text is in the voice of a single woman or a chorus of 'Daughters of Jerusalem' is already a matter for comment. More interesting, perhaps, is that in this period the early Christian tradition of identifying the female Spouse with the individual soul, whether male or female, is continued.

Many critics have commented on the implications for heterosexual men of identification with a nubile woman. As Ivy Schweitzer puts it, 'Puritanism explored feminine positions and abstract female figures that could – with some conditioning, and with considerable effort, and with mixed results – be occupied by men.'[10] Of necessity, for a man to read 'as a woman' means to imagine himself into the stereotypes that his culture associated with women. For Bernard of Clairvaux, femininity could signal weakness of any kind: thus he associates the female sex of the deer and the youth of the fawn (2:17) with the weakness of God in incarnation. In the patriarchal society of early modern England commentators did not need this precedent to stress the passivity and receptivity of the Bride. This emphasis tended to confirm the gendered stereotypes of women, but there were spiritual advantages for men in assuming female-gendered weakness.[11] For Puritanism, the spiritual benefits were even more tangible: humility and weakness called forth the Holy Spirit to produce a divine strength in the believer. As this book will demonstrate, for many Calvinist theologians the mechanics of salvation— justification and sanctification—were vividly demonstrated in early modern marriage law whereby marriage involved the husband taking on the debts and sometimes even transgressions of his bride, and compensating for them. Thus Calvinist commentators enthusiastically interpreted the Bride's expression of weakness in 1:4 ('Draw me, we will run after thee') as the human being in a state of total depravity calling on the strength of God without which he could not follow Christ. Identifying with what was culturally perceived as feminine hopelessness became a stage in an individual's salvation: 'the weaknesses and dangers of femininity could be turned to sources of valuable obedience and a useful sense of inadequacy'.[12] The marriage union with Christ was offered as the aim of the Gospel-preaching in many evangelistic sermons, particularly after the Restoration.[13]

Of course, there were problems with this gender inversion, not least the assurance from male commentators that the earthly marriage which they were using as a comparison always produced a blissful solution to the problems of the bride. Marriage as the most profound relationship that a human being could experience was one of the great discoveries of the Reformation: Richard Sibbes describes it as 'the sweetest passage of our life', and although many Protestant divines protest that the love described in the Song of Songs is far superior to that enjoyed with a real woman, the warm experience of marriage informs much of their commentaries.[14] Ivy Schweitzer quotes John Winthrop's journal which describes a spiritual experience in which God 'ravished' his heart. It is accompanied with a rather smug assumption about his own wife's marital bliss: 'my soule had as familiar and sensible society in him, as my wife could have wth the kindest husband'.[15] There is no doubt that seventeenth-century stereotypes of gender colour the interpretation of the Song of Songs. The Spouse is appropriately weak at key stages of the book, such as the mini-narrative of chapter 5 treated in the fourth chapter of this volume. However, there are many other points at which she is described in strangely aggressive and masculine terms, such as the first comparison with the Spouse in 1:9: 'I have compared thee, O my love, to a company of horses in Pharaoh's chariots.' In 6:13 'the company of two armies' is apparently to be seen in her person. In 6:10 she is 'terrible as an army with banners'. There is no doubt that in the seventeenth century this militant aspect of the Bride is important: it helps to make the text useful in political discourse, where military strength is an advantage, and is easily associated with the triumphant Bride of the latter chapters of Revelation, which seventeenth-century prophets were to use as a key to unlock what they saw as the prophetic application of the Song of Songs. In the seventeenth-century spiritual journal, a different kind of spiritual writing, Tom Webster perceives ministers whose masculinity was 'ambivalent' in the sense that they had also to fulfil a 'motherly' function to their flock, enjoying the ability to express their feminine side in the language of the Song of Songs.[16]

I would like to suggest, however, that seventeenth-century readings of the Song of Songs enabled men to have it both ways, in that the Spouse depicted there is a 'virile Bride' as Shawn M. Krahmer designates her, following Bernard of Clairvaux.. He points out that in the Song of Songs the Spouse overcomes her feminine weaknesses, and so functions, typologically, as virile. Her femininity is important—after all, with so many metaphors to choose from, the Biblical writer selected this one—but Bernard designates her a *fortis femina*, a term he also applies to Sophia, the figure of wisdom, the Virgin Mary, and his own Pope, Eugenius III. The context for Bernard's exposition of the Song of Songs is the imminent launch of the second crusade in 1145, which he actively supported: the similarities between this situation and that of Protestant commentators in the early-seventeenth century, facing a religious war in Europe, are obvious. Bernard was an authority often cited by early modern commentators on the Song of Songs. Krahmer concludes, 'in patriarchal societies when men appropriate to themselves feminised roles the picture is not feminine, but a feminised masculine'.[17] This composite gendered identity is, I think, the source of the ease with which seventeenth-century men appropriated the image of the Bride. Of course, such an appropriation by men somewhat limited the potential impact of the Song of Songs on the respect in which real women were held. However, as Chapter 5 of this book demonstrates, seventeenth-century women were empowered by the focus on the Song of Songs. Along with men, they could participate in the privileges afforded to the weak woman in the Song of Songs, privileges such as overwhelming divine love and especial access to the person of Christ. The most discernible effect is in the number of seventeenth-century women who, like the Bride, became authors, and they wrote their love for Christ in the language of the Song of Songs:

> Away base world, hence shadowes, hence away
> you shalbee noe corrieualls to my loue
> for hee is fresh as is the flo^urye may
> & truly constant as the turtle doue
> His breth like beddes of roses cheere the morne,
> His hayres reflex the sunne beames doth adorne.[18]

Carnal and spiritual readings

Debates about meaning focus on the perennial issue of what kind of text we are dealing with in the Song of Songs: various critics read it alongside writing from different places and different times. There seems to be some kind of consensus that the text dates from the fourth or third century BC.[19] There is no agreement, however, over what the genre of the text is: there have been confident assertions that the Song of Songs is a kind of Syrian epithalamion, a *wasf*, just as confident assertions that it is a parody of a *wasf*, and similarly confident assertions that the poem is not a *wasf* at all.[20] Origen of course believed that in inspiring the Song of Songs, God was initiating the genre of the epithalamion.[21] Without secure knowledge of what genre the author thought he was using it is very difficult to engage in definitive literary criticism. A recent critic has suggested that several of the statements are ironic, or even humorous, a judgement that would completely alter the perceived thrust of the text: sensitivity to tone, particularly in a poem, is a crucial element in the making of meaning.[22] To read the Biblical text as ironic seems to have been a non-starter in the early modern period. Commentators are divided between those who see the Song of Songs as a poem with a historical context, an epithalamium for the wedding of Solomon, and those who find this suggestion untenable, such as Joseph Stennett, who at the turn of the eighteenth century points out that the Tower of Lebanon which figures in the text was not built at the time of any of Solomon's weddings.[23]

However, for the most part, early modern commentators agreed on the key issue: the Song of Songs was a canonical Scriptural text, and therefore directly inspired by God. Sometimes, bizarrely, they decided that the Song of Songs had to be inspired by God simply because it was apparently so transgressive. Dudley Fenner, having pointed out several absurdities, concludes with exasperation that the supposed Solomon is guilty of fornication: 'he deferreth the marriage unto a long day ... and he is in the meantime in his hilles of frankomsence'.[24] Following Origen's magisterial second-century interpretation, most people in the early modern period found aspects of the text 'unworthy of God', and therefore, as the book had the status of sacred text, it was to be allegorised.[25] It did not help that so many commentators insisted on the impossibility of the literal meaning of the words. Some Reformers, such as Theodore Beza, could not accommodate an historical origin for the text in the marriage song of Solomon: this would tie interpretation too closely to carnal modes of interpretation, to do with a sexual relationship between a man and a woman, a sexual relationship, moreover, which had been denounced in I Kings 11, which begins, 'King Solomon loved many strange women, in addition to the daughter of Pharaoh.'[26] This belief had the advantage that there was no need to find sources and parallels for what were unique, divine words. Sebastian Castellio, theologian in Calvin's Geneva, decided in 1544 that the book was to be taken literally and was therefore immodest and obscene, but this opinion was greatly to the detriment of his career. Replacing him in the seventeenth century as the target for learned introductions to versions of the Song of Songs was Hugo Grotius, who posited a secular origin to the Song, even if it could be 'laudably adapted' by the people of God as an allegory.[27] The introductions to early modern paraphrases and commentaries are peppered with warnings about a correct readerly disposition towards the text. The preface to George Wither's 1623 verse paraphrase is typical; 'Let no man therefore presume to sing, or repeat, in a carnall sense, what is here spiritually intended; upon paine of *Gods* heauie indignation.'[28] The production of a 'correct', non-sexual meaning was a kind of test of a reader's spiritual state; as Edward Reynolds, member of a committee to produce the *Annotations on the Old and New Testament* authorised by the

Westminster Assembly declared, 'none can read with danger of infection, but those who bring the plague along with them'.[29] Samuel Woodford was even more dramatic, using George Herbert's words at the start of *The Temple*:

> Avoid Prophane, avoid! for such as you
> There is no place, or listning here;
> They're Mysteries, which we sing, and but a few
> Receive them with a well-purg'd ear.[30]

The interesting feature of these prohibitions was that they indicated that the censor had himself read the Song of Songs in a carnal way, if only to ascertain which aspects of the text were a problem. It is possible to isolate the particular verses which commentators of the early modern period identified as potentially corrupting. For example, the Westminster Assembly annotators found verse four of chapter five, 'My beloved put in his hand by the hole of the door, and my bowels were moved for him' potentially arousing: 'to an impure fancy this verse is more apt to foment lewd and base lusts, than to present holy and divine notions'.[31] Verse thirteen of chapter one, 'A bundle of myrrh is my well-beloved to me; he shall lie all night betwixt my breasts' clearly caused some concern, as Simon Patrick anxiously commented in the late seventeenth century: 'The bosome of all chaste Women is inaccessible to any hand, but that of their Husband'.[32] In the twentieth century, Paul Ricoeur dares to identify which verses a 'good Freudian' will discern as describing sexual intercourse. This tongue-in-cheek exercise serves to illustrate the limitations of Freudian interpretation in the context of a historical study: whereas he lists 2:16, 'my beloved is mine, and I am his; he feedeth among the lilies' as an explicit statement of lovemaking, any mention of 'lilies' merely brings forth musings on chastity from early modern commentators, who are at least on the conscious level wedded to a symbolic reading of the lily as an emblem of sexual purity. For an early modern reading of 5:1, 'I am come into my garden, my sister, my spouse', which Ricoeur sees as the sexual climax of the book, see Chapter 4.[33]

Of course, as Ricoeur's judgements indicate, assumptions about marriage, sex and the body are vital to any interpretation of the Song of Songs, and perhaps no discourse is more specific to the influence of culture than the love song, which assumes specific criteria for the desirable body. On the whole, of course, the Biblical text does not detail which dimensions or proportions of the body are found beautiful. Description is entirely encoded in metaphor such as that used of the woman's hair in 4:1, 'thy hair is as a flock of goats, that appear from Mount Gilead', a simile which may or may not have meant something to the author, and which interpreters struggle to make sense of (although Snoopy in the Peanuts cartoon seems to know what it means and even used it in a love letter to his girlfriend).[34] The blazons of the female body are particularly apt to give away commentators' cultural preferences. In early seventeenth-century

Italy Giovanni Diodati confidently comments on 4:3 ('Thy lips are like a thread of scarlet'): 'Thinne and vermilion lips are a most remarkeable part of corporall beauty.'[35] For most of the twentieth century, connoisseurs of women's beauty would not agree with him. Uninformed as to what it is about the lover's breasts that is particularly beautiful, and knowing only that she is 'all fair' (4:7), commentators supply their own cultural assumptions about female breasts: 'these brests are variously opened' as the editor of the 1657 *Annotations* puts it. In sixteenth-century England Dudley Fenner assumed that the Bride's breasts were 'plumpe, round, fayre, and full of good nourishment'.[36] Things had obviously changed in women's fashions nearly a century later in Scotland when, using exactly the same text, James Durham carefully explained the appearance of the Bride's breasts to his readers: 'they are like young Roes, not too big; for, when breasts are too big, it's a deformity'.[37]

Perhaps wisely, Dudley Fenner described attempts to find a secular genre for the Song of Songs as 'poison', declaring it *sui generis* and interpreting it only with the aid of other Scriptures.[38] Nearly one hundred years later John Reeve denounced those who read it as a secular love-song as 'venomous Creatures', whose reading extracted 'the rankest Poyson from the sweetest flow'rs'.[39] This strategy neatly avoided the admission that the text itself, and all subsequent interpretations of it, were riddled with cultural assumptions. Those who believed that the text was indeed inspired by God implicitly accepted an allegorical reading of the text, and therefore could ignore the enculturated rhetoric if they chose, although their readings are none the less culturally constructed. As George L. Scheper points out, Reformed theologians such as Martin Luther and, in England, William Whitaker, who expressed their hostility to allegorical readings, nevertheless produced their own allegories of the Song of Songs.[40] William Whitaker argued that there was a broader meaning for the word 'literal' which meant something like 'in its fullest sense': thus the literal meaning of the Song of Songs included the allegorical meaning. In the seventeenth century James Durham, whose very popular commentary was in the library of John Owen, went even further to argue that the allegorical meaning of the Song of Songs was, actually, the literal meaning:

> I grant it hath a literal meaning, but I say, that literal meaning is not immediat, and that which first looketh out, as in Historical Scriptures, or others which are not figurative, but that which is spiritually and especially meant by these Allegorick and Figurative speeches, is the Literal meaning of this Song.[41]

Traditional interpretations of the Song of Songs

It helped that there was a certain amount of cross-cultural agreement on what the allegorical meaning of the Song of Songs was. From earliest times, in Jewish interpretation, the lovers' dialogues had been seen as expressions of the relationship between God and his people. Christian interpretation adapted this reading to use the book to describe Christ and the Church. Origen in the third century was the first to see the spiritual meaning of the text as the literal, thus producing a 'bodiless text', where there was no 'literal' meaning as such: this reading was produced by identifying the two protagonists as spiritual entities, Christ and the Church, rather than physical beings.[42] The Scot James Durham, in a famous 1668 commentary on the Song of Songs, agreed with Origen. He summarised the debate about interpretation of the Song of Songs as between those who thought the Bride and Bridegroom were actually Solomon and his wife, and therefore types of Christ and the Church, or whether the whole text was actually a dialogue between Christ and the Church, expressed in metaphorical terms.[43] He proved his own preference for a metaphorical reading by demonstrating the incredibility and offensiveness of a literal reading of the text.[44]

> Types suppose still the verity of some History, as *Ionas* casting in the Sea, and being in the Fishes belly three dayes and three nights, when it is applyed to Christ in the New Testament, it supposeth such a thing once to have been: Allegories again, have no such necessary supposition, but are as Parables proponed for some mystical end.[45]

The aspects of Origen's interpretation that were to become canonical, and which were followed by the vast majority of early modern exegetes, were the reading of the love songs in two ways: as expressions of love between God and his church, and between God and the individual soul.[46] Bernard further developed this interpretation. Early modern commentators often referred to both authorities. The Song of Songs had always been interpreted to be about identity—who constituted the true people of God, and who did not.[47] Verse seven of chapter one became emblematic of the search for the True Church amongst several counterfeits; 'Tell me, O thou whom my soul loveth, where thou feedest, where thou makest thy flocks to lie down at noon; for why should I be like one who turns aside to the flocks of thy companions?' In the sixteenth century, this insider/outside theme acquired a new setting in the Europe-wide schism between Catholic and Protestant, to the extent that a commentary by the Italian Antonio Brucioli was seized on and translated by Thomas James in 1598 as testifying to the inherent anti-Papist nature of the book.[48]

There had been nearly one hundred commentaries on the Song of Songs in the period between the fifth century AD and the sixteenth century. Ann Matter explains this interest in the text as a feature of its complexity: its dual nature rendered interpretation inexhaustible.[49] In the Middle Ages, however, the readership of such commentary was of necessity very limited, not just by the circulation of the manuscripts, or by literacy, but by the perceived readership of the Song of Songs: she points out that Bernard 'clearly understands this quest [for union with God] as a special prerogative of the monastic élite'.[50] The invention of printing gave new impetus to the dissemination of versions of the Song of Songs, and a new readership. Max Engammare lists 27 commentaries printed in London in the sixteenth century (plus one in Oxford). He concludes that the Song of Songs 'occupe une place privilégiée sur la scène exégétique et religieuse de la première moitié du XVIe siècle' because of the Reformed concern with Biblical hermeneutic: the Song of Songs was seen to require extended commentary.[51] The insight of Luther that monks did not occupy a special place in the Church of God made the spirituality of the book relevant to all Christians in the Reformed church: it was thus no longer under control of the ecclesiastical authorities.[52] It could be argued that in England the political reverberations of the Reformation were not fully experienced until the seventeenth century, when, coincidentally, a mass readership was available for a large number of works on the Song of Songs. George L. Scheper finds 500 works on the Song of Songs printed in England in the seventeenth century, a number second only to the amount of expositions of the Psalms.[53] The impact of so many works concerned with the Song of Songs becoming available to an increasingly literate and politically active population in the seventeenth century who perceived the Song of Songs as relevant to their struggle is one of the concerns of this book.

Elizabeth A. Clark points out 'the pliability of allegorical interpretation in addressing ever new religious and cultural situations'.[54] She is talking about the texts of Christian antiquity, up to the fifth century AD, but the troubled politico-religious history of the early modern period led to some increasingly bizarre interpretations of the Song of Songs. Perhaps one of the most idiosyncratic was that of Martin Luther, who confidently dismissed previous orthodoxies as 'immature and strange'. For him, the Song of Songs was most holy because most political, dealing with the government of the Church of God in the world. He thought that the text could be interpreted for any church which had a godly prince, and therefore fitted his own situation in sixteenth-century Germany rather well. Thus his rendering of chapter one verse four goes like this:

> Although I am a state founded by God...yet there is no success and there are very few who desire and maintain public peace. I seem not to be a state but some sort of rabble of seditious men.[55]

Luther's interpretation has been to a large extent ignored by scholarship because of the limitations in time and space that he imposes on the Biblical text. However, Luther's commentary shows how in the early modern period Biblical texts could be seen as relevant to a country's political circumstances.[56] Indeed, John Collinges agreed with Luther in seeing a very particular application to the situation of the Church, although his concern was with England in 1646.[57]

The application of the Song of Songs to English political life in the seventeenth century is the subject of this book: it is an exploration of how interpretation of a text can be affected by historical context, and how history can be viewed through the lens of a Biblical text. The popularity of the text is not just an English phenomenon, of course. Engammare lists 30 commentaries printed in sixteenth-century Basle, 41 in Lyon, 57 in Venice and 82 in Paris, many more than were printed in England.[58] This book, however, limits itself to the use of the Song of Songs in England in the seventeenth century. The Reformed capacity to adapt the text to the very particular circumstances of time and place demand a detailed treatment of the English historical context. John Reeve, for example, announces: 'Twas Solomon's song but now tis mine' at the start of a version which could only have been written in 1684.[59] As we shall see, interpretation of the Song of Songs took on a different significance as political circumstances changed so radically in this revolutionary century.

It is important to note the existence of widely varying versions, particularly those of mid-century marginal sects like the Ranters, although they do not feature in this book: previous literary criticism has found extreme use of the Song of Songs irresistible.[60] A sacred text that cannot mean what it appears to say about human sexuality is bound to produce startling interpretations. It is almost true to say that the text was full of free-floating signifiers which did not mean what they appeared to say, and which therefore could be appropriated for any cause or opinion: as Thomas Beverley put it in 1687, the text was *'unstable as Water'.*[61] Thus many interpreters felt free to produce their own version of the Song of Songs, particularly as the book was pronounced 'prophetic' by many respected authorities. Other more devotional, and perhaps more responsible, authors were at pains to follow the tradition of mediaeval commentary, and their interpretations were fenced in by marginal notes referring to authorities who set limits to the authorised understanding of the text.[62] Some modern critics have commented on the similarities between Catholic and Protestant commentaries: this is probably a result of anxieties about legitimacy of meaning, leading Protestant commentators to follow Catholic predecessors where possible.[63] Nevertheless, the text that was a pillar of Catholic spirituality in the Middle Ages became a statement of anti-Catholic militancy in the early modern period. This book sets out to demonstrate how and why this radical change in meaning could happen.

Sixteenth-century English versions of the Song of Songs

This book is particularly concerned with that part of the seventeenth century which was overseen by the presence (or absence) of Stuart kings in England. However, it is important to give some sixteenth-century context to the use of the Song of Songs. From very early on, the text was adopted for use in the fledgling Reformation, which made sense in terms of the traditional interpretation of the text: it was about the true church and its opponents, and so was deeply relevant to a struggle between Catholics and Protestants.[64] At the cutting edge of the Reformation were John Bale and John Foxe, who had lived together in Reigate and Basle and both worked for the printer Oporinus, during the reign of Mary Tudor, in the project of creating a new literature based on the Bible. They both used the Song of Songs as a gloss on the Bride and Whore of Revelation, a practice used throughout the Middle Ages, where the Bride had been the true, Catholic church.[65] In their Protestant propaganda, they merely reassigned the referents of the allegory so that the Protestant church became the True Church, the Bride, and the Catholic church became the Whore. Ex-Carmelite monk John Bale, in exile from Henry VIII's reimposition of Catholic orthodoxy, put together the texts about Bride and Whore from the Song of Songs and the Apocalypse, expanding on them and comparing them with other Scriptures in his own paraphrase. His influential book was reprinted several times in the mid century, and his preface situates himself in a long and worthy tradition of dissenters and martyrs. In his preface he explains why he has called his book *The Image of Both Churches*:

> Herein is the true christian church (which is ye meeke spouse of ye Lambe without spot) in hir right fashyoned colours discribed. So is the proud church of hypocrites, ye rose coloured whore, the paramour of Antichrist, and the sinfull sinagoge of Sathan, in hir iuste proporcion depaynted, to ye mercifull forewarning of the Lordes electes.[66]

John N. King points out that this rather crude analysis of history dictated all Bale's works, both in prose and drama.[67] It is no surprise that his gloss on the Bride of Revelation refers explicitly to the Song of Songs.

> Thys woman the churche (as Salomons cantycles specyfyeth) ys fayre, lovelye, plesaunt, swete, wholesome, delectable, undefyled as the Mone, excellent in clerenesse as the sonne, and gloryous as an armye of menne with their banners and stremers.[68]

By contrast, the 'rose coloured whore' is connected with the Pope and Antichrist, 'the proude paynted churche of the pope or synnefull Synagoge of Sathan' as the emblems attached to the end of the 1545 edition vividly illustrate. The 'whoremongers' are the adherents of the Roman Catholic church: the sexual sins of the priests are particularly vilified. Neither does Islam escape opprobrium in Bale's text.[69]

Foxe's 1556 drama, *Christus Triumphus*, was reprinted in the 1670s in another wave of anti-Catholic feeling, as an 'apocalyptic comedy' featuring the Church

(Ecclesia), the Pope (Archierus), Antichrist (Pseudamnus), and Babylon, 'meretrix Pornopolis', who was of course a figure for Rome. There is no reference to Canticles in this text although the parable of the ten virgins awaiting the arrival of the Bridegroom in Matthew 25 is alluded to as Christ's imminent return is expected. The play finishes with an Epithalamium and chorus of the virgins.[70] Although the play is heavily indebted to Thomas Kirchmeyer's *Pammichius* which had caused a storm when acted in Cambridge in 1545, the explicit inclusion of the Bride and the marriage with Christ is Foxe's own.[71] In his famous sermons on the Song of Songs, translated into English in 1587 by John Harmer and dedicated to the champion of Protestantism, the Earl of Leicester, Beza told the same apocalyptic story, but in much more careful and academic fashion. He prefaced the sermons on the actual Song with a discussion of Psalm 45, claiming that this Psalm was 'a preface or abridgement of this booke of the Canticle of Canticles': Psalm 45, which is designated as a wedding song, much of which is in the voice of a bride to the king who 'greatly desires [her] beauty' (Psalm 45:11), became part of the texts associated with the Song of Songs. Sermons seven to ten, on Song of Songs 1:6–7, explain the problems Protestants have with the Roman Catholic church, which is likened to the Spouse's bastard brother, who, in the words of verse 6, was angry with the Bride. Seventeenth-century English Puritans were to follow Beza in spelling out the characteristics of the Bride as the true church in opposition to Catholicism.[72] Also enlisted in the anti-Catholic printing offensive was the future Elizabeth I, whose translation of Marguerite of Navarre's *Miroir de l'âme pécheresse* was introduced by John Bale in the edition of 1548. The embracing of the 'bride' metaphor by women, here the future queen of England as well as a recent queen of France, was to seem particularly appropriate in the century that followed:

It doth please the to gyve her an other name, to call her thy wyfe, & that she agayne do call the husbande, declarynge how thu hast frely manyfested the marryage of her.[73]

In particular, the anachronistic details of the early modern marriage contract imposed on the text as a way of explaining the Reformed doctrine of justification by faith were to become a source of theological conflict in the Stuart Restoration.

By the baptysme thu hast made a promes, to gyve her thy goodes and ryches, and thu agayne to take her synnes, for she hath nothynge els by herytage of her first father Adam. All her treasures, that she hath of nature, ar nothynge els but synnes, whych thu tyed upon the, and payed all her debte with thy goodes and lands. Thu hast made her so ryche, and with so great a ioynter endued her, that she knowynge her selfe to be thy woyd wyfe, doth beleve to be quytt of all that she oweth.[74]

The popularity of the Song of Songs was often expressed in terms of providing a Biblical substitute for profane ballads, in the vision of Miles Coverdale for the Psalm poems as early as, perhaps, 1535. The aspiration that ploughboys and carters should be so caught up in a godly lifestyle that they naturally sang Biblical songs for pleasure was part of a Reformation concern with the holiness of individual Christians, however humble, and it was a concern still being expressed well over a hundred years later.[75] Women who sit spinning are directed by Coverdale to the songs of other Biblical women (Miriam, Deborah, Hannah and Mary) but not, interestingly enough, to the song of the Bride.[76] It was frequently asserted that the Song of Songs contained 'hard places' that needed commentary: it was 'more darkly hyd than other partes of the scripture'.[77] Many commentaries were produced out of a conviction that every reader should be able to benefit from every book of Scripture, unlike the practice of the Jews, whose stipulation that only men over thirty should read the book was frequently quoted.[78] Dudley Fenner, who produced one of the first English versions in 1587, asserted the 'shining simplicitie' of Scripture at the same time as he admitted the need for commentary on the Song of Songs.[79] The interesting aspect of Fenner's text is that it is essentially a verse paraphrase, for use at the godly sing-songs that took place after the evening meal among the Merchant Adventurers in Middleburgh: nevertheless, he feels compelled to hedge the text around with glosses, and to provide a prose paraphrase of the argument of each chapter, followed by his own authoritative (and very long) interpretation of it.[80]

William Baldwin: the canticles or balades of Salomon, 1549

The same concern to control interpretation in seen in perhaps the first verse collection printed in English, William Baldwin's *The canticles or balades of Salomon, phraselyke declared in Englysh metres* (London, 1649). Baldwin was another of the militant authors of the incipient Reformation, writing at the same time as Foxe and Bale. He used the Great Bible title for the book, but it was already one that would offend members of his readership because of the connection of the word 'balade' with secular songs. However, Baldwin dedicated his work to the young King, Edward VI, in terms that show the seriousness of his intention:

> Would god that suche songes myght once drive out of office the baudy balades of lecherous love that commonly are indited and song of idle courtyers in princes and noble mens houses.[81]

Rather more aristocratic in aspiration than Coverdale, Baldwin echoed his friend Thomas Sternhold's dedication of his recent volume of psalm paraphrases to Edward VI: he was offering 'holye songs of veritie rather than the fayned rimes of vanitie'.[82] The necessity of substituting Biblical subject-matter for that of profane poetry was a sentiment frequently echoed in the sixteenth century, not least by Philip Sidney is his *Apologie for Poetrie*.[83] Baldwin is aware, however, that some saw only 'wanton wurdes' in the Song of Songs. He has two strategies for dealing with this. The first is to weave Protestant doctrine into the text in a way that makes the allegory clear. This is his explanation of the 'kisses' in verse 1:

> The Kisse o Christe, which I of thee require
> Thy grace, thy peace, thy love (my Love) it is:
> Whiche while I lacke, thy fathers wrath and yre,
> Condemnesh me for my first fathers wisse.[84]

The incorporation of the doctrine of original sin in the last line, together with the Protestant emphasis on faith rather than works for salvation a few lines earlier, is more than enough to defuse the eroticism of 'Let him kiss me with the kisses of his mouth'. Noam Flinker detects an apocalyptic thrust to the work, which is no surprise given the association of the bride of the Song of Songs and the bride of Revelation throughout the period: but he also sees it as having a specific political application, as *The Mirror for Magistrates* was to have in the following decade. He provides a reading in the context of the Prayer Book Rebellion of 1550, arguing that explicitly Protestant writing such as the works considered here to some extent provoked hostilities.[85] Baldwin certainly emphasises the military strength of the Bride, which was to be a feature of seventeenth-century versions. This is his aggressive-sounding version of 3:7–8:

> Beholde ye young, behold and see the bed
> Of Salomon, Christes peace wherin we dwell:
> With threscore men moste strong and myghtie fed
> Beset about, the strong of Israel
> That faythful are and wyse.
> Of whiche eche one doeth hold a cuttyng swurd,
> Expert therwith to stryke and warde in warre.

It is true that Baldwin goes on to define the 'swurd' as God's word, in the manner of Hebrews 4:12: 'the word of God is quick, and powerful, and sharper than any two-edged sword'. The battle is redefined as a mental one, in the realm of education:

> Well learnde they be to preache and teache Gods wurd,
> And with the same to kepe all errors farre
> From godly men and wyse.
> Vpon theyr thygh this swurd, Gods wurd they wear,
> Gyrded therwith for fear of enemies,
> That cum by nyght the feble for to fear.[86]

Nevertheless, the link between physical violence and the battle against error is characteristic of the mentality of Protestant internationalists, for whom the Song of Songs was a defining text, and whose activity is described in Chapter 1.

There are moments in the text when Baldwin chooses verse forms more characteristic of the secular love song which appear to reintroduce the erotic. Just a few years earlier the French poets had developed their own tradition of 'blason' in which parts of the female anatomy were listed for erotic effect. Not surprisingly, Baldwin's version of Chapter 7: 6–7, attracts such rhetoric:

> Lyke thou art in stature to the tree,
> Of Palmes, for no wayght can let thee for to grow:
> And thy brestes are lyke as semeth me,
> To clusters of grapes, that rype hang doune below,
> O my Darlyng.[87]

Apart from the use of appropriate metaphor to encode Protestant doctrine, Baldwin's second strategy for coping with 'wantonnesse', of which there is plenty in the first stanza of this poem, is to hedge the text around with marginal glosses, and with prefatory paraphrase. It is important to remember the textual context of this extract: the reader has just been told how to interpret this poem. The text is divided up into short poems like this which are prefaced with a prose version of the relevant passage of Canticles, and also with Baldwin's own interpretation of the text.[88] Unlike Noam Flinker, however, I do not believe that Baldwin successfully diffuses the eroticism of his text: in fact, eroticism seems part of the point of this section. The tangibility and sensuality expressed here is an important signifier of the completeness of the love of Christ for the soul: as we shall see, the relationship with Christ has to be robust enough during the seventeenth century to sustain the believer through persecution and even martyrdom.

The tension between spirituality and sensuality, doctrine and emotion, was to persist in interpretations of the Song of Songs: but in Baldwin's text it is possible to perceive how poetic paraphrases could draw on all the resources of sixteenth-century love poetry. Many poets chose to exercise their skill in this way. Samuel Woodford, in the preface to his version, laments the lost paraphrase of Spenser.[89] Drayton paraphrased the Song of Songs early on in a career as a secular poet. The volume of Biblical paraphrase was reprinted at the end of his career: unfortunately, he chose fourteeners as the metre for the Song of Songs.[90] One index of the popularity of the Song of Songs in the late Elizabethan period is that it was paraphrased in poetry by Gervase Markham, who was always on the lookout for a profitable enterprise. His effort was chosen to represent English achievement in this area by Francis Meres, in a book comparing English poets in each category with their classical counterparts.[91] There is little in Markham's 1596 version, dedicated to Philip Sidney's eleven-year-old daughter Elizabeth, to mitigate the erotic content of the Song, apart from a gesture at the beginning delineating the 'Argument' of the poem. Indeed, he even describes his poetic activity in erotic terms: he 'made love to Salomons holy song'.[92] This is his version of verses two and three of the Song of Songs:

> Imprint upon my lips pure livorie
> The hony pleasure of thy mouthes deere kisse,
> For why thy love, bounded in no degree,
> Exceedes the sence-inchaunting sugred blisse
> Which from the taste of wine attracted is.

In the end the residual eroticism of the text, however hedged around with commentary, is what makes it so important in the religion and politics of the early modern period. It is a text suffused with desire: not only the desire of the bride for the bridegroom's presence, but the desire of the lovers for each other's bodies. The strength of this desire survives all commentary: indeed, it is part of the meaning of the text for Puritans of the early modern period, for whom desire for God was a defining mark of their election. Calvin had described the union with Christ which was the centre of Reformed Christianity as 'holy wedlock', and desire for Christ was fundamental to his idea of the Christian experience.[93] Commentaries on the Song of Songs are full of the adjective 'love-sick', represented as a desirable state of mind for the Christian.[94] Henry Finch spells out the longing for consummation:

> In all which the Church, burning with a desire of Christ longeth, and is impatient till shee be ioined unto him. For hether tend all her passions, exclamations, testifications of her love, commendations of her spouse.[95]

This longing of the merely human for the reliably divine is characteristic of the religious discourses of the seventeenth century, whether in the political arena or in personal spirituality, and seventeenth-century Christians found this desire expressed for them in the sacred poetry of the Song of Songs. The sheer number of publications dedicated to the Song of Songs – paraphrases, commentaries, sermons – and the important subgenres it generated in spiritual autobiography and the hymn are a powerful demonstration of the appeal of the narrative, with its elements of heroism and love. This phenomenon may be linked, as Sharon Achinstein argues, with the popularity of the romance genre.[96] She suggests that the romance genre gave rise to the spirituality of the mystical marriage.[97] Perhaps both textual forms derive from an increasing sense of individual subjectivity that needs to be satisfied both in fiction and in spirituality, an empowerment of the individual that led to the mass political movements of the late seventeenth century. These political movements were often religious in origin, and often specifically linked to the Reformed spirituality of the Song of Songs. Perhaps it takes a literary text to capture the imagination of a culture in this way. Not only can it appear to speak to specific contemporary situations, but the imaginative impact of its tropes and narratives can form the hopes and dreams of a society. This book attempts to map that impact for communities and individuals in various contexts in seventeenth-century England.

1
Royal Brides and National Identity, 1603–25

At the opening of the seventeenth century there is some evidence that the English church saw itself as unique—as the true Bride of Christ in a Europe increasingly encroached on by the Whore of Babylon, the Catholic Church. What in some contexts was to become an individualistic, spiritualised trope—the Bride of Christ as a single soul—thus took on a communal, and somewhat nationalistic identity. The true Bride of Christ became the Church in a nation which in its own mythology, strengthened by the defeat of the Spanish Armada and confirmed by the events of the Gunpowder Plot, was the heroic opposer of the Antichrist. Thus, via that joint national and spiritual entity, the Church of England, which could plausibly be represented as the Bride of Christ, public discourse of the Jacobean period came perilously close to assuming that the English state itself was the Bride. Fortunately, the dominant Calvinist theology, which believed in a transnational body of believers that collectively made up the true Church, did not allow for such a jingoistic identification to flourish: and in any case, towards the end of James' reign, the discourse of the Song of Songs took on a stance that was theologically and culturally oppositional to the Crown.

On New Year's Day in the plague year of 1609, Kentish vicar Thomas Jackson preached what he called a 'New Yeeres-gift' to the City of London at St. Paul's Cross, the most influential pulpit in the City, where sermons had the relish of both news and propaganda.[1] Jackson specialised in judgemental sermons, and the occurrence of the plague was always a gift to those who enjoyed pointing out what was rotten in the State of England. His text on this occasion was Canticles 2:15, ('Take ye us the foxes, the little foxes; which destroy the grapes') and his sermon was called 'The Uncouching of the Foxe'. Clearly for Jackson much of the point of the sermon was to identify and flush out what he saw to be infiltrators in a godly state. To start with, however, he identified 'Gods Huntsmen': bishops, ministers and 'the rype and ingenuous Scholars' in both universities, as well as 'Christian Magistrates'.[2] Master of the Hunt is James I, 'seeing the kingdome of England is an absolute Empire and Monarchie and his Maiestie an absolute Soveraign'. In these post-Gunpowder Plot times, any slight doubt over the King's anti-Catholic steadfastness is waved away: 'that his religious heart should be once tainted with the least conceite of receiving the Beasts marke, far be it from anyone to conceive'(p. 6).

Jackson was using the tropes of the Song of Songs in the manner that had already been established in the sixteenth century—to comment on the progress of God's Kingdom on earth, in particular the ongoing struggle between Catholics and Protestants. Reformed England was the enclosed garden represented in the Song of Songs, and attempts to infiltrate it were divinely frustrated. Although the King had not granted everything asked for by the Puritans at the Hampton Court Conference in 1604, no-one in 1609 was seriously suggesting that James was at all contaminated by Catholicism: the previous year he had attempted to impose a new oath of allegiance on his Catholic subjects.[3] England was clearly the nation favoured by God, as the failure of the Gunpowder Plot had illustrated. Jackson invited his audience to compare what had happened in France in the previous century, for example, where Popery was not thoroughly exterminated, and the Massacre of St. Bartholomew's Day happened as a result (p. 13). William Perkins had more or less single-handedly defeated Catholic theologians, and the great fox himself—the Pope—had been thrown out of England by godly princes such as Elizabeth (much invoking of Foxe's *Acts and Monuments* here, with no pun intended). Edward VI did not even allow his sister Mary to say mass (pp. 21b–22). What remained in the seventeenth century were the foxcubs—the Jesuits, and other foreign malevolents such as Macchiavellians and Italianists (p. 18). There were still of course a few home-grown ills, like the refusal to pay proper tithes, and drinking too much. Jackson points out with great delight that such a crime is called 'foxing' (p. 18a). He concludes: 'the truth is (my good brethren) *the church of England maintaineth and professeth the whole pure and sincere doctrine of the Gospell*, and is so glorious that (like a blazing starre) it doth draw all mens eyes unto it, and even perstringe and dazle them with the shining brightnesse of it'(p. 27a). It all sounds rather smug and quaint. Little did Jackson know that in the 1630s his own son was to be reported to Laud for 'foxing'.[4] Also in the 1630s he would actually accept promotion from an Archbishop, William Laud, who was happy for an English Queen not only to say mass, but to have her own Catholic chapel. But in 1609 Jackson had summarised the religious politics represented by most interpreters of the Song of Songs rather well: anti-Catholic nationalism.

At the start of the seventeenth century, it was a commonplace that the Bride of the Song of Songs represented the true Church, and the true Church was of course the Reformed Church of England (the 'little sister' of the Bride, as in the Song of Songs 8:8, was sometimes described as the church of the colonies, but there was no doubt of the identity of her older sibling[5]). At St Paul's Cross the previous year, there had been a series of sermons by

John Downame in anti-Catholic, nationalistic vein which drew on the trope of the Bride as represented in Hosea.[6] The prophet Hosea was told by God to marry a whore as a vivid illustration of the relationship of God with the Jewish nation. In the Biblical book God tells Hosea that his spiritual bride, the Jewish nation, has committed adultery: she has gone after false gods. The Jewish nation is clearly intended by Downame to reference the English state: comments about the particular situation of England occur regularly in these sermons, such as a comment on the Wars of the Roses, and a thanksgiving for the succession of the Christian Prince who is clearly James I (pp. 63–4). Downame makes great play on the similarity between the words 'adulterie' and 'idolaterie': the faithlessness of Hosea's wife are a code in Downame's sermons for the practices of the Roman Catholic church.[7] God's intention is to redeem his nation, and on her repentance to restore her to the status of chaste Bride. The message for England is clear: no peace with Popish states! (p. 284). However, dalliance with Rome is not the only threat to the Bride of Christ. The marginal gloss for p. 275 reads like this: 'Ceremoniall imperfections of the church must not cause a separation'.[8] As is typical of Calvinist conformists, Downame is worried about the external threats of Popery and of separatism (often represented as 'schism'). He also supports the idea that every baptised infant is part of the Church, although he has to spend some effort in squaring this position with his Calvinist doctrine of the elect (p. 123). Although Downame allows for the existence of hypocrites within the Church, he in practice makes no difference between the Bride of Christ and the Church of England. This close identification of the Church of England with the State explains, I think, why Michael McGiffert thinks that there is a 'divine anglophilia' represented in what he calls the 'Hosead'.[9] Mary Morrissey argues that McGiffert has mistaken the representation of Israel as an Old Testament type representing the nation of England, rather than merely an example for England to learn from.[10] However, both critics seem to have missed the fact that, unlike the other Hoseads, which choose limited, doom-laden passages from the book of Hosea, the dominant image of Downame's treatise, and the doctrine he spends a great deal of time on using texts throughout the Scriptures, is the Bride.

Many early modern writers considered the Bride of Canticles to be a type: those who dissented decided that since a type must be a historical figure, the Bride remained a metaphor.[11] Hosea's bride did apparently have a historical existence, and as such could be treated as a type of the Church: Downame explains that the Church is both the mystical body of believers across history, and also the local embodiment of that Church, in a country and congregation (p. 117). This preoccupying concern with the Church as opposed to the State means that Downame's sermons, although designated a 'Hosead', are much more spiritually uplifting than their close relation, the menacing Jeremiad, examples of which were also given at St. Paul's Cross. When he uses the pronoun 'we' he is referring to the Church of England, marking the rather short period at the start of the seventeenth century when the local incarnation of the Church in England could confidently be identified with the Bride of Christ He celebrates her privileged position: 'if Christ be espoused unto us, to whom may we prefer our suites with greater boldnesse and confidence than unto our gracious husband? For who is more neere to us, then Christ, or who is more deare unto Christ then we, his beloved Spouse?'(p. 272). Many preachers were to follow his practice of comprehending all the processes of salvation—justification, sanctification, even perseverance, that controversial aspect of Calvinist doctrine—within the resources of the marriage trope (p 287, p. 304). Downame adopts the language of the marriage service of the Church of England for the formal commitment of the soul to Christ (p. 289). He expounds the nature of the spiritual marriage bond as a unity with God, in terms that in the later seventeenth century, when the Bride was not so clearly identical with the Church of England, were to become politically radical. The unity with God is both physical and spiritual: as Christ was both body and spirit, and united to God, unity with Him is both bodily and spiritual. Christians are united to God because of their unity with Christ (p. 289). Later in the period Puritan theologians were to argue about the philosophical details of this idea, and Laudians were to question its political implications.[12]

Meanwhile, discourses on the Song of Songs were becoming associated with the court of Prince Henry, and the anti-Catholic idealism rooted there. Joseph Hall, friend of John Donne and future bishop of Norwich, was invited by Prince Henry to become one of his chaplains, on the basis of his 1606 *The Arte of Divine Meditation*. His influence on Protestant spirituality and literature was to continue. In 1609 Hall published his prose paraphrase of the Song of Songs, dedicated to the eighteen-year-old third Earl of Essex, Henry's companion, who had just returned from a European grand tour to consummate his under-age marriage with Frances Howard.[13] The dedication to this volume, which included advice on family management drawn from Solomon's supposed other works, in particular the book of Proverbs, looks rather tactless in the light of the extremely messy end to Essex's marriage four years later.[14] But the dedication to the son of the Calvinist if controversial Elizabethan favourite serves to mark the politico-religious orientation of the work, and its prose paraphrase is extremely useful in explaining fully just what a Calvinist reader was thinking as he read the erotic prose of the Biblical text. This, for example, is the orthodoxly Calvinist interpretation of verse 4 of chapter one, 'Draw me, we will run after thee', stressing as it does both the helplessness of the human being to respond to God unaided and the irresistibility of God's power, which controls the individual's emotions:

> Pull me therefore out from the bondage of my sinnes: deliver me from the world, and doe thou powerfully incline my will, and affections towards thee: and in spight of all tentations, give me strength to cleave unto

thee: and both I, and all those faithfull children thou hast given me, shall all at once with speede and earnestnesse walke to thee, and with thee.[15]

Verse six of chapter two is rendered by interpreting the physical description of love as a metaphor for the spiritual, and by throwing in an allegorical interpretation of what Christ's two hands are doing:

Whilst I am thus spiritually languishing in this agony of desire; let my Saviour employ both his hands to releeve mine infirmitie: let him comfort my head & my heart, my judgement and affections (which both complaine of weaknesse) with the lively heate of his gratious imbracements: and so let us sweetly rest together (p. 17).

Some of the more erotic expressions of the blazon of the Bride's beauty require a more complete and traditional allegory, as in his version of 7:1: the difficult reference to 'joints of thy thighs' is neatly bypassed by referring to Ephesians 6:14.

Thou art compassed about thy loynes with the girdle of verity ... which is cunningly framed by the skill of the spirit of truth.

The attention is transferred from the thighs, which were to cause George Wither some trouble later in James' reign, to the belt around the thighs: but the navel in the next verse is a real navel, which has to be explained away as an entirely spiritual organ.

The navell, wherby all thy spirituall conceptions receive their nourishment, is full of all fruitful supply, and never wants meanes of sustenance (p. 68).

For verse three, Hall simply substitutes the traditional more decorous allegorical interpretation, the old and new testaments, for the actual discourse, which is a description of the Bride's breasts:

Thy two testaments (which are thy full and comely breasts: by whose wholesome milke thou nourishest all thy faithfull children, once borne into the light) are for their excellent & perfect agreement, & their amiable proportion, like two twins of Kids (p. 69).

The equation of 'pure, spiritual milk' with the teaching of the Church had, of course, Biblical sanction in texts like I Peter 2:2, which perhaps accounts for Hall's confidence here.

There are some interpretations in Hall's paraphrase, however, which smack of a non-traditional, and even partisan, treatment, where the Bride seems to be identified with the Church of England, admired as their leader and potential defender by 'forraine assemblyes'. This is Hall's version of 6:8–9:

> Yet thou onely art alone my true and chaste Spouse; pure and undefiled in the truth of thy doctrine, and the imputation of thy holiness; thou art shee, whome the holy Jerusalem which is above (the mother of us all) acknowledgeth for her onely true, and deare daughter. And this is not my commendation alone, but all those forraine assemblyes, which might seeme to be rivalles with thee of this praise, doe applaude and blesse thee in this thine estate, and saie, Blessed is this people, whose God is the Lord (p. 64).

There is more than a hint that Hall is thinking of seventeenth-century politics here: there are no 'forraine assemblyes', or 'rivalles' in the original. Like Downame, Hall is probably identifying the Church of England, and therefore the people of England as a whole, with the Bride. The following verse which interprets 'terrible as an army with banners', reveals a desire for a militant Protestantism rather at odds with James I's pacific policy:

> [she] is so dreadfull, thorough the maiestie of her countenance, and power of hot censures, as some terrible army, with ensigns displayed, is to a weake adversarie (p. 65).

The prince whom Hall served, Prince Henry, thoroughly approved of such militant sentiments, particularly against the Catholic nations of Europe.

The 'adversarie', as Hall termed the enemy of the Church, was how the Catholic church was figured in much anti-Papist discourse.[16] In the dreams of some English Protestants England should be seen in the Catholic-Protestant struggle for Europe as the godly champion, favoured by the Lord. A feature of Calvinist theology, anti-Catholic nationalism was also linked with an important faction in the Jacobean court which included those most closely associated with the doomed Essex rebellion in 1601, who had been rehabilitated on the succession of James I: Henry Wriothesley, Earl of Southampton, and Essex's son, Robert Devereux.[17] This faction saw Prince Henry as the successor to the Protestant idealism of the Earl of Leicester, Sir Philip Sidney and the executed Earl of Essex. Prince Henry seemed more than willing to become the Protestant champion of Europe. As the Venetian ambassador testified, 'He was athirst for glory if ever any prince was. He lent fire to the king in the affairs of Germany, and aspired to be leader of the confederate princes.'[18] The inheritors of the ideological and political agenda of Protestant internationalism had dominated the appointments to the court of the young Prince Henry on his father's accession.[19] The chivalric role of militant Protestant was one that Henry 'unreservedly embraced and consciously developed.'[20] His first public appearance as a man of arms was in the mediaevalist tournament of the Christmas season 1609–10, elaborately scripted by Ben Jonson.[21] This entertainment foreshadowed Henry's installation as Prince of Wales in June 1610, when Henry would be given his own palace and would have his own court. Many saw this appearance in the 'barriers' as his claim to being the military leader of the Protestant cause. The hero of the entertainment, played by Prince Henry, is Meliadus, which Drummond of Hawthornden decrypted as 'Miles a Deo', a suitably militaristic identity.[22] Roy Strong sees Jonson as torn between a peace-loving monarch and his warlike son, producing two catalogues of the deeds of English kings, the first a rather shorter list of masters of diplomacy, the second a more enthusiastic list of military heroes: Jonson comments, 'civill arts the martiall must precede'.[23] Elizabeth I features in both catalogues, as having created 'a wall of shipping' around England, so that it too is an enclosed garden: she became 'the ayde, or feare of all the nations nigh'(p. 970). In the second catalogue, the Prince is identified with Henry V, the monarch famously victorious in Europe, 'to whom in face you are/So like, as *Fate* would have you so in worth' (p. 971). The most recent victory to be lauded, in 26 lines of vivid poetry, is of course the defeat of the Armada (p. 972). This is the prelude to a new era, in which the '*Low Countries, France*, and *Spayne*' will be crucial. The entertainment includes a tournament, in which Prince Henry's prowess in arms is exhibited to great effect. Afterwards, Merlin pronounces a prophecy over Henry:

> And this yong Knight, that now puts forth so soone
> Into the world, shall in your names atchieue
> More *ghyrlands* for this state.

Merlin's final prophecy over the other Stuart prince and princess is similarly warlike: Henry and Charles shall fight 'the foes of God'. The beauty of Elizabeth Stuart might 'call the world to warre' in a chivalric contest over her person that added a militaristic element to any consideration of her marriage (p. 974). Henry, however, seems to have been already enlisted in the roll of honour directly after Elizabeth I, in a specifically military international context. At this period, Fulke Greville was composing his Life of Philip Sidney, a work of nostalgia for the international Protestantism of Elizabeth's reign in which Elizabeth herself was credited with an enthusiasm for Protestant internationalism that perhaps she had not always showed:

> She makes a publique League, for the defence of Religion, with the King of *Scots, Denmark*, and the Princes of *Germany*: perswades a Marriage between *Scotland* and *Denmark*; exileth all Jesuites, and Seminary Priests by Act of Parliament...Upon the loss of *Antwerpe*, she resolutely undertakes the protection of the Netherlanders.[24]

Fulke Greville's work, adulatory of Leicester, Essex and above all, Sir Philip Sidney, was designed to reveal James I's lack of interest in becoming an international Protestant champion, and it is likely that it was intended for Prince Henry: the work was abandoned after that fateful year of 1612.

The Protestant alliance in Europe which Prince Henry aspired to lead was partly itself the result of a marriage: the match contracted between the French Dauphin and the Spanish Infanta in 1611 put the Protestant world in fear of a new strength in the Catholic League. An alliance was concluded in the spring of 1612 between England and the Protestant Union, an association of German princes and free cities under the leadership of the Palatinate. The concrete result of such goodwill was the betrothal of Henry's sister, the Princess Elizabeth, to the Elector Palatine in December of that year. Both policies were very much favoured by Prince Henry: meanwhile he was trying to fend off suggestions for a Catholic bride for himself. Against his own advice to his son in *Basilikon Doron,* James was now favouring a Catholic match for his son to balance the very Protestant marriage of his daughter. The French Queen even suggested a marriage alliance with Henry to balance the impact of the Spanish match, prompting James to the most internationalist action of his reign when he promised to intervene on behalf of French Huguenots.[25] In November 1612, as the Venetian ambassador reports, Henry was preparing to reject the latest offer from Savoy, at the point when he fell terminally ill.[26]

The marriage of Elizabeth Stuart and Frederick, the elector Palatine, on Valentine's Day 1613, perhaps helped to mitigate the overwhelming grief of the militant Protestant party at the loss of their champion, Prince Henry. George Wither lamented the loss of a prince who could strike fear into the heathen:

> His very name with terrour did annoy
> All foreigne foes so far as he was known.
> Drooped for fear, the *Turkey-moon* look'd pale
> Trembled.[27]

Henry Peacham wrote a somewhat double-edged volume for the occasion of Elizabeth's marriage on Valentine's Day 1613, offering six poems of lament for Henry before the 'nuptiall hymns': as he put it, 'the head of a dead man laid in Earth, presented the first to the Table; in abundance of Mirth to put them in minde of *Mortalitie'*.[28] The trope of the Bride of Christ seemed an appropriate Biblical teaching for this occasion George Webbe, who had preached a famous 'Hosead' at St Paul's Cross a few years earlier, and who was soon to be one of the chaplains of James I, preached a sermon in his home town of Steeple Ashton on the wedding day offering Frederick as a kind of substitute for Henry.[29] He was very interested in the political implications for Europe of this wedding: 'whole Christendome is interested in this dayes businesse' (p. 3). Elizabeth of course is the Bride royall of the sermon, 'jewel of this isle and non-pareil of the reformed world' (p. 74). She is following in the footsteps of her legendary namesake, Elizabeth I, a true Bride of Christ: although she has an earthly spouse, he is 'no Antichristian husband', not a Papist (pp. 75–8). Like Downame, he takes the opportunity to denounce Separatists, and Familists, as well as Roman Catholics, as a threat to the Church of England: the true Protestant, who is also the Bride of Christ, is as royal as Elizabeth is on her wedding day (p. 60, pp. 16–17).

Andrew Willet, one of Prince Henry's chaplains, preached a celebration of Elizabeth and Frederick's marriage on 14 February 1613, which took the marriage of Solomon as its subject. He began by consoling Elizabeth for the loss of Henry with the prospect of a new husband and a newly-devoted thirteen year old brother:

> although in like manner that cruell fever did as it were put out one of her eies for the time, in the death of Prince *Henry* yet is it renewed againe, in her noble spouse: that now shee seeth againe w^t both her eies; Prince *Charles*, her deerest brother, and Prince *Fredericke* her amiable spouse.[30]

He entitled the sermon *A treatise of Salomons marriage*, and it was prefaced by his verse translation of Psalm 45, a psalm that for Beza summarised the Song of Solomon.[31] Unlike Beza, however, for whom the mystical marriage was the only possible interpretation of these texts, Willett treated the Psalm as an expression of Solomon's own marriage. He made full use of the political and ceremonial parallels of the two royal weddings, one Biblical, one contemporary:

> Others to expresse their joy, and professe their dutie, bring great and rich presents, gold, jewels, pretious stones, goodly trapped horse, massiepieces of plate, ... Nobles by their chivalrie, Courtiers by their Maskes & bravery; Heraulds by their heraldrie, Poets by their verses and poetrie, have strived to set forth the joy of this day (sig. ¶1v).

As in current interpretation of the Song of Songs, the trope of the mystical marriage allowed much scope for anti-Catholicism in this sermon. Willet briefly surveys the relative fates of Franco-Spanish royal marriages, for which he blames the twin evils of Margaret of Anjou and Bloody Mary, and German ones, deciding of course that the German matches are more likely to succeed: Denmark becomes a part of Germany for his present purposes. 'What true love can there be betweene a protestant and a Papist, a professor of the true faith, and a detester thereof?' he demands (pp. 9–10). The garden which is England has, like the garden of the Song of Songs, grown roses, lilies and violets: the roses of the Marian martyrs, the lily who is the virgin queen Elizabeth, and the violets which are love-matches like this one (sig. ¶2r). Frederick is wished all the attributes of Roman emperors:

> the pietie of *Constantine,* devotion of *Constantius* ... zeale of *Valentinian,* ... and to give instance of your owne nation, The victorious successe of *Henrie* the fifth, that married *Maud,* the daughter of King *Henrie* before named (sig. A1v).

He does not of course mean Henry V of England, who embarrassingly for Willet's thesis, married Katherine of France, but Heinrich V who uncharacteristically for a Holy Roman Emperor 'entred Rome by force, and compelled the Pope to consecrate him Emperour' as Willet reminds us in the margin (sig. A1v).

In his interpretation of Solomon's bride, Willet uses the same epithet 'the mother of Nations' which Jonson had a few years previously used of Elizabeth Stuart in his entertainment for Prince Henry: since this treatise moves effortlessly between the supposed actual marriage of Solomon and the Queen of Sheba, the mystical allegory of Christ and the Church, and the contemporary marriage of Frederick and Elizabeth, the assumption is that like Jonson, Willet sees Frederick's bride as a future Protestant empress.[32] All this bodes well for the impact of this Protestant couple on seventeenth-century Europe, and a Protestant empire is implicitly predicted. Willet, however, sounds a note of caution, in tune with the Song of Song's warning about the little foxes, that spoil the vines:

> this princely marriage, as it sheweth the sunshine of the Gospell, and by Gods grace promiseth continuance of true devotion: so we trust it shall discover all trecherous practises seeking for innovation (sig. ¶1v).

This is a very early use of the word 'innovation', which was to sum up for much of the English population the invidious impact of changes in the Church of England caused by the rise of Arminian clerics in the1630s. Willet's colleague in the Prince of Wales' household, Joseph Hall, had already, in 1608, accused the main scapegoat for those Arminian innovations in the 1630s, William Laud (currently a fellow of St. John's College, Oxford) of flirtation with Catholicism. He used the words of the Song of Songs to emphasise the status of Protestantism as the true church, despite its difficulties: 'See if the Spouse of Christ in that heavenly marriage-song do not call him, a yong Hart, in the *mountains of divisions* ... Take you peace: let me have Truth.'[33] The anti-Catholic chaplains of Prince Henry were clearly in the vanguard of the Calvinist fight against Arminianism which was to dominate religious politics in the course of the next three decades: as we shall see, the Biblical image of the Bride was to be useful in that struggle, as it had been in anti-Catholic writing.

George Gifford, John Donne, and Robert Aylett

John Donne had been close to various members of the group that espoused Protestant Internationalism. He knew Lucy, Countess of Bedford, who had been at the heart of this circle, extremely well: he was a friend of Joseph Hall, who had written prefatory verses to two of his poems: and he had been very close to Edward Herbert, the adopted son of Donne's father-in-law Sir George More, who was very prominent in the circle.[34] Donne had of course ruined his own chances of a position at the court of Prince Henry by his rash elopement with More's daughter, but he did try very hard to win favour, dedicating *Pseudo-martyr* (1610) to Henry, and being seen at every social function at Henry's court.[35] Puritan minister George Gifford was at Sir Philip Sidney's deathbed at the siege of Zutphen in 1586, represented by Greville in 'A Dedication to Philip Sidney', which circulated in manuscript after the death of Prince Henry. As the cause of 'protection of the Netherlanders'.[36] Gifford's account of Sidney's death circulated in manuscript, became famous.[37] His death in 1600 marked the moment when leadership of the Protestant internationalist cause was handed on to the Earl of Essex, and it was probably this strong connection with the Sidney-Essex faction that ensured that his *Fifteene sermons, upon the Song of Salomon* were republished several times after their first publication in 1598. Gifford had sailed close to the wind as one of the leaders of the Puritan faction in Essex: in 1586 he had been suspended for refusing to wear the surplice, and his name was frequently mentioned in investigation of the Martin Marprelate tracts.[38]

George Gifford's sermon on the first half of Canticles 5, representing as it did a strongly Calvinist view, serves as an illuminating commentary on one of John Donne's most famous Holy Sonnets. Sonnet 10 reaches out from what is figured first as a treacherous alliance, then as a state of spiritual adultery, towards a chaste devotion to a heavenly Bridegroom. In line 2 there is a distinct version of 5:2 of the Song of Songs: the Divine Lover is standing at the door, knocking, asking to be let in. The persona of the sonnet is a Christian believer taking the role of the Bride, who, like the Biblical figure, needs to 'rise and stand'. Gifford stresses, as does Donne, the gentleness of the action that Christ takes, having been rejected: Donne would prefer the door of his heart to be battered down.

> Batter my heart, three person'd God; for you
> As yet but knocke, breathe, shine, and seeke to mend.

What the Lover does next in the Song of Songs, says Gifford, is to find 'some little crevice, or hole, as through the door, to put in his hand' (p. 176). For Gifford, this is a tiny action of the Holy Spirit, more than enough to sway the human being: 'downe goeth the power of the flesh where he commeth' (p. 177). Thus, in response, the Bride rises and goes to the door to let her Lover in. Donne, however, is looking for something much more violent to get him on his feet, although like Gifford, he acknowledges that a kind of death must precede this resurrection: 'That I may rise and stand, o'erthrow me'. He is voicing a classic Reformed paradox here, which only the Holy Spirit can deal with: the Spirit has the power to mortify sinful human nature and resurrect the individual in the power of God. This particular passage from the Song of Songs had been cited by Cardinal Bellarmine as critical to the whole debate between Catholic and Protestant over the powerlessness of the human subject, as Richard Sibbes noted in 1639, in his series of sermons on the Song of Songs called *Bowels opened*:

> *Bellarmine* makes this *Objection,* and speakes very rudely, that he is an unwise man to knocke, where there is no man within to open; and that if Christ knocke, and we cannot open, it is a delusion to exhort to open, and that therefore there must needs be free-will in us to open.[39]

Sibbes' answer to Bellarmine is similar to Gifford's comment on verse 4: that the human subject has to be moved by the Holy Spirit, in what was to Calvinist theologians known as prevenient grace, before he can himself move to open the door to Christ.[40] The predestinarian implications of the doctrine of prevenient grace are softened by Sibbes' insistence that Christ approaches most people in this way. 'In many he opens their understandings in a great measure, and knocks upon their hearts, that they (as it were) halfe open unto Christ, like *Agrippa* that said to *Paul, Thou almost perswadest mee to be a Christian*. ... Away then with these impudent, ungracious Objections about Gods Decree for matter of Election', concludes Sibbes (pp. 162–3). It is this divine intervention that Donne is seeking, although he is able to conceive of it only in violent terms, perhaps because the Bride who is his soul is portrayed as in a state of Calvinistic total depravity: as Judith Stampfer points out, this means that she cannot respond to seduction, and rape is the only alternative.[41]

Gifford, like Sibbes, has a high opinion of the gentle power of the motions of the Holy Spirit; his Bride is already powerfully affected by repentance and love. The word he uses for her is 'rapt', a word very close to 'ravished', the verb Donne does not invoke until the end of his poem, and then as a kind of fantasy. From the *volta* in his sonnet, Donne is expressing the need for some powerful force to be exerted on him: as Gene Veith asserts, this poem could be seen as a celebration of irresistible grace. Explicitly taking the subject position of the loving but wayward Bride of Christ, he knows he needs to be 'chaste', but unless something violent occurs, that is not going to happen:

> Yet dearely'I love you, and would be lov'd faine,
> But am betroth'd unto your enemie,
> Divorce mee,'untie or breake that knot againe,

> Take mee to you, imprison mee, for I,
> Except you'enthrall mee, never shall be free,
> Nor ever chast, except you ravish me.[42]

Donne of course is aware of the full spectrum of meaning of the word 'ravish'. The context of sexual politics that he has carefully set up entails that the immediate effect of the word is one of brute sexual violence, a deliberately shocking end to the poem. As it stands the poem is an illustration of Romans 7:19, 'the good that I would, I do not; but the evil which I would not, that I do', a dilemma expressed in the first part of that chapter in the same terms as this poem, that the victim is married to the wrong partner. At the end of chapter seven the power of God to free the soul is celebrated: by 'dying' to the power of the sinful flesh which is the old husband, the soul is free to be married to Christ (verse 4). Donne's poem , by contrast, ends with a wish for a fate worse than death: the end of the false marriage for him is envisaged as a rape.

Donne's sonnet is wittily outrageous, and therefore probably does not represent an expression of the sincere agony of soul that most critics have read into it, but a comment on Calvinist interpretation of the Song of Songs, and the implication of its gender politics. All Calvinist commentary represents the Bride of the Song of Songs as passive, a role conducive not only to early modern patriarchy but to the inculcation of Calvinist doctrine, in which Christ does all the work of election, justification and sanctification. Donne's Bride is just not passive enough, or perhaps, as Anthony Low suggests, the male human being finds it too difficult to take a feminised role: whilst the Bride of chapter 5 of the Song of Songs is too laid back to open the door to Christ, Donne 'labour[s] to admit' the divine Lover.[43] The subject's plight is hopeless unless Christ is prepared to use a shocking amount of force to counteract the sinful activity of his errant Bride. Perhaps Donne is drawing attention to the huge imbalance envisaged by Calvinism in the power relationship between the partners in the marriage, figuring the bond between God and the believer. As William Kerrigan points out, in Donne's habitual metaphoric practice (Kerrigan connects this with the doctrine of 'accommodation') 'rape' is implicitly included in the marriage metaphor, along with 'infidelity, divorce , and ... all the things which attend earthly marriage'.[44] In the poem, the discomfort caused by use of the word 'ravish' is strengthened, not weakened, by knowledge of its current value in Puritan spirituality. Donne is surely drawing attention to its inappropriateness in spiritual discourse—can it be healthy to induce this kind of masochistic need in an individual? Richard Strier sees the violence as both divine and demonic in this poem.[45] I would argue that the desire for violence throughout the poem is demonic. There are some alarming questions raised about the implications of Puritan use of the allegory of marriage: human sexuality is too easily perverted to serve as a stable vehicle with which to convey a relationship with God. Not the least of these problems is the necessity, in the adoption of the trope of the mystical marriage, for at least half of the population to undergo a metaphorical transgendering. The poetic voice in Sonnet 10 is not as straightforwardly female as many critics have suggested. In the first part of the poem the militarily 'usurped town' for the figure of the poet, and the battle-zone which is the fraught relationship between God and the human being, suggest that this is not a woman's world, although it is very much the world of Jacobean interpretation of the Song of Songs. The final invocation of rape in Donne's poem is the more shocking for retaining a homosexual connotation. But as Gene Veith points out in what he sees as an 'essentially Arminian' poem, although divine rape is seen to have its attractions, Donne does not really believe in it, or even, I would suggest, approve of it.[46] His God probably continues to 'knock, breathe, shine and seek to mend' despite the perverse prayer that ends the sonnet: He is waiting for the voluntary response that in an Arminian view of salvation, which allows for the freedom of the will, is eminently possible.

Noam Flinker compares Donne's use of the mystical marriage metaphor in Sonnet 10 to church lawyer and poet Robert Aylett's in his *The Brides Ornaments* of 1625. It is the second meditation in Aylett's sequence, 'Of Zeale and Godly Jealousie', that Flinker identifies as most similar to Donne's poem. Jealousy of course is mentioned in 8:6 of the Song of Songs, in a chillingly powerful description: as Aylett puts it both in the metaphrase of the Song of Songs that precedes *The Brides Ornaments*, and in *The Brides Ornaments* itself: 'For Love is strong as death, and Jealousie/ Cruell as grave.'[47] A jealous God who will not allow his Bride to be unfaithful is consonant with the patriarchal husband invoked by Calvinist interpretation of the Song of Songs, and indeed with the way Donne wishes that God would deal with him in Sonnet 10. Flinker also points out that Aylett's use of the word 'ravish' in the context of a meditation on zeal invokes sexual violence.[48] But Aylett's constructions are not unmistakeably sexual, as Donne's are: and in any case, there is no evidence that Aylett is Calvinist in belief, although Flinker designates him as such.[49] The meditation on Zeal is perhaps the most radical poem that Aylett wrote: he even mentions with disapproval the zeal of Phineas, which became a much-repeated bloodthirsty Biblical precedent in the mouths of Civil War radicals to justify their violent actions (p. 17).[50] Zeal for Aylett is certainly connected with the passion which drove the martyrs to their deaths (p. 20). However, he is careful to qualify the exact kind of zeal of which he approves:

> May I not liken her to strong churlish wine,
> Which doth confound the braine, inflame the blood:
> But cool'd with water pure, and sugar fine,
> For both of them is soueraigne and good:
> Eu'n so doth *Iealousies* most fervent mood,

> Allaid with *sugar* of sweet *Charitie,*
> And coold with *sweetest Christalline* pure floud,
> The silent streames of soft *Humilitie,*
> Transcend in all good workes, of *Loue* and *Pietie* (p. 16).

This is a genteel zeal which needs diluting with humility and charity: no militant Protestantism here. Jealousy is a dangerously strong, and distastefully crude, emotion. Aylett's lack of radicalism is obvious in the stanza in which he deplores the effects of the wrong kind of zeal, which is characteristic of the rebellious and ignorant mob:

> Strange is this *zealous fury* of the rude,
> When *Ignorance* doth guide their blind devotion,
> The gathering of the froward multitude,
> When they be stirred with some fervent motion:
> All following some braine-sicke idle notion,
> With discontent, against authoritie,
> Raise *Schismes in Church, in Common-wealth Commotion;*
> Pretending all their *Conscience-liberty,*
> Alas! these be no fruits of holy *Iealousie* (p. 14).

The concern for hierarchies and class distinctions, as well as the scorn for liberty of conscience, alerts the reader to Aylett's political allegiances. In 1628 Aylett was appointed by William Laud to the Court of High Commission to push through Laud's reforms and to combat Puritanism. He was named among Laud's followers in the articles of impeachment in February 1641.[51] Such a difference in political orientation from those authors who usually concerned themselves with the Song of Songs and Spenserian allegory, such as George Wither and Francis Rous, is striking.[52] But Aylett's *Brides Ornaments* is in a rather different religious tradition from most texts on the Song of Songs of the early seventeenth century. Although he pays homage to Spenser (and Homer, and Virgil) in the Proem to the book, he criticises Spenser for being too interested in chivalry: all these authors should have focused on charity. This is not the Protestant internationalism of the Sidney-Essex group. Neither are the many women in the poem straightforwardly allegorical figures of the kind the Bride of the Song of Songs represents; Flinker comments, 'Aylett presents a spiritual quest for religious salvation by means of feminine figures who appeal to his narrator as attractive women before he can learn anything about their allegorical import.' *The Brides Ornaments* is 'a religious treatise that never quite loses sight of its carnal origins'.[53] By contrast, Calvinist treatises try hard to efface possible carnal origins of the Song of Songs. Beza and those who followed him denied a historical context for the Song of Songs in a real marriage, because this would reinforce the essential sexuality of the original text.[54] John Donne's theological opinions were in the end probably closer to Robert Aylett's than to George Gifford's or any other confirmed Calvinist, although his objections to Calvinist doctrine are not so explicit. However, Sonnet 10 is composed at a much earlier date than Aylett's poetry of the 1620s, when the political and theological counter-claims of Arminianism were more developed: in any case, it is problems with the language and imagery of Calvinism that Donne as a poet is primarily concerned with, and that Sonnet 10 draws attention to.

Donne's Sonnet 18, which probably dates from the 1620s, is an even more daring experiment in the perverse implications of the symbolic politico-religious value of the discourse of the mystical marriage. Unlike Sonnet 10, which explores the individualistic implications of the mystical marriage for the individual soul, Sonnet 18 focusses on the other referent of the figure of the Bride, the true institutional Church. If Sonnet 10 sought to expose the improprieties of Calvinist teaching on the Song of Songs by taking that discourse to an extreme, Sonnet 18 offers what amounts to an Arminian parody of the doctrine of the Bride of Christ. The poem begins in controversial enough mode, by asking God to reveal which church is the true Bride of Christ: this, of course, is the early seventeenth century interpretation of the question in 1:7 of the Song of Songs, 'Tell me, O thou whom my soul loveth, where thou feedest, where thou makest thy flock to rest at noon.' The choice is clearly between the Catholic church—'she which on the other shore/Goes richly painted'—and one other, which by process of elimination must be the Protestant church. The terms in which this church is described led Helen Gardner to date the poem in the period soon after 1620, when the Catholic forces of Europe defeated the Protestant forces, led by the Elector Palatine and his wife, the erstwhile Elizabeth Stuart, at the battle of White Mountain.[55] The overwhelming reaction of sadness by the English is expressed in Donne's description of a Spouse who, 'rob'd and tore,/Laments and mournes in Germany and here'. Potter and Simpson comment that 'Donne's dismay and bewilderment' at this event is also found in the sermons of this period.[56]

The *volta* means a change of tone as Donne invokes the courtly romance which always lurks behind the metaphor of the mystical marriage: he suggests that a quest for the Bride might be necessary;

> Dwells she with us, or like adventuring knights
> First travaile we to seeke, and then make love?

There is of course a problem in the way Donne has constructed the true Spouse as a queen of romance. He should be identifying himself with the Spouse—certainly as a high-ranking clergyman in the Church of England he should surely believe that he is part of the true Church. Instead, he locates himself as separate, and as male: in fact as a chivalric knight. This means that he apparently becomes competition for the Spouse's husband, a kind of Lancelot to Arthur's Guinevere. God, the 'kind husband', is begged not to be jealous, but to 'Betray ... thy spouse to our sights'. This would seem to be a vain hope of the God who proclaims himself a jealous God, a text frequently invoked as justifying His enclosing and protecting behaviour towards His bride in Puritan commentary on the Song of Songs. The final couplet of this sonnet, however, redefines the 'true' church in a way that is distinctly un-Calvinist, un-Protestant and even un-Christian:

> Who is most trew, and pleasing to thee, then
> When she'is embraced and open to most men.[57]

These two lines represent an absolute contradiction of the Calvinist doctrine of limited atonement, whereby Christ died only for the elect. This Bride is not exclusive about the way she distributes her favours: anyone can enter the True Church. There is no way to get around the fact that Donne has here portrayed the Bride as a whore, despite attempts by critics such as Stanley Stewart and Helen Gardner to explain the sexual impropriety away.[58] It is probably amusing to Donne that he has transformed the Elect woman envisaged by the Protestant church as Christ's Spouse into the Whore of Babylon, the caricature with which Protestants attacked the Catholic Church.[59]

What is very striking about the poem is the way the gender politics have changed from those of Sonnet 14, written perhaps a dozen years earlier. The sexual relationship in Sonnet 14 is imagined in the patriarchal terms within which Calvinists interpreted the Song of Songs, with Christ as the all-powerful male to Donne's female soul. It is true that Sonnet 18 portrays a different pair of potential lovers—the Church, the Bride of Christ, and Donne, the adventuring knight. However, the difference in the power balance is palpable. Donne is no longer portraying himself as the helpless soul of Calvinist theology, even if this portrayal in the earlier sonnet is ironic. In this poem he has free will, like the rest of mankind, to seek out his lady love, and the ability, it seems, to court her, although the success of this enterprise is not a foregone conclusion as it would be in a Calvinist predestinarian scheme: the romantic quest is a different kind of narrative that gives more agency to the human subjects, Perhaps the later sonnet reveals a change in mentality that corresponds to a movement in Donne's theology: he is now able to imagine the soul as a free, if not unerring, agent, who needs help from God but not the kind of utter domination envisaged in Sonnet 10.

Sonnet 18 was not printed in the seventeenth century: even Helen Gardner, for whom the expressions are much more orthodox, speculates that it might be thought 'too witty a poem for a man of his profession to write.'[60] Even in the 1630s, when most of Donne's poetry was published, it was probably transgressive to counter Calvinist claims for the limited number of the Elect with the assertion that a kind of promiscuity is more pleasing to God than purity. Donne's sonnet transforms God into a kind of pimp for his own wife, an extension of the marriage trope not envisaged by other expositors of the

Song of Songs.[61] There may also be a deliberate exposing here of the link between chivalry and militant Protestantism that had been so characteristic of the Sidney-Essex circle, a heady mixture of 'honour, idealism in religion and the chivalric quest for renown'.[62] By 1620, having long ago given up on a place at court, Donne had moved far from the ideological temper of the Prince of Wales' chaplains: perhaps he could now gently mock the incongruity of attempting to combine chivalric narrative and Calvinist doctrine in the metaphor of the mystical marriage. He produces a parody of this hybrid discourse that is unmistakeably Arminian in nature.

The Spanish match: waiting for the Bride

George Gifford's much more orthodox sermons on the Song of Songs were reprinted in 1620, and it is tempting to see this publication, upholding as it does the major tenets of Calvinism, as a celebration of the outcome of the Synod of Dort, which was held in 1618–19 in order to settle the serious controversy in the Dutch churches initiated by the rise of Arminianism.[63] Churchmen from all over Europe attended: James I sent five prominent men, including Calvinists such as Joseph Hall and John Davenant, as well as Lancelot Andrewes, who was one of the influential group of Arminians in England. There were five tenets of Calvinism which were disputed by Arminianism. It was fundamental to Calvinists that humanity was in a state of total depravity, totally enslaved by sin: Arminians, by contrast, held that humankind was not irredeemably sinful. By a subtle adjustment of Calvinist ideas of predestination, Arminians believed that God's election was dependent on His foreknowledge of who would believe in Him, and therefore not as mysterious and inscrutable as high Calvinists wanted predestination to be. The Calvinist idea that the number of the elect was limited, and that Christ did not therefore die for all mankind, was utterly denied by Arminians, who held that salvation was freely available to all: and for Arminians, grace could be resisted and finally lost, in defiance of the Calvinist doctrine of perseverance. By the early 1620s, the enemy for the moderate Puritan, who was inevitably Calvinist in doctrine, was the growing power of Arminianism in England, as Jeanne Shami comments: 'the anti-papist sermons across the spectrum were allied with a measure of anti-Arminian rhetoric, marking the association between Arminian doctrines of universal grace and the Catholic emphasis on human will in salvation'.[64] William Laud, future Arminian Archbishop of Canterbury, was made a bishop in 1621 and spent the rest of King James' reign at court. The King published in 1619 *A Meditation Upon the Lord's prayer*, which held to Calvinist doctrine, and actually attacked the Arminians, although his greatest vitriol was reserved for the Puritans, whom he designated 'the founders and fathers of the Brownists'.[65] However, Calvinist ideologies of Protestantism internationalism conflicted with James' strategies for peace in Europe. Much to his concern, his son-in-law Frederick accepted the crown of Bohemia in 1619: James forbad any public prayer for the King and Queen of Bohemia, let alone any public celebration of the event, and barred Frederick and Elizabeth from visiting England. Protestant internationalists struck back by engaging churchmen such as Richard Sibbes to preach their cause.[66] After the Battle of White Mountain Catholic forces gave obvious grounds for war in their invasion of the Palatinate, but far from intervening militarily, James forbad the clergy to represent the war that was now raging in the Palatinate as a religious one.[67] By mid-1622, against the background of a 'continued pulpit offensive' against his pro-Spanish foreign policy James intervened in theological matters: he issued directions to the clergy forbidding them to speak on such points of Calvinist doctrine as predestination and the irresistibility of grace, on August 4th, 1622.[68] On 15th September 1622 John Donne was commissioned to preach a sermon at St. Paul's Cross defending this action.[69] Nicholas Tyacke suggests that the King's growing inclination to Arminianism was the result of the importance for him of the projected marriage of his son with the Spanish Infanta: it made no sense to encourage the vehement anti-Catholicism of the Calvinists, although that had been his own policy in the early years of his reign.[70] Jeanne Shami claims that these royal religious policies 'exposed fault lines in the Church of England that contributed to a reconfigured Caroline church and the demise of the Jacobean order'.[71]

In many ways, royal chaplain William Loe, who objected strongly to Prince Charles' planned marriage to the Spanish Infanta, epitomised the godly Calvinist opposition to the rise of Arminianism in England in the 1620s. He had been one of the first to clash with the future Archbishop, William Laud, when he was still a humble Dean in 1617, and already insisting on railing off the altar in Gloucester, where Loe was serving as a minister. Loe seems to have been involved in the protest against Laud.[72] He delivered a series of seven sermons at St Michael Cornhill before he left England to become chaplain to the Merchant Adventurers' Company in 1619. His preface to the king suggested that 'those of the Churches Governement must abate theyr rough rigor and sternnes, & yeeld somewhat for the peace of the church, and by listening to the petitions, and counsels of many godly and well disposed men, should reforme the apparent errors and abuses crept into the church'.[73] There is no doubt that Loe was warning against Arminianism: 'godly' had by this time become shorthand for Calvinist. Soon after Loe's arrival in Hamburg he dedicated to his fellow Englishmen there a poetic version of some of the books of the Bible, including the Song of Songs. Bizarrely, his metaphrase was into monosyllables, which he described as particularly characteristic of ancient English. He chose well-known tunes for his poems and offered them to his congregation for their private use. The treatment of the Song of Songs is designated in a way that confirms its centrality in moderate Calvinist spirituality: it is 'to be used by every devout soule in his privat conference with his god'.[74] Loe's verses are extremely simple and gloss over the difficulties of the Song of Songs: broad Calvinist interpretations of the text are included in his version of it, and generalisations take the place of detail. He divides the book into poems of four stanzas each: here is the first.

> 1.
> O that thou wouldst on me so cast
> Some lookes of thy sweete love,
> That thou maist make me deere to thee
> My hart with grace to move
>
> 2.
> Thy love o Christ is farre more deare,
> And farre more sweete to me
> Then wealth, or wine, or limbe, or life,
> Or ought that I can see.
>
> 3.
> The sweete that I smell of thy name
> Is like an oyle most pure,
> And pourd it is on all thy saincts
> Such is thy love soe sure.
>
> 4.
> O drawe me, drawe me, I will runne
> To bord, to bed with thee;
> O pull me, pull me from my sinne
> O rid me, set me free (p. 79).

William Loe's songs see the start of the process that is to continue throughout the seventeenth century: he has transformed a difficult text into a simple love lyric. Phrases that need subtle interpretation, such as verse 2, 'Let him kiss me with the kisses of his mouth', are toned down—it is looking, not kissing, which is going on here—and their spiritual significance immediately explained. It is a given of interpretation that this poem is not about physical contact but about the motions of grace in the believer. Loe does not avoid the sexual connotations of the original text entirely: his Bride also longs to go to bed with her Spouse. However, the spiritual interpretation of verse four is incorporated into the poem: the Bride is being actually drawn towards purity and away from sin. Although the sub-title of *Songs of Sion* (*Set for the joy of gods deere ones, who sitt here by the brookes of this worlds Babel, & weepe when they thinke on Hierusalem which is on highe*) advertises it for use when the faithful are longing for the heavenly city, a rather more earthly kind of homesickness is suggested, especially when Loe has the words of the daughters of Jerusalem spoken by 'A forraigne congregation' (p. 98): 'forraigne congregation' here is any Protestant church which is not the Church of England. It is rather touching to imagine this international Protestant reciting his 'Monosyllabls of Great Brittains language' in a devotion which speaks to him of his home country, an England which is still broadly Calvinist and where the spirituality of the Song of Songs is still mainstream.

The supporters of Protestant internationalism were not pleased with James' plans for a Spanish Catholic bride for his son. Despite James' 1622 *Directions to Preachers*, the most persistent and troubling criticism continued to come from the pulpit: 1622 saw a succession of famous preachers reprimanded for commenting on the Spanish match.[75] Thomas Jackson joined in, in his traditional anti-Catholic vein, discerning some great corruption within church and state and making dark allusions to the appearance of the comet in 1618, which had been interpreted by many as signifying God's disapproval of the Spanish Match.[76] By contrast, in September 1622 Donne wrote to Goodyer saying that the King had over-reacted in warning the Spanish Ambassador of the hostility of the people to the match: they were already falling back on 'trust in God and the King's way'. Donne also sent a copy of his sermon approving the *Directions* to Elizabeth Stuart herself: one wonders how she received the justification of a measure intended to silence many of her chief supporters.[77] Robert Aylett ostentatiously started his *Thrifts equipage* (1622) with a disavowal of his interest in State affairs:

> I Meddle not with newes of Parlament,
> Court-Fauourites, or Kingdomes gouernement;
> On Kings secrets, and affaires of State,
> Nor know, nor need, nor care to meditate (sig. A1v).

Meanwhile, George Wither published his Epithalamia on Frederick and Elizabeth's marriage a decade previously, describing Elizabeth Stuart as the resurrected Queen Elizabeth, and prophesying the 'terror to the Whore of Babylon' that would issue from 'your blessed loynes'.[78] Peter McCullough believes that most of Charles' chaplains, who had been recruited to the Prince of Wales' court in the days of Henry, were opposed to the match. Andrew Willet was imprisoned for speaking out against it.[79] Joseph Hall joined him in gaol for his sermon at Theobalds in 1623, *The Best Bargaine*, dedicated to the Earl of Pembroke: Peter Lake suggests that Hall was a kind of spokesman for the Herberts at this time.[80] Hall's *Contemplations Upon the Holy Story*, meditations on the Bible which had been issued in instalments since 1612, dealt in 1622 with Solomon's marriages in a manner which could only be seen as relevant to the proposed Spanish and Castholic royal match.

> Sexe, multitude, nation, condition, all conspired to the ruine of a *Salomon;* ... now they were of those Nations, whereof the Lord had said to

the children of Israel, *Goe not yee in to them, nor let them come in to you, for surely they will turne your hearts after their Gods;* to them did *Salomon* joyne in love; who can marvell if they disjoyned his heart from God? ... so farre was the uxorious King blinded with affection, that he gave not passage only to the Idolatrie of his heathenish wives, but furtherance.[81]

Hall's protest at the proposed marriage of Charles to a Catholic gained momentum with his description of how Solomon built heathen temples for his wives to worship in: 'Each of his dames had their Puppets, their altars, their incense' (pp. 271–2). At this date he could scarcely have foreseen that he was actually prophesying the building of a Catholic chapel in London by a royal bride, not Spanish but French, when Charles finally married Henrietta Maria.

Henry Burton, Clerk of the Closet, who was to fall foul of his royal master for his radical Puritanism when Charles came to the throne, was not allowed to accompany Charles to Spain, to court the Infanta: the mission was considered too diplomatically sensitive.[82] Before Charles left for Spain, on 14th January 1623, William Loe preached to the prince and his father, urging the defence of true religion and military assistance to the Palatinate. Loe escaped censure by declaring, in the preface to the sermon, that he was not actually advising the King, a claim which actually fooled no-one. In the climate of anxiety and suspicion following Charles' departure for Spain, all references to marriages real or spiritual could be interpreted as having political resonance. On 19 March 1623 Royal chaplain James Rawlinson made a direct connection between Prince Charles' 'Amorous travels' to gain a bride and the 'Amatorious text' of the Song of Songs in a sermon entitled 'The Bridegrome and his Bride'.[83] Rawlinson affirms the origin of the Song of Songs in a real marriage, but declares that the mystical marriage is the more important, particularly as he is preaching in the season of Lent (p. 15). Nevertheless, he proceeds to draw politically apposite lessons from teaching on the mystical marriage. For example, the Bride should abstain from fornication with idols (p. 19); the anti-Catholic tenor of the sermon makes the application clear. There is much emphasis on the choice of Bride as being that of the father, which could be read both spiritually and carnally: however, there is a stress on divine election which would seem to indicate that Rawlinson is criticising the earthly father, James I, for choosing a non-elect bride for his son, the Infanta (p. 11). This is a complex hermeneutic: the Song of Songs is being interpreted in the traditional framework of the mystical marriage, but lessons are being drawn in the opposite direction, from the spiritual phenomenon back to the projected marriage of Prince Charles.

Charles' trip proved to be physically and spiritually perilous: none of the carefully chosen chaplains were in fact allowed to attend him when he arrived in Spain, and he did not hear a Protestant service during his stay there. On Charles' return without a bride, there was unrestrained rejoicing across the nation.[84] This sense of huge relief was shared by the royal household.

Loe presented Charles with an elegant copy of his January sermon, thereby signifying 'a thanksgiving for Charles' return from the ploys of his father's Hispanophile pacifism to an English defence of European Protestantism.'[85] The poet George Wither was also participating in the joyous welcome to Prince Charles from his physically and diplomatically difficult expedition to Spain. He wrote about it in *Britain's Remembrancer*, the first version of which he presented to Charles I in manuscript. It was finally published with some difficulty in 1628. The work started as a kind of record of Wither's experiences during the plague of 1625, together with his perception of the sins which had brought the judgement of God down on London. God himself speaks in outraged tones at the start of the work, detailing the favours bestowed on England, as an 'enclosed garden', protected by cliffs and seas:

> Is this the *Land* whom we have lov'd so long,
> And, in our love, elected from among
> The Heathen *Iles* ...
> Is this that *Iland*, which our love did place
> (Within our bosome) in the safe embrace
> Of great *Oceanus?* and, garden like
> Did wharfe about (within her watry *Dike)*
> With mighty Rocks, and Cliffes, whose tops were higher,
> Then any foming Billow dares aspire?

Given the favours He has bestowed on England, God is incredulous at how smug and pleasure-seeking she is while her Protestant neighbours in Europe are in trouble, and perceives her as ungrateful:

> Is this the *Country* which our bounty served
> With store of bread, when many Lands were starved?
> And whom we have preserved from the spoiles
> Of Foes abroad, and from domesticke broyles?
> Are theirs the *Cities*, which doe weare the Flag
> Of *Peace*, while *Rochel, Heidleberg*, and *Prague*,
> And all the Christian world engaged are,
> In some offensive, or defensive warre? [86]

Wither's God is particularly indignant that England is not more appreciative of the divine provision of Elizabeth I with her 'vertues masculine'. With these political opinions prevailing in heaven it is no wonder that God has in fact personally intervened to bring Prince Charles home safe without a Spanish bride:

> Did we but here, of late, when they had lost
> Their *Prince* (that now is *King*) when they almost
> Despair'd of his returne, for evermore,

> When he remained on th' *Iberian* shore?
> Did we accept their vowes? observe their teares?
> Compassionate their jealousies and feares?
> And send their *Darling* home, when few did know
> Whereon to build a hope it should be so?(p. 19)

This combination of opinions on the Spanish match, the Protestant cause in Europe, and nostalgia for Queen Elizabeth was often found in the Calvinist preaching of the early 1620s until it was forbidden by James.[87] When the preachers were silenced, this political antagonism was often expressed in writing on the Song of Songs: indeed, authors used their reading of the Song of Songs to confirm the divine authority of these attitudes.

It is perhaps no surprise to learn that one opponent of the Spanish match, the anti-Catholic George Wither, produced one of the most widely-read versions of the Song of Songs in the seventeenth century. His book of paraphrases and metaphrases, *The Hymnes and Songs of the Church*, with music by Orlando Gibbons, went into nine editions after it was first published in 1623.[88] Wither must have felt uncharacteristically favoured by the receipt of a royal grant of the copyright on this volume from King James: he was also granted the right to have his volume bound with every psalm book in metre. Needless to say, this would have made him a very rich man, but the Stationer's Company, senior members of which owned the rights to the psalms, refused to co-operate. In *The Schollers Purgatory* of 1624 Wither defended his right to the royal patent. He also found it necessary to defend his paraphrase of the Song of Songs. It appears that some critics found the combination of the content of the Song of Songs and Wither's lyric verse forms rather too erotic: one particular verse was found to be obscene. This was Wither's rendering of chapter seven verse one:

> Thou *Daughter* of the Royall Line,
> How comely are those *Feet* of thine,
> When their beseeming *Shooes* they weare·
> The curious knitting of thy *Thighes*,
> Is like the costly Gemmes of prize,
> Which wrought by skilfull workmen are.[89]

The particular phrase in question was 'knitting of thy thighs': the Authorised Version had 'joints of thy thighs'. Apart from pointing out that there was very little difference between the two phrases, Wither found himself insisting that he himself had never been sexually excited by any of his work on the Song of Songs:

> I protest before God (at whose throne I shal be judged for it, if I lye) I
> doe not remember that I had one immodest thought (so much as cast

into me) by meanes of any expression in that holy Song, during the tyme I was busied thereabout.[90]

In fact, like other authors dealing with the Song of Songs, Wither had taken care to warn his readers to approach the text in the right spirit: 'Let no man therefore presume to sing, or repeat, in a carnall sense, what is here spiritually intended; upon paine of *Gods* heavie indignation.'[91] However, he employs a daring argument to his detractors: the Song of Songs, it seems, is written particularly for young lovers, who would respond particularly strongly to a text composed in this mode (p. 52). To the criticism that children, or the unlearned, or 'the vulgar' will misunderstand the book, Wither retorts that Holy Scripture cannot be withheld from anyone on these grounds (p. 56). In short, he considers his lyrical version 'as proper, as modest, and as perspicuous as most prose Translations' (p. 57). Wither's protestations are the more difficult to believe in the light of his publication of the year before, *Faire-virtue, the mistresse of Phil'arete* (London, 1622). This is a series of love songs and sonnets written to a superlative woman, and in the Stationer's epistle to the reader (which Wither confesses he actually wrote himself) he keeps the reader guessing as to whether the work is allegorical or not:

> Whether therefore, this Mistresse of Phil'arete, bee really a *Woman*, shaddowed under the name of Virtue: or Virtue onely, whose lovelinesse is represented by the Beautie of an excellent *Woman:* Or, whether it meane both together; I cannot tell you (sig. A4r-A4v).

Wither's mistress is rather familiar to a reader of his version of the Song of Songs. She is heavenly born, and is celebrated with a blazon of her beauty, just as the Biblical bride is in chapter seven, a blazon which also includes her navel, and her thighs. The phrasing with which her thighs are described vitiates the claim that this is a poem written long ago in Wither's youth:

> I perceivd the curious knitting,
> Of those ioynts were well be fitting (E3v)

The knitting of the thighs was precisely the phrase which was perceived to be obscene when used of the Bride in Wither's 1621 version of the Song of Songs. 'Her two twinlike louely Breasts' (sig. E1r) also sound like the breasts of the Bride, but in Wither's poem they are certainly not equated with anything as sober as the Old and New Testaments. They apparently reduce him to a panting wordlessness, although being Wither this is a relative wordlessness: he describes them for a further two pages, including an erotic incident when her bodice became unlaced and one breast fell out. At this point the reader begins to doubt the warning at the start of the poem, which is very similar to the admonition at the start of Wither's version of the Song of Songs, and which uses the familiar argument that any profanity is in the reader's mind:

> If you bring a modest minde,
> You shall nought immodest finde.
> But, if any too severe,...
> Let him know thus much from me,
> If here's ought prophane, tis he (C2r).

One curious feature of Wither's paraphrase of the Song of Songs, and perhaps a strategy to make it fit his interpretive scheme more neatly, is the way the poetic text is divided up into short songs which do not necessarily fit with chapter divisions. Each short song is given its own tune, which is conveniently provided. Thus Wither is able to separate out the last six verses of chapter three as his twelfth song, and give it a warlike flavour. His preface instructs us to read it as a manifesto for militant Protestantism, portraying Christ going out in power to preach the Gospel, whilst the Church is 'defended by the Sword of Gods Word, against Infidels, Heretickes, and all the Powers and Terrours of the Kingdome of Darkenesse' (p. 49).

> His bed (which loe is Solomons)
> Threescore stout men about it stand:
> They are of Israels valiant Ones;
> And all of them with Swords in hand.
>
> 2
> All those are men expert in fight:
> And each one on his thigh doth weare
> A Sword; that terrors of the night
> May be forbid from comming there (p. 40).

Protestant internationalists made much of this passage from Canticles which for them justified the use of force in a holy cause. Contrast the interpretation of verse 6 of chapter 3, 'Who is this that cometh out of the wilderness like pillars of smoke, perfumed with myrrh and frankincense?' by the French Catholic Nicholas Caussin in 1634: for him this verse described the assumption into heaven of the Virgin Mary, who was 'wholy spiritualized, wholy vapour, al perfume, al spirit, and had nothing of body, massinesse, or earth'.[92] For Protestant internationalists, this verse described the splendid military power available to the Bride: supported by spiritual strength, but all too physical in nature.

On the whole, the pieces of narrative in the Song of Songs are rendered rather better by Wither than the actual love poetry, but he does have some rather difficult vocabulary to deal with. The most effective passage is probably that which was found to be 'obscene': this is the following stanza.

> Thy *Navell*, is a Goblet round,
> Where Liquor evermore is found.
> Thy faire and fruitfull *Belly* showes
> As doth a goodly heape of Wheat
> With Lillies round about beset;
> And thy two *Brests* like twinned Roes.

Perhaps it is significant that Wither has more or less abandoned allegorical or liturgical scheme for this, his seventeenth Song: he tries to convey only 'the mutuall interchange of affections betweene the *Bridegroome* and his *Bride*; and those sweet contentments they enioy in each others Loves' (p. 53).

The eroticism of Wither's poetic but literal version is perhaps proof of Stanley Stewart's observation, that 'the literal meaning of the Song of Songs had its own integrity, and this helped preserve a vitally erotic tradition'.[93] Despite Wither's refusal to be sexually aroused, it seems that readers continued to find the text erotic: so much interpretation of the Song of Songs was carried on in the reign of James I with the explicit intention of removing or reinterpreting the erotic content of the book. The Puritan reading, as we have seen, gained its own momentum, implicated as it was in the particular religious politics of the period. Yet a literal translation, not completely overwhelmed by commentary, and restored to its original status as poetry, could still, it seems, register as transgressively erotic. Future poets were to exploit the eroticism of the poem whilst clinging to its status as sacred text.

2
The Mysticall Marriage, Martyrology and Arminianism, 1625–40

There was a whiff of politically-informed wit in the text chosen for John Donne's sermon at Denmark House, for 26 April 1625. King James' body was still lying in state there. The text was Canticles 3:11, '*Goe forth ye Daughters of Sion, and behold King Solomon, with the Crown, wherewith his mother crowned him, in the day of his espousals, and in the day of the gladnesse of his heart.*' There followed much talk about the mystical marriage of King James with Christ, now consummated by the union of James' soul with Christ at the King's death: the imagery of sexual fulfilment usually accompanied the death of a martyr.[1] In the equation of James with Solomon lay a distinct challenge to some of the militant Protestant ideology which had been embraced by many Puritans. Solomon was famous as the man of peace, in contrast to his father: James of course had deliberately followed a pacifist policy, in contrast to his predecessor, who was perceived as a military champion for the Protestant cause, or at least, as we saw in the last chapter, presented as such by the Protestant internationalists of James' reign.[2] Donne is deliberately detaching the rhetoric of the mystical marriage from the politics of Protestant internationalism, and perhaps from the spirituality of martyrdom itself.

John Donne received a celebratory medal from the Synod of Dort on his way home with the Earl of Doncaster from a visit to Elizabeth of Bohemia, in 1620, but despite being close to supporters of Protestant internationalism such as Sir Thomas Roe and Lucy, Countess of Bedford, it is unlikely that he would have wholeheartedly embraced the Canons of Dort.[3] The idea that God welcomes many into the Church rather than limiting the effects of His atonement to a few, portrayed in deliberately shocking manner in Sonnet 18, is frequently reiterated in Donne's sermons, in opposition to the second main point of doctrine resolved at Dort. Moreover, the context for these disagreements is often his own comments on the Song of Songs, within which his anti-Calvinist point becomes even more striking, given the Calvinist domination of interpretation of this Biblical book. As early as 1624 he was preaching a distinctive reading of the trope of the mystical marriage. Donne himself often used the doctrine of the mystical marriage in his sermons, perhaps because rather than in spite of the potential for rhetorical shock effect inherent in the metaphorical linking of sexuality and spirituality. He seems to have enjoyed extending the image, and pushing it to logical but preposterous conclusions—an approach to metaphor used in a great deal of his poetry. He describes the very act of preaching to his congregation in terms that invoke sexual intercourse: 'The purpose of his mariage to us, is to have children by us: and this is his abundant and his present fecundity, that working now, by me in you, in one instant he hath children in me, and grand children by me.'[4] John Cotton was to appropriate female physiology in the same way, but Donne's use of the trope of the mystical marriage is not limited to the range of interpretations in Puritan commentary, which is not a surprise, given the way his poetry and even his preaching resists categorisation.[5] Jeanne Shami runs through the number of different politico-religious opinions that have been attributed to Donne: 'Donne of the puritan imagination; Donne the "Calvinist Episcopalian"; Donne the conformist; Donne the avant-garde conformist; Donne the Arminian.'[6] Peter McCullough gives up the attempt, describing him simply as 'muddled'.[7] What is surely true is that Donne does not offer a crude 'signpost' to his own position, a practice which Anthony Milton describes as characteristic of religious discourse in this period: or if he does, he offers other signposts in conflicting directions.[8] I have suggested that one of the distinguishing marks of politico-religious position in this period, which often does function as such a signpost, is a particular interpretation of the Song of Songs: Donne, as we shall see, deliberately espouses a complex hermeneutic of the Song of Songs, which resists any Puritan categorisation.

In a sermon on Hosea 2:19 to a real bride and bridegroom, Robert Sands and Margaret Washington (servant to his patron Lady Doncaster) Donne resists the classic identification of the bride with the enclosed garden, in the interests of sexual equality and pastoral responsibility: 'The body is the temple of the Holy Ghost; and when two bodies, by mariage are to be made one temple, the wife is not as the Chancell, reserv'd and shut up, and the man as the walks below, indifferent and at liberty for every passenger.'[9] Elsewhere he even suggests that God has had to dignify the state of marriage by adding exalted metaphors and allegories to it, because in itself it is humiliating and burdensome: he points out the inconveniences for Christ of being married to a human being.[10] This is an original and slightly anarchic interpretation of the Song of Songs: more traditionally, the Song was thought to have its superlative title because it dealt with the highest experience known to humanity, marriage.[11] In more orthodox fashion, Donne in 1624 stressed the privilege for the soul that the mystical marriage with God represented: 'God hath made love to thy soule, thy weake soule, thy sick, and foule, and sinfull soule.' However, instead of seeing this as a mark of special election, Donne constructed this love as a reason for humility, and hope for the rest of mankind: 'so much does God delight in man, so much does God desire to unite and associate man unto him; and then, what shall disappoint, or frustrate Gods desires and intentions so farre, as that they should come to him, but singly, *one by one*, whom he *cals*, and *wooes*, and *drawes* by thousands, and by whole Congregations?' The point is made again later in the same sermon, but this time more startlingly, as an interpretation of Canticles 8:6:

> Set me as a seale upon thy heart, and as a seale upon thine arme, says Christ to all us, in the person of the spouse; in the Heart, by a constant faith, in the Arme, by a declaratory works; for then are we sealed, and delivered, and witnessed; that's our full evidence, then have we made sure our salvation.

In Calvinist thought, the concept of the 'seal' was a spiritual one, either an act of God or an inward assurance of faith mediated by the Holy Spirit: it confirmed the admission of the soul into the company of the Elect. For Donne the seal is something that can be seen by others: it is a good work that bears witness to the inner salvation. Also, the seal is anything but exclusive:

> But these seales being so many, and so universall, that argues still, that which we especially seek to establish, that is, the *Accessiblenesse,* the communicablenesse, the sociablenesse, the *affection,* (shall I say) the *Ambition,* that God hath, to have us all. [12]

Donne has actually envisaged two seals, one inward and one outward, one for the heart and one for the arm, as the text of the Song of Songs indicates: the evidence of inward faith is 'declaratory works', good works that declare the status of the individual as Elect. Such a statement shows Donne refusing to repeat the commonplaces of Calvinist theology, whereby outward signs, and good works in particular, are not an accurate sign of the individual's elect status.[13] On 1 April 1627, in a sermon to Charles I, Donne confirmed his opposition to the Calvinist wing of the church, and perhaps to those Parliamentarians who had opposed Charles in the 1626 Parliament. His sermon was on the text 'take heed what ye hear', and he spent a fair proportion of it addressing Charles' subjects, warning them against subversion. They were not to speak against the Church or the State: to speak against the King was to speak against God. In this context Donne advanced a novel interpretation of the mystical marriage, whereby the King had a responsibility to protect the honour of his wife, and Christ would similarly not allow His church to be spoken against.

> The Church is the spouse of Christ: Noble husbands do not easily admit defamations of their wives. Very religious Kings may have had wives, that

may have retained some tincture, some impressions of errour, which they may have sucked in their infancy, from another Church, and yet would be loth, those wives should be publikely traduced to be Heretiques, or passionately proclaimed to be Idolaters for all that. A Church may lacke something of exact perfection, and yet that Church should not be said to be a supporter of Antichrist, or a limme of the beast, or a thirster after the cup of *Babylon,* for all that.[14]

This passage had most obvious application to the King's young wife, Henrietta Maria, a Catholic: she was not to be considered a heretic. But the use of the metaphor of the mystical marriage allowed Donne to imply that the Catholic Church too was a true Bride of Christ, although lacking in 'exact perfection'. The language he identifies here as illicit is that employed in anti-Catholic polemic since the Reformation, particularly in that inspired by the Song of Songs. It may be a tactful gesture to Henrietta Maria that calls forth this concession, as elsewhere Donne has no hesitation in calling the Pope Antichrist.[15] It is rather typical of Donne to move via the vehicle of his metaphor, the protecting love of the divine husband for his bride, to a controversial statement like this: as Donne well knows, the Biblical attitude of the Husband to his Bride is that he wants her to be 'without spot or wrinkle', pure within and without.[16] However, it is almost as if he is delighting in interpreting Biblical references to the mystical marriage in ways that are well outside of the usual Calvinist paradigms.

With the death of King James a struggle ensued over the king's posthumous reputation and beliefs, particularly in the context of the growing influence of Arminianism. Richard Montagu, a royal chaplain, had provoked a huge outcry with his 1624 book *A gagg for the new Gospell? No: a new gagg for an old goose*, in which he tried to show that Catholic doctrine was not far removed from that of the Church of England. The significance of this manoeuvre, as Anthony Milton points out, was that it exposed the theological weaknesses in the alliance between Calvinist conformists and Puritans that had guaranteed the harmony of the Church of England so far. The conventional rhetoric of this alliance combined attacks on Rome and assertions of the internal unity of Reformed doctrine: in fact, the two preoccupations of most post-Reformation discourse on the Song of Songs.[17]

There was in Parliament an opposition prepared to fight for English Church as it was currently constituted, internal contradictions notwithstanding, and to denounce all threats as Catholic-inspired. Protestant internationalists saw Montagu's book as distinguishing the Church of England from other Reformed churches of Europe, a very bad thing in their terms.[18] Protestors referred the matter to the House of Commons, but King James granted Montagu the right to defend himself, and appointed Francis White, dean of Carlisle and prominent member of the increasingly influential Durham House group of Arminian churchmen, to oversee Montagu's defence.

Montagu's book was published after James' death in 1625 as *Appello Caesarem*: White was consecrated Bishop of Carlisle at Durham House in 1626. As the title implies, the book claims throughout the backing of the King and of the Church of England for opposition to the key Calvinist doctrines of predestination and perseverance. Montagu also supports the doctrine of free will. It is not a surprise that he declares his refusal to accept the deliberations of the Synod of Dort, declaring 'the Synod of Dort no obligation to us'.[19] Such opinions were deeply offensive to the godly, despite the fact that Montagu was, technically, correct: the canons of Dort had never been officially ratified for England.[20] However, Parliament had Montagu in its sights, and in every Parliament until its dissolution in 1629, Arminianism was deplored: people like William Prynne made sure those outside Parliament knew about it.[21] The 1625 Parliament saw an attempt to adopt the canons of Dort into a Parliamentary statute.[22] A 'committee for Montagu' was appointed that included John Pym, to investigate Montagu's new book. On Thursday 7 July 1625 they declared it 'a factious and seditious book', deploring the slighting of the Synod of Dort, and declared the danger to England's church: 'the fire kindled in the Low Countries by Arminianism like to be kindled here'.[23]

Francis Rous, who took part in the debates in the House of Commons as MP for Truro, took it on himself to reply to *Appello Caesarem*, using the words of James I himself in a more Calvinist incarnation.[24] He was close to the Parliamentarian John Pym: they were brought up together on the borders of Devon and Cornwall, and Pym followed Rous to Broadgates Hall, Oxford, and the Middle Temple.[25] In the early 1620s Rous had showed his religiously-motivated concern for the English State in the treatise *Diseases of the Time, Attended by their Remedies* (1622). It was dedicated to Benjamin Rudyerd, the Earl of Pembroke's representative in Parliament and thus committed to godly Protestantism at home and the support of the international Protestant cause abroad.[26] A hint of Rous' later career as a defender of individual liberties, and as enthusiast for the Song of Songs, is seen in his contempt for hierarchy and approval for egalitarianism: 'It was not the appointment of Gods first Creation that Princes should goe on foot, and Fooles ride on horsebacke, but by *Adams* fall, rich folly takes place of poore wisdome.' With satisfaction Rous looks forward to the time 'wherein every man shall bee seated in his right place, even according to true, reall, and inward excellence' (pp. 321–4). Perhaps as Speaker of the Nominated Parliament just over 30 years later, Rous felt that this desire had come true. In 1623, however, such Utopian dreams were still far off, and his publication of that year, *Oile of Scorpions,* was rather more closely focused: contemporary disasters such as plague, poor trade, poverty, piracy, the defeat of Elizabeth of Bohemia and even the weather were identified as the punishments of God.[27] Again, moral obloquy and a dalliance with Catholicism were seen to be the main causes.

Nicholas Tyacke suggests Francis Rous as 'the ideological spokesman of the Calvinist gentry'.[28] *Testis veritatis*, Rous' 1626 reply to *Appello Caesarem*, attempts to produce King James as undeniably Calvinist, in opposition to Montagu, drawing for a great deal of his evidence on James' 1619 *A Meditation Upon the Lord's Prayer*, one of the last securely Calvinist writings that James authored. Rous seized on Montagu's volume as evidence of a Catholic plot to take over the realm, seeing Arminian doctrine as a precursor of Catholicism, and even accusing Spain of fomenting the design: 'Whosoever will bring in *Popery*, into a country strongly fixed in the *Protestant Doctrin*, must not presently fly in the face of the whole *Protestant Doctrine*, but his onely way, is to worke into it by these degres of plausible *Arminianisme*'.[29] Rous pillaged the works of James I and the articles of the Church of England to refute Montagu's claims on predestination, perseverance and freewill. Moreover, he quoted Catholic sources to make clear just how different Catholic theology was from Protestant. He located the appeal of Arminianism as its liminal status between both religions, in 'a kind of twilight'. (p. 84). As a doctrine it gloried in the ability and freewill of the human being to please God without divine assistance, like Catholicism, and yet it was classed, misleadingly in Rous' view, as Protestant. Rous was elected Member of Parliament for Tregony in 1628: he continued his attack on Montagu and other Arminians, together with a group that included John Hampden, John Pym and the indefatigable anti-Arminian campaigner Christopher Sherland. On 26 January 1629 he initiated discussion on Arminianism, repeating his accusation in *Testis veritatis* that it was a Trojan horse for Popery: 'I desire first that it may be considered what new paintings are laid upon the old face of the whore of Babylon to ... draw so many suitors to her.' Christopher Sherland joined in defence of Calvinism: 'We have a religion that is worth the loving with all our hearts. It was sealed with the blood of martyrs, and kept by miracles.' On 2 March, King Charles succeeded in dissolving Parliament, despite Denzil Holles' efforts to keep the Speaker in the Chair: the last words that were heard in the Chamber for eleven years were Holles', and apart from opposition to the grant of tonnage and poundage to the King, he wanted to voice the House of Commons' sentiments about Arminianism: 'Whosoever shall goe about to innovate any thing in Religion, to bring in either Popery or Arminianism ... let him be accounted a capital enemy of the king and kingdom.'[30]

Rous was certainly not going to allow any inroads of Catholicism to remain uncontested. In 1630 Matthew Wilson published the pro-Catholic *Charity Mistaken*. Rous's response, *Catholic Charity*, begins with a description of the Bride, the true Church:

The Spouse of Christ Jesus, when shee shines in Love, shee is amiable in Beauty, precious in the eye of her Husband, powerfull with God her

Father, prosperous in her owne spirituall health and vigour, and prepared for her consummate marriage in celestiall glory.[31]

By contrast, the Church of Rome is described as 'the mother of spirituall fornications, and in her is found the bloud of all that are slaine on earth: The power of Rome crucified the Lord Jesus, it slew millions of the Martyrs'(p. 387). Not surprisingly, Rous' volume was suppressed, and he complained that Laudian censorship was the cause: it was finally published in 1641.[32] One publication that Rous was able to print in 1631 was a text that was in many ways the apotheosis of Reformed thinking on the Song of Songs: *The Mysticall Marriage: Experimentall discoveries of the heavenly Marriage betweene a Soule and her Saviour.*[33] In traditional style, Rous' treatise is premised on the identification of the Bride with an elect and pure Calvinist Church. The difference in 1630s publications on the Song of Songs is that the threat to the Bride can no longer be securely located as outside the enclosed garden which is England. Rous' book is dedicated, with a gesture typically both inclusive and exclusive, 'To The Bride The Lambes Wife' (sig A2r), i.e. the true Church. An apparently democratic note is immediately struck: this treatise is for everyone, at least everyone who 'belongs'. The sense that not everyone is part of this privileged community is underlined by the introductory epistle to the reader, justifying Rous' choice of the subject of the Mysticall Marriage:

> Our Communion with Christ is a fastning of the soule to a mighty and impregnable Rocke that makes her stedfast, even against the gates of hell. ... For into this Sanctuary the Avenger may not enter. There is a chamber within us, and a bed of love in that chamber, wherein Christ meetes and rests with the soule, and the force of friends, or men, either dares not or cannot breake in ... An omnipotent lover gives an excessively conquering, and unconquerable safety (A3v–A4v).

From the start, spiritual intimacy with Christ is offered in the context of opposition and persecution, motivated by Satan himself. As if to compensate for the infiltration of the Church of England by hostile elements, Rous stresses the spiritual protection afforded to the orthodox. This is the curious double aspect of Puritan interpretation of the Song of Songs: for those within the magic circle there is a bed of love, for those outside, an 'impregnable Rocke'. There is not too much within the Biblical text of the Song of Songs to suggest external threats that require such protection, although much is made of the 'little foxes' who attack the vines (2:15) and are often depicted as coming from outside. Henoch Clapham had identified them definitively as Catholic foxes, 'Romish *Reinards*, spoilers of our Church', and in his 1603 treatise on the Song of Songs it was Queen Elizabeth who was charged with the defence of the garden of England from what sounded suspiciously like the Spanish fleet.

Yea, when her Maiestie hath appointed some to hunt the sea-foxe at sea:
we heare sometimes how they upholde the Foxe in his ravine: at least,
they winke at the sea-foxe, while he teares our sheepe, fleeces them of
their wooll, causeth the marchant sheepe to keepe at home in their fold,
when for the good of our land, they should be pasturing abroad. Take us
these Foxes, saith God to our Queene.[34]

Many viewed the religious politics of the 1630s, however, as the story of
the infiltration of the 'little foxes' into the garden of England. Later in his
treatise Rous himself sees the 'little foxes' as infiltrators from a huge enemy
force, who are well dug in: 'There are some little foxes that have strong
holdes, and these will ask some strength, to be digged out and taken.
Remember that thy warfare is against the whole Nation of the Canaanites,
thou maist not suffer a little one to live'(pp. 206–7). This is to give the 'little
foxes', who clearly have the status of minor pest in the Biblical text, an enormous and frightening influence, and perhaps illustrates a certain paranoia
amongst Puritans, whose self-image is still that of a hounded and persecuted
'little flock'.[35] The mystical marriage, however, offers both intimacy and
protection to the soul. Any model of marriage with a Calvinist and therefore
totally sovereign divinity will be a thoroughly patriarchal one in which the
husband is all-sufficient and the wife is truly a damsel in distress. The attrac-
tion of such an imaginative scheme for any community that perceives itself
as a minority subject to attack is obvious; John Foxe had used it to great
effect in depicting the travails of the unfortunate Ecclesia rescued by Christ
in his Latin play of 1556, *Christus Triumphans*.

Rous offers as another reason for the importance of his work in *The
Mysticall Marriage* that it offers what amounts to experimental proof of the
faith of Christianity:

> it presents to the view of the world some bunches of grapes brought from
> the land of promise, to shew that this land is not a meere imagination,
> but some have seene it, and have brought away parcels, pledges and
> earnests of it. In these appeares a world, above the world, a love that
> passeth human love, a peace that passeth naturall understanding,
> a joy unspeakable and glorious, a taste of the chiefe and soveraigne good
> (sig. A5v).

The allusion is to the twelve spies sent by Joshua to bring back evidence of
the plenty that was awaiting the children of Israel in the land of Canaan.[36]
It is crucial that the believer is not yet in heaven: it appears, however, that
he or she can experience on earth some of the transcendent delights that
can be expected there. Rous is not as cautious as some writers, like Gifford,
who imagine the relationship with Christ on earth as one of betrothal rather
than marriage.[37] He has to concede that technically the full consummation

will only come in heaven, but asserts that this betrothal, this 'inchoate marriage', far exceeds earthly marriage: 'even this betrothing compared to earthly marriages, casts a shadow of darknesse on them' (p.46). Much more optimistic than some writers, he sees human existence in relationship with God as entirely happy. His treatise articulates many of the most important aspects of Puritan spirituality, crucial to the anti-Arminian context in which he is writing. A great advantage of using the traditional interpretation of the Song of Songs, which as we have seen saw the text through a Calvinist filter, was that the author could refer to controversial matters in a kind of code: after all, he was merely expounding a Biblical text in a manner that had been orthodox for the best part of a century.

The Mysticall Marriage is not a commentary on the Song of Songs as such, although it incorporates many of the ideas and wording from other such texts. What Rous has done is to reconceptualise the entire Gospel in terms of the marriage between Christ and the soul. It is probably the usefulness of the marriage metaphor in this particular context that led to its power and ubiquity in the first half of the seventeenth century. Donne, for example, preached on Ephesians 5: 25–7 at a christening, '*Husbands love your wives, even as Christ loved the Church, and gave himselfe for it, that he might sanctifie it, and cleanse it, by the washing of water, through the Word: That he might make it unto himselfe a glorious Church, not having spot, or wrinkle, on any such thing; but that it should be holy, and without blame.*' With pleasure Donne takes this verse as a summary of the Gospel, and takes the time to work through the details of the text, relating them to key events such as Christ's justification and sanctification of sinners through his own death: 'It were pity to make too much hast, in considering so delightfull a thing, as the expressing of the love of Christ Jesus to his Church.'[38] Rous has gone further in working through the metaphor of marriage. He has drawn together many of the Scriptural allusions to the Bride—the Dedication, of course, refers to the vision of the Bride as the perfect Church in Heaven at the end of time, as in Revelation 19:7, where the marriage and the Feast that accompanies it is seen as the consummation of all things. *The Mysticall Marriage* begins with a summary of the Gospel redolent of some of the key texts of the New Testament; John 3:16, so often used to encapsulate the Gospel, Ephesians 5:25–7 and Hebrews 10:19–22. John 3:16—'for God so loved the world, that he sent his only beloved Son'—is completely rewritten:

> The Sonne of God so loved the soules of men, that hee would make them a wife, and marry them. And that hee might make this wife fit to be brought into his Fathers house, hee left his Father to come to his wife, that he might cleanse her from spots & blemishes, and present her pure & glorious to his Father. By his precious blood he purgeth her from her guilt, & by his spirit he purifieth her from her uncleannesse; and both of these hee bestoweth on her in his marriage with her. And then the

soule thus washed, hath boldnesse to approach unto God, through her husband, the Sonne of God, who hath loved her, and given himselfe for her, and given himselfe unto her. For God beholds her, and she beholds God, as one with his Sonne, even as his Sonnes wife (pp. 9–12).

Of the three Biblical passages referred to here only Ephesians makes direct reference to the marriage metaphor, and yet it is very easy to incorporate each stage of the reconciliation process into the marriage narrative, something John Donne did not feel the necessity to do. In Rous' deeply patriarchal view of marriage, the figure of the Redeemer is easily assumed into the husband eager to do all that is necessary for his wife's acceptance with her Divine father-in-law. Miraculously the mismatch of God and man is transformed into unity, through Christ's heroic action.

By contrast, the model of marriage that Donne is offering is much more equal. At the start of Sermon V Donne promised a negotiation between two fundamental relationships laid down by God, between Prince and Subject, and between husband and wife. Ironically, it is the defiantly non-Royalist Rous who seems to equate 'Prince' with 'husband' as the powerful half of the equation. Donne, however, envisages a more mutual relationship, in spite of what he wryly admits to be normal seventeenth-century gender relations:

> Now, that submitting, of which the Apostle speakes of here; is a submitting to one another, *a bearing* of *one anothers burthens:* what this submission is on the wives part, is expressed in the two former verses; And I forbeare that, because husbands at home, are likely enough to *remember* them of it; but in the duty, in the submitting of the husband, we shall consider first, what that submitting is, and that is *love, Husbands love your wives;* Even the love of the husband to the wife, is a burthen, a submitting, a descent; and secondly, the patterne and example of this love, *Even as* Christ *loved his Church.*[39]

He goes on to express the saving actions of Christ in redemption as 'a burthen, a submitting, a descent', in contrast to the distinctly princely conduct of Christ in Rous' account. It is striking how similar the two passages are in terms of the processes of justification and sanctification they describe: yet the tone and rhetoric is entirely different. For the actual process of 'washing' Donne temporarily changes the metaphor so that the Church becomes a 'Hospitall' full of sick people, thus stressing the unpleasant implications of Christ's gift of himself to humanity.[40] By contrast, the gift of Christ in Rous' account is to his bride, and it is a kind of romantic, if not erotic, surrender: the painful, sacrificial aspect of that love is not stressed as it is in Donne's sermon. Rous' Christ is a romantic hero: the 'delight' that Donne confesses as he rehearses the Gospel story is of a rather subtle, more profound kind.

It comes as no surprise that Rous had turned his hand to Spenserian romance in his youth. *Thule, or Vertues historie* was written by him when he was 16, and published in 1598. It is full of powerful knights who leave home in search of brides. This is Aidon in search of Viceina:

> This knight was moved by this damsels fame,
> And with his mothers leave departed thence,
> Vowing by heavens-makers fearfull name,
> As long as life should stay, or lively sence,
> Not ever to returne from whence he came,
> Before (as signe of his benevolence)
> He shall salute this Lady face to face,
> And with his armes that Saint-like Nymph embrace.[41]

Aidon rescues Viceina from a fate worse than death (any woman who actually loses her virginity in this romance is hopelessly corrupted, and beyond saving). There is a great deal of romantic love here, accompanied with much kissing and embracing. However, no couples actually consummate their love in this text: Aidon is killed, as is Arnian just before his marriage. Fidamour and Eumorphos go through a wedding ceremony, but Rous' interest is captured by the tilt immediately afterwards: the Book ends after an evil enchanter is dragged down to hell.

The mature Rous had not lost his penchant for romance. At the end of the love story in chapter 1 of *The Mysticall Marriage*, Rous describes the love between Christ and the soul, drawing heavily on the Song of Songs.

> Yea tell him resolutely thou wilt not leave him untill thou here a voyce in thy soule, saying; *My wellbeloved is mine, and I am my wellbeloveds*. To this end bee still gazing on him, and still calling on him; *Kisse me with the kisses of thy mouth*; Yea kisse my soule with such a kisse of thy spirit, that they may be no longer two, but one spirit: say to him whom have I in heaven but thee, and whom have I desired on earth besides thee? My soule thirsteth, and panteth for thee the living God. Tell him that thou art sicke of love (pp. 14–15).

Rous is incorporating verse three of the sixth chapter of the Song of Songs, verse two of the first chapter, and verse eight of chapter five ('I am sick of love') as well as other utterances from the Psalms. All this is of course entirely to be expected within the Reformed tradition, and Rous does not even feel the need to cite his references. What is more daring in chapter 1 is that Rous consciously recuperates sexual desire for his purpose of demonstrating the strength of the love between Christ and the soul. He uses the morally ambivalent word 'lust' in a defiantly transgressive manner, drawing attention to the sexual connotations of the word: 'Looke on him so, that thou maiest lust after him, for here it is a sinne, not to looke that thou maist lust, and not to lust having looked'(p. 13). For justification, Rous cites Galatians 5:17, 'The flesh lusteth against the Spirit, and the Spirit against the flesh' to argue that there is a spiritual equivalent of fleshly lust:

> it lusteth against the flesh; but it lusteth after spirituall objects; wherof Christ Iesus is the chiefest. Let thy spirit then looke and long, and lust for this Lord who is the spirit, the chiefest spirit; let it cleave to him, let it hang about him, and never leave him till hee bee brought into the chambers of the soule (p. 14).

Rous is quite clear that he is using the language of morally ambivalent sexual desire, but he has complete confidence that the spiritual experience he describes is absolutely separate from the fleshly phenomenon.

The second chapter of *The Mysticall Marriage* is a fully imagined exposition of the extended metaphor of Romans 7, which offers another application of the marriage trope. The sinful soul is depicted as being married to a false first husband, who has to die in order that the soul can be married to Christ. St. Paul identifies the first husband as the Law, the strict covenant of the Old Testament, whose power has been killed by the death of Christ. Rous' application is rather more daring in that he characterises the first husband as 'lust'. It is clear that his wider application is to fleshly desires in general, but perhaps he singles out the word as clarification of his previous point: unspiritual lust is an evil, and for Rous to be married to it, in his extremely patriarchal view of marriage, is to be a prisoner in a 'slavish marriage'. Rous offers a vivid image of a soul forced to work all day and be a sexual object at night:

> If it be in the morning, there is a bargaine of profit imposed on her, and this lot of bricke must be made that day, and about it must the soule goe, being pierced throgh with the thorns of covetousnesse, by the violent hand of her false husband, that she may have no leisure, respiration or rest. And if at night the soule be weary of this dayes worke, and would faine goe to bed with the body, the night is lusts day (pp. 32–3).

Only the death of Christ as personally applied can deliver the soul from earthly lust and allow her to experience spiritual lust: the believer has to give consent to the death of the first husband. The rhetorical depictions of marital misery, it appears, are given in order to persuade the soul to give her consent to the marriage with Christ (pp. 34–5). It is then that the mystical marriage can take place, and it is an experience that Rous imbues with the qualities of a romance:

> She will looke on dead lust as on a loathsome carkasse; and shee will loath the remembrance of her former not loves but adulteries: she will be

like one awaked from a foolish dreame, or an inchanted love, and shee will wonder that shee hath so long beene bewitched with vanity, folly, sinne and misery (p. 41).

The soul has found her true love.

Rous attempts to describe the state of bliss enjoyed by the soul married to Christ in the following chapter, drawing on all the resources of Biblical language to describe plenitude: 'she is filled with the waters of life, with the oyle of gladnesse, with the new wine of the kingdome of God, with the joy of the holy Ghost, even a joy unspeakable and glorious' (p. 60). Of course, the text of the Song of Songs is useful here: 'being thus lovely, the bridegroom kisseth and embraceth her with spirituall visitations, he tells her his counsailes, and his eyes are ever toward her, even when hee seemes to be turned from her: For she is set as a signet upon his heart, and much water cannot quench his love'(p. 61). As an intellectual justification for such overwhelming fullness of experience, Rous deploys an aspect of the marriage relationship not mentioned in the Bible. As the bride of Christ, Rous declares, she is joint-heir with Christ of all God's riches (p. 59). Although Romans 8: 17 does indeed mention the idea of the Christian being joint heir with Christ, it is as a child of God and therefore as Christ's sibling that this comes about, rather than as his wife. The move from 'child' to 'bride' is consistent with Rous' practice in this volume of producing a scheme which assimilates much Christian text and doctrine into the experience of the marriage relationship. By contrast, Anthony Low notes that George Herbert deliberately avoids the marriage metaphor, moving seamlessly into the language of childhood and infancy at the point where a deeper expression of intimacy is expected by the reader.[42] Whatever the reason for Herbert's choice, his use of a non-politicised religious language certainly made his poetry available to a wider constituency than would have been the case if he had used the terms of the mystical marriage: his poetry was as popular with Royalists as with Puritans, whereas Rous' treatise is at home in an aggressively Calvinist culture.

Rous' treatise made clear the problem of the spirituality of the mystical marriage for Archbishop Laud and the Arminian hierarchy of the Church of England. Chapter six listed the privileges of the soul married to Christ, one of which, cited again and again in the seventeenth century, was the joy of pillow-talk:

There are some mysteries and secrets which thy husband wil whisper unto thee by his spirit in the bed of love, and then let him that hath an eare, heare what his spirit saith … Goe into this Sanctuary, and there receive Oracles and Answeres; for there shalt thou finde resolutions of those things that were before too high and too hard for thee (pp. 184–5).

If aspiration to divine secrets were not enough of a presumption in the eyes of Laudians, the second privilege, drawing as it does on the famed susceptibility of a passionate man to the woman with whom he has a sexual relationship, was irreverent and delusional: 'If thou want any thing now aske it, for in these heates of love, thy husband will deny thee nothing' (p. 193). With such total command of Divine generosity goes, of course, unlimited power, and Rous does not even try to avoid sounding subversive: 'If thou doe first seeke a kingdome: wherefore whatsoever thou askest, be sure to aske this kingdome' (p. 195). Bliss is of course the promised end of all romances, and Rous offers the extremes of physical desire to the believer. 'Let these kisses of Christ Iesus kindle in thee such a fervent love of Christ, that thy soule may pant to bee united to him in a perfect and consummate marriage'(pp. 24–5).

Chapter seven of Rous' treatise, 'The signes, and markes of the true and right visitations of the heavenly Bridegroome' explored a topic strictly marginal to commentary on the Song of Songs but one which the logic of the mystical marriage dictated to be necessary. A doctrine of inclusion and exclusion such as many Puritans derived from the Biblical book distinguished sharply, as we have seen, between Catholic and Protestant, between elect and non-elect, between holy and profane. Nowhere in the text, however, was there any suggestion as to how to distinguish between included and excluded categories. The problem was widespread in Calvinism, where it was crucial to identify the elect soul, and in the first decades of the seventeenth century there were many treatises published on what were called 'the marks' or 'the signs' of election. One of the first and most authoritative treatises on this subject used the Song of Songs as the key text for such identification.[43] Nicholas Byfield, the well-known Calvinist minister in Chester and Isleworth, where he preached often to Sir Thomas Hoby, produced no less than 'sixteene infallible signes of a child of God' in a 1614 sermon which was reprinted several times before 1637. However, although these signs may well have been infallible if discerned, none of the sixteen functioned very well as signs, as they were impossible to verify. They ranged from 'holy desires', such as desire of death, to 'spirits 'of prayer and adoption, and four different kinds of love: perhaps the criterion that most nearly approached an outward sign was number twelve, right use of the Sacraments.[44] In 1623, just before he was silenced by royal command, Thomas Gataker, stressing the need to examine oneself to ascertain ones own sincerity, offered ten 'notes of sinceritie'. The first three—universality, uniformity, ubiquity—showed a genuine attempt to find an outward criterion for judging sincerity, but the other seven included 'desire of Grace' and 'love of God' and were impossible to judge from the outside.[45] Adam Harsnett's 1630 sermon *A touch-stone of grace* was reprinted three times later in the decade, and also promised 'infallible evidences'. The main one offered, however, was obedience, and as Harsnett, opponent of Laud, admitted, 'An Hypocrite may go far in Outward Obedience'.[46] Rous' own 'signs' do not function too well as signifiers either: they are identified as light, joy and holiness, in each case a particular variety of light, joy and holiness that is spiritually discerned. Perhaps the most visible sign is what Rous coyly describes as 'fruitfulnesse'. Although he does not specify what he means by this his comment suggests powerfully a woman who has had sex, is now enjoying a kind of afterglow, and who has been made pregnant:

> Wherefore if with light and joy, the soule doe feele, that the spirit of Christ, by spirituall heate, power, and love, have wrought a powerfull, and fruitfull holinesse in her, let her know that Christ Iesus himselfe hath beene with her (p. 276).

The more mystical and inward these 'signs' were perceived to be, the more dependent they were on the articulation of a privileged rhetoric deemed to indicate the soteriological status of the soul. This rhetoric increasingly incorporated the text of the Song of Songs and the implications of the doctrine of the mystical marriage into definitions of the 'elect'.

The subject of martyrdom had become incorporated into the spirituality of the Bride of Christ through the dominant text of sixteenth-century English Protestantism. In John Foxe's *Acts and Monuments,* the idea of marriage with Christ had been associated with martyrdom, as we have seen: martyrs viewed the day of execution as their wedding day, the day when their union with Christ was to be fully brought about. Rous' fourth chapter stresses the context of persecution and the bliss to be expected by those who are martyred: 'When the Bride suffereth most for her love to the Bridegroome, the Bridegroomes love must needes be most increased to the Bride; and consequently the fruits & benefits of his love' (p. 83). John Donne had subscribed to the Foxean view of the marriage experience of the martyrs, as he made clear in this sermon at Lincoln's Inn quoting from Canticles 5:2:

> That peace, which made the blessed Martyrs of Christ Jesus sleep upon the rack, upon the burning coales, upon the points of swords, when the persecutors were more troubled to invent torments, then the Christians to suffer … That sleep, which is the sleep of the spouse, *Ego dormio, sed cor meum vigilit, I sleep, but my heart is awake.*[47]

Elizabeth Isham, reading John Foxe's *Acts and Monuments* in the 1630s, found comfort in the words of 'Bradford, that blessed Marter', who conceived of death as the consummation of the mystical marriage:

> If in prison are so many mercies. how many are there in the pallace. If the wicked have so many benefits what is store prepared for thy Servants. O Lord if thy children find such joy comfort in that place of teares, and mourning. what shall they find in day of the mariage.[48]

John Foxe's massive work appeared only once in the 1630s, but much of the rhetoric and ideology of his volume was easily available, in a digest produced in 1613 by Clement Cotton, for those who could not afford the rather expensive original. Cotton was a layman, a member of the Drapers' Company, who nevertheless had impressive theological credentials: he had translated Calvin, and produced one of the most popular concordances in the early seventeenth century.[49] *The mirror of martyrs in a short view* is how most early seventeenth-century readers appropriated Foxe, and the connection between martyrdom and the mystical marriage is perpetuated there.[50] To confirm the conceptual link between the Song of Songs and martyrology, the first page of the text is taken up with three verses from the Biblical book, verse three of chapter six ('I Am my welbeloveds, & my welbeloved is mine') and verses six and seven of chapter eight:

> Set me as a seale on thine heart, and as a signet upon thine arme: for *Love* is strong as death ... Much water cannot quench *Love*, neither can the flouds drowne it: if a man should give all the substance of his house for *Love*, they would greatlie contemne it.[51]

These verses of course are classic articulations of the motivation of the martyr. The Preamble spells out the connection between the martyr's experience and the soul's status as Bride of Christ:

> shee esteems the prison a Pallace; fetters of jron, Ornaments of fine Gold: the darkest dungeon, a delightsome dwelling; rather then shee will violate the chastitie of her faith to Christ her onely Spouse, she will willingly endure headding and hanging; yea burning and broiling (sig. ¶3r).

Following this is a dedication to Elizabeth Stuart, linking her name with that of Elizabeth I: the link between Protestant internationalism, martyrology and the Song of Songs is thus made explicit (sig.¶1v). In the 1615 edition the dedication is to another woman inextricably linked with Protestant internationalism: Lucy Countess of Bedford, who was at the centre of the political grouping attempting to continue the heritage of the Sidney-Essex faction into James' reign. In the 1630s editions, perhaps in response to the increasingly hostile publication environment, the dedication is to the Drapers' Company, and the page of quotations from the Song of Songs has disappeared altogether.

Encoding resistance in the mystical marriage metaphor

Despite the large numbers of commentaries on the Song of Songs before the publication of Rous' treatise in 1631, the 1630s as a whole did not see publication of this kind of text, perhaps because its political associations were obvious to any reader, or censor. Interpretation of the book was the province of the anti-Laudian, anti-Arminian constituency, who used its tropes and dynamics to affirm their own Calvinist spirituality, and define a transgressive Other that was explicitly Catholicism, but which could often be read as Arminianism. Joseph Hall, now Bishop of Exeter, republished his 1609 paraphrase of the Song of Songs, but it was carefully hidden away in a volume of wider Biblical commentary: his love for the text was to resurface in devotional publications of the 1640s.[52] The spirituality of the mystical marriage emphasised spiritual experience rather than obedience to Church and State authority, so important to Laudians: it could even be used to undermine such authority by its emphasis on the privileged relationship to Christ of the individual believer. Application of the teaching on the 'marks' of the children of God, so typical of Calvinist thought, could be used to divide those united by Reformed teaching from those espousing Arminianism: this was not where the Laudians wanted the fault-line in the English church to run. They were more concerned to separate Puritans with their tendencies to dissident church practice from Calvinist con-formists, who often acquiesced in Laudian reforms.[53] In practice, the 'reforms' seem to have been counterproductive; they united these two constituencies against Laud. Tom Webster suggests that there was a category of 'conformable' godly ministers who were effectively driven into nonconformity, or outright hostility, by Laud and his reforms, but who should not be called 'Puritan' as such: they were driven into alliance with more convinced Nonconformists by the events of the 1630s. He offers a model of social drama to help explain what happened to the godly clergy in the 1630s. In response to a crisis, he suggests, the clergy will pray against an external threat: what happens then is a reaffir-mation of the identity of the group and the alien nature of the threat.

> The group is turned further inward, joined by a starker definition against the external object. The breach is not healed, but is made, in a sense, more external.[54]

The rhetoric of the Song of Songs, which was used throughout its history to define identity and difference, played a key role in group dynamics within the clergy of the 1630s. Calvinist commentary on the Song of Songs could allow the godly reader to identify threats to the true Church, and join with his colleagues in the Bride of Christ to pray against them.

One site of conflict in the 1630s was the identity of conformity: where exactly was the fault-line between those loyal to the Church of England and those who could not longer be deemed orthodox? A giant of early Stuart spirituality whose conformity has been the subject of modern scholarly disagreement was Richard Sibbes, whose sermons on the Song of Songs were printed in the 1630s. In one sense he was clearly 'conformable': he was pre-sented by the crown to the perpetual curacy of Holy Trinity, Cambridge, in 1633. His modern biographer, Mark E. Dever, is at great pains to stress his conformity, insisting that his career and the tenor of his writing rules out radicalism.[55] Richard Sibbes was somewhat of a Puritan celebrity during his life. Having died in 1635, he himself appeared in Samuel Clarke's English martyrology of 1652. What Clarke said of the English divines in his 1651 *A generall martyrologie*, detailing persecution and martyrdom across Europe, may have been his view of Sibbes, as a kind of martyr: 'our Modern Divines, ... though they were not Martyrs, yet may they well be stiled Confessors, in regard of the great Persecution and Sufferings, which most of them met with-all whilest they lived here'.[56] Mark Dever points out that Clarke's *Life* is very brief and does not include an account of a deprivation of Sibbes' Fellowship and Lectureship in Cambridge, which appears in the *Life* of Preston in the same volume: in fact, asserts Dever, correctly, no such double deprivation happened.[57] However, Dever is refusing to acknowledge that Nonconformists and Calvinist conformists tended to unite in the face of what they perceived as Laudian threats to the integrity of the Bride of Christ.

Sibbes died in 1635, and many of his works were published posthumously in 1638 and 1639, when religious politics had polarised further. In 1639, his sermons on chapters four, five and six on the Song of Songs appeared: *Bowels opened, or, A discovery of the neere and deere love, union and communion betwixt Christ and the Church, and consequently betwixt Him and every beleeving soule*.[58] In many respects these sermons followed traditional Reformed interpretation of the Song of Songs: the difference was in the context for the publication of such commentary. Whereas Jacobean Christians had claimed the inclusivity of the text for the Church of England, and interpreted the Catholic Church as the transgressive Other, the English church under Charles I and Laud had increasingly become aware of its own fragmentation. Interpretation of the Song of Songs, which as we have seen, tended to locate and identify the true Spouse of Christ, was dangerous in this political context, and very few preachers attempted to do it in the 1630s. By 1639, Sibbes was safely dead, and he had been a conformist all his life, so publication of this text might not have appeared risky, particularly as he deliberately eschewed prophetic interpretation of the Song of Songs, and argued for its relevance in all times.[59] However, within the fevered politico-religious climate of the late 1630s, his sermons identified the enemy within rather than tending to national unity: in this sense they helped to intensify the social drama taking place within the English church. Even the traditional stress on the same privileges for 'every particular member' (p. 5) of the church resonated as controversial within a Church of England where episcopal privilege was emphasised.

Sibbes has chosen to focus on chapters four, five and six of the Song of Songs, the section which contains the narrative of the sleeping and neglectful Bride, and which became the locus for many distinctly Puritan doctrines. Verse 1 is seen as the opportunity to rehearse the rhetoric of martyrology:

> if *Christ* be with us, the flames nor nothing shall hurt us. If in a dungeon as *Paul* and *Sylas* were, if *Christs* presence be there by his spirit to inlarge our soules; all is comfortable whatsoever (p. 41).

However, Sibbes suggests a disturbing and rather contemporary application for the sleepiness of the Church at the start of chapter 5. He conceives of it as indifference towards the growth of abuses in the Church:

> Worshipping of images arose from reserving the pictures of friends; and after that were brought into the Church. Invocation of Saints arose from some of the Fathers figurative turning of their speech to some that were dead. ... Nothing in Popery so grosse, but had some small beginnings (p. 94).

The message is clear: there are innovations in the life of the 1630s Church of England which are indicative of the beginnings of Popery. This of course has enormous implications for any equating of the Church of England with the Bride of Christ: and Sibbes continues with the story of chapter five to make the point very clearly. The Bridegroom is knocking at the Bride's door, as He does in chapter 5 of the Song of Songs, an action that Sibbes equates with the privileges given to England since the Reformation:

> Now what meanes of knocking hath hee not used among us a long time? ... For *Mercies,* How many deliverances have we had (No Nation the like, we are a Miracle of the Christian World,) from forreigne invasion, and Domesticall conspiracies at home? How many mercies doe we enjoy? *Abundance together with long peace, and plenty* (p. 155).

Despite this, says Sibbes, some have refused to move to let Christ in. The possibility of the Christian community in England fragmenting is real. Sibbes identifies the threat by his naming of the Watchmen who torment the Bride in later in chapter five, as 'governors of the Church and state' (p. 293). The identification with the Laudian regime is an extremely easy one to make in the late 1630s:

> as wee see in the story of the Church, especially the *Romish Church,* they have excommunicated Churches and Princes: but not to speake of those Synagogues of Satan, come wee nearer home and wee may se amongst our selves sometimes those that are Watchmen and should be for encouragement, They smite and wound the Church, and take away her vaile (p. 295).

It was the Pope who excommunicated Elizabeth I, but those mentioned here who 'should be for encouragement' but who are wounding the true Church are surely bishops of the Church of England.

After Sibbes' death in 1635 his writings became increasingly appreciated by anti-Laudians, much to the regret of his modern biographer, Mark E. Dever, who does not seem to realise that to be anti-Laudian is not to put conformity to the Reformed Church of England in doubt.[60] The publication of *Bowels Opened* received specific comment in Clarke's 1652 martyrology, extracted from John Dod's introduction to the work. Dod had seen the manuscript of these sermons while Sibbes was alive, and insisted that it be published, declaring:

> I consider these Sermons a very profitable and excellent help both to the understanding of this most dark and Divine Scripture, as also to kindle in the heart, all heavenly affections towards Jesus Christ.[61]

This accolade from a 'convinced Nonconformist' helps to produce a Richard Sibbes who has more in common with radical divines than Mark Dever would like to admit. Sibbes had of course entrusted the editing of his works to Philip Nye and Thomas Goodwin, and their growing radicalism may help to account for the widespread use of Sibbes' works by Nonconformists. Nye was convinced by 1633 that kneeling at the Sacrament was idolatrous and abandoned his lectureship, leaving for Arnhem. Goodwin resigned his living at Trinity to Sibbes and at the end of the 1630s, joined Nye in Holland.[62] There is no doubt that the story Sibbes finds in the Song of Songs is absolutely in tune with narratives produced by 'convinced Nonconformists' that also drew on the Biblical book: the true Church included even those deprived of their Church of England livings, whilst it was defended by God against the 'popish innovations' of Laud and his followers.

The subtitle to Sibbes' book, *A discovery of the neere and deere love, union and communion betwixt Christ and the Church, and consequently betwixt Him and every beleeving soule*, contained a phrase that became crucial to interpretation to the Song of Songs in the seventeenth century, and to political use of it. 'Union and communion' became a phrase that described the absolute intimacy of the relationship between Christ and every true believer, found in the Song of Songs:

> Now from this union of persons comes a communion of all other things whatsoever, *I am my Beloveds and my Beloved is mine* (p. 444).

It was Calvin who had identified this union as a 'sacred wedlock', but this relationship was not only for the spiritual élite, as it had been in monastic communities.[63] In Reformed theology, the mechanics of salvation were perceived as taking their effect by union with Christ. Justification—the remitting of a believer's sin—and sanctification—his achievement of holiness—were communicated to human beings by their union with Christ.[64] This union was constructed in terms of seventeenth-century marriage law. Here is Sibbes' statement of one implication of such union, a statement very similar to Francis Rous' in 1631, but one which was to become a cause of controversy in the Restoration because of the lack of responsibility this doctrine demanded from the individual believer:

> *The Wife is taken with all her debt, and made partaker of the honours, and Riches of her Husband.* Whatsoever hee hath is hers, and he stands answerable for all her debts, so it is heere, we have not only the name of *Christ* upon us, but we partake his honours, and are *Kings, Priests,* and *Heires* with him. ... There is a blessed change betweene *Christ* and us; his honours and Riches are ours; We have nothing to bestow on him, but our Beggery, sinnes, and miseries, which he tooke upon him (p. 48).

Inheritors of Laudian ecclesiology at the Restoration were to find in this doctrine worrying evidence that believers in the mystical marriage did not feel the need to take the blame themselves for crime or debt.[65]

This kind of writing was perpetuated after the Restoration, perhaps in opposition to the reassertion of church hierarchy, but it began in the late 1630s as a gesture of resistance to Laud. These gestures often took the form of posthumous republication of works by one of the great giants of early-seventeenth century Puritanism. Three of John Preston's sermons, including an influential one reprinted in 1648 as *The mysticall match between Christ and his church*, appeared in an edition by Thomas Goodwin, this time in collaboration with Thomas Ball, to whom John Preston had bequeathed his pupils in godly religion, and who himself had a strong record of defiance of the Laudian regime.[66] Preston had been preaching in the late 1620s, and he had had a vision of a union with Christ which was at the same time more absolute than any earthly relationship, and yet was imaginatively conceived in the terms of a seventeenth-century marriage:

> there is a reall union, when CHRIST sends his Spirit into the heart; therefore thou must consider, whether thou have the Spirit of thy Husband dwelling in thee or no, for except thou have the holy Ghost to dwell in thy heart, it is impossible that there should bee any match, for there will bee alwayes jarres and dissentions betweene you, when thou hast the same Spirit, then there is the same will, the same desires, you love and hate the same things; therefore in considering, whether there be a match or no, this is a great thing, it will not deceive you, consider whether thou have the Spirit of thy husband.[67]

The usefulness of the marriage metaphor for Preston is in the tangibility it suggests for a spiritual union: he links it with the witness of the Holy Spirit, which is the affirmation to an individual that he or she is saved (p. 11). In fact, marriage with Christ is not an optional extra for the particularly holy Christian: the marriage ceremony is seen as the rite of baptism (p. 5). Preston compares the man without Christ to the woman without a man: no-one to speak for her, no-one to counsel her (p. 25). The mystical marriage for Preston does not so much feminise the male Christian as make him hyper-masculine, enable him to be united with the ultimate male. Preston's evangelical appeal to his audience presents union with Christ as an ideal of plenitude that must have seemed particularly attractive in the 1630s:

> lastly consider, how faire a life you shall live with him. … In that security, that you neede feare no enemy; whereas other men have a thousand feares, a Christian hath this benefit, hee makes the Lord his dread, that hee need feare nothing; but he is delivered from the hands of all his enemies. Consider with what contentment thou shalt live, that thou hast such a husband … that shall fill thy soule, that when thou hast him, thou needest not thirst after any thing besides (pp. 30–1).

Mocked and criticised by Anglicans in the Restoration, this kind of thinking strengthened opposition to the Laudian regime, and ate away at its hierarchical principles. If the mystical marriage offered such a cornucopia of spiritual benefits, it is difficult to see what necessary function the institutional church fulfilled: and for those who turned their backs on the Laudian version of the Church of England, as so many who taught the importance of the mystical marriage did, the structures of the narrative of the Song of Songs implicitly offered happiness and protection.

The writings of Sibbes and Preston contained the substance of much mainstream, Calvinist conformist spirituality, in which as we have seen, the mystical marriage was an important element. However, for 'Convinced Nonconformists', those firmly opposed to conformity on principle, seen by Tom Webster as the heirs of Arthur Hildersham, himself an author of a commentary on the Song of Songs, and John Dod, the imagery of the Song of Songs was central. John Dod managed to survive through the 1630s as a nationally-respected divine despite having been ejected from the Church of England as early as 1607: he was supported by Northamptonshire gentry, and the autobiography of Elizabeth Isham, sister of the Royalist and Laudian Justinian Isham, reverals how admired he was in all circles. She found him much more interesting to listen to than more orthodox preachers.[68] In this more radical category could be counted the Rogers dynasty—John Rogers, author of the famous *Seven Treatises*, and his son Daniel, both of whom the 85 year old Dod remembered with affection to John's grandson Samuel in 1638.[69] Also included in the extended family were Samuel's cousin Nathanael Rogers and his uncle, Adam Harsnett. Daniel Rogers was lecturer at Wethersfield, Suffolk, as his father had been before him (Stephen Marshall had filled the gap between Richard's death in 1618 and Daniel's appointment in 1625). However, at a diocesan visitation in 1631 he was asked to subscribe to articles confirming the government and liturgy of the Church of England, and on refusal to do so was suspended.[70] His son Samuel kept a spiritual journal in the tradition of his grandfather, and his anti-Arminianism is clear throughout, as is his tendency to encode his experiences in the language of the Song of Songs.[71] He seems to have thought Charles I to be a Catholic, as he prayed for the king's conversion on March 6th 1636. On 13 August he lamented the fact that 'idolatrous superstitious Arminians.have prevailed lamentably within these 7 years' and the following day he expressed his longing for Christ in an idiosyncratic expression adapted from 2:5 of the Song of Songs: 'ravish me with thy flagons'(pp. 66–7). In the autumn of 1636 Samuel conceived a longing to go to New England, and this seemed to induce a greater desire for Christ, stimulated by the 'sweet incouraging spirit' of Adam Harsnett and a sermon on the mystical marriage by a Mr. Fuller: 'ravish my soule with loves' he writes on 2 September, 'some of thy marriage love, oh my husband' he demands on 1 November. On 4 October 1637, having heard an admirable sermon by the anti-Laudian Dr. Richard Holdsworth the day before in Cambridge, he met an Arminian on the way home: the antidote for him was to 'lye down in Xs armes'(p. 195). In 1638 he denounced Laud and Wren as 'those 2 cursed traitors to X' (p. 163). Alone in a godless household, the Song of Songs articulated for him an inner drama: the text itself turned him inward to a place of unity with God and his elect, and enabled him to identify and resist the enemy.

By 1638, however, Samuel Rogers was no longer lonely: he was chaplain to Lady Mary Vere, whose home in Hackney offered him the access he desired to a wide community of godly preachers. Lady Mary Vere had an impeccable godly pedigree: an ancestor of hers, William Tracy, was one of the martyrs in Foxe's volume. Her husband Horace had been a dominant figure in the English army in the United Provinces of Holland in the 1620s: his troops used the liturgy established by the Earl of Leicester in Elizabeth's reign, until Laud suppressed it in the early 1630s. Simon Adams identifies this army as the last English institution loyal to the cause of Protestant internationalism.[72] Mary Vere was a friend to many ministers from different wings of the Reformed church, and lobbied her brother-in-law Edward Conway for the promotion of clergymen as diverse as future Archbishop James Ussher and radical Puritan John Davenport. Richard Sibbes dedicated a book to her, and she welcomed John Dod into her home, which became a living emblem of the unity of conformist and Nonconformist Calvinists in the face of Laudian opposition.[73]

To identify a military enemy, as Protestant internationalists had done, is to make a significant psychological step in redefining group identity, but perhaps the ultimate move in this social drama is the employment of the rhetoric of persecution and martyrdom. The language of martyrology, with its marriage imagery and its polarising tendencies, was by the 1630s assuming the context of persecution by the Arminian hierarchy, which had taken the place of Catholicism as the silent 'other' of the Song of Songs: of course, to many, Arminianism was identified with the Catholic threat. The growing dissension within the Garden of England was epitomised by the fate of

Burton, Bastwick and Prynne in the late 1630s. Henry Burton had travelled a long way since he had served in Prince Charles' household as Clerk of the Closet, a colleague of William Loe. Dismissed by the new King Charles for accusing William Laud of being 'popishly affected', he too, like Francis Rous, attacked Montagu's book *Appello Caesarem*, in *A Plea to An Appeale* (London, 1626). He continued publishing throughout the 1620s and 1630s in opposition to Laud and Arminianism, prefacing his works with dedications to Charles I, his erstwhile employer, and publishing in Amsterdam for much of the 1630s. On the 31st anniversary of the Gunpowder Plot at St Matthew's, Friday Street, a traditional occasion for freedom of speech on anti-papist rhetoric, Burton went rather too far: he preached two sermons attacking the institution of bishops in the Church of England as inherently papist.[74] The sermons were published in Amsterdam with a lengthy dedication to Charles, protesting at various 'innovations' imposed by Laud:

> alterations in setting up of Altars, Images, Crucifixes, in bowing to the Altar: in putting downe afternoone Sermons on the Lords dayes in sundry Diocesse: in allowing no other Catechising, but by bare Question and Answer out of the Booke, without expounding of the maine Principles of Religion to the ignorant youth and people.[75]

Samuel Rogers read and re-read these sermons with fervour: for him they reaffirmed his allegiance and loyalty. 'My heart and portion be with those that contend for the faith, whether in life or death.'[76] Burton was of course charged with sedition, and eventually joined in prison by his future fellow-sufferers.[77] On hearing of his imprisonment Samuel Rutherford predicted a new age of persecution for the Church.[78] Thomas Ball joined in a public fast on behalf of Burton, Bastwick and Prynne.[79]

William Prynne was not charged with the writing of any particular work, but he had been extremely busy writing several explicitly anti-Arminian treatises in the 1620s. In 1626 Stephen Marshall's network of godly divines were distributing copies of the work that was eventually published as *The Church of Englands old antithesis to new Arminianisme* in 1629.[80] More violently anti-episcopalian tracts followed in the 1630s. His attack on female actors in *Histrio-Mastix* (1633) was taken to be criticism of Queen Henrietta Maria for her own participation, and that of her ladies in waiting, in Walter Montagu's *Shepheards Paradise*: he was found guilty of sedition, and sentenced to life imprisonment, a £5,000 fine, and the notorious ear-cropping. This harsh punishment did not, however, stop him writing. John Bastwick had also written a great deal against Laud's church in the 1630s, but most of it was in Latin: he was however charged with the writing of *The Letany*, a book prompted by his dire situation, imprisoned in The Gatehouse and neglected by his gaolers. The full title, however, which directly criticises the bishops, gives some indication of why he along with the other two were given the harsh punishment in 1637 that Prynne had already undergone four years earlier. This time, Prynne's ears, lightly cropped in 1633, were completely butchered.[81]

John Knott has described how Burton, Bastwick and Prynne deliberately evoked the rhetoric and behaviour of the Foxean martyrs.[82] They also appropriated the textual practices that were used in Foxe's *Acts and Monuments*, and were to be part of oppositional textual strategies for the rest of the seventeenth century: accounts of interrogations, personal letters, and last speeches before suffering.[83] Their master-stroke was to use the rhetoric of martyrdom without actually having to go through the experience of execution. This apparent contradiction exposes the social function of the rhetoric of martyrdom: if it can reasonably be employed, the beneficial effects of strengthening a group from within and demonising the opposition without can still be achieved. The use of the mystical marriage metaphor in the description of martyrdom, for example, was justified in Foxe's volume by the Reformed belief that the closeness of a relationship with Jesus Christ was brought to consummation by the believer's death. Yet Burton on the scaffold on 30 June 1637, who was only to lose his ears, could still see his day of suffering in these terms: 'never was wedding day soe welcome and joyfull a day as this is'.[84] Adopting the Foxean martyrs' description of their martyrdom clothes as 'wedding garments' he describes his wife's present to him of new gloves as 'wedding gloves'. His wife is also able to participate in the language of the Bride: 'shee was more cheerefull of this day, then of her wedding day' (p. 28). Burton's description of his time in the pillory drew on the words of the Song of Songs to suggest the experience of the Bride even at the point of earthly persecution: he finds himself strengthened by the 'wine of consolation' and declares 'if the world did but know his goodness, and had tasted of his sweetness ... al would come and be his servants' (pp. 25–6). Samuel Rogers and his friends identified closely with Burton at the start of July 1637, and his diary recorded their mourning for Burton's fate.[85] Of course, the survival of these 'martyrs' did not only guarantee a glorious homecoming at the end of November 1640, their 'wedding night' as Henry Burton's supporters called it: it allowed the martyrs themselves to present their experiences at leisure with rhetoric carefully chosen for appropriate resonances. Thus, in one of the first autobiographies of the seventeenth century, a genre which became inextricably linked to martyrology, Henry Burton described a woman in the welcoming crowd who said 'Oh sir, this is a glorious wedding day... but your wedding day upon the pillary was more glorious.'[86]

The use of the tropes of martyrology are to be expected in the most militant of the anti-Laud activists: perhaps more surprising was their imployment in late 1630s biography as demonstrated in its familiar seventeenth-century form: the funeral sermons of 'eminent Christians' who were offered as exemplars for lay members of the Church. Funeral sermons were frequently published, and it was difficult to object to them, but in this period of strict Laudian censorship the combination of solid Puritan sermon with an exemplary Puritan life could be very powerful, particularly if the subject of such celebration was known for political or religious opposition to the Church hierarchy. The title of John Ley's funeral sermon for Jane Ratcliffe, *A patterne of pietie*, stresses the importance of her example for imitation by the readers, and Peter Lake has identified its anti-Laudian character, an instinct supported by the fact that Samuel Clarke, the martyrologist, later included it in his strategic volume celebrating classic Puritan lives, *A Collection of the Lives of Ten Eminent Divines* (1662), which had a distinctly political function in the ecclesiastical politics of the Early Restoration.[87] Of course, in 1662, Samuel Clarke's aim was to redraw the boundaries of the Established Church, which had expelled so many Puritans on Black Bartholomew's Day, to include the godly—the Presbyterian godly at least. Jane Ratcliffe was a wealthy and well-known citizen of Chester, who had enjoyed the distinction of being celebrated by Nicholas Byfield, under whose ministry she was converted, as 'marked even with everie one of the signes' of God's election: his famous sermon of 1614, *The Signes*, was dedicated to her.[88] John Ley's sermon for her stresses her passion for God in terms used by the martyrologists: 'Her love to God was *strong as death,* Cant. 8. 4. yea, and much stronger, so that Death could not affright her; for she desired daily to look death in the face.'[89] One of Byfield's sixteen signs had of course been this very desire for death: Ley quotes from a piece of writing that she left at her death, entitled 'Why I desire to dye' (p. 432) .On her husband's death she does not seek remarriage, because she is 'so devoted to her Lord Christ' (p. 430). Although under threat of suspension from the Sacrament for refusing to kneel, she gave the matter serious consideration before deciding that her original decision was right. Lake summarises the political impact of this sermon as 'the rejection of Laudian or conformist claims that puritan goodness...could not but lead to non-conformity and disorder' (p. 146). Clarke's implicit claim is that certain kinds of Puritan should be valued members of the Church of England.

Like Ley's sermon for Jane Ratcliffe, funeral sermons in the late 1630s took on many of the characteristics of martyrology, including the tropes from the Song of Songs. They often represented, in their commemoration of a godly lay person by one of the clergy, one aspect of an alliance between anti-Arminianism in its secular and ecclesiastical incarnation. Funeral sermons by Richard Sibbes were particularly influential. He had clearly been close to some of the main Parliamentary opponents of Arminianism in the 1620s: Pym had been given a funeral ring at his death. The enterprise in which clergymen and Parliamentarians had been united from 1626–1633 was the support of godly preachers. Four merchants, four lawyers and four clergymen, one of whom was Richard Sibbes, had together constituted the Feoffees for Impropriations, a committee elected to raise money to fill vacant lectureships and parish appointments with soundly Calvinist men. Within the space of eight years they funded eighteen preachers in eleven counties, collecting £6,361 6s 1d.[90] They funded lecturers at a kind of seminary at St. Antholin's, Budge Row, which attorney-general William Noy advised the King to take charge of, as the Feoffees were 'bringing up of youth as they please'.[91] It was a condition of their appointment that nominated clergymen sought no change in the government of the Church of England. Despite this, Laud quickly identified the Feoffees as a target, and recorded satisfaction in his diary when their activities were suppressed by decree in February 1633.[92] Sibbes had known Pym's colleague Christopher Sherland, who had been one of the lawyer-members of the Feoffees, and preached his funeral sermon in 1632: Sherland was also a friend of Northampton preacher Thomas Ball.[93] Five years later Sibbes' sermon was published as 'Christ is Best', and Sherland is celebrated as 'a holy and blessed man', 'a hearty and true Promoter of the Cause of Religion'.[94] Sir Thomas Crewe was another member of the Northampton godly community, a Parliamentarian and member of the Feoffees, who was memorialised by Richard Sibbes in 1638, in *The Brides Longing for her Bride-Groomes second comming*. Crewe's Parliamentary career had begun in 1604 and he had sat as MP for 5 different constituencies, being made Speaker in 1624 and 1625. He was appointed to the ecclesiastical high commission in 1625, an appointment renewed in 1626, 1629, and 1633. He had consistently espoused an oppositional politics: he had presided over the debate caused by the publication of *Appello Caesarem* in 1625. Sibbes summarises his career in this way:

> But this worthy man ... would not be scorned, or turned out of his course by any man; hee was a Child of Wisedome, able to justifie what hee did, against the spirit of grosse and proud prophanenesse, and against an emptie, formall, dead, cold profession. Hee had not onely the Word of God to backe him, but his owne excellencies, and the sweetnesse that hee felt and found in his Christian course, to defend him.[95]

Crewe's funeral sermon had two London editions as well as a Banbury edition: the writer of the prefatory epistle said that this publication 'hath with a long and longing desire bin wished and waited for by sundry', presumably since Crewe's death in 1634 (sig A3v). The text that Sibbes chose for the sermon was Revelation 22;17, chosen especially with Crewe in mind: '*The Spirit and the Bride say, Come, and let him that heareth, say, come*'(p. 111). Sibbes' message is that the elect Church does not fear death, and longs for the second coming of Christ, 'the Marriage-day': the sermon, characteristic of the spirituality of the mystical marriage, extols an inward, ecstatic relationship with God, a 'sweet entercourse that is betweene Christ, and his Spouse':

> These desires, are the breathings and motions of the Spirit in the soule, tending to further union. Even as motion tends to rest, so desires tend to the uniting unto the thing desired. The Churches desires here, are the immediate issue of the soule, and therefore undissembled; and they shew the true character of a Christian soule (p. 29).

It is the existence of these desires that marks out the elect, and Sibbes concludes his sermon on Crewe with the example of Paul preaching before the Roman governor of Judea.

> Why, let, *Felix* tremble, and let the World tremble; but let every Christian, that hath made his peace with God, rejoice … Let us looke up, and lift up our heads with joy, for our Redemption draweth nigh (pp. 109–10).

To a Puritan reading this in Banbury in 1638, Sibbes is promising deliverance from an oppressive authority that is unmistakeably identified with the Laudian regime.

The importance of Foxe's history of martyrdom in the struggle for the identity of the English church is confirmed by the fact that the Bishop of Norwich Richard Montagu, who had begun that great controversy in the 1620s, published posthumously his own volume of *Acts and Monuments* in 1642, when the argument in England was almost lost, for the next eighteen years at least. The difference between his view of the Church and that propounded in expositions of the Song of Songs is shown in the full title for the work: *The Acts and Monuments of the Church before Christ Incarnate*. The very idea that the Church could exist before the coming of Christ was anathema to those who believed that the Church was His Bride: Montagu argued that there always had been a visible church in existence, that the Synagogue was indistinguishable from the Church, that good works were acceptable to God even in pagans. Nothing could be more objectionable to those who believed that the predestinating love of God singled the Church out from the rest of corrupt humanity, protected her and gave her privileges and especial favours which demanded complete devotion and spiritual-mindedness in return. A generation brought up on the social drama articulated in interpretations of the Song of Songs were not to be convinced by a 'martyrology' that affirmed only an undiscriminating inclusion.

By the end of the 1630s the terms of the mystical marriage were well established as a kind of oppositional code to the Laudian hierarchy of the Church of England. The trope of the Bride as the true Church was used to affirm the history of the English church with its legacy of martyrdom. Various verses of the Song of Songs were used to give Biblical sanction to Calvinist doctrine in opposition to Arminianism, as we have seen. The result of this thinking was to give definition to an elect within the Church of England who were marked out by spiritual signs of God's favour and a rapturous experience of God's love. Thus treatments of the Song of Songs became a textual expression of a kind of radical Puritan romance. Sermons and treatises on the Song of Songs had the advantage of not using explicitly political language in the 1630s, a period when censorship was being heavily enforced.[96] Yet the cultural associations of the book were with the anti-Catholicism and Protestant Internationalism of the previous reign. Ordinary believers were reminded of a different era when the Church of England could be identified with the Bride of Christ for its purity of doctrine and resistance to foreign infiltration. Many of them believed that true religion elevated all its members to a state of intimacy with Christ that the Laudian regime, with its emphasis on ceremonial and its railing off of the altars, seemed to deny them: they wished to draw the boundaries for the sacred in a different place, a boundary that would definitively exclude Catholicism.

One of the first sermons to the Long Parliament which marked the beginning of the end for the Laudian regime, given on the solemn fast that marked the anniversary of Queen Elizabeth's accession to the throne on 17 November 1640, put forward the idea of a radical covenant with God that would purify the nation of the abuses of the 1630s. Cornelius Burges, friend of John Pym, represented the Laudian regime as the 'Babylonian captivity', and represented this covenant with God, that would bring them home to Zion, as a marriage:

> This Covenant is a marriage-Covenant, and there is no marrying with God, so long as your former husband, your base corruptions, your swearing, riot, drunkennesse, uncleannesse, pride, oppression, and what ever else your soules *know to be the plague of your own hearts,* remaine alive and undivorced.

For those prepared to go forward with God in this way, there were unparalleled privileges:

> We know how it is with a wife married to a loving husband. They loved one another before marriage, and many expressions of a speciall love passed betweene them, but they never enjoyed one another fully till the marriage was solemnized. Then, there is not only a more intimate manifestation of fervent, intire, loyall, chaste love; but a further enlarging and stretching out of mutuall affections to each other, than they could possibly have beleeved they should ever have reached unto, till now experience assure them of it. And even thus it is between us and God. [97]

As we have seen in the previous chapter, the Song of Songs could also be read as legitimising military effort in such a cause. It is no wonder that what was often seen as a God-given victory to the forces of Reformed Protestantism in the Civil War was to bring about, in the Interregnum, a renewed confidence that God saw them as the Bride of Christ in England. Francis Cornwell, writing in 1645 and looking back at the 1630s, summarised the support for anti-Laudian activists offered by Song of Songs discourse:

> when I lay in dolefull desertion, in the time of my imprisonment, for opposing that devised forme of Worship (which the Prelates had corrupted with their Popish innovations, by putting in, and leaving out, what they pleased) ... the first comfort that I received, for the assurance of the pardon of my sinne, and justification in the sight of God, was from reading this excellent Treatise of Mr. *Fox*.[98]

However, what Cornwell had learned about the mystical marriage from Foxe, which he excerpted from *Acts and Monuments* into his own treatise, was the sentiment summarised in the subtitle to his volume: *The loyall spouse of Christ hath no head, nor husband, but royall King Jesus*. It was exactly this sense of an independence from earthly authority that radicals found so empowering about their reading of the Song of Songs, and Laudians so subversive.

3
Emblematic Marriage at the 1630s Court

The 1630s saw very few publications specifically concerned with the Song of Songs: as we have seen, the text was deeply implicated in a religious politics that was oppositional to Archbishop William Laud, and he was in charge of the licensing of the press in this period. Many of the publications around the court were, however, preoccupied with a marriage that was not exactly mystical but which had symbolic resonance for Royalists—the marriage of Charles and Henrietta Maria. The contrast between the popular Puritan discourses treated in the last chapter, and the élitist literary texts that dealt with marriage at court, goes some way towards illustrating the gulf opening up in the spiritual imagination of Puritan and courtier in the 1630s. In 1638 one 'new' version of the Song of Songs was licensed for publication, but it was not part of the populist Puritan tradition; it was in Latin, by Gilbert Foliot, a twelfth-century Bishop of London, selected from ancient manuscripts by the royal librarian, Patrick Young, famous reorganiser of the King's Library. Gilbert Foliot's concerns are those of mediaeval Catholicism, to bolster the spiritual and moral authority of the Roman Catholic Church. Typical of this emphasis is his interpretation of verse five of chapter one, which had become since the Reformation a proof-text for the doctrine of original sin. The bride's 'blackness' in 'Nigra sum, sed Formosa'(I am black, but lovely): is glossed as the sufferings of the early Church through persecution, following commentators such as Bede.[1] This pro-Catholic publication was hardly likely to appeal to radical Puritanism, or constitute any threat to the absolutist regime of Charles and Laud. Works by 'godly' ministers in general, and treatises of commentary and interpretation in particular, were not favoured by Laud's censors: William Prynne later accused Laud of deliberately hindering the education of the people by denying them aids to Scriptural study.[2] It is no surprise, then, that treatises of the Song of Songs in its Reformed interpretation, of the kind which had proliferated in the earlier decades of the century, were not printed in the 1630s, when publication was dominated by Laud.[3]

In any case, Puritan interpretation of the tropes of the mystical marriage was not going to be a useful feature of any court where Henrietta Maria played a dominant role. Its anti-Catholic hermeneutic was unacceptable to her, of course, and to most of the Court itself. In any case its broad symbolic structure was far too unsubtle to function at this élite level. Henrietta Maria formed alliances, if temporary ones, with both Catholic and Protestant (even Puritan) nobles, and the main political factions at Court supported either Catholic France or Catholic Spain.[4] Also, the immediate referent of any figure of the Bride was most obviously the royal bride Henrietta Maria herself, and she preferred a different set of tropes for use in her own personal iconography. As Jessica Bell has shown, she found visual associations with the Virgin Mary useful in projecting her own image. Her mother Marie de Medicis even included them in portraits sent to facilitate royal marriages: 'the qualities that the Virgin had in abundance were all attributes with which a queen would be only too happy to be associated: queens had to appear as pillars of society who were worthy of public respect: but their primary role at court was to produce an heir, preferably male'.[5] Neither of these qualities was in English Puritan hermeneutic associated with the Bride of the Song of Songs, who was an icon of resistance to a persecuting society, and whose lovemaking was, paradoxically, virginal, and therefore by definition without issue. Individual women at Henrietta Maria's court such as Lucy Hay, Countess of Carlisle, and the Duchess of Chevreuse, were anything but virginal (they were both well-known as mistresses of important men) and as Malcolm Smuts has shown, they exercised in their own right the kind of political power that rendered redundant the dependence of the individual soul on her divine Husband that is so powerfully set forth in populist, Reformed interpretations of the Song of Songs.[6] The tropes of the Song of Songs had had a previous life in Catholic discourse, however, and this chapter traces this use in court writing of the 1630s. It also looks at some versions of the marriage trope by poets of the 1630s and 1640s who were aware of differing interpretations of the tropes of the Song of Songs in literary tradition.

Henrietta Maria propagated her own kind of piety in the 1630s court. Nicholas Caussin was the author of a text that in translation came to define its Catholic piety, *The Holy Court*: it described the implications of Christian Neoplatonism for courtly behaviour. *The Holy Court* was originally written for Henrietta Maria's brother, Louis XIII: the first volume of the English translation was printed in Paris in 1626, dedicated to Henrietta Maria, who was now the new Queen of England, and the five-volume project was completed in 1638. Caussin's frontispiece could be interpreted allegorically: blind Cupids tumbled from pedestals, allegorical figures represented the arts and sciences bearing suitable emblems.[7] All was centred on the devout figure of the monarch. Explicitly a treatise for 'men of quality'—those who 'be among men as mountaines over valleys'—it exhorted them to 'be mountains of perfume, of which *Solomon* speaketh in the Canticles'.[8] The treatise was explicitly Roman Catholic in allegiance. Caussin designated Protestantism a sect, with its roots in disobedience and rebellion (p. 656). He mocked the appeal to Scripture, and appealed throughout to the example of Catholic martyrs (pp. 68–9). He reversed the Protestant characterisation of the Catholic church as the Whore, asserting its status as the Bride; 'Your Ministers in the false glasse of their Doctrine represented the Romane Church to you, this lovely and chast spouse of Heaven, as a monster composed of al sorts of abominations' (p. 60).

The kind of piety set out in Caussin's book is based on doctrinal and social principles in complete opposition to popular Puritanism. The sense of spiritual equality for all which is encoded in Puritan interpretation of the Song of Songs often led to a despising of courtiers and court life, and the first topic Caussin tackles is a belief he acknowledges to be widespread, 'that the court and dovotion [sic] are ... things incompatible'(p. 1). Such a belief he equates with a catastrophic breakdown of the normal link between nobility and virtue, a breakdown typical of madness or chaos. It is also in defiance of God, who elevated the King and the court to their high position (p. 2). Caussin cannot resist expressing the opinion that the physical attractiveness of the nobility is 'a fayre shop for the soule', although he is clearly rather ashamed of such a superficial point, and hastily justifies it: 'the bodyes of Noble and Gentle men are ordinarily better composed, and as it were more delicately moulded by the artful hands of nature' (p. 7). Everywhere Caussin validates the sense of sight as a reliable indicator of more hidden virtues. Beauty is affirmed as a positive sign of piety, and evidence is produced to show that Jesus and Mary were physically beautiful (p. 20). Virtue is much more visible in great men, and that is a positive thing: God gives physical beauty to such noblemen to give them more authority (p. 11, p. 20). His concern is for harmony of signification: he explains away the biblical prejudice against riches, and concludes that, after all, the poor do not have time to be good (pp. 15–16).

A court ideology so much in opposition to the spirit of English interpretation of the Song of Songs would seem to preclude the appearance of the Biblical book in court writing: and yet Danielle Clarke has suggested *Partheneia Sacra*, a Catholic emblem book of 1633 which is deeply indebted to the Song of Songs, as 'the text which most clearly exemplifies the Queen's influence and interest'.[9] Its author, Henry Hawkins, was the brother of James, translator of *The Holy Court*, and he was a Jesuit priest who in James I's reign had been imprisoned and exiled. However, in Charles I's reign he seems to have existed in London very comfortably, under the protection of several influential Catholic friends, such as Endymion Porter.[10] He translated several works of Catholic spirituality, including Stephen Luzvic's emblem book *The Devout Hart* (1634). *Partheneia Sacra* was an emblem book of his own composition.[11] Christian Neoplatonism, which Erica Veevers has characterised as the dominant philosophy of Henrietta Maria's court, found its natural expression in the religious emblem.[12] Fundamental to emblem theory is the Neoplatonic idea of correspondences: earthly entities related to spiritual entities in a stable hierarchy. Thus the drawings which accompanied the poems in *Partheneia Sacra* symbolised spiritual truths which were expounded in Hawkins' poetry.

The sub-title of *Partheneia Sacra* is *The Mysterious and Delicious Garden of the Sacred Parthenes*: the link between the garden and the Virgin (Parthenes) makes the invoking of allegories from the Song of Songs inevitable, as much Catholic interpretation of the Song of Songs saw the enclosed garden as an emblem of the Virgin herself. This equivalence is spelt out in Hawkins' 'Epistle to the Parthenian Sodalitie': the Garden is a symbol of the Virgin, but so are the other twenty-two emblems illustrated within it. Karl Josef Höltgen assumes that the book was written for a group of devotees of the Virgin existing secretly in England.[13] Erica Veevers points out just how like such a 'sodality' was Henrietta Maria's court: in 1632 she began a chapel in the grounds of her palace at Somerset House for the Arch-Confraternity of the Holy Rosary, a cult of the Virgin started by the Capuchins, who had special permission from the Pope to operate a centre in London. Henrietta Maria was the first member.[14] Hawkins addresses an introductory epistle to the 'Parthenian Sodalitie' which celebrates, in the words of the Song of Songs, a change from an anti-Catholic regime: 'now then the winter past of melancholie thoughts, the showers blowne-over and quite vanished, of teares of persecution' (sig. A1v). The garden is the dominant emblem, and it is a garden much elaborated on—there are violets and sunflowers as well as roses and lilies, and there are valleys and hills, and obelisks, pyramids, arches, pillars and other garden architecture. It is a palace garden, with sumptuous garden furniture: one that even surpasses Eden, as Satan is not allowed there (p. 12). The imagery of *Partheneia Sacra* is drawn from a mediaeval tradition that identified the Virgin Mary with the Garden of the Song of Songs, as well as elements within it. The 'extra' emblems not found in the Song of Songs are based on mystical names for the Virgin, such as 'stella maris' and 'porta coeli'.[15] As the book progresses, says Michael Bath, 'an allegorical image of the Virgin is being composed out of the miscellaneous varieties of the natural world'.[16] The text of the Song of Songs 4:7 gives the interpretive framework for this emblem book, which is also a traditional meditation on the Virgin; 'Thou art all fair, my love'.[17] Within a Neoplatonic scheme, every beautiful image can ultimately be related to the Virgin.

In his Preface to the Reader Hawkins worries that his choice of the emblem form might 'seeme prophane' (sig A2v). What his particular version of the emblem allows him to do is to dwell on the vehicle of the metaphor: at least half of each of the twenty-four divisions is spent lovingly describing the visual appearance of the symbol, rather than moving immediately away from the image to consider the hidden meaning as, for example, Francis

Quarles would do in his 1635 *Booke of Emblemes*. J. E. Secker points out that there is some very early naturalistic description in the 'Essay' section on the symbol of the Mount:

> Mountains are one of the gallantst things in Nature. ... The verdures give forth themselves delicious to behold, like a Landskap in a table, with al the greenes to be found in the neck of a mallard, heer a bright, there a dark, and then a bright and a darke againe...with the lights and reflections caused through the dawning of the day in the morning or twylight of the evening (pp. 226–7).[18]

Michael Bath shows that Hawkins' writing is full of images of perception, and references to actual paintings.[19] An untroubled relationship between physical sight and spiritual insight is of course fundamental to emblem theory, and this is a marker of the breach with Puritan spirituality. Danielle Clarke has suggested that Marian literature of the 1630s is concerned with surfaces, and that Puritan writers such as Henry Burton and William Prynne abhorred this concentration on appearances, finding such writing implicated in sexual voyeurism.[20] Hawkins in 'The Proeme' to the book finds himself able to give a physical description of the Virgin Mary herself, an extremely un-Puritan thing to do:

> Nor yet was She destitute of the guifts of Nature likewise, while a certain Divinitie of beautie dazeled the aspects of men. The bashful forhead soft and gently arose; beneath the black and archie browes shined forth the bright lamps of Her eyes, which how powerfully they pieced and penetrated the heavens, who knows not? The nose most gracefully inflecting, made a handsome kind of pillar to her forhead; lips somewhat thinner, the receptacle of a meeke elocution, and celestial graces (sig. A5v).

Implicated in the emphasis on physical beauty is a concern with material richness that is politically charged, as in the description of the rose, 'the Princesse of flowers':

> To speak of the fires of its Carnation, the snow of its white Satin, the fine Emralds, cut into little toungs round about, to serve as a trayne to wayt upon it; of the Balme and ambergrees, that breathes from this little crop of gold (p. 20).

This is writing for the aristocratic élite, for whom wealth and luxury are not necessarily a hindrance to piety, as these attributes so often are in Puritan teaching. It is no surprise when Hawkins shows his political sympathies directly, as in 'The Character' of the bee, which muses on the superiorities of a monarchical system (p. 71). Puritan spirituality tends to ignore the contingent circumstances of outward appearance, whose associations may be alienating to the readership in terms of class and lifestyle, and focus on the spiritual meaning of the emblem, which for them is axiomatically accessible to everyone.

What is perhaps slightly strange about Hawkin's interest in the Virgin Mary is the number of emblems that deal with symbolic images of Mary's conception of Jesus. In one way this is hardly surprising; a book that represents Mary as the enclosed garden, her virginity apparently unpenetrable, is almost inevitably fascinated with the mechanics of the Immaculate Conception—how did God bypass her defences? The processes depicted are of course not gynaecological, nor even theological: but there is a concentration of interest in the metaphorical representation of such an event in Hawkins' Emblems. This is a very un-Puritan interest, one which focuses again on the complexities of the image: the interpretation, a key doctrine of the Catholic Church, is a given, but there is obvious flexibility in how the Immaculate Conception might be represented. Ten of the twenty-four emblems in the volume deal in some way with this event. The first uses a metaphor from the Song of Songs, 4:16: 'Come thou south wind and blow upon my garden', which is the text of the motto on the Emblem of the garden (p. 13). The garden is shown very satisfactorily enclosed by a high fence: but above the fence is the South wind, blowing down on the garden. The text of the Poesie makes the problem, and its solution, obvious, in terms that are horticultural but which have an obvious reproductive analogy:

> But it was clos'd: Alma's shut up, we know,
> What Gard'ner then might enter in to sow?...
> The Holie-Spirit, like a subtile wind,
> Peercing through al, only a way could find.
> As th'Earth brought forth at first, how 't is not knowne;
> So did this Garden, which was never sowne (pp. 13–14).

The penetration of the Virgin by the Holy Spirit is figured in other rather less Biblical ways in other Emblems. In 'The Pearl' a it appears that a phallic ray is descending from God into the open shell of the oyster. 'The Discourse' explains:

> The *Virgin-Mother-Pearl* itself... opened her Virginal soule, at her mysterious *Annunciation*, in the Spring of the yeare, by the quiet shore of her tacit and silent contemplation, to receive the heavenlie Deaw ... that is, to conceave that precious *Pearl, Christ Jesus*, in her womb ...after the opening thus of her free consent, and her Angelical soule, the Celestial deaw of the *Holie-Ghost* descended into her, and so the infant-*Pearl* was divinely begot in the virginal womb of the Virgin-mother-*Pearl* (p. 192).

The Immaculate Conception is also portrayed as the 'inflammation' of the rose, which blushes and conceives (p. 25): as the dove mating with the Virgin (p. 207); as 'Light condens'd' which in the mysterious process that made Manna appear, produces Christ the bread of life in the womb of Mary, figured here as a ship (p. 254). Here, the concentration on the image allows for a prurience that does not usually attach to the doctrine of the Immaculate Conception: an unhealthy focus on the practicalities of conception, metaphorically figured and visually represented, cannot help but draw attention to physical processes rather than deep spiritual truths. But, as every early modern reader of poetry knows, sex always happens in a garden.

Paul Ricoeur identifies several places where 'a good Freudian' should detect sex happening in the garden of the Song of Songs.[21] Of course, a post-Freudian reader is not necessarily going to respond in exactly the same way as a seventeenth-century reader, but it is worth examining one of these instances as treated both by Henry Hawkins in *Partheneia Sacra* and by Francis Quarles in his *Booke of Emblemes*. In the emblematic works the text cited is verse 16 of chapter 2, although verse 3 of chapter 6 is almost identical: 'My beloved is mine and I am his: he feedeth among the lilies.' For Hawkins of course the lily is another emblem of the Virgin Mary, and his emblem is at the centre of a series of discourses expounding the similarity between the Virgin and the lily, focusing on the virtue of chastity (according to Gordon Williams, the modern association between the lily and the vagina was not current in the seventeenth century).[22] This verse for Hawkins is emphatically not about sex, in contrast to other emblems which describe the conception of Christ: the Discourse before the emblem itself explains that Jesus is feeding at the Virgin's breast, surrounded by the metaphorical lilies which are her virtues and which are part of the enclosure which keeps her chaste (p. 34). The image however shows a stylised lily being offered up to a symbol of God by a strange knobbly cloud-like being from whom a human arm protrudes and who is identified by the Poesie as the Virgin herself. The focus is very definitely on the Virgin as lily, and stem to stamen the flower is anatomised as parts of the Virgin's soul.

Quarles' naturalistic image, by contrast, looks at first sight a great deal more sensual. His lovers are sitting very close together in a lily-planted garden. The sumptuous palace and terraces very prominent in the background of the picture rather overwhelm the effect of the lilies, incidentally making nonsense of Christ's command to consider the lily as more beautiful than anything else. However, the lily is definitely not the focus of Quarles' emblem: his poem mentions no flowers at all. Rather, the unity of Christ and the soul is described and celebrated. This is done in distinctly sensual terms. The first image used is that of two streams flowing together, a relatively cool and passionless metaphor if Quarles had not described the separate watercourses as 'wanton'. The second stanza, however, leaves restraint behind.

> Ev'n so we met; and after long pursuit,
> Ev'n so we joyn'd; we both became entire;

No need for either to renew a suit,
For I was flax and he was flames of fire (p. 257).

For Quarles, this is a verse about passionate unity. The first five stanzas of his accompanying poem are indistinguishable from a love song. His expository task is clearly to elaborate on the central metaphor here: the mystical marriage. The emotional and sensual content of the love song is overlaid by some theology and Biblical imagery in the final stanzas:

> I'm his by penitence; he mine by grace;
> I'm his by purchase; he is mine, by bloud;
> He's my supporting elm; and I his vine:
> Thus I my best-beloveds am; thus he is mine (p. 258).

In Quarles' emblem the relationship between image and poem is simply that of elaborating the central conceit, in the manner, perhaps, of a sermon. No decrypting is necessary.

These two renderings of the same Biblical verse show completely different uses of the emblem by their authors. For Hawkins the Biblical verse alludes to a complex sign system around the Virgin Mary. His rendering on the one hand explicates what is happening in that verse, whilst on the other hand it embeds the verse in a wider symbolic structure of his own composition. Complexity of interpretation is part of the pleasure here, and part of the point. The Latin mottoes, for example, remain untranslated. Understanding of these mysteries is for the élite only. By contrast, Quarles' anthropomorphic rendering of the Divine husband and the earthly Bride as lovers in an admittedly courtly garden needs no code-breaking. It is obvious that sex of a kind is going on here. The task of the poet is to redefine intercourse as a phenomenon of the soul: emotions may be engaged, but not bodies. In such an enterprise, naturalistic emblems may be considered as rather more of a hindrance than a help: the diagrammatic emblems of *Partheneia Sacra*, even when illustrating such mysteries as the conception of Jesus, are not nearly so erotic.

The origins of the emblem are multiple, in discourses ranging from esoteric symbol to commonplace proverbs. These are two figures of speech that would seem to require very different interpretive strategies, but Michael Bath concludes that it is actually impossible to distinguish hieroglyphic theories from rhetorical theory about figures; they are all seen as ways of communicating, like the simile.[23] As Hoskins declares, 'similitude ... is the ground of all emblems, allegories, fables, and fictions'(p. 54). Michael Bath insists that the Renaissance saw these literary figures as 'a single way of representing moral experience', and traces attempts to link emblems with Biblical verses in earlier English theorists.[24] He concludes that there was a stock of material for Renaissance emblematists that included humanist commonplaces, proverbs, and hieroglyphics: the Bible, which could be seen as an emblem book in its own right, added to this stock. In rhetorical theory of the Renaissance, knowledge of things is assumed to be fundamental to good oratory: the source of such knowledge is not questioned. Nicholas Caussin's compendium of emblems, ranging from esoteric ancient Egyptian texts to recent Christian symbols, illustrates this. Michael Bath concludes that arcane Egyptian symbols and mystical Christian icons are being treated as essentially the same thing: 'hieroglyphica swallows up allegoria' in this work.[25] Attempting to distinguish between the disparate elements of his book, Caussin decides that the symbolic element of the emblem is more clearly interpreted than in other figures, allowing it to communicate a more profound *sententia*.[26] Of course, a literary form which is 'an untidy body of signifying practices' allows for a variety of uses: the relative importance of image and text may be envisaged very differently. For George Wither, by instinct a populist communicator, it is his verses which are the 'illustrations' within his emblem book, not the pictures: the poetry 'quickens' the images, which otherwise lose their capacity to instruct.[27] The emblem form could harness various kinds of literary excitement at the same time, however con-tradictory these could appear; from the aristocratic élitism that surrounded the devise, to the esoteric mysticism of alchemical symbols, to the pagan secrets of hieroglyphics, to the 'Adamic language' that could be claimed for a system of natural signs. That the religious emblem was not completely alien to Puritans at least in the 1590s is shown by the fact that Andrew Willet, who figured largely in chapter 1 as Calvinist chaplain to Prince Henry, pro-duced one of the first emblem books, in English and in Latin, dedicated to that 'best patron', the Earl of Essex, in 1592. His emblems are of three types: allegories, histories and natural symbols such as animals. He insists that all of them are grounded in Scripture; there are no visual illustrations but that is because of the cost rather than any ideological objection.[28]

Francis Quarles' *Emblemes* 1635

The emblem was one genre which could be used for educational purposes, had been employed as such by Puritans, yet was closely associated with Royalism, and therefore could be safely published in this period when Laudian censorship was very active. The most popular treatment of the Song of Songs in the 1630s appeared in Francis Quarles' *Emblemes*, published at a time when Quarles was privately composing anti-Laudian eclogues.[29] This seventeenth-century best-seller went into 18 editions in the next 90 years, despite costing the princely sum of 5s when first published. As Ian Green points out, this volume succeeded despite the risk of Puritan hostility. Quarles' subject matter was explicitly Catholic—he had taken most of his plates from two Jesuit emblem books, *Pia Desideria* (1624) and *Typus Mundi* (1628). The sacred emblem form involved engraved images, in Quarles' case representations of God and Christ, the latter as a winged Cherub: and charges of violation of the second commandment against graven images, which Diarmaid McCulloch has identified as so important for Reformed Protestants, would have seemed inevitable in a decade in which it was still controversial to insert illustrations into Bibles.[30] It was the Jesuits who were the foremost users of emblematic images, and their printing press at Lyon produced some of the most famous illustrated books in the early modern period, much to the anger of the Protestant community there.[31]

Francis Quarles suggested an equivalence between the emblem project as a whole and the task of interpreting Scripture. He equated the emblem with the specifically Biblical literary form of the parable, and also with the mystical esoteric form of the hieroglyphic:

> An *Embleme* is but a silent Parable. Let not the tender Eye check, to see the allusion to our blessed Saviour figured in these Types. In holy Scripture, he is sometimes called a Sower; sometimes, a Fisher; sometimes a Physician: And why not presented so as well to the eye as to the eare? Before the knowledge of letters God was known by *Hieroglyphicks:* And, indeed, what are the Heavens, the Earth, nay every Creature, but *Hieroglyphicks* and *Emblemes* of His Glory?

Within a parable, the reader is accustomed to distinguishing types of Christ—Quarles lists the sower, the fisherman, the doctor. The application of this biblical, word-centred technique of literary criticism is suddenly broadened by Quarles to include the secular, non-verbal text of Nature—earth, sky, animals. These are described by Quarles as a different kind of language, as hieroglyphics, but although by the 1630s this word could already designate incomprehensible nonsense, Quarles, like a good Protestant, presents breaking God's code as an unproblematic task. There are no difficulties envisaged for the reader, either—only the 'pleasure' which Quarles wishes for him.[32] The equation of sacred symbols of Egypt with Biblical stories that teach Christian doctrine is not perceived as odd in this period; perhaps it was this aspect of the emblem, that it was capable of carrying complex meanings, which led Quarles to choose emblems from the Song of Songs for his volume. He had shown great interest in the Song of Songs in the 1620s, and produced a verse paraphrase of it, with explanatory glosses. The purpose of the volume was, as he stated to his readers, 'to invite you all to the wedding' of the Bridegroom Christ with the Bride his Church.[33] Availability of pictures may have encouraged him to represent the text in emblem form. Most of his illustrations were copied from two Catholic emblem books, *Typus Mundi* by students of the College of Rhetoric of the Society of Jesus and the 1624 *Pia Desideria*, by Herman Hugo.[34] Thirteen of the plates from *Pia Desideria* are illustrations of the text of the Song of Songs, which means that much of books IV and V are concerned with this Biblical book. The Catholic origins of Quarles' source text, which includes long quotations from the Fathers within every emblem, are obvious: Quarles has translated and selectively included a few of these quotations within his emblems, even adding extracts from the Fathers to emblems in Books 1 and 2 where his source text did not include any. Even more potentially transgressive is the fact that the figures in the illustrations evolved from erotic emblem books which featured an adventurous Cupid: thus Christ and the Bride are a boy and a girl, and the boy retains the chubbiness and the wings of his original.[35] Given the popularity of the volume, these poems and these images must have been the way that many readers in the seventeenth century engaged closely with the Song of Songs: a tantalising thought, as so much of the rhetoric of this volume—a combination of words and images—differs from widespread Calvinist commentary.

The optimism about the project expressed by Quarles at the start of his work is not entirely unalloyed. The original introduction to the volume was the poem which introduces books three, four and five of Quarles' emblems, 'The Entertainment'.[36] At first reading it is a warning very much like those which often preface versions of the Song of Songs. It summons as readers only those who have experienced the second birth and who are not seduced by the pleasures of the flesh:

> ALL you ... whose chast eare
> No wanton songs of Sirens can surprize
> With false delight ...
> Whose souls can spurn at pleasure, and deny
> The loose suggestions of the flesh draw nigh:
>
> And you whose am'rous, whose select desires
> Would feel the warmth of those transcendent fires,
> Which (like the rising Sun) put out the light
> Of *Venus* starre, and turn her day to night.

This warning cannot apply only to the emblems on the Song of Songs as there are others contained in books three, four and five. This is a prohibition that has nothing to do with possible sensual reactions to the Biblical text; it is highlighting a carnal problem with the emblem form itself. For the Puritan reader there is a double jeopardy lurking in emblems which tell the story of the Song of Songs. Readers are accustomed to being ordered to interpret the Song of Songs in chaste spiritual fashion: but here there is also the peril of images, which could also distract from and corrupt the Word. Thus Quarles' warning has a double edge. The challenge is not only to read the message of the mystical marriage aright, but also to be able to use visual emblems properly. Inevitably for Quarles, reading an emblem poem involves contact with a visual image: visual images were more often associated with the sinful human flesh, or with Catholicism. The answer for the reader is to use the illustration with care, merely as a means to understand something more about God, and not to dwell on the visual image. Quarles advocates as little time as possible spent looking at the emblem:

> Shake hands with earth, and let your soul respect
> Her joyes no further, then her joyes reflect
> Upon her Makers glory.[37]

Ernst B. Gilman has observed this tension between word and image in Francis Quarles' work, and equated it with a kind of Protestant iconoclasm. Certainly, Protestant practice differs from Jesuit theory, where word and image were believed to mirror each other.[38] Gilman perceives a problem for Protestants in the use of the image: 'no longer a mirror of the divine, [the image] reflects the anxieties of our own attempts to decipher it'. [39] So much for the concept of straightforward translation of a language of hieroglyphics, an idea which clearly appeals to the Protestant Quarles as a function of the emblem.

It is in fact difficult to see how the emblems based on the Song of Songs in Quarles' text could be regarded as hieroglyphics, which need interpretation, at all. The situations chosen for *Pia Desideria* are on the whole those that can be easily assimilated into the narrative of a love relationship between Christ and the soul. Thus Emblem 9 of book 4 is entitled '*O that thou wert as my brother, that sucked the breasts of my mother, I would find thee without, and I would kisse thee*' (Canticles 8:1). The accompanying poems, both in *Pia Desideria* and Quarles' *Emblems*, offer thoughts suggested by the concept of the soul embracing the young Christ:

> Illustrious Babe! how is thy handmaid grac'd
> With a rich armfull! how dost thou decline
> Thy Majesty, that wert so late embrac'd
> In thy great Fathers arms, and now in mine! (p. 222).

There is very little decoding needed here. Quarles is entering into the imagination of the Bride as she fantasises about embracing Christ as a baby. Any difficulties in this scenario are ignored by the poet. Hester Black suggests that the conversion of the lovers into small children in the engravings helps to negate the eroticism of the Song of Songs, and in fact, in this illustration the female Soul is embracing the child Christ much as a child would do a doll.[40] Emblem 1 of Book 5, based on 5:8, '*I charge you, O daughters of Jerusalem, if you find my beloved, that you tell him that I am sick of love*', is an excuse for a Petrarchan-style delineation of the effects of being 'lovesick' and temporarily abandoned by the lover, in stanzas reminiscent of a hundred second-rate Elizabethan poems:

> O tell him, that his cruelties deprive
> My soul of peace, while peace in vain she seeks;

> Tell him those damask roses, that did strive
> With white, both fade, upon my sallow cheeks;
> Tell him, no token doth proclaim I live,
> But tears, and sighs, and sobs, and sudden shrieks (p. 250).

Rather more felicitous is the love-poetry which accompanies Emblem 3 of Book 5, based on Canticles 2:16: *'My beloved is mine, and I am his'*.

> Nor Time, nor Place, nor Chance, nor Death can bow
> My least desires unto the least remove;
> He's firmly mine by oath; I his by vow;
> He's mine by faith; and I am his by love;
> He's mine by water; I am his by wine;
> Thus I my best-beloveds am; thus he is mine (p. 258).

This represents one of the few poems in which Quarles sounds something like George Herbert. These straightforward verses, however, do not really fulfil the function of the emblem poet as stated at the start of Quarles' volume. Rather than decoding an image, the poet is developing it, giving larger expression to the sentiment which is already explicit in the illustration. This has the effect, I would argue, of giving greater importance to the image, whereas truly Protestant emblems 'point away from themselves and thus declare their own insufficiency'.[41] Rather than the brief 'hand-shaking' envisaged by Quarles, a glance which is quickly followed by concentration on the explanatory poem, the text merely serves to throw significance onto the original image, to which the gaze returns. Thus, the reader becomes very aware, for example, of the gorgeous garden in which the lovers are seated in Emblem 3 book 5, or the beautifully-proportioned interior of the palace in which the girl is cradling her baby in Emblem 9 of book 4. Gilman notes that the poems of *Pia Desideria* are in some ways as superficial as the engravings: 'the sensual texture and mythological decoration ... in the Jesuit verses had echoed the rapturous feeling of the plates'.[42] Perhaps the Protestant iconoclast is right to emphasise the corrupting effect of images.

Protestant anxieties about Song of Songs texts focus on the interpretation of particular rhetorical images, rather than the problem of using images itself, which Gilman discerns in many of Quarles' emblems.[43] The Song of Songs, after all, is a set of images, a succession of smaller metaphors based on the overarching allegory of the mystical marriage. God has chosen these poetic images in order to communicate something particularly holy: there cannot therefore be a problem with the use of these images as such. However, William Gouge, introducing Henry Finch's commentary in 1615, stresses 'the manie Rhetoricall allegories, and hyperbolicall metaphors which are hard to be understood and rightly applied'. Of course, such a discourse requires a commentator, and Henry Finch, being a learned lawyer (if not a minister) is qualified to restore 'perspicuitie', that quality which Reformed views of the Biblical text require, to this admittedly obscure book.[44] The more allegorical the Song of Songs text is perceived to be, the more interpretive work there is for Quarles to do, and the more he differs from his Catholic original.

Karl Josef Höltgen, in opposition to Ernst Gilman, wants to see this emblem book as an indication of Quarles' sympathy with Catholicism: he compares the emblem with the spirituality of Ignatius Loyola, equating the illustration with the composition of place, the poem with the meditation, and the final epigram with the colloquy.[45] However, Puritan spirituality is too hostile to surface appearances to be dealt with satisfactorily in this scheme. It is true that Quarles calls his poems 'Meditations', although as we have seen, they do not always dwell harmoniously on details of the image in the way Catholic spirituality recommends: but they are meditations in the Joseph Hall tradition, whose *Arte of Divine Meditation* Joseph Brinsley recommended for illustration, but whose consciously Protestant meditation threw less emphasis on the materiality of the sign.[46] There is no resemblance at all between the colloquy, which in Ignatian spirituality turns the lessons of the meditation into a prayer, and Quarles' epigrams, which seize on any aspect of the emblem that will afford matter for rhetorical wit, whether it is consistent with the message of the poem or not. In any case, as Robert Wilcher has pointed out, in the mid-1630s Quarles is anything but Catholic in allegiance: his volume *The shepheards oracles*, written in the 1630s but not published until after his death in 1645, shows a resolutely anti-Catholic and even anti-Arminian position, as his dialogues between 'Nullifidicus' and 'Pseudo-catholicus'(p. 36) and between 'Arminius' and 'Philamnus' (p. 60) make very clear.[47]

Superficially, then, Quarles' *Booke of Emblemes* might be seen as a publication facilitated by the religious art and literature of the 1630s court. However, a comparison with Henry Hawkins' *Partheneia Sacra* shows Quarles' work to be much more in sympathy with Puritan interpretations of the Song of Songs than the Laudian censors perhaps realised. Despite, or perhaps because of, the aristocratic trappings in Quarles' engravings, his emblem book was popular with a wide readership who would be familiar with, and probably receptive to, the populist interpretation of the Song of Songs on which Quarles' poems depended. The difference between the two volumes perhaps helps to illustrate the diverse function of Court literature compared with that of works designed for the mass market in what Ian Green calls the publishing drive towards 'entertaining edification' in the seventeenth century. Its consumers were the growing number of the relatively well-educated and relatively well-off (after all, Quarles' *Emblemes* were quite expensive). Samuel Pepys spent an entertaining evening with the Earl of Sandwich in January 1660, reading Quarles' emblem book and eating turkey-pie: there is little evidence that he was Puritan in sympathy or behaviour (althought the Earl of Sandwich, Sir Edward Mountagu, was) but clearly he was able to understand those many emblems which depended upon a Puritan understanding of the mystical marriage.[48] By contrast, for Henrietta Maria and her Catholic entourage the Song of Songs was about something else entirely: the mystical marriage, surrounded with esoteric symbolism, was between one earthly woman, Mary, and a divine lover. The élitism and the Mariolatry of Hawkins' emblem book would have been repugnant to the majority of the English people.

The 1630s court masque

As we have seen, the Puritan doctrine of the mystical marriage was not the dominant interpretation of the Song of Songs at the English court in the 1630s. Nevertheless, marriage itself retained moral and political significance, often in literature which retained a direct connection to the emblem. The rest of this chapter moves away from consideration of the Biblical book, to a survey of how marriage was used as an image in courtly culture of the 1630s. In doing so I hope to illuminate the differences in assumption and outlook between court literature and popular theology.

Devout Humanism as expressed by Nicholas Caussin is compatible with Neoplatonism, and Erica Veevers has shown how under the patronage of Henrietta Maria these combined as Christian Neoplatonism to produce the distinctive art of the 1630s court.[49] Both the emblem and the masque, characteristic courtly literary forms, owe their form to Neoplatonic philosophy. Many critics have noticed the link between masque and emblem form. D. J. Gordon shows that masques had their origins in emblem literature.[50] Danielle Clarke notes the reference to masque culture in *Partheneia Sacra*:

> Have you seen a statelie Mask in Court, al set round, and taken up with a world of beautiful Ladies, to behold the sports and revels there? Imagin the *Starres* then, as sitting in the Firmament, to behold some spectacle on Earth.[51]

Emblematic images were an established part of stage imagery in the masque, and several masques, such as *Chloridia, Tempe Restored* and *Luminalia* provided emblematic settings for Henrietta Maria that mirrored emblems associated with the Virgin Mary.[52] Both emblematists and masque writers had a tendency to turn the real persons of the King and Queen into emblematic figures, a significance associated with their married status. Kevin Sharpe has stressed the importance of marriage in literature of the Caroline court, arguing that Charles I consciously propagated his view of good government through the Neoplatonic representation of his marriage as a union of souls.[53] Courtly authors reflected that emblematic image back to their monarch. Even George Wither in the dedicatory epistle of his *Collection of Emblemes* to Charles I, and the queen he calls 'Mary', finds, somewhat surprisingly, that they are an emblem of unity between the Protestant and Catholic church, although he has to do some violence to gender relationships and to traditional anti-Catholicism to demonstrate it: they are both *'Daughters* of the Spouse *Divine'*.[54] Jonson in his masque put on for the King's northern progress in 1634, *Loves Welcome at Bolsover*, uses Charles and Henrietta as his emblematic example of mutual love in a Neoplatonic scheme which echoes the circle seen by Ficino as the emblem of God and man in unity.[55]

Thomas Carew's *Coelum Britannicum* was based on Giordano Bruno's Platonic dialogue, *Spaccio de la Bestia Trionfante* (1584), which argues against mistaking the representation of the Idea for the Idea itself. Carew's message is different, but both works start with the same dramatic situation. Jupiter has repented of his previous immoral lifestyle, and has cleansed the heavens of the impure pagan gods. The vacant spaces are to be filled with new stars, to consist of appropriately Neoplatonic virtues. Carew had more topical and practical concerns than Bruno, and his masque has direct relevance to 1630s politics: Joanne Altieri has shown that he was interested in the slippage between the ideal Platonic world and the real world of the 1634 court.[56] Mercury sets up the basic plot and nominates Charles and Henrietta Maria as the first new stars.

> First you succeed, and of the wheeling Orbe
> In the most eminent and conspicuous point,
> With dazeling beames, and spreading magnitude,
> Shine the bright Pole starre of this Hemispheare,
> Next, by your side, in a triumphant Chaire,
> And crown'd with *Ariadnes* Diadem,
> Sits the faire Consort of your heart, and Throne;
> ...
> So to the British stars this lower Globe
> Shall owe its light, and they alone dispence
> To'th' world a pure refined influence.[57]

At this point of conventional praise to the King and Queen the disruptive figure of Momus enters. In Carew's masque, the role of Momus, God of Satire, is expanded to include references to events in the real world. Joanne Altieri points out that the masque was danced on 18 February 1634, the day after the two-week trial of William Prynne for writing *Histrio-mastix*. She finds in Momus' list of mock-allegations against himself a parody of the accusations against Prynne:

> My name is *Momus ap-Somnus-ap-Erebus-ap-Chaos-ap-Demorgorgon-ap-Eternity*, My Offices and Titles are, The Supreme Theomastix, Hupercritique of manners, protonotary of abuses, Arch-Informer, Dilator Generall,

Vniversall Calumniator, Eternall plaintiffe, and perpetuall Foreman of the Grand Inquest (p. 178).

Momus is not as impressed by the reformation in heaven as Mercury is, and rattles off a list of mock reforms which critics agree are meant to recall reforming measures recently instituted by Charles I:

Monopolies are called in, sophistication of wares punished, and rates imposed on commodities. Injunctions are gone out to the Nectar Brewers, for the purging of the heavenly Beverage of a narcotique weed which hath rendred the Idaeaes confus'd in the Divine intellects, and reducing it to the composition used in *Saturnes* Reign. Edicts are made for the restoring of decayed house-keeping, prohibiting the repayr of Families to the Metropolis, but this did endanger an Amazonian mutiny, till the females put on a more masculine resolution of solliciting business in their own persons, and leaving their husbands at home for stallions of hospitality (p. 182).

'No masque,' claims Kevin Sharpe, 'had represented immediate politics so precisely', giving a list of the royal proclamations which are being satirised here.[58] Altieri claims that William Noy, chief prosecutor of William Prynne, was responsible for most of the courtly reforms, and that this is another reminder of the trial just finished.[59] It is Momus who introduces to us the famous emblem of marital unity, Carlo-Maria, which Jupiter has created to keep his wife and himself on the path of marital fidelity:

to eternize the memory of that great example of Matrimoniall union which he derives from hence, [he] hath on his Bed-chamber doore and seeling, fretted with starres in capitall Letters, engraven the Inscription of *CARLO-MARIA* (p. 183).

As elsewhere in the court masque, the emblem of the two-in-one which is the royal marriage signifies unity and harmony, a message all too relevant to Jupiter and Juno, on whose ceiling Charles and Henrietta Maria have already been made into decorative and exemplary stars.

As in Bruno's dialogue, Riches, Poverty and Fortune then compete for a place in the heavens, and here we see Neoplatonism coexisting well with Caroline court culture. Ripa's 1611 *Iconologia* can be used as a crib-text for the symbols and emblems of the *Coelum Britannicum*. As might be expected, Riches and Fortune get rather short shrift from both Mercury and Momus, but so too does Poverty. Poverty makes a rather familiar pitch for pre-eminence, citing pure weight of numbers, and the fact that poverty often produces virtue:

The numerous Armies, and the swarming Ants
That fight and royle ... , are all my Subjects,

> Thay take my wages, weare my Livery:
> Invention too and Wit, are both my creatures,
> And the whole race of Vertue is my Off-spring (p. 195).

To Puritan auditors, this might represent a legitimate claim, but Mercury is having none of it. He redefines Poverty's virtues from the point of view of privilege:

> Wee not require the dull society
> Of your necessitated Temperance,
> Or that unnaturall stupidity
> That knowes nor joy nor sorrow; nor your forc'd
> Falsly exalted passive Fortitude
> Above the Active: This low abject brood,
> That fix their seats in mediocrity,
> Become your servile mind; but we advance
> Such vertues only as admit excesse,
> Brave bounteous Acts, Regall Magnificence (p. 196).

Poverty is just too ugly and too boring to populate a British heaven: her hair is a mess and her clothes are patched. In the devaluing of the visual typical of Puritan culture, these signs of material turpitude in a Neoplatonic scheme could signify the opposite in spiritual and therefore more important terms, as we have seen: the Biblical Bride is 'black, but comely', a verse taken in Puritan commentary to mean that despite the deformities wrought by sin the Bride is still beautiful to God.[60] In Neoplatonic culture, however, spiritual worth is signified by obvious physical worth, such as noble status and beauty. At the end of *Coelum Britannicum*, Charles I is depicted as the epitome of heroic virtue. Henrietta Maria's eyes sparkle in the sky more brightly than the previous stars and the heat of their love releases the British heroes for the dancing which takes up the greater part of the evening. The combined beauty, aristocracy and virtue displayed in the patterns of dance is part of the ultimate harmony symbolised by the emblem of Carlo-Maria, the royal couple who preside at the ending of the play—Momus has slipped away.

Despite his final absence, Altieri argues that it is Momus who is more attractive to the audience.[61] After all, Carew himself took Momus' role. She argues that Mercury is not allowed simply to praise. He has to know the truth about what is really going on at court, which is conveyed by Momus, the ultimate peeping Tom:

> My privileges are an ubiquitary, circumambulatory, speculatory, inter-rogatory, redargutory, immunity over all the privy lodgings, behind hangings, doores, curtaines, through key-holes, chinks, windowes, about

all Venerial Lobbies, Skonces, or Redoubts, though it bee to the surprize of a perdu Page or Chambermaid (p. 178).

As Sarah Poynting has shown, the Court at this time was certainly more like the bawdy society portrayed by Momus than the idealised Neoplatonic picture we are left with at the end of the masque: the gossip surrounding ladies-in-waiting Dorothy Seymour and Eleanor Villiers details the kind of activities going on 'beyond hangings, doores, curtaines' at court.[62] Kevin Sharpe believes that the triumphal ending of *Coelum Britannicum* does not efface Momus' words: 'the compelling force of these dialogues is by no means eroded by their final transcendance in apotheosis, spectacle, or dance ... their words remain with us throughout the performance'.[63] It is doubtful, however, whether a modern critic has ever experienced the performance conditions of the seventeenth-century masque—the length of the spectacle, the amount of dancing, and the sheer over-indulgence in food and drink at such occasions testified to by many witnesses. It is not surprising that Puritans could not assume that masques were understood to have a moral function. In Calvinist thought original sin has caused such a disruption that there is no untroubled relationship between human art and divine truth: if the decadent courtly setting for the masque were not bad enough, its complex imagery and use of visual stimuli would have damned it in Puritan eyes[64] Thomas Carew, however, did achieve immediate publication of his masque, so it is possible that a less-than-flattering view of the royal couple that could even accommodate irony was accessible to a contemporary readership. Martin Butler suggests that the very choice of an emblem which shows the joint triumph of the King and Queen, as in Aurelian Townshend's *Albion's Triumph* of 1632, could reflect on the King's favourite, Lord Treasurer Weston, who was known to be an opponent to the Queen: certainly, his was an embattled position in 1634.[65]

Nevertheless, the royal marriage was made to bear a significant interpretative weight in the Caroline court masque. Kevin Sharpe has argued that marriage was used by dramatists of the Court, particularly William Davenant in *The Temple of Love*, to mitigate an emphasis on chaste Platonic love that was fashionable at court. *The Platonic Lovers,* a play of 1635, exposes Platonic love as hypocrisy—rather than the consistency of signification required by Neoplatonic theory, this kind of pretence is a mask for immorality. The dedication to Jermyn, who had recently seduced one of the Queen's maids of honour, makes the point. Marriage, to which all the characters become reconciled, is again the answer. But it is not only the reconciliation of soul and body, passion and love, that marriage offers, but a wider reconciliation which can operate politically. In 1640 *Salmacida Spolia* offers the royal marriage as part of the answer to impending civil war.

The importance of the royal marriage to the imaginative scheme of *Salmacida Spolia* is underlined by the fact that this is the only Caroline masque to be danced by both king and queen together; as Sharpe says, 'the king and queen actually presented their own union, as the active virtue to be emulated'.[66] However, the royal couple would seem to have some work to do in overcoming the state of disorder represented as the scene opens, 'a horrid Sceane appeared of storme and tempest'. The Fury who presides over this scene, and summons her sisters to 'incense/The guilty and disorder Innocence' is explicitly attempting to bring an end to the peace of the 'too much happy Ile' which is Britain. Although Karen Britland draws attention to the European aspect of the masque, and points out that the known female troublemakers Marie de Medicis and the Duchesse de Chevreuse had recently arrived in England, many readers assume that the Fury is commenting on the state of England and Scotland, which in January 1640 were on a war footing, when she indicts the dissatisfied, and particularly those traitors masquerading under the name of religion, as the cause of future conflict.[67] The choice of Latin proverb from which the title of the masque is taken, 'Salmacida Spolia sine sanguine sine sudore' is explained at length by Davenant:

> For the first *Melas* and *Arevanias* of *Argos*, and *Troezen* conducted a common Colony to *Halicarnassus* in *Asia*, and there drave out the barbarous *Carie* and *Lelegi*, who fled up to the Mountaines; from whence they made many incursions, robbing and cruelly spoyling the Grecian Inhabitants, which could by no meanes be prevented. On the top of the right horne of the hill which surrounds *Halicarnassus*, in forme of a Theater, is a famous Fountaine of most cleare water, and exquisite taste called *Salmacis*: It happened that neere to this Fountaine one of the Colony (to make gaine by the goodnesse of the water) set up a Taverne, and furnish'd it with all necessaries, to which the Barbarians resorting (entised by the delicious taste of this water, at first some few, and after many together in troops,) of fierce and cruell natures, were reduced of their owne accord to the sweetnesse of the Grecian customes.

Such a victory, 'without blood, without sweat' as the proverb has it, must have sounded rather good to the king who, when he was not rehearsing the masque in December 1639, was meeting with his Council of War to make preparations for battle. In fact, the Earl of Northumberland told his sister that the King spent more time on rehearsals for Salmcida Spolia than on anything else.[68] On 4 January 1640 John Egerton Earl of Bridgewater wrote to Secretary Windebank saying that he was finding it difficult to raise £500 to lend Charles for the prosecution of the Bishops' War in Scotland. He must have found it somewhat galling that the King spent so much time rehearsing a masque whose preliminary costs amounted to £1,400.[69] Puritans at court were also offended by its performance on Sunday. Martin Butler lists the masquers who eventuallly became critics or opponents of the king and comments that 'the élitism of the masque, its esoteric symbols, its almost mystical ceremonial and its representation of the king as a god who effortlessly reduces discord to harmony' indicates 'a dynasty isolated and remote from the nation at large'.[70]

Within the masque, the victory is obtained when the 'beloved people' invite their king, Philogenes, 'lover of the people', to take his throne, and suggest to him that he has to stay calm in the face of the unrest of his people (presumably not the 'beloved' people, but the other sort):

> If it be Kingly patience to out last
> Those stormes the peoples giddy fury rayse,
> Till like, fantastick windes themselves they waste,
> The wisedome of that patience is thy prayse.

The clinching manoevre is the descent of Henrietta Maria from heaven, the cue for much music and dancing, and the final song is addressed to them both:

> All that are harsh, all that are rude,
> Are by your harmony subdu'd;
> Yet so, into obedience wrought,
> As if not forc'd to it, but taught.

With such an outbreak of universal peace and harmony it seems odd that at the first performance of this masque, 21 January 1640, one observer congratulated himself at not having attended the very splendid event, as 'the disorder was never so great at any [masque]'.[71] Indeed, few attended the second performance, as the Sidneys' solicitor, William Hawkins, wrote: 'the hard usage of people at the former dancing kept many off now'.[72] Disorder, it seems, eventually triumphed in life as it was not allowed to do in art. Martin Butler concludes that 'Salmacida Spolia attempted to build bridges but finally failed'.[73]

In the end of course the Neoplatonic figure of marriage, with its signification of mutual harmony, could not save Britain from civil war. It is an intriguing suggestion by Richard McCoy that it was chivalry on the part of the militant Protestant constituency that brought England to civil war, a courageous effort for truth against an entrenched repressive regime. He argues that it was successors of the Sidney-Essex group and their militant approach to religion who caught the imagination of the Protestant nation in 1640, as they had not done in 1601.[74] This religiously-motivated chivalry is embodied in a very different model of spiritual marriage, that of the Song of Songs, a text popular with allies of the Sidney–Essex circle, as we have seen in Chapter 1. Verses in the Song of Songs had been used in the Jacobean argument for armed struggle in the fight against Catholicism in the Thirty Years War: many in the Parliamentary army saw their fight as another holy struggle against Catholicism. The Bride herself is formidable, but she is a much weaker partner in the mystical marriage between Christ and the Church. What the mystical marriage means is that Christ will always be available to protect the true Church out of his love for her. The neo-Platonic values of harmony and hierarchy are not celebrated here: the authorities are to be resisted where necessary, and God is not always on the side of beauty or greatness. The mystical marriage is not a model relevant only to aristocracy: all Christians can partake of the beauty and power of the Bride, which is a gift to all believers, however ugly and powerless, from Christ their husband. Human capacity and will is not important: external signs are not reliable in this spiritual realm, within which it is imperative to operate. It is not surprising that a Court steeped in Neoplatonic systems had difficulty understanding other methods of interpretation at work in the country, such as the Puritan understanding of the mystical marriage.

Sex and gardens in Royalist poetry

The signification of marriage in Court culture and literature was very different from its function in Calvinist spirituality and literature. In the court, the trope always conveyed an implicit or explicit compliment to Charles I and Henrietta Maria as the living emblem of the perfect earthly marriage. One of the meanings of the symbol was harmony, a quality that could be applied to national politics as in *Salmacida Spolia* or domestic gender relations, as in the epilogue written for *The Tamer Tamed* by John Fletcher, one of the court's favourite playwrights.[75] A performance of this play was, twinned with *The Taming of the Shrew* in a court performance of 1633.[76] Fletcher's play inverts the action of *The Taming of the Shrew* to produce this moral point:

> To teach both Sexes due equality;
> And, as they stand bound, to love mutually.[77]

This message of 'equality' is radical even by 1630s court standards: more usually, 'mutuality' was seen to be the meaning of the emblem that was the marriage of Charles and Henrietta Maria. Even so, this interpretation of the ideal marriage is very different from the spiritual ideal of the mystical marriage, which goes out of its way to stress the lack of equality, and indeed of mutuality, between the two partners, God and the individual Christian. Also radically different was the place of sexual relations in the two models. As we have seen, marriage was often applied as the antidote to ideas of Platonic love in the 1630s court, in which spiritual love transcends the physical: it represented a mean between sexual promiscuity and celibacy, whereby physical intercourse was a necessary element of marital love. In a third and distinct view, the sexual relationship which at times is portrayed with frankness in The Song of Songs is relegated by Puritan interpreters to the status of metaphor; all descriptions of physical intimacy are to be interpreted as expressions for the depth of the spiritual love between Christ and the Church.

It is no surprise that court poets and dramatists steer clear of explicit references to the Song of Songs, however much they seem preoccupied with marriage itself. The different hermeneutics of court culture and popular Calvinist culture on this particular topic are partly a product of different political positions, but there were, of course, many Calvinists at court. David Norbrook has resisted attempts to categorise the masque as necessarily involving a specific politics, pointing out that Laud did not like masques and that other more Puritan figures were not necessarily opposed to them.[78] However, as we have seen, the Neoplatonic systems of imagery on which the masque was based validated the visual as a reliable sign of the spiritual: neither the specific and complex interpretations of the Song of Songs tradition nor the Calvinist propensity to emphasise meanings which undermined the usefulness of visual imagery was particularly suited to the genre of masque or emblem. Poetry, however, which operated on a range of rhetorical effects not necessarily related to symbolism, was perhaps flexible enough to handle the complexities of signification in the Song of Songs, and poets continued to be attracted to the poetic text of the Biblical book.

Thomas Carew was known as a poet rather than a masque writer, and he wrote several wedding songs for the marriages of friends and acquaintances. Altieri's observation that he was interested in the clash of ideal and reality is fully justified in these poems, which progress quickly from the spiritual ideals of marriage to issues connected with sexual consummation. His advice to Carew Raleigh, second son of Sir Walter, is to extinguish all lights on his wedding night in order to make the sexual relationship more exquisite; there is a distinct suggestion that the experience will pall rather quickly otherwise.[79] To Thomas Killigrew, marrying Cecilia Crofts on 29th June 1636, he represents the priest's religious office as a mechanism to allow him sexual intercourse:

> From the misterious holy touch such charmes
> Will flow, as shall unlock her wreathed armes,
> And open a free passage to that fruit
> Which thou hast toyl'd for with a long pursuit.

The consummation for the bride is described with relish, with graphic details of blood and shrieks.[80] For John Lovelace, marrying the fifteen-year-old Anne Wentworth, later the dedicatee of Richard Lovelaces's *Lucasta*, going to bed with his bride is a rather more decorous prospect, 'to revel in Loves sphere':

> They know no night, nor glaring noon
> Measure no houres of Sunn or Moon,

> Nor mark time's restless Glass.
> Their kisses measure as they flow,
> Minutes, and there embraces show
> The hower's as they pass

None of these aristocratic marriage-beds has anything to do with a garden, and there are no invocations of the Song of Songs, which is not surprising in poems that focus on the sexual consummation which interpreters of the Song of Songs do their best to exclude. The clearest echo of the Song of Songs in Carew's verse is in his famous erotic poem 'The Rapture', an irony which has to be deliberate: Paula Johnson describes the relationship of the Song of Songs to this poem as 'far-off, but also very near'.[81] Here, Paradise is indeed a garden, with the flowers, streams and breezes that are part of the furniture of the Biblical book: it is also an enclosed garden, and the name of the mythological giant who guards the entrance, Honour, prepares us for the idea that it is a metaphorical garden. As in much Song of Songs discourse, particularly Roman Catholic in origin, chastity is being figured here. However, this is not an idealised, or even authentic, virtue: from the beginning, Honour is depicted as 'a Masquer', 'a stalking Pageant'. Like the devices engineered by Inigo Jones, Honour is a man-made thing, and not the messenger of God that many suppose him to be: these are designated in class terms, as 'the servile rout/Of baser subjects', presumably those who have not had the advantage of seeing how easily fearsome spectacles can be manufactured for court masques. The garden, it seems, represents the body of the beloved, a fact reinforced by Carew's designation of parts of her body as physical entities:

> I'le seize the Rose-buds in their perfum'd bed,
> The Violet knots, like curious Mazes spread
> O're all the Garden, taste the ripned Cherry,
> The warme, firme Apple, tipt with corall berry:
> Then will I visit, with a wandring kisse,
> The vale of Lillies, and the Bower of blisse:

At the start of the poem, Carew's desire was encrypted in a kind of feminism, comparing the enclosure of the garden, 'free woman', with the enclosure of common lands by possessive landowners; within the garden, female deities are supposed to reign, 'Queens of Love, and Innocence,/Beautie and Nature'. However, as the sexual fantasy becomes more explicit, all pretence of mutuality disappears: the woman becomes the object of invasion and pillage, and the poet is the one performing all the actions. This garden is indeed a sacred space: no spies, or the peeping Toms envisaged in Carew's masque, are able to gain entrance.[82] However, this garden differs from the

Song of Songs in that the key partners in marriage, husband and wife, are words never mentioned here:

> All things are lawfull there, that may delight
> Nature, or unrestrained Appetite;
> Like, and enjoy, to will, and act, is one,
> We only sinne when Loves rites are not done.

Carew knows that his Elizium is the very opposite of the Biblical garden. In this context, his invocation of the Song of Songs has an ironic resonance that helps to point his message, which is that true innocence, as opposed to the masque emblem Honour, is about free sexual enjoyment. The words of the Song of Songs, as opposed to their interpretation in various Christian traditions, could be used to express the kind of joyous sexual intercourse Carew intends to portray in 'The Rapture', although it must be said that the Biblical text is far more expressive of mutuality than Carew's poem. One comment of Carew's draws attention to the futility of using sexual terminology to describe divine love for the soul, whilst denying the importance of the act itself:

> And so our soules that cannot be embrac'd,
> Shall the embraces of our bodyes taste.

Contrary to Puritan or indeed Catholic doctrine, the soul cannot feel rapture in any way that can be meaningfully compared to sexual intercourse. Implicit in 'The Rapture' is the scorn of traditional modes of interpretation of the Song of Songs. There is a delicious irony in invoking Biblical discourse to support Carew's argument for sexual promiscuity. Silently, the Bride of the Song of Songs joins the catalogue of 'ten thousand Beauties' including Petrarch's Laura and Odysseus' Penelope who are imagined making up for lost time and abandoning their chastity for a life of unbridled promiscuity.

Perhaps the poet who most skilfully trapped the echoes of the poetic tradition in his own verse to stunning, if complex effect was Andrew Marvell, who seems to have started his career as a poet in homage to the lost ideals of the 1630s. His commendatory poem to Richard Lovelace's *Lucasta* in 1648 laments the loss of courtly literary culture. The date of composition of 'The Nymph Complaining for the Death of her Fawn' continues to be debated, but it has a particularly strong elegiac tone, so much so that it has been interpreted as a response to the execution of King Charles, or a lament for the loss of the country's innocence in Civil War, as well as the nymph's complaint for her lost virginity.[83] Many critics have sensed the presence of allegory, a perception underlined by the many references to the Song of Songs in 'The Nymph Complaining'; Nigel Smith lists six references at different points in the poem.[84] Allegory is probably too restrictive a scheme into which to force this resonant and highly allusive poem, but the widespread belief remains that it is about much more than the death of a fawn, a suspicion heightened by the generic starting-point of the poem, which is the 'death of a pet' lament, as practised by Greek and Roman writers, and most recently, in the sixteenth century, by John Skelton's 'Boke of Phyllyp Sparowe'. Such poems would explore issues of emergent sexuality under cover of childish innocence. For such a theme the employment of the ambiguous text of the Song of Songs is irresistible. Rather than a use of particular meanings associated with certain images, Marvell's technique is here to use various well-known elements of the Song of Songs—roses and lilies, turtle-doves, skipping deer, gardens—which inevitably recall an entire context, and could be summarised as 'sanctified sexuality'. The aura of holiness mixed with sensuality in which 'A Nymph Complaining' is presented is vital to a poem which explores the representation of innocence. Rowland Watkyns' poem, 'The Holy Maid' has profound similarities of style and content with 'A Nymph Complaining': both poems are concerned with the holiness of a young girl.[85] Its language is similarly sensual, which is not a surprise from a Laudian minister whose poetry is often explicitly anti-Puritan, yet its dying subject is explicitly Christ the Bridegroom.[86] The maid rejects earthly love in what is easy to read as a sublimation:

> My love ascends a higher sphere;
> Where honor, beauty, pleasures be
> Inthron'd, and full of constancie.
> My Beloved's white and ruddy,
> My red sins made him all bloody: ...
> His mouth breathes roses; and no bliss
> Can equal his delicious kiss.[87]

The 'red' and 'white' which in Charles and Henrietta Maria's court are evocative of chaste passion are here given their religious context—they are the colours of the martyr. By contrast, Marvell's nymph takes pleasure in a loving animal: there is no attempt to allegorise the sensual physicality of the poem. Robin Skelton may not be right in his suggestion that Marvell had seen 'The Holy Maid', but the contrast between the two poems shows that 'The Nymph Complaining' is a re-writing of the experience of the Song of Songs, including straightforwardly physical sensuality in a representation of holiness.[88]

It is guilt with which the poem begins, however, firmly located with the civil war 'troopers', who seem to be Parliamentarian in allegiance. The crime of the soldiers in shooting an innocent fawn is discussed for the first 24 lines, and the possibility of forgiveness is raised, but ultimately discounted:

> There is not such another in
> The world, to offer for their sin (lines 23–4).

The guilt is firmly associated with the scarlet of the blood in which they might want to wash their hands: it is the colour of the sinful stain with which each is imbued. The next section of the poem begins 'Unconstant Sylvio', associating the girl's lost lover ineradicably with both sin and red stain. But of course, the substitute who takes Sylvio's place in the girl's heart is her 'deer', and much effort is spent representing the animal as entirely innocent, and therefore much more worthy of love than 'false and cruel men' who by now include the troopers, and Sylvio himself. This takes the form of an attempt to make the fawn whiter-than-white; it feeds on milk and sugar (55) and becomes 'more white and sweet then they'(58). The nymph's reaction to the fawn's whiteness is to turn red, to blush. Danielle Clarke has identified the frequency of the use of the female blush as characteristic of the 1630s collapse of different discourses, of sexuality and of religion, into each other, so that even in holy women such as the Virgin, the blush is interpreted as a sign of suppressed sexuality.[89] This collapse is what tends to happen in seventeenth-century interpretation of the Song of Songs although it is not always recognised: Andrew Marvell is of course alert to this, and signifies what is happening Clearly, it is the girl's hidden or unconscious sexuality that is being indicated in 'The Nymph Complaining', and it comes to the surface when the nymph compares herself with the fawn for whiteness. She has difficulty asserting that the fawn's foot is whiter than her own hand, and the quick move to generalisation—'Nay, any lady's of the land'—is clearly an attempt to diffuse a sense of guilt.

The private, overgrown garden to which the poem moves has been interpreted by many critics as the nymph's own mind, and surely it is a representation of her unformed sexual awareness. Two kinds of flowers grow there—lilies, which by convention and by the colour-coding of the poem we interpret as figures of innocence, and roses. Lilies and roses had been the joint emblem of Charles and Maria, signifying in the 1630s the blend of purity and passion which produced the perfect marriage.[90] The red of the roses would associate these flowers with the guilt of the men at the start of the poem; but at this stage in the development of ideas, red acquires a beneficent significance. The fawn has a natural inclination towards the lilies, but therein lies a problem: when the fawn is amongst the lilies it is impossible to discern its shape. The whitening fawn amongst the white lilies becomes a kind of white-out, and the nymph cannot find it. It is only when the fawn moves towards the roses that it becomes clearly defined again, and in the next part of the poem the red functions as a counterpoint to the white, defining it, identifying it and producing an attractive mix of colours. To anyone familiar with the Song of Songs the fawn's next move is a surprise, and it is a slightly painful one. In the Song of Songs at the moment of total union—'My beloved is mine and I am his'—it is the lilies that the lover moves towards, and eats: 'he feedeth among the lilies'.[91] There is an imperceptible shock as the fawn eats the roses, the more so as the fear that the thorns will hurt the fawn is registered by the nymph: 'its lips ev'n seemed to bleed' (l. 84). However, the redness on the fawn's lips turns out to be not a sign of inward damage, but a part of a rather different signifying system. The red dye from the roses has coloured the fawn's mouth, relieving the by now oppressive whiteness which had engulfed it: moreover, in a gesture of innocent sensuality, the fawn transfers the redness to the lips of the girl:

> then to me would boldly trip,
> And print those roses on my lip (lines 85–6).

A poem from Richard Lovelace's posthumous *Lucasta* volume of 1659 also has Love feeding on red things—cherries, roses and plums—but here the context is a garden remote in time, 'In the first Age' as the title has it, where like Carew's Elizium there were no rules, and no marriage.

> Love then unstinted, Love did sip,
> And Cherries pluck'd fresh from the Lip,
> On Cheeks and Roses free he fed;
> Lasses like *Autumne* Plums did drop,
> And Lads, indifferently did crop
> A Flower, and a Maiden-head.[92]

The equation of a girl's virginity with a flower that can be 'cropped' as easily gives away the moral imperatives of Lovelace's poem. The conclusion reveals that the poem was in fact an elaborate seduction strategy, and that as Chloris did not co-operate, the poet has settled for masturbation instead. 'The Nymph Complaining' cannot be reduced to a blatant concern with sex. It is clear that in 'The Nymph Complaining' roses are as beautiful and as morally irreproachable as lilies. The fawn was well on the way to becoming 'lilies without, roses within': yet it remained 'pure virgin'. The rose, which is associated with passion, and which in the context of the poem could stand for guilty passion, stained red like the crime of the troopers, is rehabilitated for pure innocence.

In Marvell's Elysium, where the dead fawn ends up, creatures may be whiter than white; he now lives 'With milk-white lambs, and ermines pure'(l.108) and swans, and turtle-doves, and presumably with other white creatures. However, the memorial statue that the girl orders for him, although made of alabaster, cannot represent the essential purity of the fawn. The poem ends with a failure of representation. In this world it is not possible to represent true innocence innocently: what happens if the worldly poet tries, as we saw in this poem, is that the innocent subject disappears. Modes of representation associated with guilt and passion must be employed. Indeed, an important part of the fawn's being is its innocent sensuality: as in many 'pet' poems, it sucks its milk from the girl's fingers, as well as 'kissing' her. However, to delineate these aspects is to represent faithfully, and conventional modes of description which ignore the implication of innocence with sexuality are doomed to fail: for all that, the subject of the poem, the fawn, remains innocent, despite the fact that the girl and perhaps the poet also have failed to represent that innocence properly.

If Marvell is right, it is not satisfactory to close down the sexuality of the Biblical text. Sexual innocence on its own will signify only absence of love. Only an integration of the physical passion expressed in the words of the Song of Songs with spiritual purity will produce a correct reading. The significance for a reading of the Song of Songs, that text that from its inception had been used to designate insider and outsider, sacred and profane, is profound. Both the sacred and the traditionally profane are present within Marvell's garden, if not for long: they are the materials for creating the final image of profound innocence and beauty, however transient that might be. But 'The Nymph Complaining' also says something about allegory. Although an allegorical interpretation is suggested in several places, allegory is manifestly too rigid a scheme to use on the poem: in any case to reduce the poem to another, different narrative, as Puritans and Catholics alike did for the Song of Songs, is to destroy the work of art. The process of Puritan commentary on the Song of Songs during the seventeenth century is on the whole a story of an attempt to make the text say something other. A Catholic emblematist like Thomas Hawkins, using the resources of rhetoric and image, tried to recapture art and beauty for the Song of Songs in *Partheneia Sacra*, and his aristocratic audience, appreciative of the role that art and beauty could have in holiness, responded. Perhaps what made Quarles' *Emblemes* so popular with a mass readership was that despite its reductive, and orthodox, allegorical message, the sensuality of the visual image and occasionally of the poetry itself remained, reminding the reader of the beauty and complexity of the text of the Song of Songs.

4
From Annotations to Commentary: New Spectacles on the Song of Songs

This chapter investigates the peculiarly influential text of the Song of Songs in the Interregnum by looking at its representation in the aids to Biblical interpretation that proliferated in the first half of the seventeenth century. Biblical commentary was itself politicised, almost from its inception in English Reformed thought: what is charted here is a phenomenon that was at its most intellectually influential in the 1640s and 1650s after the collapse of Church of England authority. This chapter looks in detail at some of the mid-century interpretations of the Song of Songs, and then discusses the tradition of commentary that continued into the Restoration. The significance of a particular interpretation of the Song of Songs was maintained until the end of the century, and within certain Dissenting circles, well beyond.

Between 1612 and 1647, five editions of a Biblical dictionary, initially authored by Thomas Wilson, were printed: it was much the most popular of such exegetical aids, and drew on Continental scholarship to comment on the use of important 'ecclesiastical' words.[1] It had an appendix offering separate dictionaries for those Biblical books perceived as particularly intransigent: Hebrews, Revelation, and of course, the Song of Songs. This dictionary was 'specially made, to give some light to the darkesome booke of Salomon's song, called the Canticles'.[2] In the fourth edition of 1635 this sub-dictionary stretched to 17 pages. In the sixth edition of 1656, when two other authors added material, the section on Canticles was 86 pages long, accounting for most of the increase in length between the two editions. Something had changed during the 1640s in the perception of the importance of the book of the Song of Songs. The necessity for a larger glossary was brought about by the increase in commentary on the Biblical book: and this phenomenon in turn was profoundly related to the political upheavals of the 1640s. Foucault's observation on the nature of commentary is relevant here: 'it allows us to say something other than the text itself, but on the condition that it is this text itself which is said, and in a sense completed'.[3] This chapter will show that some commentaries on the Song of Songs appear to say something radically other than the text itself. Although this brings some interpreters into direct conflict, what is surprising is that there is clearly in the 1640s a substantial readership for even some of the most idiosyncratic interpretations. Commentators on the Song of Songs, that 'darkesome booke', have license, in the 1640s, to interpret it with great freedom. Limits on interpretation are set by a community of readers who decide whether a version remains in some sense a saying of the Biblical text, and that they can therefore use it and quote it with Scriptural authority. These limits are of course historically and politically constituted. In the political fragmentation and changing historical circumstances of the 1640s there are many different groups of readers available, and therefore many versions of the Song of Songs in circulation, some of which come into conflict with one another. The focus of this chapter is on the Presbyterian/Independent readership which seems to have been the primary market for aids to Biblical interpretation; some more extreme attitudes to the Song of Songs are described here and in the next chapter, but they should be seen in the context of a more mainstream hermeneutic.

Official attitudes to all exegetical aids to Scripture underwent a transformation at the start of the decade. One of the first achievements of the Long Parliament, now confident in its status and power, was the setting up of a Grand Committee for Religion in November 1640, which set about unpicking the decrees of the Laudian establishment. Edward Dering's notes as chairman offer details of the composition of the committee, its role and its progress. He lists three issues for consideration by committee: the first two concern the suffering of ministers under Laud's authority, and in particular which doctrinal questions had been put to them on ordination. However, the third injunction quickly became the major part of the Committee's proceedings: 'to examine abuses in bookes, in licensing, in printing, in forbidding them'.[4] One of the forbidden books under Laudian censorship had been the Geneva Bible, which in fact had not been printed in England since 1616: copies had been smuggled in from Holland, after importation had been forbidden in 1630, when, Laud argued, the popularity of the Dutch Geneva Bibles became a threat to the English printing industry.[5] David Norton argues that it remained the version most used in England, but not because of any relative superiority of its translation over that of the King James Bible of 1611: in fact, distinguished divines such as Daniel Featley and William Gouge declared the Authorised Version to be the most correct translation.[6] The popularity of the Geneva Bible amongst English readers was clearly the product of its annotations.[7]

The Geneva Notes had been under attack since the Hampton Court Conference of 1604: it was the perceived subversiveness of some of the notes that led to the drive for the new translation. Demanding that there be no annotations added to any new version of the Bible, James I attacked the Geneva annotations at the Hampton Court Conference: 'some Notes very partial, untrue, seditious, and savouring too much of dangerous and trayterous conceites. As, for example, Exodus 1,19, where the marginall Note alloweth Disobedience unto kings. And 2 Chronicles 15,16, the note taxeth Asa for deposing his mother, only, and not killing her'.[8] In 1641 the bookseller Michael Sparke complained that 12,000 quarto Bibles with notes had been imported from Holland, but that the importers had been summoned before the Laudian Court of High Commission and had their Bibles seized: 'more punishment for selling a 4[to] Bible with Notes, then 100 Masse Books in the High Commission'.[9] In the mid-1640s Archbishop Laud noted in his account of his trial that 'now of late these notes were more commonly used to ill purposes than formerly'.[10] However, William Prynne suggested, listing the measures taken against 'the Bible with Notes' that it was the principle of annotation, rather than the anti-monarchical nature of individual notes, that was politically unacceptable to Laud: like Mary Tudor, he suppressed annotated Bibles 'for feare that the Notes in them should overmuch instruct the people in the knowledge of the Scriptures'.[11]

Given this political animus, it is perhaps surprising that the Committee for Religion did not attempt to revert to the use of the Geneva Bible in 1641: but market forces were moving in a different direction. Some London printers, who clearly saw a marketing opportunity, petitioned the Committee for the right to affix the Geneva notes or other annotations to the King James version, which was the only one that had been printed in England since 1616. In fact, nine hybrid versions which published Geneva notes alongside King James text were printed from 1642–1715, some of them in Holland. The extremely Calvinist nature of the Geneva notes is perhaps even more obvious when they are juxtaposed with the Authorised Version. For example, 5:5 of the Song of Songs, 'my hands dropped with myrrh, and my fingers with sweet-smelling myrrh, upon the handles of the lock' is glossed with obscure Calvinist relish, 'the spouse who should be anointed of Christ shall not find him if she thinke to anoint him with her good works'.[12] A more satisfactory solution was that of the Committee for Religion, who commissioned a new set of Annotations to accompany the text of the King James Version.

A team of ten scholars received personal invitations from Sir Edward Dering to embark on the work. They represented a range of what could still, in 1641, be seen as mainstream Calvinist scholarship, from a Puritan, anti-Catholic tradition. John Ley, President of Sion College in 1645, annotated the Pentateuch, and the Gospels: William Gouge, opponent of Laud, worked on the Old Testament from Kings to Esther: Meric Casaubon annotated the Psalms; Francis Taylor, Proverbs: Edward Reynolds treated Ecclesiastes and the Song of Solomon: the assiduous Puritan scholar William Gataker was 'exceeded by no Commentator, Ancient or Modern' in his notes on Isaiah, Jeremiah and Lamentations: Francis Pemberton was responsible for the first edition's notes on Ezekiel, Daniel and the minor prophets: Daniel Featley, anti-Catholic controversialist, annotated the Epistles of St. Paul; John Downame and John Reading, chaplain of Dover castle, dealt with the rest of the Bible.[13] Most of these divines became members of the Westminster Assembly, which perhaps explains why they had the time to embark on such a large undertaking: they were apparently paid a daily allowance of four shillings for Assembly business, for which they were perhaps envied but definitely ridiculed by their opponents.[14]

The Preface to the 1645 edition of the resulting *Annotations Upon All the Books of the Old and New Testament* sets the work at the end of a grand narrative from Catholic darkness to Reformed light where the events of the 1630s are obliquely alluded to as a fleeting shadow. Four stages are described in this process: the reformation of preachers: the availability of vernacular Bibles: the necessity of Annotations: and the preparation of this particular volume of Annotations. The thrust of the praise for vernacular Bibles is a concern for the wellbeing of the less powerful sections of society, including women. The statute of Henry VIII's reign prohibiting the reading of the Bible to certain classes is indignantly quoted: '*no woman, Artificers, Apprentices, Journey-men, Servingmen, none of the degrees of Yeomen, or husbandmen, nor labourers*'.[15] Between stages 2 and 3 of their argument the Calvinist doctrine of the perspicuity of Scripture, with its theoretical accessibility to all readers, has to be reconciled with the necessity of interpretative notes. For this rather difficult negotiation the metaphor of annotations as 'spectacles' is employed: ironically, in a more optimistic age, the same metaphor had been used by Calvin to describe the function of the sacred text itself in enabling readers to discern God more clearly.[16] By the mid-seventeenth century, it seems, the reader needed the annotations in order to correctly manipulate the aid to spiritual vision which is the Bible. 'The Scriptures may have their use, and force on the affections of ignorant Readers': but there are awful consequences if Scripture is not 'fenced with an Orthodox exposition', particularly the difficult books of Genesis, Job, Canticles, Ezekiel, Daniel and Revelation. Origen, it is suggested, would not have castrated himself if he had read 'a Marginall Note upon *Matt. 19.12.*'. (The note in the Geneva Bible might well have helped any would-be self-mutilator, insisting that castration is only a metaphor for 'the gift of continencie' and that in any case, this gift is very rare: after all, none may 'rashly abstain from' that Protestant institution of marriage.) The Preface to the 1645 Annotations is, however, optimistic about the fact that much good English scholarship is available to prevent the heresies and 'fond fantasies' that might result from the reading of an unannotated Bible.[17] The Geneva Notes are by no means rejected in this enterprise, but pronounced 'Sound and Orthodox in Doctrine': the 1611 controversy over the Notes is rehearsed, and the part played by one of the team of annotators, John Ley, in defending the Geneva Notes, is proudly paraded. In view of the present dominance of the King James version, it is concluded, there is a need for a new pair of spectacles with which to read the text.[18]

According to the Preface, the group of ten set about their task with meticulous scrupulosity. They consulted translations of the Scripture in other languages, and 'made special use' of the new Geneva Annotations, published in Italian in 1641 by John Diodati, and the *Annotations Upon the Whole Bible* by Theodore Haask, which was published in Dutch in 1637. We are told that the team met daily to confer on their work: where there were disagreements, these were catalogued and referred to a particular day of discussion on the controversial issues. The whole endeavour was conducted in a spirit of prayer and devotion, although the divergent political opinions of the assembled scholars must have made for lively discussion at times, especially after the outbreak of the Civil War: John Reading had Royalist sympathies, and Edward Reynolds, who was to become Bishop of Norwich in 1660, refused to take the Oath of Engagement. Daniel Featley, who had impeccable anti-Arminian qualifications, was a chaplain to the King, and spent time in prison for communicating with Archbishop Ussher who was with the King at Oxford. In fact, an Advertisement of three pages at the start of the Annotations is given over to a discussion of some of Ussher's notes which take for granted the existence of bishops. The Advertisement begins and ends in a spirit of impeccable charity towards Featley, who was dead by the time the volume appeared: in parenthesis, however, are three pages of ferociously anti-Episcopal argument, introduced by the words 'But the truth is, the foundation of such an *Prelacy* is rotten.'[19]

Perhaps the team of annotators was too meticulous for the printers and readers eagerly awaiting the results of their labours, for on 11 January 1642 the Parliamentary Committee for Printing, established in February 1641 when it was clear that the scrutiny of publication would be too onerous for the Committee of Religion with its other tasks, commissioned another set of Biblical annotations—the translation of John Diodati's *Pious Annotations*, for which the English annotators expressed so much respect. These were the only Annotations to become a best-seller in seventeenth-century England, and there is some evidence that the publisher, Nicholas Fussell, had crammed print onto the page in order to make the quarto edition of over 1,200 pages affordable by families.[20] The 1643 edition is prefaced with a handsome portrait, beneath which is a poem in praise of the annotator, offering the reader a chance to meet him:

> Reader looke well on Diodati, more
> Uppon the Golden worke he stands before.
> Lest in the Scriptures Labyrinth thy minde
> Should snare and lose itself, heer thou mayst finde
> A Clue that will through each mysterious storie
> Lead thee from earth up to the throne of Glorie.

As in the Preface to the 1645 Annotations, the epistle from the translator to the reader stresses the importance of Biblical commentary as a code-breaker for the ordinary Christian. 'Here is nothing with-held, God hath revealed for the benefit of the meanest.' For this scholar, the language of the Song of Songs, 'the *Bridegrooms* language', is the authentic, empowering voice inviting the ordinary believer to read and understand even the most profound mysteries of faith.[21] Paradoxically, one distinctive aspect of the Bridegroom's language was that it was not perspicuous: it needed an interpreter. The interpretation of the Song of Songs became in this period a kind of exemplum for the necessity of mediated reading. The preface to Matthew Poole's 1683 commentary, making the case for Biblical commentaries and annotations, quotes St Bernard on the Song of Songs: 'here is an excellent Nut but who shall crack it? Heavenly Bread but who shall break it?'[22] Protestant interpreters agree with Catholics that the Song represents the closest communion and highest degree of holiness available to a human being. However, this élitist enterprise conflicts somewhat with the Reformed imperative to make the Song available for interpretation to all readers. The next section of this chapter looks at four sets of annotations—the 1645 *Annotations Upon All the Books of the Old and New Testament*, and the three previous works they expressly consulted—and their mediation of the cryptic text of the Song to the ordinary believer.[23]

Of course much of the material in previous volumes of Annotations praised by the English team had to receive the primary mediation of translation. John Diodati's *Pious Annotations* was not published in English until 1643, and *The Dutch Annotations Upon the Whole Bible*, which had been commissioned by the Synod of Dort, not until 1657. The epistle to the 1648 edition of Diodati's *Pious and Learned Annotations* takes as 'reall confirmation of their usefulnesse' his estimate that 'many thousands' of Diodati's notes had been simply translated and used by the English annotators. This claim was hotly disputed in the preface to the 1651 edition of the English *Annotations*, which was larger than the 'greedily bought up' edition of 1645.[24] It was pointed out that not all the annotators could read Dutch and Italian: neither volume had been available in translation whilst most of the work was done. In fact one of the team, Francis Pemberton, was judged to have made too much use of Diodati's work: he was dropped from the editorial team, and his notes for Ezekiel, Daniel and the minor prophets were redone by someone whom Baxter calls 'Bishop Richardson' for the 1651 volume. The compiler of the annotations from the Song of Songs was a very different case. Scholar and influential churchman Edward Reynolds, 'the pride and joy of the Presbyterian party', became Dean of Christ Church on the fall of Oxford in 1646. He refused to take the Engagement Oath administered by the Independents in 1650, and remained in the wilderness until the late 1650s, when the collapse of the Republic brought alive Presbyterian hopes of power and influence. His 1658 *Works* were praised by that militant Presbyterian satirist, Robert Wild: like the poet, Reynolds was also a supporter of General Monck, although unlike Wild, he followed his hero into acceptance of Royalist domination at the Restoration, becoming Bishop of Norwich, a move which even Anthony Wood sees as a betrayal of his fellow Presbyterians.[25] It is probably an Anglican pride which moves Wood to declare that the Annotations completed by Reynolds are the best in the volume, but he does have an impeccable Nonconformist source, quoting Matthew Poole for that opinion. Edward Reynolds' annotations are certainly less politically inflammatory that those of his Italian and Dutch colleagues, a fact that may reflect his career as, depending on the observer's post-1660 religious allegiance, a notorious timeserver or, alternatively, a steadfast moderate.

In any case, the three mid-seventeenth century sets of annotations agree on the basic method of approach to the Song of Songs, which is of course allegorical: there is no disagreement that the text, 'under the type of Solomon and the Queen' is actually about the relationship between Christ and the Church.[26] Diodati, the most flagrantly Calvinist of the commentators, insists from the start that the text is applicable to 'every faithfull soule'. This is the very phrase which had been suggested in the first annotation on the Geneva text of the Song of Songs, and following his predecessors, Edward Reynolds makes this application his second annotation. In fact this tradition of dual application, the metaphor of the Bride as both Church and individual Christian, went all the way back to the famous second-century commentary of Origen.[27] Only the Dutch annotations did not make this individualistic option clear at the very start of the commentary, allowing in the notes on verse 2 the alternative meaning of the Bride to be 'his chosen ones', a gloss which allows room for the application of the Song to every believer. Despite the presence of the individualistic type of the Bride in Catholic commentary, there was a strong tradition of monastic use for the Song of Songs, which at least limited potential Brides to a spiritual élite. It was the application to all believers which was both central to Reformed spirituality and repellent to Stuart absolutism, as became clear in controversies over the text of the Song of Songs in the 1670s.

The tension observable by modern readers in commentaries on the Song of Songs is in turning what appears to be an erotic poem into a very different kind of text, one which has to be spiritually edifying and applicable to the individual believer. As Diodati's Preface to the book puts it, 'whatsoever is spoken in this booke in poeticall and figurative terms, must be directly referred to spirituall meanings, to which it perfectly and properly belongeth; whereas if it should be turned any other way, there would be nothing but monstrous absurdities'. The mid-seventeenth century versions are following in a long tradition of this kind of muscular interpretation, and adopt many commonplaces of Patristic exegesis into their work with ease. In fact, as John Barton has recently pointed out, there is no ancient interpretation of the work that is not allegorical.[28] The work that had to be done by Protestant commentators was in transforming traditional Catholic interpretation into a hermeneutic that was distinctively Reformed. From the start of the commentaries this exegetical method is obvious, in the notes on the first five verses of the Authorised Version of the Song of Songs.

The first five verses of the Song of Songs

1:   The song of songs, which is Solomon's.

2:   Let him kiss me with the kisses of his mouth: for thy love is better than wine.

3:   Because of the savour of thy good ointments thy name is as ointment poured forth, therefore do the virgins love thee.

4:   Draw me, we will run after thee: the king hath brought me into his chambers: we will be glad and rejoice in thee, we will remember thy love more than wine: the upright love thee.

5:   I am black, but comely, O ye daughters of Jerusalem, as the tents of Kedar, as the curtains of Solomon.[29]

The necessary condition of the marital union between Christ and the individual believer is, of course, that person's salvation. Salvation is often referred to in commentaries as the 'betrothal' between Christ and the soul, whilst acceptance into heaven constitutes the consummation of the union. As we shall see, the delay between contract and consummation causes varying degrees of anxiety and discomfort in different readers of the text. The terminology of these first five verses offers several opportunities to confirm the peculiarly Protestant conditions for salvation. Verse 5, as interpreted by Reformed commentators in a culture in which there were very few people of colour, is a transparent statement of justification by faith, as in the Geneva version's note on the word 'blacke': 'The Church confesseth her spots and sin, but hath confidence in the favor of Christ.' The Bride is not justified by works, but by faith.[30] Moreover, her salvation is not brought about by her own efforts, as in the note on 'draw me' in verse 4: 'the faithfull confesse that they cannot come to Christ except they bee drawn'. As Beza had pointed out, the depraved nature of the human heart meant that all 'good motions', or divine impulses, had to come from God himself: the incapacity of the human being to move towards God unaided was axiomatic to Calvinist teaching.[31] Elizabeth Isham describes her Calvinist understanding of this verse rather well in her manuscript 'Booke of Rememberance', started in 1638:

> I had porposed of reformeing my selfe. yet I slacked. it being out of my mind for it was not in my power to performe the same. and yet I find my owne dullnes. But as thou hast /now\ given unto me to will. so I trust thou wilt give unto me to perfect. (therefore I) say \by/ with the spouse in the canticles Draw me and I will run after thee.[32]

Reynolds in his 1645 version follows these early Geneva notes rather closely. Where he differs from the other three sets of annotations is that he does not share their perception of a threatening environment for the Protestant

Christian. It is a feature of Reformed theology's inherent divisiveness that vocabulary within the blandly joyful opening to this book can be construed as suggesting oppositional categories. The Dutch gloss on verse 3's 'virgins' as 'the elect' begins to suggest a category of the non-elect that is named by Diodati in his note on verse 4: 'This seemeth to be added for to exclude hypocrites, which are in the externall Church, from these holy desires, and meditations'. Inclusion of the ordinary true believer seems to imply exclusion of everyone else, as in Reynold's note on 'chambers', in the same verse: 'the secret joy, that is not known to the world'. The spiritual doctrines of the Reformation are perceived as creating a political backlash involving physical danger to the believer, as had been the case in so much of Europe over the previous century. Somewhere in verse 5 the Geneva annotators discern 'domesticall enemies', whilst Theodore Haask sees 'danger amongst false brethren'; more paranoid than his fellow commentators, he expands his note to cover 'tyrannies and persecutions'. Reynolds' relatively peaceful interpretation may reflect the optimism of the early 1640s, when it must have seemed to Calvinists that their time in opposition was over.

Diodati takes the opportunity occasioned by the wording of the first five verses to descant on Calvinist spirituality. His note on verse 4 finds a profound interaction between the human and the divine: 'thy Spirit shall not work in us by an insensible motion, without any interchangeable or voluntary action on our side, like unto weights which are drawn up by engines, but it shall cause us to move and will as thou doest, and after thee'. This kind of conscious union is clearly the kind of relationship that the mystical marriage is intended to symbolise. However, at a very early stage Diodati utters a note of caution, even on the rapturous words of verse 2, 'let him kisse me':

> The Bride, namely the Church desires, that Christ who hath contracted a spirituall marriage with her, the accomplishment of which is deferred untill eternall life, should come in the mean while at severall times to give her more expresse assurances of his grace, should draw neerer to her with more intimate approaches of his presence and power, and should give her more lively inspirations of his Spirit, which is as it were the breath of his mouth.

The kisses are, it seems, the Bride's favourite fantasy, and the marriage is very definitely not consummated on earth. The Geneva Bible, however, blithely represents the Song in entirely positive terms: it is a representation of the desire of the Church for Christ, but there is no hint of frustration or deferment here. Rather, the vision expressed in the Preface to the Song of Songs is one of absolute fulfilment available to every individual believer:

> In this Song Salomon by most sweete and comfortable allegories and parables describeth the perfite loue of Iesus Christ, the true Salomon

and King of peace, and the faithfull soule or his Church, which he hath sanctified and appointed to bee his spouse, holy, chaste and without reprehension. So that here is declared the singular loue of the bridegroom toward the bride, and his great and excellent benefits, wherewith he doth enrich her of his pure bounty and grace without any of her deservings.

Diodati, perhaps chastened by nearly a century of Protestant experience not quite living up to this idyllic picture, qualifies the absoluteness of this spiritual blessing somewhat. It is 'not so much ... the ordinary state of the elect'; it is, in effect, a foretaste of heaven. The acknowledgement of the uneasy state of the Church, between earth and heaven, seems to need some justification. Diodati's gloss on verse 16 of chapter 2 turns its famous statement of total communion with Christ—'My beloved is mine, and I am his'—into an explanation of why this communion is not absolute, and inserts an agreement to Christ's absence on the part of his Bride which is wholly inauthentic to the original text.

the Church gives herselfe wholly to Christ, and doth embrace and lay hold on him by a lively faith, though he reside in heaven, in glory: to which corporall absence she voluntarily consents.

This reading is in fact from the corrected 1648 edition. The uneasiness of the interpreter is perhaps accentuated by a mistake in the 1643 edition, which reads, 'though we reside in heaven'. The joy of the Bridegroom and the Bride as described in the Song of Songs is mitigated by this insuperable problem: Christ and his Church are in reality not yet fully united. The commentators strive to present the experiences of bliss as ample compensation: yet the slightly peevish tone of Diodati's preface discloses the problem for the Church.

On the one side it is fitting for her to desire with ferventness to relish these first fruits, and on the other side, that the times and meanes to obtain them are at Christ's free appointment, and when it pleaseth him: though he never quite deprives his elect of them in this world, so they be desired with a holy zeale . .. but if she be slack and negligent therein, the occasion is lost, and there follow great troubles and afflictions.

In this account it is possible that the believer may actually never lay hold on the experience of the Bride: the fullest commitment to desiring 'these first fruits' will simply ensure that she is never totally deprived of them. In the worst case scenario allowed for here, which seems to be complete deprivation, the blame will be firmly on the side of the human partner in this relationship. The Preface to the 1645 Annotations identifies these 'vicissitudes' of the mystical marriage as the subject matter of the Song, with no embarrassment about the cause of the marital difficulties, which is 'Christ manifesting of himself to, or hiding his affections from, his Church in this world'. The image which encapsulates the deferral of the enjoyment of Christ's presence and the imperfect state of the union between Christ and the soul is that offered in 2:9: 'he standeth behind our wall, he looketh forth at the windows, shewing himself through the lattice'. For the Geneva annotators, this verse had been emblematic of mystery and concealment: the wall was the wall of flesh under which Christ's divinity was hidden, the lattice, or 'grates' as the Geneva version put it, signified 'that we can not have full knowledge of him in this life'. Diodati makes this an illustration of the mystical nature of spiritual discernment; 'though I doe not see him openly, which is a thing reserved for the life everlasting, yet I apprehend him by faith'. Reynolds is rather more hopeful, although it is unclear whether the deferral of presence here is within the text or beyond the grave: 'he was neerer now than before on the mountains, but not so neer as he will be'. The Dutch annotators fully embrace the ambiguity, moralising the process of deferral and placing it within a scheme of God's providence: 'here is shown the steps or degrees, whereby Christ manifesteth his love unto the Church, not equally all at once, but according as he knows it to be good for us'. Francis Rous had used a metaphor that was to become a favourite in the early modern period for the impeded view of the Bridegroom, the 'crany.' 'The Bridegroome here doth but looke in upon the soule at a crany, and the soule seeth him but by glimpses, but there shall she behold him face to face; and this beholding as it is full, so it shall also be perpetuall.'[33]

Chapter 5 and the narrative fragment

These anxieties are developed and explored in the fragment of continuous narrative at the heart of the Song of Songs, at the beginning of chapter 5. As E. Ann Matter observes, 'The Song of Songs is striking in its unresolved hints of narrativity', but this section has always attracted interpretation as an almost self-contained story about deferred union.[34]

> *1:* I am come into my garden, my sister, my spouse: I have gathered my
> myrrh with my spice; I have eaten my honeycomb with my honey;
> I have drunk my wine with my milk: eat, O friends; drink, yea, drink
> abundantly, O beloved.
> *2:* I sleep, but my heart waketh: it is the voice of my beloved that knock-
> eth, saying, Open to me, my sister, my love, my dove, my undefiled: for
> my head is filled with dew, and my locks with the drops of the night.
> *3:* I have put off my coat; how shall I put it on? I have washed my feet;
> how shall I defile them?

4: My beloved put in his hand by the hole of the door, and my bowels were moved for him.

5: I rose up to open to my beloved; and my hands dropped with myrrh, and my fingers with sweet smelling myrrh, upon the handles of the lock.

6: I opened to my beloved; but my beloved had withdrawn himself, and was gone: my soul failed when he spake: I sought him, but I could not find him; I called him, but he gave me no answer.

7: The watchmen that went about the city found me, they smote me, they wounded me; the keepers of the walls took away my veil from me.[35]

This little story begins with an experience of plenitude. The relationship between the two protagonists is not just the erotic one of bridegroom and bride, but of brother and sister. The apparently incestuous relationship is ignored by commentators: all are delighted to explain that Christ took human form, and therefore became a sibling of the Church. The garden which Christ enters in verse 1 has already been glossed in the previous chapter as the Church itself, turning this conjunction into an intimate experience of profound union. The sexual connotations of the 'garden enclosed' are reinforced by the Italian and Dutch annotations for verse 12 of chapter 4, stressing the traditional signification of garden as the virginal soul: the next chapter, then, is a sexualised encounter, described in terms of utter fulfilment of the senses: all three seventeenth-century commentators record the alternative translation of the last clause of verse 1 as 'be drunken'. Only Grotius spells out the declaration of sexual satisfaction in verse 1, however, and his commentary represents an extreme, as we shall see later.[36] Diodati goes so far as to say that this is a new experience of ravishment for the Bride. He has already however identified the honey, wine and milk, as all three seventeenth-century commentaries do, as 'good works': in this account it is Christ who is achieving fulfilment, taking pleasure in the actual holiness of his Church. The Geneva Notes concentrate on the bliss of the Bride: the 'banket' described in verse 1 is for the elect. Likewise, the seventeenth-century commentators cannot resist the extraction of a Calvinist dynamic from the pronouns in verse 1: 'Christ calleth all these portions here mentioned, his portions' declares the Dutch annotator, 'as without him we can do nothing'. Diodati spells out the mechanisms of Calvinist sanctification: Christ 'comes by a speciall grace to visit her, taking a singular delight in her good works, proceeding from the ground of his grace and the manuring of his Spirit, whereby they are properly his own'. Edward Reynolds abbreviates, assuming the voice of Christ for a moment: 'I have taken pleasure in the works done by my grace', turning any sexual fantasy here into one of a somewhat narcissistic character. The extraction of the doctrine of grace from Chapter 5 is so important to the Geneva annotator that he identifies the Bride's transgression later on in this story, for which she is severely to be punished, as the independence and presumption typical of Catholic attitudes to holiness; 'The spouse who should be anointed of Christ, shall not find him, if she thinke to anoint him with her good workes'(note e, chapter 5 verse 5).

Built into all the hermeneutic shapings of the narrative is the typical Calvinist juxtaposition of divine presence with divine absence; the 'vicissitudes' of Edward Reynolds' preface, what the seventeenth century often called 'desertions'. A treatise on these 'spirituall desertions' was published in 1639 and issued several times in Edinburgh and London throughout the Interregnum: on its front cover was Canticles 5:6—'I opened to my beloved, but my beloved ... was gone'.[37] Joseph Symonds' treatise is extremely thorough, exploring first of all whether the desertion is real or merely perceived subjectively by the believer. Both are options in Symonds' extensive scheme. He then details all the possible causes of such a spiritual state, in what amounts to a profound work of Puritan psychology. In the commentaries the three annotators take pains to stress that the blissful communion of verse 1 of chapter 5 is in response to the fervent desires of the Church: Edward Reynolds' account stresses the instantaneous nature of Christ's response to the Spouse's desires. By orthodox Calvinist doctrine, however, this ideal state of things cannot last: and it is, of course, all the Spouse's fault. She falls into a kind of post-coital sleep, glossed by the Dutch annotator as 'carnall ease and security'. What follows is an illuminating description of how Christ is envisaged, within Calvinist spirituality, as awakening the human being who is overwhelmed with concerns of the flesh ('worldly cares' in Edward Reynold's terms) to spiritual desires. It seems in verse 2 that the Bride has locked the Bridegroom out of her bedroom, creating the prototype for the Christ who stands at the door and knocks in Revelation 3:20. The 'knocking' of Christ and the subsequent 'opening' by the Bride is interpreted for the 1640s English readership by Edward Reynolds: Christ initiates communion with the soul 'by the motions of his Spirit', and the believer responds to Christ 'by receiving those motions'.

Motions

'Motion' is a word intimately bound up with the spiritual history of English Protestantism since the Reformation: the term has already featured in this book, and will again in the Epilogue. Cranmer had used it in his 1549 Prayer Book, in one of the Collects that had no original in the Catholic liturgy, the collect for the first Sunday of Lent. The Protestant observer of Lent must resist the sensual impulse of the flesh, but not in a spirit of self-denying stoicism. Instead, in the correct Protestant relationship to Christ, there will be access to a new kind of impulse: 'Give us grace to use such abstinence, that, our flesh being subdued to the Spirit, we may ever obey thy godly motions in righteousnesse, and true holinesse'. In its origin the word is probably a translation of Calvin's term 'mouvement', a favourite of his in his *Institution of the Christian Religion*. The 1561 version posits several kinds of 'motions', including sensual and demonic ones, but the desirable kind of motions are 'the motions God doth inspire in men'.[38] In Book II, Calvin describes the way that these divine motions act in human beings.[39] George Gifford's testimony to the divine presence at Philip Sidney's death-bed was that Sidney felt extraordinary 'inward Motions and Workings'.[40] In the poems 'Artillerie' and 'The Method' George Herbert also uses the term 'Motion' to describe the way God communicates. Herbert even argued that if a murderer could be proved to have acted on a divine motion, he should be acquitted.[41] He was commenting on a treatise translated by Nicholas Ferrar, and sent to him for approval: the treatise was Juan de Valdes' *110 Considerations*, perhaps the most bald statement of the necessity for and irresistibility of divine impulses, 'motions'.

This circular movement by which the believer reflects back to Christ the very impulses of love and grace which he had received from Christ in the first place is seen by Reformed commentaries on the Song of Songs as the prime subject of the book. In 1654 Samuel Petto tried to formulate the theology of these impulses in *The voice of the Spirit. Or, An essay towards a discoverie of the witnessings of the spirit*, to which he attached a practical application of his treatise, *Roses from Sharon, or Sweet Experiences*. The epigraph of this volume quoted two verses from the Song of Songs, Cant. 4: 16, 'Awake, O north wind; and come, thou south; blow upon my garden, that the spices thereof may flow out. Let my beloved come into his garden, and eat his pleasant fruits': and Cant 7:12, 'Let us get up early to the vineyards; let us see if the vine flourish, whether the tender grape appear, and the pomegranates bud forth: there will I give thee my loves.' The experiences of A.M., who in true Song of Songs fashion, felt God speaking to him in his bed at night, are distinctly physical: 'my heart was in a kinde of heate, or wonderful glowing' (p. 16). A.M. describes 'motions' and charts ways to resist them: it is possible to ignore them, put difficulties in the way of obeying them, or mistake their source and consider them to be your own ideas and insights (p. 29).

Edward Reynolds himself had recently explained the significance of poetic words in producing divine impulses, in an enlistment of rhetorical motions—figures of speech—for the power of divine motion. In his *A Treatise of the Passions and Faculties of the Soule of Man* (London, 1640) he posited a powerful combination of Reason, Imagination and Invention which could produce a 'kind of heat and rapture' identical with 'the *Poets* Divine Raptures'.[42] The poet can become a go-between in the relationship between Christ and the believer: the divine text produces 'heat and rapture' through its imaginative mecha-nisms, which produce divinely inspired motions in the reader. The impor-tance of literary form in divine discourse had been investigated by another member of the editorial team for the 1645 Annotations, David Reading; his *Davids Soliloquie conteining many comforts for afflicted minds* (London, 1627) had been a study of the spiritual and rhetorical power of the book of Psalms. In fact, these two books, the Psalms and the Song of Solomon, were regarded in the seventeenth century as having particular power to move the emotions, as Francois de Sales stated as far back as 1609:

> There are certain words, with [sic] have a particular force and efficacie to content and satisfie the hart in this behalf: such are the daintie sighes, and passionate complaints, and loving exclamations that are sowed so thick in the psalmes of David; the often invocations of the sweet & delightful name of IESUS; the lovely passages which be expressed in the Canticle of Canticles.[43]

Such a Catholic rhetoric could easily be adapted to explain the power of Reformed reading of the Scriptures. In the 1648 edition of Diodati's *Pious and Learned Annotations,* the Ramist analysis added before the Song of Songs adds a stylistic criterion for the excellence of this book: its message is communicated 'more fitly by resemblances', 'more pathetically in expressions' than any other Biblical book, and is therefore 'more clearly to humane capacity then either the 45 Psalme or any other Psalme'.

The subsequent drama between the Bridegroom and the Bride in chapter 5 has plenty of 'heat and rapture' and is conducted in terms of 'motions'— physical motions such as the movement of Christ's hands to open the door, psychological motions such as the Bride's instinctive response to him, spiritual motions when she finally opens up and is willing to receive him. Of course in the text of chapter 5 only one movement that is not an external gesture is recorded, in verse 4: that too is a physical motion, one which operates as a metaphor, translated in the Geneva Bible as 'Mine heart was affectioned towards him'. In the allegorical scheme with which this text is interpreted, however, all physical motions have a metaphorical register. Thus, the movement by the Bridegroom's hand towards 'the hole of the door' has an irresistible sense of penetration, into the bedroom of the Bride, and therefore into her being. All the seventeenth-century annotations pick up this masterful gesture, although they translate it into spiritual terms. For Diodati, the significance of this gesture is 'A description of Christs power, to work that inwardly by his Spirit in a faithfull man, which outwardly he commandeth by his word.' This is the Dutch annotation on the same movement: 'so moving and touching their hearts, by the efficacy, and power of the Spirit, as that he rouseth them up to a fervent longing after him'. This is the essential Calvinist paradox: at the heart of Calvinist spirituality is a relationship between Christ and the soul, yet it is a relationship initiated and carried on by one party only. The doctrines of predestination and perseverance dictate that however profound the spiritual union between Christ and the believer, and in spite of the extended metaphor of the Bridegroom and the Bride which describes it, this is not a genuine relationship: it is axiomatic that the human being has nothing with which to respond to God that is not already given by the Holy Spirit. The metaphor of 'holy rape', used with disturbing frequency in the seventeenth century, is the result of combining the imagery of the mystical marriage with the theology of Calvinism. There is more than a suggestion of this sexual dominance in this passage, as glossed in the Dutch annotations to verse 5:

> the call and operation of Christ by his Holy Spirit in the hearts of believers hath exceeding great power, and that they being sensible thereof in their hearts by true faith and repentance (as sweet-smelling spices) do prepare themselves to receive and entertain their Bridegroom ... her heart being anointed with the oil of grace, and so all locks and bolts, that is all impediments and hindrances being removed, the Bridegroom might come in unto her without molestation, to enjoy the fruits of his grace, which she had received from him,

The modern reader might feel that the 'molestation' which has somehow crept in to the text here is hardly likely to be a problem for the Bridegroom, divine as he is, although such transgressive thinking is denounced in the 1651 *Annotations* as the 'foul ugly rottennesse' that 'some have belched here'. It is, it seems, possible to mistake spiritual motions for physical ones. Samuel Petto recognises the problem of trying to distinguish between the witness of the Spirit and 'the impulsings of Satan', but can only offer what is a rather circular argument: 'Reall tasts that the Lord is gracious, cause the soule to disrelish carnal delights, and imbitter those sweets to it.'[44] An over-literal interpretation which causes physical gratification will already exclude that particular reader from the charmed circle of 'the elect' who have experienced true spiritual pleasures. It is one thing to praise the metaphorical register of this divine poem as intended to be particularly effective with human readers: it is quite another to shift consideration of the spiritual tenor of the motion, towards over-emphasis on the verbal vehicle, with its physical connotations.

In any case, by the time the Bride has got round to opening the door (verse 6) the Bridegroom has got tired of hanging around outside it. Diodati comments, in the penitential tones of the Bride, 'Christ did suspend and keep back this rich communication of his free grace and spirit which hee offered me, if once I had received it in time.' The Dutch annotations here surely owe more to painful personal experience than to the dynamics of the narrative, which stress the neglect of the Church, rather than of God: 'this is one of the sorest and greatest troubles that do befall the children of God, when God seemeth not to hear their prayers, although they cry and call day and night unto him.'

Anti-Catholic commentary and hostile reactions

The commentators differ in their interpretation of verse 7, particularly in their identification of who the 'watchmen' represent. This is not the first time the watchmen have appeared in the Song. In chapter 3 verse 3 the annotators have already recorded their suspicion of these authority figures. For Diodati, they are godless, secular authority:

> great worldly wise men, who have the care and government of States and Common-wealths, while the night of this life listeth: But have no light of the kingdome of heaven, neither can they give a man any directions towards it.

The Dutch annotation gives two interpretations, one of which corresponds to Diodati, whilst the other, similarly negative, finds a target closer to home: 'teachers and ministers who are dumb dogs'. By comparison, Edward Reynolds registers only mild disapproval: 'The watchmen here, are such as should have directed her to the Bridegroom'. It is no wonder that the commentators leap to identify those who wound the Church at the end of her traumatic experience of loss in chapter 5 as their favourite bugbears. The Geneva version, which had glossed the watchmen as neutral authority figures in chapter 3, comes off the fence in chapter 5 to identify them as 'false teachers, who wound the conscience with their traditions', a clear reference to the Catholic enemy. Diodati identifies a secular state authority, hostile to religious commitment, which 'Seeing me inflamed with zeale to seek after Christ, did persecute and torment me, through Gods permission for punishment of my negligence.' The Dutch version really goes to town: 'Hereby is intimated, that God sometimes suffereth his Church to be persecuted and oppressed by Tyrants, and wicked Governours, yea also by false Teachers, and Hereticks, to chastise her for her drowsiness and negligence.' This is the lowest point of the Bride's fortunes: she is wounded and humiliated, without her veil, which has been seized by the watchmen (the Dutch version points out the significance of this action for sexual shame). The Bridegroom is nowhere to be seen, and He escapes the expository blame for this episode, which falls not only on the watchmen but on the Bride herself: God allows this suffering as a just punishment. Edward Reynolds is so convinced of the heinous sin of 'neglecting Christ' that he allows the Spouse very little sympathy at all, to the extent of exonerating the watchmen: his reluctance to identify an authoritarian hate figure may reflect the apparent absence of an enemy for the Presbyterian Church in the early 1640s in England. After all, the Parliamentary State who had commissioned these very annotations could hardly be seen as a persecutor, and the demise of the monarchy and Laudian authority must have seemed absolute in the year of publication of the first edition of the Annotations, which was also the year of the execution of Laud. The 1655 edition of the Christian Dictionary, in its special section for the Song of Songs adds to earlier versions which had offered for 'watchmen' the alternatives of 'Popish Prelates' or 'godly ministers' and is positively expansive: 'Pastors which watch over the City of God, wherof some be negligent and blinde, as false Priests and Prophets, Popish Prelates, ignorant guides, and idle Shepheards under the Gospel.'[45] In fact, both sets of English annotations, although nearly a century apart, are less keen to identify a political enemy than the Continental versions: the 'little foxes who spoil the vineyards' in verse 15 of chapter 2, a locus classicus for the enemies of the Church, are heretics in the Geneva version and false teachers in the 1645 Annotations; in the Dutch and Italian versions they are also rulers and tyrants respectively. Surprisingly, the Song of Songs had always been interpreted by Christians as what Ann Matter calls an 'insider/outsider' text: the earliest commentaries identified the Jews as the enemy, whilst in the High Middle Ages it was different branches of Christianity which were identified.[46]

Despite the restrained tone of Edward Reynolds' contributions, the 1645 Annotations were a target of later Anglican critique, and Royalist satire. Simon Patrick was offended by the lack of negative comment in the Annotations on the sin of sacrilege. He lists several verses where there was opportunity to mention this heinous crime, but where the annotators 'slipt over it'. He spends pages on the Biblical warrant for condemnation of the sale of bishops' lands, identifying several Scriptures as particularly apt for this purpose, but wilfully ignored by the annotators.[47] The title page of Sir John Birkenhead's *The Assembly-Man*, published in 1663 but composed in 1647 and circulated in manuscript, has a frontispiece representing Independent and Presbyterian elements in the Westminster Assembly. A Puritan, presumably representing an Assembly member, treads underfoot volumes of Fathers, Councils, and Casuists, and of course, the Book of Common Prayer. By contrast, on a shelf above his head (labelled 'Classicall' to indicate their essentially Presbyterian nature) are neatly stacked volumes of Diurnals, Votes and Ordinances, a Concordance, a copy of Geneva Notes and a Directory for Worship. Within the pages of *The Assembly-Man,* the 1645 Annotations come in for the satiric humour which Sir John Birkenhead vents on the Westminster Assembly, despite the fact that the work was never a formal product of that organisation.[48] 'They have lately published Annotations on the Bible, where their first Note (on the word Create) is a libel against Kings for creating of honours.'[49] In fact, their first note, on verse 1 of Genesis, manages to find occasion for adverse comment on the use of the royal 'we':

> that Courtly phrase is so much younger than the beginning of all things, that is was not taken up untill the tyranny of one person becoming odious to the people, succeeding kings, to gaine the good will of their Subjects, made show of moderating their soveraign authoritie by ruling rather by others counsell then by their own self-wils.

This note is surely more libellous than that quoted in Birkenhead's satire. However, it is clear that critics did not feel the need to read the Annotations themselves in order to repeat Birkenhead's criticisms, which focus on notes he considers self-evidently risible; the careful explanation that Jacob, in Genesis 27:9, ordering two goats for dinner, used one carcass to make sauce, as one goat was more than enough meat for his supper; and in the note on Matthew 2:16, the criticism of Herod for condemning two-year-old infant boys to death without 'legal Tryal'. These three chestnuts are copied in to the Bodleian copy of the 1645 Annotations by its 1712 owner, George Coningesby, along with this judgement of the entire volume: 'Commonly they follow the *Geneva* Margin, as those Sea-men who understood not the *Compass* crept along the Shore'. A later owner, presumably Anglican, has felt the need to distinguish Edward Reynolds' annotations as superior to the rest, quoting Anthony Wood: 'it was wished by many learned Men of the Presbyterian persuasion, that the rest had been all wrote *pare filo & eruditione*'.[50]

The Song of Songs and radical prophecy

Edward Reynolds may well have been a deliberately conservative choice for the notes on the Song of Songs, to avoid possible embarrassment to such an august and authoritative commissioning body as the Westminster Assembly. By 1642, a correlation was already obvious between commentaries on the Song of Songs and more radical Puritanism. 'The old Separatist' Henry Ainsworth (as Simon Patrick called him[51]) had written, as 'his last farewell to his friends' a version of the Song of Songs in metre, followed by Annotations: the judgement of the preface to the work, published shortly after his death, in 1623, was that 'he hath sung sweetliest in this'.[52] This work was reprinted in 1627 together with his annotations on the Pentateuch and the Psalms, and although it did not appear throughout most of the 1630s, it was republished in 1639 when the end of the regime was in sight. Ainsworth's commentary was not explicitly Separatist and was exceptionable only in the 1630s, when an extremely Reformed and Calvinist interpretation of the Song of Songs, having much in common with Francis Rous' 1631 *The Mysticall Marriage*, began to look unorthodox in the context of the increasing anti-Calvinism of the church hierarchy. The most popular commentary of the 1640s was, however, explicitly political, written by John Cotton before he left England in 1633.[53] John Cotton was particularly fond of the Song of Songs, and marked his arrival in America by preaching on it. His commentary was published in two editions in the 1640s, interspersed with volumes such as *The Keyes of the Kingdom of Heaven* (1642), *The Way of the Churches of Christ in New England* (1645) and *The Way of the Congregational Churches Cleared* (1648), which set out his vision for an Independent church. The first of these texts was actually commissioned by the Westminster Assembly and was very influential on men like John Owen, who were beginning to initiate and establish Independent congregations in England.[54] Cotton claimed, however, that the publication of his commentary on the Song of Songs was unauthorised, and it is certainly unorthodox. According to the front cover, the commentary on the Song of Songs is aimed at 'such as endeavour and thirst after the settling of Church and State, according to the Rule and Pattern of the Word of God', an appropriate designation for what is a millenarian vision. Cotton is not reluctant to apply political meanings to the text, which is seen as 'Lively describing the Estate of the Church in all the Ages thereof, both Jewish and Christian, to this day'. As Luther had done, Cotton gives contemporary referents for many of the entities named in the Song of Songs: Luther himself is the garden, fenced in with a hedge by the protection of Elector John (p. 171). The 'beds of spices' are sites of other Protestant communities, including Zurich, Strasbourg, Brussels, Berne and Geneva. As for the English church, it was '*beautifull as Tirzah* in King *Henry* the eighths time, *comely as Jerusalem* in King *Edward* the sixths time, *terrible as an army with banners* in Queen *Elizabeth's* time.'(p. 176). Perhaps it is not surprising that this commentary is explicitly hostile to the Laudian church, naming it as a 'concubine' and not the true Spouse: they have ministers 'thrust upon them without their liking or consent'(p. 186) and are corrupt in their doctrines of the Sacrament, and predestination (p. 188). Anthony Tuckney, Master of St. John's in 1655, tells us that Cotton treated the Song of Songs as a prophecy of the state of the Church from Solomon's time to the seventeenth century because he had been convinced by Thomas Brightman's commentary.[55]

Thomas Brightman was perhaps the most politically influential Bible commentator of the 1640s, and the one most freely acknowledged as a prophet, despite the disadvantage of having died in 1607. Brightman's annotations on the Song of Songs, *Scholia in Canticum Canticorum,* had been published in Basle, in 1614. In 1644 it was translated and published in London as part of his Complete Works, but a separate edition of the annotations of the Song of Songs was published in the same year, although the pagination made clear that this edition had simply reused the plates from the larger volume: the printer for both was John Field. *A commentary on the Canticles or the Song of Salomon* shows the same boldness about predicting the future of the church as his commentary on the Revelation, also republished in the1640s, had done. 'The Epistle to the Reader' is a bit squeamish about 'this Propheticall and particular application', admitting that Brightman does not follow any other interpreters, but pointing out that 'the difficulty of the Allegory hath occasioned such variance amongst the Interpreters, that it may almost be said; as many men, so many mindes'.[56] In a Ramist table at the start of the volume, Brightman offers a history of the chosen people of the Old Testament and the New Testament (the Church Legall and the Church Evangelicall). From very early on in the text the book becomes prophecy on the part of Solomon, although history, of course, for Brightman, so that by the beginning of chapter 5 we are at the year 336. The 'sleep' of verse 1 is explained in ecclesiastical terms: 'this drowsinesse crept in the time of *Constantine...*

the sharpest sighted Pastors could not use their outward senses: not perceiving how ambition crept in among the Bishops, and not onely that, but now they began to consecrate Temples to Saints'(p. 1031). Along with verse 2, which describes, apparently, 'the doctrine of free justification by Christ alone decayed at that time', this language would resonate in the 1640s with memories of Laudian practice and doctrine. The commentary follows with a list of Holy Roman Emperors, some who had helped to shut Christ out, as the Bride does in verses 2 and 3, others who had tried to let him in. Verse 6 is an easy text on which to fasten a Puritan doctrine of the Church Invisible. The watchmen, in Brightman's terms, are different from the rather kindly English policemen-type figures he perceives in chapter 3 verse 3, who would have directed the Spouse to the Bridegroom had they known where he was. These more sinister beings are 'the Ecclesiasticall Teachers and Rulers', who persecute the church and force her underground: her plight is not so bad, as she inhabits a metaphorical wine cellar, where the Bridegroom sustained her for centuries with apples and wine, while the 'harlot of *Rome*...[boasted] so much of her visibility since her first beginning'(p. 1035). Verse 7 describes the Spouse's efforts to communicate her misery, through St Bernard's commentary upon the Canticles, and the prophetic utterance of Hildegard of Bingen: Brightman had included substantial extracts from her prophecies in his commentary on Revelation. Brightman has incorporated the first verse of chapter six into the end of chapter five: other commentators such as Henry Finch had felt similar freedom to rearrange the order of the text, although he had not asserted, as Brightman does, that this particular verse refers to the invention of printing.

By chapter 6 the commentary has reached 'things present', where Brightman finds the Song of Songs particularly apposite. After 1563, he argues, the church was divided into queens, concubines and virgins. Amongst the queens he rates the churches of England, Ireland, Scotland, the Low Countries, Geneva, Switzerland and Thrace; 'concubines' are 'others cleaving to their opinions' and include the Germans, the Danes, the Spanish church and the Swedish church. 'Virgins', ranked lowest because of their lack of intimacy with the Bridegroom, are Anabaptists, Libertines, Antitrinitarians and Arians (p. 1048). The final chapters of the commentary deal with the state of the Church in the end times, but Brightman specifically refuses to put a date on the second coming of Christ, although suggesting that the time was drawing near (p. 1077). However, we are confidently told that Rome shall be utterly destroyed about the year 1650, a date considerably nearer to Brightman's 1640s readers than when he first penned it at the start of the century (p. 1051). The remorseless teleology of the prophetic versions, which inevitably end with the fall of Rome and the conversion of the Jews, represents a very different interpretative framework of the Song of Songs than the ones produced by mid-century commentators, for whom the text was an emblem of the lack of closure to be expected from the godly life.[57]

Nathanael Homes, following Brightman's general methodology, published in the early 1650s his own commentary on Canticles, which he used to interpret the extraordinary events of the 1640s, and to claim that Brightman had been right about predicting the end of the Pope's power in 1650. This prophetic interpretation he considered the literal sense of the Song of Songs.[58] His particular allegiance to the Independent party, however, rendered his interpretation triumphalist and deeply controversial. The Presbyterian Edmund Hall quarrelled violently with his Brightman-esque claims, contained in Homes' sermon before the Lord Mayor on the day of thanksgiving appointed for victory at the battle of Dunbar.[59] Hall's rather different view of how the prophecies relate to 1650 is not surprising: in 1651 he was in prison for attacking Cromwell. The sub-title of his book, *A Presbyteriall glosse upon many of those obscure prophetick texts in Canticles*, gives away his Presbyterian position.[60] Hall's pro-monarchical view was that the grandchild of James I would utterly defeat the Pope (p. 102); since Charles II secretly promised the French in 1670 to convert the country to Catholicism, and since his brother became an openly Catholic king, Hall's prophetic gifts were obviously not of the best.

The Brightman and Homes commentaries represent one extreme in interpretative strategies for the Song of Songs, the use of the text as a politico-religious allegory with specific referents in space and time. There was an illustrious precedent for this: Luther's *Lectures on the Song of Solomon* had used the same strategy, although for a different place, and a different time. Luther would not have quarrelled with this distancing, however: 'any state in which there is the church and a godly prince can use the song of Solomon's just as if it had been composed about its own government and state'. Many later commentators would have agreed with Luther that the real subject of the Song of Songs is 'the greatest of all human works, namely, government': few of them in the following century, however, would have shared his love affair with authority.[61] As we have seen, interpretation of the political message of the Song of Songs varies with the allegiance of the commentator, as between Nathanael Homes and Edmund Hall. Moreover, the extreme polarisation of religious politics during the century after Luther meant that believers were often in the situation of having to defend themselves against authority rather than to experience its protection: rulers usually end up, as we have seen, within the category of the watchmen who attack the Bride in chapter five. Thus the sensual enjoyments delineated in the text are seen as supporting the Bride's perilous political situation, much as Brightman's commentary saw her sustained with wine and apples during her period as the Church Invisible. There is a great deal of scope for subversive religious politics in interpretations of this book, and it is no surprise that radical interpreters are attracted to it, such as the radical Independent Joshua Sprigg and the Fifth Monarchist Hanserd Knollys.[62]

As Brightman notes at the start of his commentary, 'the comparisons of this song are taken from such things which do chiefly tickle up the senses' (p. 982).

Any commentator with pretensions to orthodoxy—and that designation includes all of the authors mentioned in this chapter so far—would refute a literal reading of the sensual experiences, which would turn the Song of Songs into a 'hot carnall Pamphlet' (the disapproving designation of the 6th edition of the Christian Dictionary).[63] Combined with the dynamic of persecution found within the text, such a literal reading could give powerful expression to a transgressive sect, as Noam Flinker has described its appeal for the Ranters. The freedom of interpretation guaranteed by the allegorical status of the Song of Songs allowed the assignations of radically different meanings to the textual metaphors. Thus Joseph Salmon assigns the role of the Bride to the true Ranter, whilst Puritan religion is seen as fornication with the Harlot. As we have seen, this partial interpretation of the text had been a feature of all Reformed commentary: but Ranters added to their particular bias a belief in the potential holiness of the sexual act which made the Song of Songs one of their favourite intertexts. Both Laurence Clarkson and Lodowick Muggleton, on finally disowning their Ranter allegiance, blamed the inclusion of the Song of Songs in the Bible as the reason for their error.[64] Clarkson explained, 'I was ... proving by Scripture the truth of what I acted; and indeed *Solomon's* writings was the original of my filthy lust, supposing I might take the same liberty as he did, not then understanding his Writings was no Scripture.'[65] As Sebastian Castellio had asserted in the previous century, the Song of Songs had no divine authority, and was merely an erotic love song.

Ranter use of the text of the Song of Songs represents only one very small fraction of the wide readership the book found in the 1640s, but it was an interpretation waiting to happen. The Reformed tradition of interpreting the text as a description of unconditional Divine love for each individual human believer, offering the possibility of a palpable relationship with Christ to the reader, was fertile ground for the antinomian tendency in radical Puritanism. Also, the radical split between tenor and vehicle, meaning and word, which allowed eccentric or bizarre interpretations of the Song, had already been prepared for by centuries of allegorical hermeneutic which Luther, for example, found absurd.[66] Again and again prefatory epistles acknowledge the instability of the meaning of the Song of Songs, and the infinite possibilities of interpretation. As the dedicatory epistle to Brightman's commentary flippantly suggests, one man's interpretation is as good as another's: 'as many men, so many mindes'. The radical individualism of the subject matter of the Song of Songs was mirrored in the radical freedom of interpretation offered to the individual reader. It was against such hermeneutical anarchy that the learned compilers of annotations struggled in the years of individual freedom after 1642. Even Edmund Hall, opposing his own apocalyptic reading to that of Nathanael Homes, continued to insist on the essential perspicuity of the difficult texts that included the Song of Songs, quoting Augustine's famous metaphors for the different levels of interpretation: 'It is a sin to be wilfully negligent in the search into those Prophecies, which give light to the times we live in ... there the Lamb may wade, and the Elephant may swim'.[67] All he himself needs to interpret these 'hard places', are the Scriptures themselves, and the Fathers. It is ignorance that is the cause of heresy and schism, insists the Scottish Presbyterian Andrew Simson, introducing his 1655 edition of Wilson's *Christian Dictionary* to 'the Christian Reader'.[68] His much enlarged dictionary for the Song of Songs draws on several famous commentaries, including Ainsworth's, Brightman's, and the English Annotations, showing that authority had attached to some radically different interpretations. The point of the Annotations, particularly in books such as the Canticles, was to mediate between the direct apprehension necessary for a salvific reading, and the judgement of scholars needed to prevent the 'dangerous misconstruction of an imprudent inconsiderate Reader'.[69] The second edition of Diodati's work, *Pious and Learned Annotations*, dedicated fulsomely and loyally to Charles I in 1648 by the publisher, Nicholas Fussell, sees in this kind of commentary a solution to the sectarianism of the 1640s: 'in these last and perillous times, heresies on the one side are sprung up, schismes and factions on the other, and that there is a kind of Atheisme, irreligion, and profaneness in most, yet all of these mask't and shrowded under the name of Christianity, and confirmed by texts of holy Writ, wrested and misunderstood ... these dangerous delusions are no ways better prevented then by hearkening to Learned and pious Divines, who use all the lawfull, just and ordinary meanes for a true understanding of holy Writ.'[70]

Restoration commentary on the Song of Songs

It is perhaps inevitable after the political and religious upheavals of the 1640s and 1650s that the prefaces to Biblical commentaries increasingly recommend themselves less as helps to individuals in ascertaining their own divinely inspired reading of Scripture than as necessary aids to the control of sectarianism and political subversion. Presbyterian Matthew Poole's huge Latin commentary, *Synopsis Criticorum,* is dedicated, with political correctness, to Charles II, who had provided Poole with a flattering licence.[71] Despite the fact that the year of its publication, 1669, was a year of great Nonconformist unrest in London, and the beginning of a polemical attack on Nonconformity and its traditions of exegesis by Anglicans such as Simon Patrick and Samuel Parker, the list of subscribers to the edition is extraordinary: no less than eight bishops are listed, along with pillars of the establishment such as the Earl of Bridgewater. Simon Patrick himself is mentioned twice. The *Commentatorum in Canticum* in volume 2 is filled with references to Ainsworth, and there are a few notes from the Dutch Annotations. However, there are just as many references to Grotius, whose historicised commentary of 1644, *Annotata ad Vetus Testamentum*, asserted that the text was primarily a love song, and in the process of interpreting the text took pains to stress the sexual connotations of many of the phrases; verse 1 of chapter 5, for example, is glossed as the Bridegroom congratulating himself on having achieved sexual consummation.[72] Like Grotius, Poole ponders on the meaning of the sexual metaphor, and quotes Grotius' opinion that the mystical marriage is an ancient heresy revived by the Anabaptists. Poole also refutes the methodology of Cotton and Brightman who interpret the book as specific prophecy.[73] The political danger of following their approach is seen in the commentary of Thomas Beverley, an Independent who was imprisoned for much of the 1680s. He used Brightman and Cotton's basic framework but also asserted his own interpretation; 'I have freely dissented from them, whenever I see Reason', he comments in 1687. Strangely, he himself perceives the radical instability of a text interpreted in this way; 'The Song, and several parts of it, *unstable as Water,* having no consistent Figure of their own, shall receive Shape from every Vessel the Interpreter brings to it.' Thus, his prophetic and poetic version of the Song of Songs portrays, for Beverley, the kingdom of Christ flourishing on earth in the year 1772.[74]

With the careful rejection by Poole of Cotton and Brightman's volumes, the two great planks of prophetic commentary on the Song of Songs, the potential of his volume for use in radical politics is much reduced, particularly as the text was in Latin. Simon Patrick's contemporary blast at Nonconformist interpretation of the Song of Songs was clearly not meant to include Matthew Poole's learned commentary. 'Nothing is so sweet and pleasing to flesh and bloud, as for a man to hear how much a great Prince is in love with him, and how freely he loves him, how his heart beats in Heaven toward him: and especially how careful and compassionate he is toward him in a persecuted condition', grumbled Patrick in an accusation of antinomianism against Nonconformists, in 1669.[75] However, Patrick's disgust at Nonconformist commentary and annotation was clearly not aimed, as Laud's was, against the very principle of exegetical aids, as he became one of the most prolific and well-known Anglican commentators on the Scripture. His *Paraphase on the Song of Solomon,* published in 1700 accepts that the text should be applied to Christ and his love for the church in general, rather than the individual believer in particular. It eschews a very specific or very mystical interpretation: 'it hath been famous for the shipwrack of many great Pilots: who went too far, as I conceive, and sought for more there than is to be found; and therefore miscarried'.[76] Thus his paraphrase for Chapter 1 verse 4a, 'Draw me, we will run after thee' goes like this: 'Appear then in thy Power, Majesty and Glory, and by thy mighty Grace and love attract me and all my people to thee: which will make the whole World most readily and cheerfully devote themselves unto thy service'.(p. 2). This rational and good-humoured tone continues throughout the book, evening out, as he promised, the extremes of love and despair, and, it must be said, destroying the power of the book's poetic texture as well as its potential for radical politics.

In one respect, however, Patrick's volume does resemble Nonconformist commentary of the same period. In 1683 the first part of the English redaction of Poole's learned commentary was published, unfinished, at his death in Amsterdam (he had fled there, believing himself to be one of the targets of the Popish Plotters). *Annotations upon the Holy Bible. wherein the sacred text is inserted, and various readings annex'd, together with parallel scriptures* seems to promise the scholarly commentary of *Synopsis Criticorum*. In fact, the English volume retains the remnants of his Latin apparatus with its references to ancient languages, as well as the original principle of annotation, but there is an irresistible momentum towards paraphrase. This is part of the gloss on verse 4 of chapter 1.

> We will not receive thy Grace in vain, but will improve it and co-operate with it, and stir up all our strength to obey thee. Christ, my Husband, and Lord, the King of his church, as he is oft called, the King of Kings &c. Heb. has caused me to come, by drawing me as I desired. He hath answered my Prayer. Where I may most freely and familiarly converse with him, and enjoy him, he hath taken me into most intimate communion with himself.

Here, I would suggest, the idea of annotation as empowering the individual to interpret Scripture for herself is beginning to give way to the self-standing volume of commentary which promulgates a specific view of Scripture, and to some extent replaces it. This principle had been clear in the enlargement of the 1645 Annotations, which had originally been designed for the margins of the King James version: although that short volume sold well, there was a demand for a fuller commentary, and inclusion of the actual text of Scripture, which was satisfied in 1651. The section on the Song of Songs in the 1651 edition is very much fuller than that of 1645, and the characteristic movement from third person commentary to first person paraphrase is already noticeable in the gloss on chapter 1 verse 4: 'Not onely kisse, that is, call and invite, but command, and work effectually, not onely by discovering the glory sweetnesse and spiritual excellencies that are in thy self, and thy administrations, which is but morall fruition, and is found in any attractive object, but also by inclining my heart to follow thee, which indeed is the right drawing of the heart ... Else I move not: Not onely come down to me, and dwell with me, but lift me up, that where thou art, I may be also.'

Norton suggests that the popularity of Notes was due to the fact that unlearned Christians actually found the Bible incomprehensible without them.[77] In effect, the seventeenth century sees a move from exegetical aids such as the *Christian Dictionarie* to full-blown, self-standing commentary, as the title of the 1651 edition advertises: *Annotations upon all the books of the Old and New Testament this second edition so enlarged, as they make an entire commentary on the sacred Scripture : the like never before published in English.* In effect, this mediation between the sacred text and the unlearned reader (commentaries in Latin continue to pursue the scholarly course) produces a new text, one that is more comprehensible, and in line with the politics and beliefs of its intended readership. The instability of the Song of Songs renders its commentators' alignment with particular religious policy more transparent, as we have seen.

Four editions of Poole's commentary, finished by other Nonconformist scholars, were published by the end of the seventeenth century, and they sold in great numbers. But perhaps the commentary that was to fix Nonconformist interpretation of the Bible for several centuries—it is still available on the Web today—was Matthew Henry's Presbyterian commentary.[78] His interpretation of the Song of Songs, the apotheosis of one hundred and fifty years of Reformed interpretation, was published in 1711 as *An Exposition of the Five Poetical Books of the Old Testament,* and later formed part of his famous commentary on the whole Bible. Henry includes the Biblical text, which should perhaps fix his interpretation to specific words and phrases: however, he treats it in larger segments, with pages of commentary between the Biblical verses, which allow a free discursive interpretation rather than comments on individual words. In effect, each section of commentary reads like a sermon (and may well have started off like that) in which literal meaning is very soon left behind for a more rhetorically compelling narrative. This is part of two complete folios on chapter 5 verses 2–8.

> She still calls him her Beloved, being resolv'd, how Cloudy and Dark soever the Day be, she will not quit her Relation to him, and Interest in him. 'Tis a Weakness upon any Apprehension, either of our Own Failings, or of God's withdrawings, to conclude hardly as to our Spiritual State. Every Desertion is not Despair. I will say, Lord I believe, help my Unbelief...tho he leave me, I love him, he is mine.

As each section gathers rhetorical impetus, awareness of alternative interpretations is lost: in effect, the Biblical text is rewritten as an authoritative, inward, spiritual narrative, and all trace of the erotic, multivalent, love song, which had occasionally surfaced to trouble the reader, is erased. The 'motions' for which the Song of Songs is famous are reproduced in the rhetorical motions of the commentary's narrative: but there is no doubt about what the motions mean or in what direction they are meant to move the reader. Henry's commentary closes down interpretations of the Song of Songs to the single one of a meditation on the believer's relationship with Christ. Moreover, rather than the constant 'vicissitudes' which were, according to earlier commentary, both the content and the elliptical form of the text, Henry's narrative has acquired an ending—no less a climax than the end of the world, in anticipation, at least. Whereas mid-century commentaries saw the final verse of the book as a repetition of longing for the presence of the Beloved—as indeed it is, literally, a repeat of 2:17—Henry takes the longing to a different level, an eschatological one.

> But those that truly love Christ long for his second coming, because it will be the crown both of his glory and their bliss. The comfort and satisfaction which we sometimes have in communion with God in grace here should make us breathe the more earnestly after the immediate vision and complete fruition of him in the kingdom of glory. The spouse, after an endearing conference with her beloved, finding it must break off, concludes with this affectionate request for the perfecting and perpetuating of this happiness in the future state.

What Henry has done is to pick up the cues from the prophetic texts which link the Spouse of the Song of Songs with the Bride of Revelation 22, who calls for Christ to come and defeat Antichrist. Matthew Poole, in a period when, as Warren Johnston has shown, Biblical apocalypticism was still a common mode of interpreting history, had glossed the last verse of the Song of Songs with verses from the last chapter of the Bible. By the time Henry produced his commentary the church in England was no longer commonly thought to be in battle with Antichrist in the shape of the Pope, and the second coming of Christ was looked forward to as a personal devotional fulfilment.

The popularity of Henry's commentary through the centuries looks like, and is claimed as, a concern with the Biblical text, but in fact it represents the death of the Reformed ideal of 'perspicuity'. Glossed over, rather than glossed, are the 'hard places' for which the Song of Songs had been notorious throughout its life in the Jewish and Christian canon. The Biblical text of the Song of Songs is simply resistant to the kind of immediate assimilation by the ordinary believer that is the model for popular Nonconformist reading of the Bible, so it has to be replaced by a text that will fulfil these requirements. Of course, within this authoritative rewriting of the Biblical text, political application is perilous, especially in consideration of the struggle of eighteenth-century Dissenters for legal recognition in the political mainstream. Henry's commentary distances itself from the history of radical interpretations of the Song of Songs, and concentrates on a spiritual reading as disengaged from contemporary politics as the likes of Simon Patrick would have it to be. Perhaps the most vivid illustration of the shift of the context for interpretation from political persecution of the State to spiritual transactions with God is the conclusion of Matthew Henry's commentary on the passage in chapter 5 we treated earlier. Although the Watchmen may be hostile instruments of the State—Presbyterians had many political and legal battles to fight in the early eighteenth century—the Bride passes over their mistreatment in silence, for her priority is not political resistance but the love story between herself and the Bridegroom. This is Henry's interpretation of verse 8.

tell him that I am wounded with Love to him, Gracious Souls are more sensible of Christ's Withdrawing, than of any other Trouble whatsoever. *Languet Amans non languet Amor.*[79]

This last is a quotation from a pornographic novella by a twelfth-century monk, in which the beautiful Alda, closely guarded by her father, is given an education in the arts of sexual love by Pyrrhus, dressed as a woman to gain entry to her prison. Fifty-seven years previously, the inclusion of a passage from a secular romance in what was purportedly a sacred text had given Milton one of his most powerful tools with which to attack the king's integrity in *Eikon Basilike*. By the beginning of the eighteenth century no such radical disjunction is perceived between the words of a sacred text and those of a profane one: both can be employed in God's purposes. The presence of rhetorical strategies in giving power to the holy discourse of the Bible is openly acknowledged. So too is the link between spiritual 'motions' and 'emotion', now the word for the way the human being is 'moved'. Such acceptance of human characteristics into the interpretation of a divine text moved perilously close to the acceptance of the Song of Songs as an erotic love song: Henry's strategy, to as it were replace the sexually explicit language with a narrative of the romance between Christ and the soul, is one way of dealing with an interpretive framework that had completely changed since the early seventeenth century, when the radical separation of sexual and spiritual could be taken for granted, and when the text itself had become a means of polarising readers into opposing categories: godly and Papist, holy and profane, revolutionary and conformist. The potentially subversive 'spectacles' through which the text of the Song of Songs was read in the 1640s had become heavily rose-tinted by the early eighteenth century. The book of radical prophecy had been turned into romance, a love story between Christ and the reader.

5
The Seventeenth-Century Woman Writer and the Bride

This chapter charts the effect of the reading of the Song of Songs by women over nearly one hundred years of intimate engagement with the Biblical text, in the Reformed strategy of interpretation described in the previous chapter. Although the material presented here ranges widely over the whole of the seventeenth century, this chapter is placed at a particular point in the book as a whole, in the treatment of the 1650s when the tradition of interpretation of the Song of Songs described in the previous chapter became hegemonic in England. It is then, I argue, that the story of women's use of the Song of Songs becomes part of mainstream narratives about the growth of authorship beyond élite literary circles, and therefore part of the larger subject of this book, which is not primarily about gender. Some of the entrances into authorship described here turned out not to be channels into a wider participation by women in literary authorship, but a manifestation of a particular political and religious situation, and therefore a kind of 'dead-end' in terms of women's literary history, However, the important phenomenon that is the subject of this chapter takes its place alongside other paradigms of women's authorship, in differing religious and political contexts.

Given the dearth of writing authored by women in early modern culture, the privileging of an authorised female voice in the Song of Songs gave women readers what was often their sole opportunity to respond to something like female authorship. In some cases, this experience turned readers into writers; the reading of the Song of Songs by women had a substantial impact on women's authorship in the seventeenth century. One of the first anthologies of women's writing, the second 'Lampe of Virginitie' in 1582 of that multi-volume testimony to Reformed women's religious culture *The Monument of Matrones,* was published within the spiritual framework of a gendered vision of the Bride of Christ: on the front cover the coat of arms of Elizabeth I in prime position at the top of the volume is mirrored by a very feminine image of the Bride in the opposite position, the bottom centre. This engraving of the Spouse is surrounded with the text 'Hir lamps of love are coles of fire and a verye vehement flame of the Lorde. Cant.VIII Chap'.

This is a translation of the Latin version of verse 6 of the eighth chapter of the Song of Songs: the Geneva version has 'the coles therof are fyrie coles, and a vehement flame' whereas the Latin word for 'coles' is 'lampadas'. The very word 'lampe' which is so important to the overall scheme of the book is taken from the parable of the wise and foolish virgins in Matthew 25, who are waiting for the bridegroom for whom it is vital to keep their lamps alight. The opening prayer reinforces the application of the parable of the ten virgins to the readers of the volume, and the dedicatory letter emphasises the status of Queen Elizabeth as the Bride of Christ. The epistle to the specifically female reader explains why Biblical writing, including the text of the Song of Songs, has been included:

> that looking in this glasse of the holie lives of their foremothers, they may christianlie conforme and adorne themselves after their good examples, and become for their rare vertues verie beautifull spouses in the sight of their spirituall bridegroome Jesus Christ.[1]

Much of the language used about the relationship between reader and book is that of the exemplary text: there is much use of the metaphors of 'pattern' and 'mirror'. It is obvious that Thomas Bentley began the project as a collection of writing by women, and only added the biblical and liturgical matter after finding little women's writing.[2] Gender is clearly an important part of his methodology: he wants women to identify with writing by other women, including Elizabeth's translation of Margeurite de Navarre's *Miroir de l'ame pecheresse*. The female reader is instructed to identify with the female writer:

> With the most gratious Souereigne Ladie Queene *ELIZABETH*, to muse divinelie of the inward love of the soule towards Christ their spouse.[3]

The reader is also told to identify with Lady Jane Grey facing execution, or with Anne Askew facing martyrdom, or with Elizabeth Tyrwhit in her daily prayers and meditations.

Never in this volume are women readers expressly encouraged to imitate the women writers in their authorship activity, but such a move would be merely one step beyond that which Thomas Bentley suggests as providing useful activity until Christ returns, 'giving us in the meane season diverse gifts and talents to occupie and imploie'.[4] There is certainly evidence that in the century after *The Monument of Matrones* women drew on the text of the Song of Songs not only as subject matter, as a way of describing a relationship with Christ, but as a model for their wider activity as authors of poetry and prophecy. The text is also available for a gendered polemic, as evidence in a general argument for greater equality with men. The recognition of the gendered body of the Bride in this way weakens the allegorical status of the text, in that she becomes available particularly to women as an embodied, female character with whom to identify. Such a reading inevitably offers the love story of the Song of Songs as a model to women for their relationship with Christ, which in turn leads to questions about the explicit eroticism of the text: perhaps it might even, as Sharon Achinstein has suggested, affirm women's sexuality and help to voice female sexual desire in a period when such articulations are rare.[5]

Certainly, Thomas Bentley was not alone in finding little women's writing extant by the late sixteenth century: much of what he found was out of print, and he was consciously promoting a rather rare commodity.[6] The situation was little better during the early years of the seventeenth century. A mere handful of works by women came into print before the Civil War, and several of these were marketed as 'mother's legacies'— documents whose primary readership was apparently the author's children, and which were usually introduced by prominent men.[7] As Wendy Wall has shown, the combination of the limited audience, apparently the author's own family, and the recent decease of the author herself, offered one space for women's authoritative writing in which the bounds of her submission to men were not deemed to have been transgressed.[8] It was impossible to accuse a dead woman of the self-display, deemed inherent in the activity of authorship, which for women was often seen as akin to bodily display: publication of her writing was seen as equivalent to prostitution.[9] It is important too that these 'mother's legacies' were prose works, with no rhetorical or literary virtuosity on show. The writing has the dramatic effect of 'last words', assumed to represent absolute sincerity and truth. Despite the affective possibilities of the genre for feminine grief, and for the preservation of the personal voice of the dying woman in language, these documents were unremittingly moralistic and didactic.[10] Psalm-like meditations in prosaic metre were often added as appendages to the prose texts, as if to indicate what the acceptable limits of woman's literary activity might be. Thomas Goad, who edited Elizabeth Jocelin's *The mothers legacie, to her unborne childe* in 1624, ignored her poetry, and her notes on divinity, in order to publish an unfinished treatise which fitted perfectly into his construction of her in his prefatory 'Approbation'. He is pleased that this treatise shows no sign of her dangerous knowledge of history and languages, 'these her lines scarce shewing one sparke of the elementary fire of her secular learning'.[11] Such gendered limitation on scholarship in general and literary writing in particular seems to have effectively restricted publication by women. The collapse of print censorship between 1640 and 1642 ensured a flood of what would have been previously unlicensed publications, particularly from godly men who had been denied expression by Laudian licensers.[12] Those who had been silenced by strict censorship during the 1630s might have included women who had aspirations to authorship. However, there was no immediate increase in publications authored by women in the early 1640s: cultural prescriptions against women publishing their work permeated too deeply. There was to be no releasing of the floodgates as women prevented from publishing their theological, or indeed literary, works before 1640, sent them to the press.

However, in the 1640s, a few women showed that they had taken to heart the teaching on the perspicacity of Scripture enshrined in the production of the English *Annotations*, which specifically extended the right of reading and interpreting Scripture to women. The annotation to Deuteronomy 21:8 in the Geneva Bible had already given mothers the responsibility to instruct their children, and Charmarie Jenkins Blaisdell argues that noblewomen enjoyed the opportunity to debate Scripture, and to espouse the Reformed cause.[13] The priority in Reformed Bible commentary to give access to the text to marginalised groups meant that all women were offered the intense identification with characters in the biblical story that Reformed reading assumed. Elizabeth Isham, for example, in her 1638 manuscript 'Booke of Rememberance', used identification with King David to legitimise her own feelings in the face of melancholy, and the expression of such feelings in rhetoric.[14] Female biblical characters were made available to women authors as role models, and there is a great deal of evidence in women's writing that they used them as such. Mary Pope's main appeal throughout *A Treatise of Magistracy* (1647) is to the authority of her own interpretation of Scripture, 'having good warrant out of Gods word' both for her message and for her right to give it as a woman (sig. C2v). Her volume is full of Scriptural examples of women who have contributed to the work of God, or who have authoritatively spoken the words of God to their community: the women who helped Moses build the Ark of the Covenant; Abigail, who helped to save her husband Nabal; and even Eve. In Pope's epistle to Parliament, in which she specifically asks Parliament to bring the King home from house arrest in Holdenby House (sig. C1r), her role model is the woman of Tekoah, who, in 2 Samuel 14, spoke to David on behalf of Absalom, to bring him home from exile. As Sharon Achinstein has pointed out, feminist scholarship has been alert to any traces of women writers identifying with other women in terms specifically of their gender.[15] However, in this period there is a lack of evidence of women writers having read and appreciated the work of other women. The use of biblical figures in texts of female authorship therefore constitutes an important element in the forging of a female tradition of writing.[16] Female poets such as Anne Southwell recognise the Biblical singers such as Debora as predecessors in the activity of female authorship.[17]

The Bride of the Song of Songs is explicitly offered to the individual soul as a model for an intimate relationship with Christ in the mainstream interpretation of the text of the Song of Songs outlined in the previous chapter, and this would seem to offer a privileged place to female readers of the biblical text. However, in the first half of the seventeenth century, there are few instances of women explicitly claiming the Bride of the Song of Songs as a female predecessor in the way that women like Deborah and Anna, also speakers of biblical poetry, are commonly used to authorise female writing.[18] Part of the reason for this lack may be the insistence by commentators that the text should not be read as a conversation between a real women and a real man. This claim was axiomatic to arguments for the canonical status of the Song of Songs: too much consideration of a historical context for the lovers' interchange led to awkward questions about their sexual activity, when their marital status was uncertain, as we have seen. Because the literal meaning of the book was incompatible with teachings of Scripture on marriage, and therefore seen to be absurd, it necessarily qualified for an allegorical reading.[19] Even if a supposed origin for the work in the love of Solomon for his Queen is posited, as in the 1645 *Annotations*, instructions to readers to interpret the text as a spiritual allegory quickly leave any sense of individual human speakers behind, and in some cases a historical reading in terms of the life of Solomon is explicitly condemned.[20] In the face of consistent identification of the Spouse with the entire Church, male and female, it was considered transgressive to draw attention to the femininity of the major speaker in the book that is often called, rather inaccurately, *The Song of Solomon*.

In the early part of the century, male commentators had seemed deaf to the female-gendered voice of the Bride. Henry Finch's commentary of 1615 insistently applied the text to 'the Christian man': even verse 9 of chapter 4, 'thou hast ravished my heart, my sister, my spouse', is interpreted 'He doth behold us as the brethren of Christ'.[21] But then, his text is advertised as 'perused and published by William Gouge', whose views on the relationship between men and women were paraded to the world in 1622 in *Of Domesticall Duties*. There he elaborated on 'the generall head of all wives duties': subjection to their husbands.[22] Despite this, he vigorously refused the label misogynist (sig. ¶3r). However, concern about the woman's 'subjection' may be what this kind of reading of the Song of Songs demonstrates: the intimacy of the Bride with the Bridegroom suggested by the text offers an overturning of the early modern hierarchy whereby God is superior to men, who are superior to women.[23] Sylvia Brown argues that Thomas Goad, (chaplain to the Archbishop of Canterbury) who edited Elizabeth Jocelin's manuscript Mother's Legacy for publication in 1624, deleted a reference to the mystical marriage because the trope potentially offered too much spiritual privilege to women, (the natural referents of the term 'Bride') and therefore threatened patriarchal hierarchies.[24]

Women poets and the Bride

As one might expect, it was women poets who responded to the feminine voice of the Bride, rather than male ministers. Aemilia Lanyer's women-oriented *Salve Deus Rex Judaeorum* (1611), is a poem dedicated to various élite women and expressly takes the subject position of a woman speaker.[25] It contains some women-centred interpretations of the Bible such as *'Eve's Apologie'* (ll.761– 832) which is followed by a vindication of Pilate's wife and a sympathetic address to the women at the foot of the cross entitled 'The teares of the daughters of Jerusalem' (ll.969–1000) in which their compassionate behaviour is explicitly contrasted with male cruelty. Lanyer's evocation of the Resurrection is accompanied by two stanzas labelled in the margin *'A brief description of his beautie upon the Canticles'* (ll.1305–20). Appropriately enough, this is for the most part a version of the woman's description of her lover in chapter 5 of The Song of Songs, although an extra metaphor for the lips, 'like scarlet threeds', is imported from the blazon of the woman in chapter 4. The first sight of the risen Christ is offered in the context of the love affair with the Church:

> This is that Bridegroome that appears so faire,
> So sweet, so lovely in his Spouses sight.

The extract ends with the relationship being redefined as between Christ and the first person plural pronoun:

> His lips, like Lillies, dropping downe pure mirrhe,
> Whose love, before all worlds we doe preferre.[26]

Lanyer has recently christened Margaret Countess of Cumberland, her main addressee, as 'Deare Spouse of Christ': here she revels in the identification between her chosen readership of aristocratic women, herself, a court musician's wife who needs patronage, and the biblical Bride.[27]

Anne, Lady Southwell, writing in manuscript in the 1620s, uses biblical women—Debora, Abigail, Jael and Judith—to boost her confidence as a 'weake female' who dares to write poetry.[28] Two manuscripts survive of Southwell's long poem on the Decalogue, and the second, British Library MS Lansdowne 740, meditates more intensively on the position of the woman writer, and takes comfort in the figure of the biblical Bride. In the face of the scorn heaped by men on the early seventeenth-century woman writer, and especially the prophetess, she asserts the appropriateness of expressing her love of for Christ in the terms of the Song of Songs:

> Away, base world, hence shadows, hence away.
> You shalbee noe corriualls to my loue
> for hee is fresh as is the flou^rye may
> & truly constant as the turtle doue
>> his breth like beddes of roses cheere the morne,
>> his hayres reflex the sunne beames doth adorne.

She also has to confront a Puritan disapproval of poetry, and although she very strongly disapproves of printed publication, she does assert her right to use verse, as the divine Lover in the Song of Songs did:

> & though some amorous Idiotts doe disgrace it
> in making verse the packhorse of theyr passion
> such cloudes may dimme the sunne but not deface it
> nor marvell I that love doth love this fashion
> > To speak in verse, yf sweet & smoothly carried
> > to true proportions love is ever maryed.[29]

This view of Southwell's poetic activity within the privileged space of the garden of *The Song of Songs* is confirmed by her curate at Acton, Roger Cox, who seems to have been sent her poetry in manuscript. In his elegy for her he memorialises her poetic activity in a pun on her name:

> The South winde blew upon a springing Well:
> Whose waters flowed & the Sweete streames did swell.[30]

This is an explicit use of Canticles 4:16 to create the image of the inspired woman poet, safe in the enclosed garden from any unholy intrusion, open only to the breathing of the Holy Spirit which inspires her with holy poetry. Given her interest in the Song of Songs it is no surprise, perhaps, that Anne, Lady Southwell was a moderate Calvinist and Protestant internationalist: she was a friend of Daniel Featley and her second husband fought under the command of Horace Vere in 1620s Europe. Like other Protestant internationalists she uses the image of the Bride to talk about the true Church of God.[31] However, she also uses it very particularly to strengthen the position of women, as we shall see later in this chapter.

Female prophets and the Bride

In the first half of the century these uses of the Song of Songs by women were isolated: but from the 1640s onwards the start of the dramatic phenomenon which was the prominence of women's prophetic utterance drew attention to the potential empowerment that identification with the Bride of Christ offered to women. Mary Pope, author of *A Treatise of Magistracy* (1647) and two prophetic tracts, was a relatively orthodox writer, who thought her right to offer a prophecy was bolstered by spiritual claims to special treatment by God.[32] She represents herself as being 'an observer of the ebbings and flowings up and downe of Gods providence' over twenty years, and has 'gotten understanding'.[33] She seems to have obtained some kind of prominence in the church, 'God having made me a Mother in Israel'. Parliament, to whom she wrote so often, ignored her: she funded her own publications out of the salting business left her by her husband, and hired someone to present copies at the doors of Parliament.[34] She must have been known in London Presbyterian circles, as George Thomason, a potential sympathiser given his involvement in the 1651 Presbyterian Plot, supplies her full name at the end of his copy of her tract, and her address, The Harrow, in Friday Street. However, although she begins her work with fairly orthodox appeals to the precedent of Biblical women, her writing shows a transition to the kind of prophetic language used by the better known prophetesses of the late 1640s, suggesting that she has an important message from God to Parliament. Whether or not she was 'mother' to any particular church in London, her pamphlet is figured here as her child, prompting the idea that she is united to Christ in the mystical marriage. In one of her final appeals to Parliament, dated 27 January 1647, she announces 'there is a child to bee brought forth, which is neither Presbyterian nor Independent', a child to whom Parliament should listen.[35] She represents herself as in travail in the epistle to Parliament at the start of this book: 'this child shall not be abortive, but shalbe brought forth in due time, and borne a goodly child'. She raises the mysterious question of the fatherhood of this 'child': 'there has been much contending to find out who are the true parents of it', but as she designates herself 'the Handmaid of the Lord', and insists that God has given the words to her, the question of the tract's original authorship is not hard to solve (sig. B4r). She looks forward to an apocalyptic 'marriage of the Lamb', when the whole church shall share in her closeness to Christ (p. 130).

Despite Parliament's apparent neglect of Pope's petition, by the late 1640s, women prophetesses seem to have gained some credibility.[36] The status of prophetesses in the middle of the century is shown by the number of men willing to risk their reputations by introducing women's prophetic publications: in the case of Elinor Channel's prophecy, her discourse seems merely a vehicle for Arise Evans to offer his own thoughts, which constitute more than half of the 1653 pamphlet attributed to her.[37] In Hugh Peter's recommendation of Mary Cary's prophecy in 1651, we get some insight into the perceived source of the power of women's words.[38] Sue Wiseman points out that he raises the issue of her femininity, an aspect Mary Cary herself glosses over.[39] He compares her with conventionally learned women, Elizabeth of Bohemia and Anna van Schurman, who know foreign languages: however, he says 'this my countrywoman speaks the best language'.[40] He represents her pamphlet as 'the spouse's wish and longing' and quotes Canticles 8: 14 as a kind of summary of Cary's discourse: 'Make haste, my beloved, and be thou like to a roe or a young hart upon the mountains of spices.' Clearly his idea of authorised women's writing is the voice of the Bride from the Song of Songs. Mary Pocock, a close friend of John Pordage who in the Interregnum had led a radical community in Bradfield, Berkshire, had explicated the marriage trope to describe the relationship between King and Parliament in *The Mystery of the Deity in the Humanity* (London, 1649).[41] The Bride is the

Commons: the Upper House constitutes the king's daughters, other actors in the marriage scenario enacted in Psalm 45, which Beza had explicated as an introduction to his sermons on Canticles as 'a summe and abridgement of this whole Canticle'.[42] In the same work, Mary Pocock makes a statement of gender equality: 'Male and Female are all one in Christ ... the Lord is no respecter of persons' (pp. 44–45). For this radical community, where women played a prominent role, the spirituality of the Song of Songs was equally available to men and to women.

Anna Trapnel

There is no doubt that in mainstream culture of the late 1640s and 1650s women were perceived as being particularly open to the Holy Spirit, and one way of describing this close relationship with the divine was in the biblical words of the Song of Songs.[43] Despite the interpretative effort to annex the figure of the Spouse for Christian men earlier in the Reformation, there was clearly a sense that femininity could offer special access to the status of Bride of Christ. The best known prophetess of the period, Anna Trapnel, dated her genuine spiritual experience from the age of 14 when she heard Hugh Peters speak on the mystical marriage: 'he opened the marriage Covenant that is between God and his spouse'.[44] True to the discriminating power of the trope of the mystical marriage, she immediately discerned that despite her precocious spirituality she did not know God as she ought: a period of intense anxiety and grief was brought to an end on the first of January 1642. At this point she claims to have felt the Holy Spirit witnessing to her soul in the words of verse 3 of chapter 6 of the Song of Songs: 'Christ is thy wel-beloved, and thou art his' (p. 9). Two days later her mother died, and her aunt, suggesting that she should replace one intimate relationship with another, told her that now she must labour to be married to Christ: her modest answer, that she hoped she was already married to Christ, precipitated hours of 'terrible hell' because of the conditional nature of her reply, at the end of which she experienced what she calls the 'sealing' of the Holy Spirit. Thereafter she experienced the bliss characteristic of a prophetess: 'raptures of joy', and 'ravishings of spirit'(p. 12) and she began expounding Scripture to those who were close by.

   Although she accepts that this conversion narrative is written in a gendered voice, Sue Wiseman has questioned whether in her prophetic utterances Anna Trapnel was speaking as her self, a woman, or whether she was speaking 'for' God, and therefore not engaging with patriarchal authority in a way that makes sense to modern feminists.[45] Diane Purkiss has suggested that prophetesses find authority for their voice in the seventeenth-century marriage law of the *femme couverte*, in which the husband is responsible for the crimes or debts of his wife. As we shall see in the next chapter, this law was explicitly cited by Nonconformists later in the seventeenth century to describe the freedom from guilt they experienced on being 'married' to Christ. Purkiss suggests that women who consider themselves 'Brides of Christ' cannot at the same time belong to ordinary husbands, but this is I think a misreading of Jane Lead's *A Fountain of Gardens*. Jane Lead is not actually harbouring murderous impulses when she desires 'the death of the First Husband, who for so long hindered my Marriage with the Lamb'.[46] In Romans 7:4, and in Jane Lead's 1696 text, the 'First Husband' is in fact the law which condemns the believer's own sinful 'flesh', and this has to be destroyed by baptism before he or she can truly be united with Christ.

Another problem with the authorship of Anna Trapnel's prophecies is that the documents we have seem to have been copied down by an amanuensis while Trapnel was in a trance, a task that was acknowledged to be difficult, particularly when Trapnel was singing rather than praying.[47] Her words, then, might be considered as a hybrid discourse: when the amanuensis could not properly hear what she was singing, he presumably supplied the gaps with material that a prophetess would be expected to say in the radical context of Fifth Monarchist religious politics. An untitled folio volume in the Bodleian library, which has been characterised by James Holstun as marking her September 1657 separation from the Fifth Monarchists meeting at Allhallows' Church with a radical group, was probably produced in this way.[48] It helps to clarify radical thinking about the significance of the figure of the Bride for prophetic women, and demonstrates the power of the trope to function beyond the pages of what had been considered a rather limited allegory. The first page of the first section—dated October 11 1657 at 9 o'clock precisely—sets out the role of the Spouse which is, alongside the Holy Spirit, to sing of Christ—to 'bring/Tydings unto the world of/Christ the most glorious King'. This role for the Spouse is extra-biblical, particularly in terms of her equality with the Spirit, and goes rather beyond the Bride's role in the Song of Songs. In fact soon after the start of her poem, Trapnel is situated in exactly the situation of the Spouse in chapter 5 of Canticles—being attacked by the watchmen: 'they at her do strike. For they did tear and rent the vail /Of Christs beloved Wife'. Not present in the original text, but a key feature of Trapnel's discourse, is the fact that the unspecified enemies— 'they'—are attacking her for her song, her praise of her Lover.[49] Trapnel's song makes much of this criticism, as perhaps a reader might expect from a prophetess who has been attacked for her utterances. One of their specific criticisms is a literary one—they object to one of the similes she uses. In fact, this simile, the pomegranate, which her discourse compares to 'his temples', and 'his locks', is straight out of Canticles 4:3, and 6:7, 'as a piece of pomegranate are thy temples within thy locks'. Trapnel's text graciously explains to her detractors that this is an Emblem, and that she must use emblems to describe Christ, although he is 'above/All Emblems'. Some of the biblical metaphors are used in her description of Christ, although it must be said, they are the less exotic ones—his eyes are 'Dove-like', he is like the cedar, his countenance is 'like Lebanon' (Canticles 5: 15). Some of this early discourse, on the second page, is taken straight from Canticles: 'Ten thousand can't compare' with Christ (5:10), she is 'ravish'd' with his eye (4:9), 'O how lovely is he!' (5:16). The mini-narrative in chapter 5 is reinterpreted as a story about the perfume imparted by Christ which causes her to follow him: there is no blame here for the Spouse as in the commentaries, but the episode where Christ disappears from outside the door is seen as an instance of the 'drawing' process desired in 1: 4:

> After him she did go.
> She knows the King had been there,
> It was his very touch,
> Because the King had drawn her heart,
> She therefore loved much (p. 2).

The importance of the Spouse's song is emphasised throughout this section. Trapnel herself, or her scribe, has obviously received the text of the Canticles as a female-authored document, and it is the role of the Bride as singer that is appropriated for her. Clearly this identification with the Spouse of Canticles helps to validate her prophecy at this key point in the volume. The Song of the Bride is referred to later in the volume as a way of constructing the text itself: a paraphrase of parts of Canticles is included, so that Trapnel's poem is grounded in the authority of the Bride's song, from which it branches out (p. 14). At one point this poem seems to be identified as the same kind of discourse as the song of Deborah, and another biblical woman, Jael, is mentioned as the heroine of Deborah's song (p. 69). The choice of these figures is clearly meant to authorise and reinforce the author's femininity here as in other female-authored texts: Trapnel's spiritual song is described as wine, and as butter, a commodity that featured in Deborah's song.[50] However, no point about the validity of women's discourse in general is being made. Midway through the volume a conventional condemnation of women's utterance as 'idle talk' occurs, (p. 211) and a criticism of women as being too ready to speak. Moreover, Eve is censured as a representative sinning woman:

> ... he made Creation rue,
> Through the yeilding of *Eve* to that
> Which did so tempt and ensnare;
> And therefore, Hand-maids, you ought now
> To have the greater care.
> O let some learn what evil hath been,
> And how it actively doth grow;
> And do not you go tattling, and
> With such a tongue to and fro.

The affirmation and validation of Trapnel's prophecies is found in the extraordinary women of the Bible: that affirmation is not extended to women in general. In fact, women's own words will always be unacceptable: the lesson to be learnt from Eve's example is that female human utterance should be replaced by divine discourse.

> This should learn Females to be slow of speech
> To have very few words from self,
> Because this Sex had such a first voice,
> But to look to the Lord for help (p. 211).

Trapnel thinks that her power as a prophetess is in emulating a divine feminine voice in the Scripture: as an extraordinarily receptive woman, her voice is that of the Spouse. She is an exception to the majority of women, who can ventriloquise the speaking voice of the Holy Spirit. Her long fasts, which brought no physical harm to her, were miracles which proved that her body was unlike that of any other woman. Ironically, this is far from the spirit in which Reformed commentary interpreted the mystical marriage, as a privileged relationship with Christ for all believers, accessible in theory to all women.

Poetic 'babes' of the Bride

The Bride of the Song of Songs was also an inspirational figure for more mainstream women of the 1650s. An Collins has been described as everything from Catholic to Quaker, but her *Divine Songs and Meditacions* (1653) actually celebrates the current Independent establishment as the fulfilment of the vision of the English Reformation.[51] Moreover, the Discourse at the start of the work rehearses her theological beliefs in the terms of the Catechism produced by the Westminster Assembly, placing her in the mainstream of Presbyterian/Independent thinking. Early in the volume she claims the role of the Bride in Canticles 5 and rehearses its narrative, as is typical of this kind of spirituality, in terms of a spiritual drama between herself and the Christ who knocks at the door of her heart.[52] Her rather free lyric poetry is perhaps intended to represent the spontaneity of the inspiration of the Holy Spirit, in opposition to the 'frozen forms long since compos'd' which probably refer to the liturgies of the Church of England.[53] She describes her own poetic activity in terms of her enclosure in the garden of the Song of Songs:

> ...As a garden is my mind enclosed fast
> Being to safety so confind from storm and blast
> Apt to produce a fruit most rare
> That is not common with every woman
> That fruitfull are.[54]

Here, she is denigrating the child-bearing capacity of ordinary married women compared with her exceptional experience as the unmarried spiritual bride of Christ. It is not clear what 'fruit' she is producing, but she is imitating the strategy used by influential men earlier in the century, such as John Donne and John Cotton, of seeing spiritual offspring from her relationship with God: perhaps she is thinking of her poems, as she calls them 'the offspring of my mind.'[55] For An Collins, spiritual marriage and spiritual reproduction are clearly superior to their fleshly equivalents. The importance of physical chastity is inescapable: Peter Stallybrass has spelt out the importance of the enclosure of the Song of Songs as a common figure for virginity in the early modern period, and An Collins exploits this association to the full.[56]

The tendency to compare real men rather unfavourably with the divine, perpetually eligible bachelor is developed in the work of another anonymous poet, 'Eliza', who developed the poetic and religious potential of the Song of Songs for women.[57] Like An Collins, 'Eliza' saw her poems as her 'Babes', the offspring of her marriage with Christ. Published as 'Eliza's Babes' in 1652, the volume elaborated on the gendered implications of the relationship between Christ and the individual soul as expressed in Canticles. The spiritual bliss she experiences leads her to turn down several earthly marriage offers, which she consistently describes as 'thraldome', and her poem 'The Bride' makes this choice seem rather logical:

> Sith you me ask, Why born was I?
>   I'll tell you; twas to heaven to fly,
> Not here to live a slavish life,
>   In being to the world a wife.
>
> When I was born, I was set free,
>   From mortals thraldom here to bee;
> For that great Prince prepar'd a bride,
>   That for my love on earth here dy'd.
>
> Why not I then earths thraldom scorn,
> Sith for heavens Prince I here was born?[58]

This noble spiritual aspiration is somewhat fleshed out by a poem entitled 'The Lover' in which she purports to sit down with a friend and discuss sweethearts.

> Come let us now to. each discover,
> Who is our friend, and who our Lover,
> What? art thou now asham'd of thine,
> I tell thee true, Ime not of mine...

> For He's the purest red and white,
> In whom my soule takes her delight;
> He to the flowrs their beauty gives
> In him the Rose and Lilly lives.

As the poem proceeds, using the language of the Spouse's blazon in the Song of Songs, the spiritual language shifts into a carnal register, and Christ mutates into Cupid:

> His pleasant haire with seemly grace,
> Hangs by his faire sweet lovely face,
> And from his pleasing eyes do dart
> Their arrows which do pierce my heart.[59]

'Eliza' is no An Collins, crippled with illness and with no real marriage prospects, but is from a good family with connections at court, and she does in fact marry, a match that is arranged for her and which initially she deplores: subsequent poems record that she is pleasantly surprised by this worldly experience. But this is surely an instance of Sharon Achinstein's observation that 'in female vocalisation of desire for God, female desire is also transvalued, sanctioned, and given full expression without subordination to patriarchal norms'.[60] The poetry of this anonymous woman reveals the existence of a feminised erotic ideal, sanctified and spiritualised by the biblical text but probably mobilised by Petrarchan poetry and the language of the romance, particularly popular with women in the court circles within which 'Eliza' moved.[61] 'Eliza' exploits to the full the way that her own spiritual desires, expressed in a supremely feminine register derived from the Song of Songs, free her at least in spirit from enslavement to the patriarchal institutions that would otherwise control her life.

The spiritual journal and marriage with Christ

'Eliza's poetry seems to combine sacred and profane imagery: but in more orthodox religious discourse such as commentary and sermons an impermeable barrier between carnal and spiritual interpretation of the Song of Songs seems to have been assumed. The continued warnings about profane readings of the Song of Songs suggest a belief in the attainability of an entirely holy interpretation. An essential part of correct reading was a de-sexualisation of the text, implying a de-gendering of the main characters within the Song of Songs. The many references to gendered bodies were explained in abstruse allegorical terms. The 'breasts', for instance, which frequently recur in the text, are interpreted as the Old and New Testament in most commentaries. However, during the 1650s there is evidence from other kinds of texts that this exclusion of gendered interpretation was no longer absolute. One 1658 publication revealed a male-sanctioned model of female devotion based on the Song of Songs: *A wise virgins lamp burning; or Gods sweet incomes of love to a gracious soul waiting for him Being the experiences of Mrs. Anne Venn.* The longer title offers key pieces of information, showing that it was adopting the pattern of male-approved publication familiar from the 'Mother's Legacies' genre earlier in the century. This woman is related to a prominent man, '*(daughter to Col. John Venn, & member of the Church of Christ at Fulham)*'. Her writing is in manuscript, composed in her closet, and she is already dead: it is '*written by her own hand, and found in her closet after her death*'. All these circumstances give this discourse maximum political effect. The self-display involved in publication, so abhorred in the female sex, is avoided by the fact that this writing was doubly private—in her closet, and in manuscript—and that the deceased Anne Venn is now unable to take advantage of any praise or publicity forthcoming from this printed work. All this is emphasised in the preface by her editor, well-known Independent minister Thomas Weld, and her exceptional devotion is characterised in the words of the Song of Songs: 'having...*found her beloved, she took him, and caught him, and held him, and would not let him go,* Oft saying with the Spouse, *Let him kiss me with the kisses of his mouth, for his love is better than wine*'. (sig A3v). Her spiritual diary, kept since the age of nine, is a fascinating record of the ecclesiastical journey, rather familiar in the Interregnum, from the Church of England to Presbyterianism to Independence, sprinkled with the names of famous preachers of the day such as Christopher Love, Walter Cradock and Stephen Marshall. In March 1654 at the age of 28 she utters a prayer, in effect a petition to become a Bride of Christ:

> The 11th of this first Month the Lord drew out my heart very much to beg of him to manifest himself in the relation of Husband to my soul, more and more letting him to find and feel what it was experimentally to be embraced by him, and gathered up into more intimate communion with him (p. 239).

Her prayer is clearly considered by her editor to be answered within the text, although her meditations are less a description of 'what it was experimentally to be embraced by him', as sermon notes from the many Independent services she attended, at Westminster Abbey and elsewhere, in which a frequent subject is the loveliness of Christ, the subject of treatises in the late 1650s by Presbyterian Thomas Watson and Independent John Owen.[62] Notable towards the end of the diary is the manner in which a sermon by her Fulham pastor Mr. Knights on Psalm 43:7, 'Thou hatest iniquity', is transformed by her note-taking into a sermon on the beauty of Christ (pp. 322–326). However, the contents of her diary are not quite as rapturous as suggested in the preface: she certainly does not reiterate the particularly erotic words of Song of Songs 1:2 as Weld claims. Weld's representation of Venn as continually using the words of the Song of Songs, a discourse clearly identified by him as signifying exemplary femininity, is actually his own construction of her devotional language. Weld's status as prominent Independent minister implies that in the 1650s, the rhetoric of the mystical marriage became the approved spiritual discourse for women.

The practice of keeping manuscript diaries as Anne Venn did seems to have blossomed from the mid-1650s, although Tom Webster traces a tradition of journal-keeping from Richard Rogers' 1603 *Seven Treatises*.[63] In 1652, Isaac Ambrose, as part of his treatise on the entire Christian life, *Prima, Media, Ultima*, prescribed the recording of 'Evidences' and 'Experiences' as crucial to the middle part of a Christian's life. In his sample record, the Evidences are proof to the Christian that he is saved. Experiences are both good and bad: some are political, some are social, some are of the deepest spiritual nature and correspond to the intimacy with God and the desertion by God charted in the Song of Songs. Ambrose's definition of 'Experiences' is 'Real proofs of Scripture-truths' and the examples he gives us chart a reading of Scripture that is profound in its engagement with the text.[64] Life experiences as validated by the scriptural text constitute proof—'evidence'—of God's work in the life of the believer. Not surprisingly, his experience of spiritual bliss in 1641 is linked to texts concerning the relationship between Christ and his Bride in Canticles and Revelation. Samuel Petto's 1654 *Roses from Sharon, or Sweet Experiences* was a record of his relationship with Christ, using the language of the Song of Songs. John Beadle's *The Journal or Diary of a Thankful Christian*, based on a 1633 sermon, followed in 1656, confirming the advice to record every spiritual experience, and the Scripture that gave rise to it.[65] Women seem to have made particular use of this practice: funeral sermons for women often mention such journals. Edmund Calamy's 1657 sermon for Mrs. Elizabeth Moore, which included her own 'Evidences for Heaven', 'proofs' that she was saved taken from the experiences of her own life, became a seventeenth-century bestseller, and must have confirmed the idea that the manuscript journal was ideal feminine writing practice.[66] Samuel Clarke's exemplary lives of women often contain excerpts from their journals as evidence of their holiness.[67] Manuscript diaries from Presbyterian and Independent women around this period confirm that in their personal devotions they are encouraged to construct themselves as the Bride of Christ.[68] Several women record in their manuscript journals feelings of spiritual bliss, in conjugal terms, including Mary, Countess of Warwick, friend to John Beadle, and patron to many ejected nonconformist ministers.[69] Her chaplain John Woodruffe's digest of her journal takes care to include her visits to powerful politicians such as Chancellor Hyde and Court aristocracy, including the King and Queen, and to exclude much of her personal devotion. The original journal is in fact far more preoccupied with her relationship with Christ than with her relationship to aristocratic human beings. Even Woodruffe, however, records her reading of the Song of Songs in January 1668. Her favourite quotation is from Canticles 7:12, which had been the epigraph for Samuel Petto's 1654 volume, 'there will I give thee my loves'. This is Mary Rich's response: 'it pleased God to affect exceedingly my heart, and to make me with pantings and breathings of soul to beg that God would this morning give me his love'.[70] 'There' in the Song of Songs is the vineyard: for Mary Rich it is her 'wilderness', where she spends many hours in communion with Christ. Canticles 7:12 features frequently in her diary, although it is usually excised by Woodruffe, who does, however, record her statement that her 'soul was ravish'd with desire', a phrase straight out of Ambrose.[71]

Elizabeth Turner, née Broadnax, whose father was a Cromwellian general, and whose Independent family was prominent in encouraging nonconformist resistance to persecution in Kent, also left a spiritual journal. It started on May 9th, 1658, and continued until 1677, by which time it had become a yearly assessment of her spiritual condition made on 14 February—her wedding day. Earlier in her marriage, however, a different kind of wedding had been more important to her. She includes in her journal entry for 22 January 1666 an 'amazinge covenant' based on the marriage service, marking her betrothal to God: 'I doe heer wth all my power accept thee for my head & husband: for better for worse, for all times & conditions: to love honor & obey thee before all others ... neither life nor death shall part betweene thee & mee.'[72] Words like 'ardent', 'ravishing', 'precious' and 'longings' permeate her discourse in the early part of the diary. It must be said that her many pregnancies, the worry of educating her children, stepchildren and nephews and nieces who became her responsibility on the death of her brother and sister, somewhat modified the rapturous tone later in life. Ollive Cooper, a Presbyterian from Nottingham, who struggled with breast cancer and an abusive husband, recorded, in orthodox spiritual journal fashion, her 'evidences' of salvation, and also her frequent renewals of her covenant with God. Her journal contains just one poem, a version of the second chapter of the Song of Solomon, verses 1–6:

> I am the rose of sharon faire
> The lilies of the field
> Theres none with thee that can compare
> Thou causest me to yield
>
> As appletrees amongst the trees
> Soe is my love for faire
> amongst the sones theres none that can
> with my belovd compare
>
> He brought mee to his banquet house
> Our covering was love
> Stay mee with flagones comfort mee
> for i am sick of love

with apples faire and beautifull
and pleasant to my taste
he fed me theare while with both armes
wee lovingly imbraste.[73]

The vivid, erotic discourse of the Song of Songs seems to have inspired in this ordinary Nottinghamshire woman the desire to express her own feelings for Christ in a poetic register. She is clearly appropriating this language in a more than metaphorical sense: the sensual words of the Song of Songs signify spiritual feelings that are almost tangible. Along with many other women, she uses biblical words that are easy to translate from their 'literal' meaning to their 'allegorical' meaning in the love of Christ for the soul: the images she uses for her own poem do not require a complex hermeneutic to describe her own spiritual experience. The words she adds of her own are those of response to the words of the Bridegroom in the biblical text; 'Thou causest me to yeild', 'theres none that can/with my belovd compare', words that are as at home in a spiritual register as in a romantic one. The conclusion of her poem is in a mutual embrace, an ending which is perhaps incorporated from some version of the romance genre; certainly this piece of writing constitutes a rare essay into literary writing by a woman of 'the middling sort' who has not had a literary education.

Some modern critics have characterised such writing as escapist fantasy, but this somewhat dismissive attitude does not lead to a careful reading of women's manuscript writing in context. Julia Palmer was the wife of a radical Presbyterian minister, and her manuscript 'Centuries', two hundred lyrics composed between 1671 and 1673, and dated in spiritual journal fashion, explore the same register of feelings as the more conventional spiritual journals, connected to her loving relationship with Christ. In this type of lyric, as opposed to paraphrase, it is inevitable perhaps that language from other types of love poetry will intrude into the strictly biblical register. There is no doubt that Palmer would have eschewed the reading of romances, and romantic poetry, as an ungodly Royalist practice, yet she often employs sub-Petrarchan diction: 'It is a sweet tormenting pain/To burn in strong desire' (p. 127).[74] The power of the biblical tropes describing the mystical marriage seems to sanctify for Palmer the associated romantic discourse that is often drawn into her poetry. She constantly describes herself as 'lovesick' and 'longing', contemporary words for desire which of course are validated by the text of the Song of Songs. Many poems chart her desire to die and to be with Christ, a state of mind which is the logical extreme of the piety of the mystical marriage, where full consummation is always deferred until death. One poem, addressed to Mr. H., expresses her consistent longing for death, and then records her indignation at being rebuked by a mere mortal:

Oh pity Lord, a love-sick soul
Doe thou my state, sweetly condole

> And take mee up, with thee to dwell
> Out of this dark, and durty, cell
>
> But stay a while, what's this I hear
> Thers one that would put me in fear
>
> As if in longing, to be gone
> I were, most grosly, in the wrong.[75]

Julia Palmer's indignation is unsurprising in view of the number of sermons which have lauded the desire of Christians, and Christian women in particular, to be with Christ. One of the earliest and most popular biographies of a woman, *A Christal Glasse for Christian Women*, was of Katherine Stubbes, wife of popular author Philip Stubbes, who died in 1592, at the age of 19. This pamphlet was reprinted throughout the seventeenth century, and according to Ian Green, 'provided a model to women of what a "godly" life should be like'.[76] The pamphlet records with approval her willingness to die, to forget her earthly husband and child, and to murmur her love and longing for Christ even when she appeared to be asleep: 'Oh my sweet Jesus, Oh my love Jesus, why not now: sweet Jesus, why not now'.[77] Elizabeth Turner at times also passionately longs for death, and attributes this longing to her ecstatic experience of Christ's love.[78] Julia Palmer feels justified in desiring death, in spite of Mr. H's claim that it is legitimate to ask for long life. Occasionally, however, Palmer does apparently achieve a kind of fulfilment on earth: some of her titles, such as number 32, 'The soul in an extasy of admiration, at the beauty of Christ, and the sweetness of communion with him', reveal the potential for an almost sensual bliss in her relationship with Christ, and perhaps explain the frequency and depth of her longing for a consistent sense of Christ's love for her. The final poem of her two Centuries incorporates words from the Song of Songs and ends with the last words of the Bible at the end of the book of Revelation:

> Oh deerest Jesus, come away
> My soull doth faint, with thy delay
>
> Oh take thy steps, both larg, and wide
> And quikly, fecth away thy bride
>
> Who would from hence, faign be releas'd
> To solemnize the mariage feast
>
> And ever take repose, and rest
> In her deer bridgrooms, sacred breast

Till in his arms, shee be, intwin'd
What comfort, can shee, take, or find
....
Come, Lord Jesus, come quikly.[79]

There is no consummation here, except in the vividly-realised imaginative vision of future heaven. There is an incipient literariness in the poem which at the same time is deeply bound up with the true words of Revelation, and ultimately with the Song of Songs: the rhyme and rhythm, while simple, add to the urgency of the expression of desire. Despite its closeness to the spiritual journal in its dated form, this document is not, as those manuscripts so often are, limited to the prose description of states of mind: it attempts to replicate in literary strength and passion those states of mind. Julia Palmer felt her 'Centuries' important enough to leave to two well-known Nonconformists, Joseph Biscoe and James Pitson: she clearly felt that her poems contained spiritual truth but it would be interesting to know if other readers agreed that her experience could be counted as valuable spiritual 'evidence'.[80]

The mystical marriage and political resistance

Julia Palmer's poetry charts a particularly troubled period for Nonconformists in England, the period leading up to the Declaration of Indulgence in 1672, and could be seen as an escape from difficult circumstances. However, in Julia Palmer's 'Centuries', poems of spiritual intimacy alternate with overtly political poems. State Papers show that the Declaration was a strategy by the Charles II's government to defuse possible Nonconformist opposition to the third Dutch War: Julia Palmer's writing demonstrates that she at least was not persuaded, despite the fact that her husband received a licence to preach at the Declaration of Indulgence.[81] Her manuscript reveals that in this period, the piety of the mystical marriage is certainly not an introspective, quietist phenomenon. For Julia Palmer, it is a strategy for survival in a period of persecution, as it had been for martyrs of an earlier period. Julia Palmer's poems and Elizabeth Turner's journal both express fears of a French-led Catholic invasion of England and a subsequent return of the experience of martyrdom. The anti-Catholic writer of *The Christian Life and Death of Mistris Katherin Brettergh*, another account of an exemplary young woman dying in childbirth in 1601, sees her joy in Christ and her longing for death as proof of the truth and effectiveness of the Protestant religion under great stress:

It must needes be a divine Religion and a truth comming from God, that thus can fill the heart and mouth of a weake woman ... with such admirable comfort. And a wretched conceit, and mere Antichristian, is that religion which so hateth and persecuteth this faith.[82]

The politicised spiritual discourse of the mystical marriage is shared by another group of women from a radical Presbyterian context in Scotland, a coherent group characterised by anti-popery and opposition to Indulgence from the Crown, just like Julia Palmer. David Mullan has recently uncovered fifteen autobiographical manuscripts from late seventeenth-century Scotland, where radical Presbyterians suffered more violent persecution than their sisters south of the border.[83] In his edition of several of these manuscripts, most of which have been preserved by transcription, David Mullan help-fully lists the Scriptures quoted in these narratives, and the Song of Songs figures prominently. Many of these women, who come from differing class backgrounds, were politically involved in resistance to the Crown. Marion Fairley's husband William Veitch was involved in the Pentland Rising in the 1660s and remained politically opposed to the Stuarts to the extent that he landed with Monmouth's forces in 1685. Henrietta Lindsay was the devoted stepdaughter of the Duke of Argyll; he was executed in 1685 after the abortive rebellion that was meant to coincide with Monmouth's efforts in the West Country. Both these women clearly intended that their journals should have a wide circulation, and eighteenth-century copies of Marion Fairley's still exist, implying that this was indeed the case.[84] These women are all Covenanters, and it is their habit to renew their commitment to Christ on regular occasions: Mullan speculates that these narratives provide a wider context for this repeated covenant.[85] However, the Scottish journals share the vocabulary and structure of those from the English Presbyterian/ Independent context, where the regular taking of the Covenant was not so prominent. The origin of these journals from both countries is, I think, that traced in Ambrose's *Media*: in the imperative to record spiritual experiences, both as evidence for the writer that she is saved, and as encouragement to other Christians. Sarah Savage, a member of the famous Henry family, Cheshire Presbyterians, wrote many volumes of a spiritual journal, some of which survive in later copies and were clearly circulated: in her journal she herself records reading other women's 'lives' which do not seem to have been printed publications.[86]

In the very long journals which have been discussed so far, external event, whether calamitous or propitious, is subordinated to the writer's perception of her ongoing relationship with Christ. All these journals read more as the record in minute detail of the relationship between the writer and Christ than as diaries in the more conventional sense with their descriptions of daily life and external occurrences, which makes them frustratingly opaque as an historical source. Ollive Cooper, having given a short but intriguing account of the circumstances of her difficult first marriage, comments scorn-fully that 'temperall favours' are 'but the dark side of gods goodness' before reverting to the (for her) more compelling narrative of the love between her-self and Christ.[87] Contemporary readers would of course have more idea of the events which were the backdrop to the spiritual narrative, and which are clearly intended to be a significant element. The years after the Argyll rebellion, when Henrietta Lindsay's husband was fleeing from justice in Holland, and before his triumphant return with William of Orange, were clearly full of incident for her: she obliquely alludes to events in Windsor, London, Amsterdam and Rotterdam. However, the drama of her narrative is in her perception of Christ's absences and presences, a drama no doubt underlined for contemporary readers by their understanding of how spiritual favour interacted with temporal favours. Such a drama of withdrawal and disclosure is precisely that which seventeenth-century interpreters discerned in the Song of Songs, as we have seen in the previous chapter, and so it is not surprising that Henrietta Lindsay frequently employed the words of the biblical book. David Mullan comments on her frequent employment of a metaphor in Chapter 2 verse 9, 'my beloved... looketh forth at the windows, showing himself through the lattice', which he feels to have been influenced by a reading of James Durham's popular commentary on the Song of Songs.[88] The metaphor of the lattice through which Christ can be imperfectly discerned captures the elusive nature of Christ's dealing with the believer during the hostile events in the world, or the spiritual opposition of Satan, of which these women are so conscious. Henrietta Lindsay's detailed journal charts every appearance of Christ to her, however veiled, as well as the spiritual attacks of the enemy. Here is her description of 'a hid enjoyment' that she experienced while visiting the Court at The Hague in 1687:

> one half-hours access to the Son of God, who in the remotest corners of this earth and in the hardest circumstances than most of the world would think possible to bear up under, yet O quhat lot can he not sweeten and make delightsome, quhen his blessed countenance ... is felt and found in it (p. 321).

A paragraph of quotations from the Song of Songs follows. What is remarkable is the confidence with which she assumes she can stand in for the Bride in all the erotic utterances of the book, whether directed to her from her lover or vice versa: at one point she even rewrites verse 3 of chapter 2, 'as the apple tree among the trees of the wood, so is my beloved among the sons' so that it reads 'daughters' rather than 'sons'.[89]

Perhaps the most exquisite use of the Song of Songs in this Scottish context is a verse paraphrase dedicated to the Countess of Caithness by Barbara Mackay.[90] Mary Sinclair, Countess of Caithness, was the sister of the Duke of Argyll. Barbara Mackay was from a devout Presbyterian family, whose allegiances were complex: her brother, Hugh Mackay, was a major-general with James II's army, but landed with William in 1688 and became his commander-in-chief in Scotland.[91] Whatever Barbara's specific allegiances (her husband was a royalist soldier) her manuscript was included in James Wodrow's collections relating to the persecution of Presbyterians in

Scotland: the page before Barbara's paraphrase is headed, 'D. Of Monmouths Declaration'.[92] It may be that Wodrow, who collected these documents in the early eighteenth century, knew more about Barbara's specific allegiances: however, the status of the Song of Songs as an archetypal text of anti-Catholicism with a well-established function of strengthening a readership in persecution may have been enough for Wodrow's purposes. That Barbara Mackay was indeed anti-Catholic is shown by her own poems included at the end of the manuscript: 'The authors confession off faith', fol. 27v, includes anti-priest sentiment and anti-transubstantiation remarks.

The importance of the Song of Songs is clear in the dedicatory verse to Mary Sinclair: 'Of all that ever I wust in my time/I have herein the Marrow to you sent' (fol. 9v). The Song represents the most important truths that Mackay has learned. The introductory verse gives the framework within which the Song should be interpreted:

> This sweet dealgoue that point out the Love
> Betwixt the creature and his Lord Above (fol. 10r).

In the paraphrase, however, as in the Biblical Song of Songs, there is no mention of Christ at all. Just occasionally there is a touch of theological interpretation, such as when the wall or lattice behind which the lover is obscured is described as being the result of sin (fol. 11r). In true Presbyterian fashion, there is a reference to predestination as God's decree inserted in 5:12: the lover's eyes are described as washed so that 'he can always see/ What e'res the lot off all he did decree' (fol. 14v). The focus of Mackay's paraphrase is not doctrine, however. The introduction to the Song of Songs explains why it is more important than any other song, 'most pretious rare' as Mackay puts it. It is a poem of overwhelming emotion, even eroticism, yet it remains absolutely chaste and legitimate:

> For puritie it is the truth most pure.
> It ravisheth, it captivates, it charmes
> All sound affections in the beloveds armes (fol. 10r).

Verse paraphrases of the Song of Songs tend to preserve the eroticism of the text simply because there are so many sense impressions that are part of the imagery, and the two lovers' bodily presence is so strongly realised. Mackay's verse is even more sensual than that of most paraphrases of the Song of Songs as her brief expansions of the text can emphasise the physicality of the love affair. Thus 1:13 is paraphrased quite closely, in a way that does not hint at an allegorical meaning of the verse:

> As bundle of Myrrh from the spicie tree
> My sweet beloved he is so to me

> He shall ly down with pleasure and delyte
> Between thy breasts and there rest all ye night (fol.10v).

There is no mention of beds in the original text of 8:3, and Mackay's version supplies a setting all too recognisable as the site of physical love:

> When I would sleep in his beloved bed
> His holy hand would uphold my head
> And that my Joy might all ye more increase
> His glorious right hand might me still embrace (fol. 16r).

What Barbara Mackay has learnt in her life, the thing that is most precious, is that for her Christ is a real and sensuous presence. Because the Song of Songs is holy, she can use its extravagant language, and even elaborate on it, without the fear, particularly strong for women, that she will be carried away into excessive and illegitimate emotion.

Divine lover versus earthly husband

One of the benefits of using the Song of Songs for these women is as an outlet for a strong desire that is couched in entirely feminine terms. One of Julia Palmer's poems most indebted to the Song of Songs, Poem 41, begins with a celebration of lack of inhibition:

> Come now my soull, let Loose on Christ
> thou needst not fear excese
> When thy afections ar att high'st
> his love deserves no lese.[93]

Puritan women in particular were taught to avoid excess of emotion, particularly for their children, who were very likely to die.[94] Mary Rich blames her own romantic longings, fostered perhaps by her reading of romances in her youth, for her disillusionment in marriage: 'it was not safe to let my heart ever again too freely to go out unto any person or things of this world'.[95] Elizabeth Jekyll's diary records her sense of sinfulness at loving her husband too much: the Puritan God is jealous of any earthly being who might take first place in the affections of a believer.[96] For Palmer, who was married to a Presbyterian minister, Christ threatens to replace the figure of her earthly husband, a potentially transgressive feature of her spirituality perhaps detected by Mr. H. However, this type of devotion for women seems to have been encouraged by Nonconformist leaders in the Restoration: in 1672 Thomas Vincent spoke to a convention of Presbyterian women on the theme of *Christ the Best Husband*. In a departure from commentary earlier in the century, he stressed that women in particular are called to be Brides of Christ (p. 2). To encourage the women present to that role he points out that Christ does not ask a dowry, he will never seek a divorce, and he will never lead them on until he has gained his wicked will (pp. 24–6). Sharon Achinstein suggests that this kind of Nonconformist teaching used the Song of Songs 'to shore up monogamous heterosexual relations within the realm of the family' in the face of Court libertinism.[97] It is true that in the Restoration Christ is constructed as the ideal Nonconformist husband, in opposition to the rakes of the Court: but this reinforces the danger that, given the expressed benefits of a spiritual marriage as opposed to a physical one, a spiritual woman such as 'Eliza' might turn her nose up at a mere mortal, be he never so holy.

The literary tradition in which many of the versions of the Song of Songs originated, whereby the Biblical poetry was seen as a substitute for 'rebald songes', as schoolmaster John Wharton asserted in his preface to Jude Smith's paraphrase of the Song of Songs in 1575, only confirmed that love for Christ was spiritually superior to love for ordinary men.[98] Elizabeth Melville, Lady Culross, developed this literary tradition by writing a sacred parody of Marlowe's famous love lyric, in which Christ the shepherd calls to the soul, his beloved:

> Come live [with me] and be my love
> And all these pleasurs thou shalt prove
> That in my word hath warned thee
> O loath this life and live with me.

The place that the shepherd is gesturing towards is not an earthly Arcadia, but a heavenly Paradise: the rest of the song makes clear the choice that is to be made between sacred and profane love.

> Thy heart is mine I bought it deir
> Then send it not a whooring here
> This lawless lust and love prophane
> Such pleasures false shall end in pain.

In the first assessment of Elizabeth Melville's practice of sacred parody, Sarah Ross has described this poem as drawing on a popular tradition to subvert the values of secular love poetry, whilst adhering to its structures: 'it exemplifies her use of verse to enact Calvinist doctrine and to critique secular Petrarchism, all the while exhibiting a delicate handling and love of poetic language, metre and form'.[99]

Of course, the economic security provided by earthly marriage ensured that most of Thomas Vincent's listeners would not use his teaching to scorn human suitors, and most of Elizabeth Melville's readers would not entirely eschew human passion. However, Lilias Dunbar's journal shows how her espousal to Christ could interact with more tangible marriage offers. Here, the experience of the mystical marriage confirms her in her resistance to an unwelcome suitor:

> The next day after I had received his letter, when I was seeking the Lord in secret, I found the Lord Jesus manifesting his love to me with his kingly power so that my soul was ravished with love to him, and my heart made his captive and no other's.... I gave no answer to that letter. I was made to believe without doubting that he to whom my soul was espoused would be a provider to me in temporal things.[100]

Elizabeth Isham's fifty-thousand-word 'Booke of Rememberance' seems to have been partly conceived as a way of explaining to her family her life-long resistance to earthly marriage.[101] When marriage negotiations with John Dryden, uncle of the poet, were broken off for financial reasons in 1632, 23 year old Elizabeth Isham distracted herself with Sidney's *Arcadia* and Spenser's *Faerie Queene,* as well as with spinning and making lace: when tempted by Satan to worry about being single, however, she comforted herself with John Randall's *Saint Paul's Triumh, or the Saints conjunction with God* (1626):

> Looke into the booke of *Canticles* with a spirituall eye, and there we shall see this Communion of the beleeving soule with Christ... there is never a stitch nor passage in it, but is from love. (31–2)[102]

What is clear is that women are being offered, and even enjoying, a spiritual experience that they are taught to call a marriage with Christ, an experience which reinforces their femininity and validates it. They are so confident of the benefits of the role of Spouse that they able to compare earthly husbands unfavourably with their spiritual Husband. Several of the authors of spiritual journals had unhappy marriages, whilst many of the other authors were frequently absent from their husbands. Julia Palmer's husband was away preaching for much of her marriage, and Elizabeth Turner's was often called to London to help defend legal cases against Nonconformists. The Countess of Warwick is very conscious of being torn between her duties to her husband and her duties to God. She is grateful for the time to pray while her bad-tempered husband is asleep, and her critique of earthly romance implies that God is jealous of a woman's human lover: 'God is so merciful ... as to throw down our idol and his rival'.[103] Earthly husbands feature very little in journals such as Henrietta Lindsay's. The Song of Songs offers the construction of a mutually fulfilling relationship that very few early modern women experienced in human and physical terms.

It is possible that Sharon Achinstein is right in positing the origins of this imagined experience in the romance genre. For Nonconformists, however, this type of writing was deeply transgressive, and certainly not on their reading lists: Mary Rich regrets the time she spent in reading romances. The Song of Songs becomes the true romance of which romantic fiction is a Satanic copy. Unable to believe that the romance genre does not hold a strong grip on the Nonconformist female imagination, Ramona Wray finds in the piety of the mystical marriage a reconciliation between two powerful states of mind: 'spiritual longings and romantic imperatives find their meeting place in the personal relationship between a male divinity and a female believer'.[104] Whether or not romance remains an imperative for the Nonconformist woman who has eschewed the snares of earthly love, it may be that the divine sanction of the book of the Song of Songs serves to keep feminine romantic feelings within her experience. Certainly women of the mid-century do not write about their husbands or lovers in the same terms in which they talk about God. Even 'Eliza', pleasantly surprised by marriage, saves her rapturous poetry for her divine Husband. This is as it should be; the earthly relationship is a pale imitation of the divine archetype expressed in the Song of Songs, which offers a woman's response to a mutually-fulfilling love relationship, sanctioned by its inclusion in Holy Writ, and available for appropriation by any believer. The results for women's self-esteem and self-expression are obvious in the manuscript and print publications of the seventeenth century.

It is tempting but inaccurate to describe these religious narratives as 'romances', as Mary Anne Schofield asserts of Quaker women's writing. She claims that translating from real-life stories into prose, borrowing from an existent and already popular literary form, the romance, these seventeenth-century accounts retell the speaker's trials and sufferings in the context of the romance heroine and her dilemmas.[105]

She finds evidence for her assertion in these words from Elizabeth Stirredge's 1711 *Strength in Weakness Manifest*:

> Oh! That desolate Place where I used to retire alone, how many times hath my Soul met her Beloved there, that hath sweetly comforted me, when my Soul hath been sick of Love; and full of Doubts, for fear my Beloved had left me, and forsaken me. But Blessed be his Name that liveth for ever, he still appeared in a needful Time.[106]

Schofield's comment is 'while outwardly maintaining the religious purpose, the language and plot situations are loaded with romance topoi and nuances.' For Schofield, the religious 'coverings approved by the male world' are merely a convention: what she sees as the romantic story-telling gives 'truer sounding of the feminine Quaker voice'(p. 64). Schofield seems to be using a model of the romance genre rather unfamiliar to the seventeenth century, where in any case romances are popular not with the radical women who write accounts of their spiritual experiences, but with a more aristocratic Royalist constituency. Ramona Wray notes that Mary Rich, countess of Warwick, read romances in her youth, a practice she later deplored: nevertheless Wray traces the persistence of romance structures in Rich's autobiography, a process which probably needs more explanation than she seems to think is required.[107] Schofield may not have noticed that Stirredge is clearly referring to the Song of Songs, with its mini-dramas of the appearances of the divine lover alternating with the Bride's perceived abandonment by him, rather than any secular text. The point is that for these seventeenth-century women the religious element is the 'romance' of their lives, although they would have refused the unpleasant word: rather than secular literary tropes, they are using the motifs of the Song of Songs, a text with a rather longer history and more favourable politico-religious associations than the romance genre which is so often invoked. The tedious, repetitive detail of the manuscript journals testify to a frustrating experience of desire temporarily fulfilled and then deferred, the very process illustrated in the Song of Songs, rather than Schofield's simplistic imposition of the romance plot on women's spiritual narratives: 'rescue occurs, the heroine is saved, the lover returns.'

The Song of Songs and women's writing

When I began this chapter I was convinced that the very existence of a poetic, Biblical text largely in a woman's voice was a decisive factor in the development of women's writing in the seventeenth century. As we have seen, there is a demonstrable link between the Song of Songs and what Michael Mascuch has called 'the advent of the diary and related forms of recording first-person discourse in writing during the seventeenth century'.[108] However, I now wonder whether in some cases the use of the Song of Songs, admittedly widespread and clearly influenced by gender, made the next stage of development in authorship—from non-literary genres such as the spiritual journal to self-consciously literary genres like poetry and a more modern conception of 'autobiography'—more conflicted for women. It is demonstrable that the text of the Song of Songs feeds into the material of the spiritual journal, but as we have seen, the origins of that genre are in providing factual material—evidence—to demonstrate the workings of God in an individual life. The profound and ubiquitous use of the Biblical text to validate the experiences of the spiritual journal only serves to delineate the factual, truthful nature of the written word and distinguish this use of writing from literary composition.

Roland Greene sees what he calls 'the refusal of invention' as a female-gendered practice typical of women's writing, but he is really considering translation and paraphrase where there is little room for creativity: it would be necessary to compare the Psalm paraphrases of, say, Philip and Mary Sidney, to establish whether there are any real differences related to gender alone.

More controversially, he asserts that most Calvinist writers 'are not interested in depicting the human psyche in any particularity', a criticism that he again applies mainly to women.[109] The terminology here, which implies that these writers are aware of the individual human psyche but decline to represent it, is a little unhelpful and perhaps lacking in historical specificity. In spiritual terms, Calvinism, with its narrative of God's approach to the soul and that soul's highly individual response to God in very particular circumstances, allows for an introspection and detailed scrutiny that surely helped to develop the modern conception of the psyche. The literary representation of such a psyche, however, is a separate development: critics tend to date the first appearance in literature of a recognisable modern subjectivity only towards the end of the sixteenth century. The conflicted attitude to literary representation which is particularly associated with women's authorship is bound to inhibit the development of literary subjectivity in women's writing. What is lost from any simplistic opposition of the truthful and the literary is any sense of the necessity of imaginative construction of the self. In its least sophisticated manifestation, this leads to the appropriation of the Biblical words of the Song of Songs without any sense of context or of speaker, as in Ollive Cooper's stanzas, which are intriguing only in the context of what the reader has learned about Ollive Cooper from the autobiographical elements of her journal. The further away from the Biblical text the poem travels, the more room there is for a sense of personal voice: Julia Palmer, whilst her repetition of some of the Biblical concepts is somewhat irritating, manages to give a sense of individual agency and distinctive personality that although not sophisticated or literary, still gives the reader a satisfaction that is based on the imaginative appropriation of a recognisably individual speaker behind the words. The more that women's writing engages with literary models, the more it is able to communicate the imaginatively-constructed sense of a speaker that all successful literature incorporates, and to use the shortcuts that are part of literary convention to suggest an individualised human origin for the text. For example, Elizabeth Melville by adapting Marlowe's secular poetry constructs the divine speaker of her poem 'A Call to Come to Christ' as lover, in the same mode as, if very different to, Marlowe's passionate shepherd.

This distinction is more obvious when applied to the determinedly non-literary spiritual journal and its closest 'literary' equivalents. Elizabeth Isham's 'Booke of Rememberance' is, like its cousin the spiritual journal, a record of her thoughts, feelings and spiritual experiences, but it is more than that. Like the spiritual journal it is intended as a record of fact, but for the benefit of readers other than herself—her immediate family, as she states at the start of her journal, with the imperative of explaining to them her decision not to marry.[110] With this purpose comes the necessity of creating a coherent and understandable character whose innermost voice the written word can be believed to be expressing. It helps that Elizabeth

Isham had recently read St. Augustine's *Confessions*, which has done so much to establish the literary conventions whereby the subjectivity of the speaker is conveyed: she refers to the *Confessions* throughout her 'Booke of Rememberance' and calls her document her own 'confessions'.[111] She also describes the inspiring role of the *Confessions* as she began to write.[112] Thus, like Augustine, she supplies detail of locations and places in which many of the incidents described in her 'Booke of Rememberance' take place. She includes depictions of many of the principal characters that help to establish them as characters in a kind of drama: that drama is continued on an internal stage with self-questioning and debate, allowing access for the reader to an engaging, imaginatively realised speaker.[113] As with Augustine, the reader is involved with the speaker's thoughts and dilemmas to a point where close identification happens: like Augustine, she does not automatically concur with the opinions of authority figures, a process which helps to establish her as a distinct and rather interesting individual.[114] The self-conscious construction of memory seems to be the key to the imaginative creation of past incidents and emotions. In Augustine's tenth book, the one that he later described as 'written of my selfe' as opposed to being dependent on Holy Scripture, he indulges in a long self-conscious reflection on the power of memory, particularly in recreating emotions.[115] The resulting document is much more like the modern autobiography than it is the spiritual journal, for instance in the recreation of the death of a friend in Book 4: likewise, in instances such as the deaths of her mother and sister, the reader has a well developed sense of the character and identity of Elizabeth Isham.[116]

Mary Rich's long spiritual journal is a good example of the limitations of the genre. Despite her élite education and wide reading the document is full of repetitious statements about her continuing and intimate relationship with Christ: even Anthony Walker, her great admirer, selected heavily for the shorter version he published as *Eureka, Eureka* in 1678. She herself used the journal as an aid to meditation on her own spiritual life. Mary Rich also wrote a kind of autobiography, which she also meditated on, but one suspects that it supplied her with a different kind of material. 'Some specialties of the life of M. Warwicke', an autograph manuscript in the British Library, surveys her life from 1625 to 1674, yet is much shorter than the journal: the journal records her writing of 'specialties of my fore-past life' on 8–10 February 1671.[117] The selected material includes external events much more than it discusses her inward spiritual condition, which nevertheless drives the whole narrative. Ramona Wray considers it to be indebted to the romance genre, as we have seen, and indeed the narrative does cover her marriage, which was resisted by her family, although it does not expose the difficulties and heartbreak she was later to experience at Charles Rich's hands, and which we know about from the journal. Wray is probably right to conclude that in the autobiography Rich depicts her marriage as part of God's plan in that it brought her into a godly family: she is always alert to ways that the providence of God might reveal itself. Isaac Ambrose considered that the spiritual journal, with its conscientious recording of diurnal detail, would fulfil this revelatory function. However, it may be that Mary Rich needed to see larger patterns and clearer directions for God's intervention in her life, and thus wrote something like the modern autobiography, with its clear narrative and selectivity of detail. The document is far more literary than the spiritual journal, reading much more like the exemplary Lives that were by now very popular in Nonconformist circles. After extensive treatment of her love for Charles Rich, in which she represents herself as the victim of plotting between her sister-in-law Elizabeth Killigrew and Elizabeth's mother, a 'cunning old woman', Rich constructs herself as the good wife, an interpretation much more clearly signposted than in the conflicted spiritual journal. God is shown to be vindicated in allowing the marriage in spite of her father's justifiable objections. What is difficult to agree with in Wray's analysis is that these structures are taken from the romance genre. Whilst her youthful passion for Charles Rich is given full weight, the consequences of their private marriage are not positive, and her love for her husband is seen as disobeying God's command.[118] The most important factor in the whole story, and the end to which the narrative tends, is not the importance of earthly love but the unfailing mercy of divine grace. Literary this narrative certainly is, in terms of its shaping and writing, but the literary genre is imitates is not the romance. Self-construction is essential to this narrative because it shows her conversion from one kind of person—specifically, the kind of person who read romances and saw plays, to a very different woman. She had been determined never to become a Puritan but afterwards, she says, 'I hardly knew myself'.[119] An important feature of this document, then, is an imaginative construction of Mary Rich both before and after conversion.

The narrative concludes in three stages: the first charts the end of their dynasty with the death of Charles' 'wild' brother Hatton in 1670 and draws the moral that both Charles and Mary were being punished for not wanting many children in their youth. Charles had been worried about money, and Mary herself had been worried about the loss of her looks.[120] The additions to the manuscript first of all describe the death of Charles in 1673 as 'the greatest trial of my life': she is comforted by the fact that she has been such a good nurse to him. The final entry records the marriages of the nieces, Ann, Mary and Essex Rich, whom she had brought up: she concludes with prayers for them and the sense that her own worldly work is complete.[121] The document is much more of an exemplary life than a romance; if anything, the 'specialties' is an anti-romance, in that it charts a shape for her life that is not dependent on human passion, but rather on repentance, conversion and a godly existence. We can supply from the journal that the love of Mary Rich's life was not Charles Rich but Christ. The journal is not a satisfactory reading experience because the literary construction of the speaker, and the shaping of daily life, is absent, as it must be if the writing is to be treated as recording the evidence for conclusions about God's dealings with the individual, in other words as truth rather than a human invention. This is a feature of many if not all of women writers' engagement with the Song of Songs in the seventeenth century: although it is poetry, because the Song is taken from the Bible it is regarded as referring to absolute truth. It is helpful in encouraging godly women to write in non-literary ways, but it is rare that the model of the Song of Songs fosters literary authorship in a woman writer.

Transgressive brides

The evidence from mainstream women's religious writing of the seventeenth century, in manuscript and in print, is that they perceive an imperative to value their status as the biblical Bride more highly than their earthly status as married women. More radical constituencies could take the subordination of earthly marriage even more seriously. In 1650 Humfrey Ellis of Winchester had published a very stern pamphlet against a serious abuse of this teaching: *Pseudochristus: or, A true and faithful relation of the grand impostures, horrid blasphemies, abominable practises gross deceits; lately spread abroad and acted in the county of Southampton, by William Frankelin and Mary Gadbury, and their companions. The one most blasphemously professing and asserting himself to be the Christ, the Messiah, the Son of God who dyed and was crucified at Jerusalem for the sins of the people of God. The other as wickedly professing and asserting her self to be the Spouse of Christ, called, the Lady Mary, the Queen, and Bride, and Lambs Wife.* According to Ellis, Gadbury used to attend the radical congregations of John Goodwin and Henry Jesse in the late 1630s. She had been married, but was abandoned by her husband. She was illiterate, and lived by selling laces and pins for gentlewomen.[122] However, she manifested the signs of a prophet: a voice spoke in her, and was accompanied by physical trembling. When William Franklin arrived in her presence she testified that he was a prophet too: at which stage sexual ambiguity raised its ugly head. He spent the night under the same roof as Gadbury, leaving her open to the charge of 'keeping a naughty house'. The court at the Guildhall dismissed the charge, but the two left for Hampshire, where, in November 1640, she claimed, according to Ellis, to be '*the Spouse of Christ, the Bride, the Lamb's wife*'. Of course, this claim designated Franklin as divine: yet in the heady years of the early 1640s, many believed in the validity of the couple's claims, and in their visions, including a respected local minister. Alarmingly, Gadbury kept asserting that she was going into labour, raising speculation about what kind of child would be born from this prophetic couple, but no baby ever appeared (p. 16). Opinion in Hampshire was fiercely divided over whether Franklin and Gadbury were immoral impersonators, or indeed Christ and his Spouse. Finally they were tried in a local court, where the focus was on the nature of their physical relationship. She denied that they had sexual intercourse, but was laughed at: when confronted with evidence of their past sexual relationships, she asserted that because both were now dead to sin, such an accusation was no longer relevant (p. 50). The court, however, found otherwise: and the author of the pamphlet is left claiming that the wickedness of this pair was worse than that of John of Leiden, William (Frantic) Hacket, or any Anabaptist.

A woman who flew in the face of contemporary culture by taking the words of the Song of Songs too literally was always going to get into trouble. From 1659 for a period of at least twenty years, Anne Wentworth used her perceived position as the Bride of the Song of Songs to resist male authority, including her husband, and the leaders of the Baptist church. In 1677 she published a defence of her conduct, *A Vindication of Anne Wentworth*. She represents the cause of their dispute as her desire to publish prophetic writing. Her husband resented her vocation, which clearly did not tally with what he expected from a wife: 'it was necessary for the peace of my Soul, to absent myself from my earthly Husband, in obedience to my Heavenly Bridegroom, who called and commanded me to undertake and finish a work, which my earthly husband in a most cruel manner hindered me from performing, seizing and running away with my Writings'.[123] Her pamphlet uses the trope of the Bride of Christ in two distinct ways. As with many polemical treatises of the seventeenth century, she posits the true Church as her own constituency, although it is not clear whom she includes in this category besides herself. It is rather a shock to see the Baptist Church with named elders, including her own pastor Nehemiah Cocks and the well-known leader Hanserd Knollys, stigmatised as the enemy, as 'formal professors' and therefore false Christians (p. 11). These were the very terms in which Hanserd Knollys in his own treatise on chapter 1 of the Song of Songs had categorised the Church of England: 'false Ministers and formal Professors' who had brought in 'Antichristian Inventions and Superstitious Traditions'.[124] However, the Baptist movement is clearly not radical enough for Anne Wentworth, particularly in its view of women's ministry. She insists that her story of oppressions by men and deliverance by God should be made public, and complains that her writings have been seized (p. 11). Her 1679 volume of prophecy, *The revelation of Jesus Christ just as he spake it in verses at several times, and sometimes in prose, unto his faithful servant Anne Wentworth, who suffereth for his name* seems to have been published by a non-mercenary female friend, who gives supporting evidence that Wentworth's husband turned out of her house (pp. 22–3). Wentworth herself complains 'I am reproached as a proud, wicked, deceived, deluded, lying Woman; a mad, melancholy, crack-brained, self willed, conceited Fool: and black Sinner, led by whimsies, notions, and knif-knafs of my own head; one that speaks blasphemy' (p. 19). What sustains her, as she makes clear in *A Vindication*, is her sense that Christ is her true husband. She records, on

3rd of the 11th month, 1670, the 'comly bands of Marriage': 'then was the full communication between Christ and my soul, the Love knot' (p. 11). Her belief in this relationship gives her endurance in her sufferings, and the drive to write: 'My heavenly Bridegroom has come, and has given me courage, with an humble boldness, and holy confidence to speak the truth in all faithfulness, and to fear no man ... his left hand is under my Head, and his right Hand doth Embrace me, his Banner over me is Love' (pp. 9–10).

Anne Wentworth might have expected the support of another radical religious community who had a history of promoting women's ministry, and who read her pamphlets: one of the few instances available of one woman commenting on another's writing. This was none other than John Pordage's group, to be designated The Philadelphian Society in 1690s London. By then they were rather less radical than they had been in the 1640s and 1650s in Berkshire when Elizabeth Poole, who was consulted by the Army Council, had been connected with them, and despite the similarity in their spiritual experiences, Anne Wentworth was too politically active for them in the 1670s. John Pordage was still putting great faith in women, and his current spiritual partner was Jane Lead, whose prophecies were to become well known. According to Julie Hirst, it was under the preaching of the antinomian Tobias Crisp that Jane Lead determined to become a Bride of Christ, and this seems to have been a common feature of female devotion within this community.[125] Jane Lead's spiritual journal, printed as *A fountain of gardens watered by the rivers of divine pleasure, and springing up in all the variety of spiritual plants; blown up the pure breath into a paradise, sending forth their sweet savours, and strong odours, for soul-refreshing* and with the epigraph of Canticles 4:16 and 6:2, describes her longing for her marriage with Christ, and the Voice of the Bridegroom that encouraged her towards that experience in November 1674.[126] Ann Bathurst, who also lived with the Pordage family, left manuscripts which have been copied and edited and placed, according to the inscription on the flyleaf, in 'Dr Heath's Library at Mrs Brackley's in Tufton Street, Westminster'. Her writing resembles a spiritual journal, beginning in 1678, but it is even more ecstatic than the more mainstream women's manuscripts from earlier in the century, and she frequently breaks into verse. Here are the first eight lines of a poem in which she celebrates her status as the Bride, in the context of her diary entry:

I know not but our own Ears are unfitt to know all that is in the Bed-Chamber with us & our King; and so not fit to be fully revealed to us, nor fitt to be heard by others who have not knowen the Same; unless we can believe tho^ we have not seen: to such I say

The Espousal Knott I've not forgot
It is of Sacred Memory

> The Nuptial Knott, yea double Knotts
> I have overliv'd to sie.
> Long since I married was in Time,
> Unto Eternity
> but Time has held us all so long
> Scarce any yet set frie.[127]

Long since 'espoused' to Christ in more orthodox fashion, Bathurst has survived to experience the full consummation of her spiritual marriage, referred to as the 'Nuptial Knott', which she describes as 'double' presumably to indicate the excess of her joy. She is more than usually coy about the bliss which she experiences in the 'bedchamber', and the suggestion of sexual experience is inescapable, even if that suggestion is there in order to suggest that intimacy with Christ surpasses earthly intercourse.

Despite the similarity in the terms in which the mystical marriage relationship is described, Jane Lead did not respond favourably to Wentworth's prophecy. In 1677, Wentworth's prophecies were much talked of in London, by 'some considerable and otherwise ingenious persons' as informers to the Secretary of State reported.[128] She had in fact written, from her home of eleven years, Kingshead Court, Whitecross Street near Cripplegate, to the King, via the Mayor of London, on 31 July , predicting a catastrophe before New Year's Day.[129] Jane Lead had read her work carefully, as her journal for 29 December 1677 reveals:

> Upon the Consideration of *A.W.'s* Prophecy, it was advised me, that we should have no part with her in divine Justice, nor be Agents in the avenging property, in desiring Plagues and Vials of Wrath to come so immediately upon the Formal Churches. It was shewn me, that it was not the Time, nor the Manner revealed yet, how they should be overturned.[130]

Lead's disapproval of the vengeful nature of Wentworth's prophecies, which conflate prophecy with denunciation of named individuals, helps to indicate that her version of the piety of the mystical marriage concentrates on the individual and spiritual application of the trope. The traditional application of the text of the Song of Songs to particular churches, the true and the false, is absent from the writing of Lead and Bathurst: their concerns are fundamentally non-political. The different directions taken by Anne Wentworth and Anne Bathurst in their spiritual writing of the 1670s indicate the range of uses that women made of the biblical book of the Song of Songs in the seventeenth century. Available to women in particular, it seems, was identification with the Bride of Christ which enabled spiritual application of the erotic text to their own lives. The number of autobiographical documents which chart this romance with the divine indicates how important and how fulfilling this biblically-sanctioned spiritual experience was in the lives of women from very different backgrounds, from mainstream Nonconformist denominations to radical sects. There is more work to be done on how this kind of spirituality intersected with women's experience of earthly marriage in the seventeenth century, but it is clear that the relationship is a conflicted one, the spiritual discourse often compensating for or comparing favourably with a less than ideal relationship with earthly husbands. When these kind of direct comparisons were made, of course, the absolute separation between the discourse of divine love and that of human sexuality which allegorical interpretations of the Song of Songs demanded became untenable. In the case of the 1650s Berkshire community, where living arrangements were unorthodox—Mrs. Flavell, who had an illegitimate child that Pordage explained away as her niece, actually shared a bedroom with Pordage and his wife—the use of the mystical marriage trope perhaps explains why Pordage was accused at one and the same time of promiscuity and of unnatural abstinence from sex.[131] Not all readers, it appears, were able to make the absolute distinction between spiritual and carnal readings of the Song of Songs that holiness demanded, and these more worldly-wise Christians were suspicious of those who claimed to experience the mystical marriage. The *schadenfreude* on prominent display in Humfrey Ellis' pamphlet about Mary Gadbury shows how irresistible the fall from superhuman holiness to all-too-human lustfulness was to many seventeenth-century readers.

The Church as Bride and women's rights

It is clear, however, that women who drew implications for their own lives from an identification with the spiritual Bride of Christ found the text of the Song of Songs genuinely empowering. In her reply to Joseph Swetnam's *The Arraignment of Lewde, idle, froward, and unconstant women*, Rachel Speght finds comfort in the Song of Songs for real women:

> not few, but many times, doth our blessed Saviour in the Canticles, set forth his unspeakeable love towards his Church under the title of a Husband rejoycing in this Wife; and often vouchsafeth to call her his Sister and Spouse, by which is shewed that with *God is no respecter of persons*, Nations, or Sexes.[132]

This is a rather subtle argument for women's equality from the feminine epithets of the Song of Songs. Speght's interpretation of 4:9 is different from Henry Finch's, quoted earlier in this chapter: it is sensitive to the female gender of the Bride. Even more claims are made for women on the basis of the feminine gender of the Bride of Christ by Anne, Lady Southwell. Her short poem from the 1620s is a particularly witty example of the 'Defence of Eve' genre. It begins with a statement of the problems of real men and real women in contemporary marriage.

> All.maried.men.desire.to.have good wifes:
> but.few.give good example.by thir lives
> They are owr head they wodd have us thir heles.
> this makes the good wife kick the good man reles.

In response to the men's contempt, Southwell relates the creation of Eve from Adam's rib to the birth of the Church through the wound in Christ's side. Not only does this rescue Eve from her traditional opprobrium: implicitly, all women are dignified simply through their ability to identify with the female-gendered Bride. The proto-feminist message of the poem depends on the Bible's choice of a female type, the Bride, to represent the Church:

> When god brought Eve to Adam for a bride
> the text sayes she was taene from out mans side
> A.simbole of that side, whose sacred bloud.
> flowed for his spowse, the Churches savinge good.

Just as the Church was born when Christ's side was pierced at the crucifixion, so the first woman was created out of a rib from the side of Adam: God confers status on real women through His choice of a female type. Lancelot Andrewes had suggested a similar manoeuvre in 1591, to prove the relative importance of Eve over Adam.

> *St. Paul* saith, *Ephes. 5.25.* that the creation of *Eve* and her marriage, is *magnum Sacramentum,* shewing us the mysterie of Christ, the second *Adam,* and his espousage to the Church, which was his *Eve* taken out of his side.[133]

The comparison of the birth of Eve and the birth of the Church had first been suggested by St. Augustine.[134] This typological pattern, however, is not always enlisted to a polemical end. Lucy Hutchinson, writing a poetic version of Genesis in her 1679 epic *Order and Disorder,* takes care to elaborate the parallel between the creation of Eve and the creation of Christ's Bride, the Church at the crucifixion. The second Adam, awakened from death, speaks to his newly-formed Bride in the language of the Song of Songs: 'My spouse, my sister,' said he, 'thou art mine'. The balance of the relationship here, however, is typical of that portrayed in the treatises of Restoration Dissenters: the unity between Christ and the Church is one of absolute strength and total weakness.

> As my victorious triumphs are all thine,
> So are thy injuries and sufferings mine.[135]

There is no room for pro-women sentiment in such an analysis, which is no surprise in a poem which is published anonymously, and which does not reveal its author's feminine gender. Southwell, however, takes the opportunity to complain that the status and love that should be the right of real women by virtue of their comparison with the female Bride is not usually forthcoming from men. The poem is framed by uncomplimentary remarks about men and finishes with a joke at their expense:

> This is a.misterie, perhaps too deepe.
> for blockish Adam that was falen a sleepe.[136]

The mystery of the marriage between Christ and the Bride, and its implications for the way they should treat their wives, is just too hard for most men to understand.

Polemic on the status of women was a feature of the earlier part of the century, culminating in the pamphlet debate started by Joseph Swetnam.[137] In the later seventeenth century Quaker women used the text of the Song of Songs to argue for the equality of men with women, particularly in terms of speaking and writing. This is particularly interesting as Quaker women use the spirituality of the Bride of Christ no more than Quaker men: the spirituality of the mystical marriage is not seen as gendered.[138] Quaker practice, however, which offered authority to many women, sometimes needed defending, as in this rather clever argument from *An Answer to the Objection of the woman forbidden to speak in the Church*.[139] St. Paul, of course, had famously forbidden women to speak in church, suggesting that they should ask their husbands at home if they want to know something: this Quaker's answer brilliantly conflates the mystical marriage with the text from 1 Corinthians 11:34.

> Christ being the head of his *Spouse,* or husband of his *Church,* the *Spouse of Christ* being united unto him, and betrothed in *Righteousness,* both asketh of him, and staying at home taketh counsell with him, though the Harlot from home, and the Stranger unto him knoweth it not (p. 16).

Applying the trope of the Bride particularly to women, the writer argues that she is privileged by this intimate relationship with Christ, has learned from her divine Husband at home, and is thus qualified to preach in public. The most famous Quaker defence of preaching women, Margaret Fell's *Woman's Speaking Justified* of 1666, has been hailed as by Catherine Belsey as evidence that women had 'found a voice' in seventeenth-century England.[140] Judith Kegan Gardiner attributes Fell's own confidence as an author to her identification as 'a mother in Israel', and charts this authorial presentation in various pamphlets.[141] However, Fell's justification of women's discourse in general starts with the argument Rachel Speght had used from the words of the Book of Canticles: 'the Lord is pleased , when he names his Church, to call her by the name of *Woman*' (p. 4). The next stage of Fell's argument is a rather greater conceptual leap, arguing from the metaphorical language of the Bible for the spiritual status of women: 'Thus much may prove that the Church of Christ is a woman, and those that speak against the woman speaking, speak against the Church of Christ' (p. 5). The final link in the argument is to show the woman who is the Bride of Christ actually speaking: 'Is not the Bride compared to the whole Church? And doth not the Bride say 'Come'? Doth not the woman speak then? ... the Bridegroom is with the Bride, and he opens her mouth' (p. 17). These arguments are the natural outcome of the increasing identification of real women with the biblical Bride over the course of the seventeenth century. This kind of thinking seems to have empowered Quaker women, who publish more volumes than other seventeenth-century women, and unlike them, do not feel disqualified by their gender from public discourse.[142] Outside of the specific arguments considered here, where women's status is the subject matter of the pamphlets, there is simply no need for Quaker women writers to preface their writing with excuses for publication or apologies for their inadequacies as women: their position as the Bride of Christ who is able to speak is simply assumed.[143] In this aspect, as in many others, Quaker women's writing is markedly different from much female-authored writing of the century.

Conclusion

In that most popular of exemplary lives of women, *A Christal Glasse for Christian Women*, Katherine Stubbes' obsessive bible reading was held up as a particular virtue for godly women to emulate:

> you could seldom or never have come into her house,, and have found her without a bible, or some other good booke in her hands. And when she was not reading, she would spend the time in conferring, talking and reasoning with her husband of the worde of God.[144]

It was inevitable that the radical and intimate engagement with text recommended by Reformed biblical commentary would result in important consequences for women who read the Song of Songs. Women's religious writing of the seventeenth century, whether in prose or verse, demonstrated a profound identification with the Spouse who is a central female speaker in this text. Whether authorised or unauthorised by important men, it was only a matter of time before this apparently allegorical figure would come to have a particular significance for real women. The gendered body of the Spouse was indicated at every turn by the sensual language of the Song of Songs, no matter how assiduous the attempts to divert attention from her flesh by assigning detailed and often absurd spiritual meanings to corporeal entities. In any case, as we have seen in a previous chapter, Protestant allegory tended to simplify the tortuous hermeneutic of Catholic commentaries, and produce the biblical text as a straightforward analogy of human sexual relationships with the mystical marriage. This chapter has traced the growth of a spirituality which seems to have been regarded as particularly feminine in character, based on an identification with the biblical Bride by many seventeenth-century women. It is clear from a study of manuscript documents that such identification offered pleasure, confidence and self-esteem in a society where such positive experiences were not easily accessible to women. The extravagant nature of the descriptions of such spiritual bliss indicates that many women found their highest earthly happiness in their relationship with Christ. In these cases, the text of the Song of Songs, so much of it in a female voice, seems to have helped women articulate a distinctively feminine experience, in a register with inescapable connections to female sexual desire.

One of the fruits of this self-confidence was the impulse to authorship: the encouragement of Reformed commentary to engage so closely with the biblical text meant that words in the feminine voice of the Bride could be adopted as one's own with minimal anxiety. This is probably the source of the confidence which David Mullan discerns in the authorship of the Scottish manuscript journals, despite the lack of published writing by women in the same period.[145] Poets and pamphleteers used the text more boldly, as direct encouragement to women to engage in authorship. The fact that a high proportion of the few surviving seventeenth-century documents authored by women appeal to the text of the Song of Songs shows how important it was, both as authorising strategy and as content for women's writing. The Bride of the Song of Songs was a poet, and her authoritative discourse became the inspiration for many of her female readers in the seventeenth century. Many women who believed they were the Bride of Christ expressed that faith in words, even if not many went further into full-blown literary authorship.

6
Politics, Metaphor and the Song of Songs in the 1670s

The last chapter has charted extensively the influence of the Reformed inter-pretation of the Song of Songs on women's writing. However, the main story of this book, to which the last chapter serves as somewhat of a subplot, is one with a broader historical import: the implications of a Reformed reading of the Song of Songs for English religious politics of the seventeenth century. This chapter shows the reaction of Anglican clergymen committed to the Restoration settlement of the Church of England to the reading of the Song of Songs that was dominant in the seventeenth century and that has been charted in this book, and describes some of their preferred alternatives. The political implications of such a reading were well recognised by many Anglican controversialists, and suspected of being one of the causes of the theological daring that inspired the Puritan Revolution. The error in Biblical interpreta-tion, as many Anglicans saw it, that led to a personal reading of the mystical marriage trope as a love affair between Christ and the individual believer, was seen as a mistake in the reading of metaphor as well as a theological misread-ing of the beneficial effects of redemption and justification for the individual Christian. This Anglican revisionism, inspired by Royalist politics, involved a profound rewriting of many of the most prized theological insights of the Reformation, and this chapter charts attempts to do just that.

One of the commonplaces of English literary history is a perceived attack on excessively metaphorical prose style in the Restoration: a demand for plainness articulated by clergymen of the Church of England who were also members of the Royal Society. Half a century ago, R.F. Jones used Thomas Sprat's 1667 text, *The History of the Royal Society,* to argue that this attack was motivated by a scientific concern for accurate representation.[1] His work was so influential that it has only to be cited for this proposition to be taken as proved, as in this recent literary history of Nonconformity: 'As is well known, this repudiation of figurative language became the orthodoxy of the Royal Society in its *History* (1667) by Thomas Sprat.'[2] However, in 1980 Brian Vickers showed that Jones' analysis of Sprat's text was actually a misreading, accusing Jones of a lack of historical awareness in an awful warning to all early modern literary scholars: 'No seventeenth-century figure wrote in a vacuum, although some modern scholars do.'[3] Vickers is certainly right about Sprat, who spends the first part of his book in a careful construction of the historical context for his prescriptions on style. In these first chapters Sprat posits an interdependence of culture, politics and language in a way that would satisfy the most rigorous New Historicist. Since 'there is an agreement between the growth of *Learning*, and *Civil Government*'(p. 29), upheaval within the latter implies the disruption of the former, a disruption that can be traced in textual practice. Thus 'the short history of learning'(p. 16) which R.F. Jones found in the first part of *The History of the Royal Society*, is actually a military history: rather than Swift's 'battle of the books' for which the whole of the seventeenth century, in the view of R.F. Jones, provides interesting intellectual background, this is the kind of warfare in which people get hurt.

The immediate context for *The History of the Royal Society* is of course a succession of one *annus horribilis* after another: the period 1665–67, with its three-fold curse of plague, fire and humiliating war, topped off with the fall of Clarendon. Nicholas van Maltzahn has vividly charted the forces for political instability operating in 1667, the context for the publication of *Paradise Lost*, of course, as well as *The History of the Royal Society*.[4] One theme of the publications of the winter of 1666–67 which Sprat draws attention to is the sense of crisis induced by the widespread belief that the nation was under the judgement of God:

> This wild amuzing mens minds with *Prodigies*, and conceits of *Providences* has been one of the most considerable cause of those spiritual distractions of which our Country has long been the *Theater* (p. 362).

Sprat blames the political instability of late 1660s England on an overdramatic religious discourse which has its roots in sectarian conflict, perhaps expressed in publications such as Thomas Vincent's *God's Terrible Voice in the City*, which laid the blame for plague and fire firmly on the ejection of godly ministers in 1662 and the implementation of the Five Mile Act in 1665. This volume had gone into six editions by 1668, which is not surprising, considering its vivid eyewitness account of both disasters.

Various targets have been assumed for Sprat's well-known prescriptions on plainness of style. Nancy Armstrong and Leonard Tennenhouse suggest he had in mind 'the florid rhetoric and Latinate polemics of Caroline intellectuals'.[5] The less well-known parts of Sprat's work which precede and follow his literary recommendations in fact answer the question: they constitute a political attack on the Nonconformists, whom he considers the inheritors of the opinions and practices of the Civil War. He calls them '*Holy Cheats*'. This phrase echoes the title of a 1661 volume by Roger L'Estrange, *The Holy Cheat*, an attack on John Corbett, Civil War activist and respected

Presbyterian, a volume that began L'Estrange's twenty-year crusade to discredit Nonconformist claims to spiritual superiority. Claiming that 'All Popular Factions take the *Church* in their Way to the *State*', L'Estrange sought to expose political intentions beneath the religious rhetoric in a sustained campaign of literary criticism.[6] It is this Tory Anglican initiative, literary critical in methodology but political in motivation, which clerical members of the Royal Society such as Samuel Parker, Joseph Glanvill and Thomas Sprat took up with such relish.[7] Brian Vickers concludes that rather than the intellectual endeavour to make pulpit rhetoric conform to 'scientific' standards of accuracy, these polemical texts reflect the need of the Royal Society to ingratiate itself with the Church of England. He suggests that at this early point in the Royal Society's history there was a real possibility of its scientific endeavours being seen as experiments in forbidden knowledge, such as alchemy, which several of its more famous members continued to practise.[8] Sprat ends his *History* with a determined attempt to link Nonconformity with the forbidden science of Astrology (p. 364 onwards), an extraordinary move which makes sense only if the treatise is read in the context of an attempt to distance the Royal Society from practices such as alchemy which, as Michael Heyd argues, was widely held to spring from the same subversive root as religious enthusiasm.[9] A letter to Robert Boyle of 11 July 1669 describes 'invectives against Cromwell, the fanatics, the Royal Society, and the new philosophy' in a speech by Oxford University Orator Robert South, a juxtaposition of hated entities which tends to confirm Vickers' point.[10]

This urgent political element in what has been seen as a controversy about prose style has also been emphasised by Derek Hirst, who uses it as the context for attacks on Nonconformist diction by Simon Patrick in his *Friendly Dialogue between a Nonconformist and a Conformist* (1667) and Samuel Parker in his *Discourse of Ecclesiastical Polity* (1670).[11] Patrick becomes increasingly unfriendly in the second and third continuations of his debate and in the final separately-published appendix, which take the opportunity to rehearse the grievances of the Interregnum in some detail, and give away the essentially political rather than literary critical nature of his attacks. Parker, however, goes so far as to suggest that a purge of prose style would solve the political problems of the nation: 'had we but an Act of Parliament to abridge Preachers the use of fulsome and luscious Metaphors, it might perhaps be an effectual cure for all our present distempers'.[12] This is an extraordinary claim, mocked by Owen in his reply to Parker, published the year before *A Discourse of Ecclesiastical Polity* which he had obviously seen in manuscript: as he points out,

'the principal Doctrines of the Gospel about the grace of God, the Mediation of Christ, of Faith, Justification, Gospel-obedience, Communion with God, and Union with Christ, are esteemed and stigmatized by some as *swelling Mysteries of Fanaticism;* and the whole work of our Redemption by the blood of Christ as expressed in the Scripture, [are] deemed *Metaphorical?* [13]

As we shall see, some of the 'fulsome and luscious Metaphors' that were particularly dangerous in the view of Tory Anglicans, were those from the Song of Songs, which were often used to illustrate exactly the doctrines in Reformed Christianity that Owen finds so precious. To focus on the general recommendations for plain style is to ignore the significance of the fact that on this point, Tory Anglicans do not generally practise what they preach: twentieth-century critics such as Brian Vickers and Roger Pooley have rightly identified a tendency to metaphorical discourse even in the attacks on metaphor, and perhaps the most famous attack on Parker, Andrew Marvell's *The Rehearsal Transpros'd,* pointed out that Parker's metaphors can be as luscious as anyone's.[14] Marvell also noticed that Parker had, suspiciously enough, cited exactly the same offensive metaphors as Patrick had done. The contemporary replies to Patrick and Parker focused on defending particular metaphors: for example, John Owen in *Truth and Innocence Vindicated* listed the metaphors that were Biblical and therefore the stylistic choice of the Holy Ghost.[15] At the beginning of *A Friendly Dialogue between a Conformist and a Non-Conformist* Simon Patrick gave a succinct critique of Nonconformist spirituality in terms of a particular set of metaphors:

> nothing is so sweet and pleasing to flesh and bloud, as for a man to hear how much a great Prince is in love with him, and how freely he loves him, how his heart beats in Heaven toward him: and especially how careful and compassionate he is toward him in a persecuted condition.[16]

The ironic tone of this observation is particularly vicious in its references to persecution, since Patrick's church was currently conducting 'a persecution of Protestants by Protestants without parallel in seventeenth-century Europe'.[17] Persecution was of course the archetypal context for Song of Songs spirituality. Although Patrick's comment is meant to indicate the self-indulgent nature of Nonconformist teaching as a whole, it is clearly recognisable as a digest of Reformed commentaries on the Song of Songs, as shown in chapter 4. In this chapter I am going to consider these metaphors in particular, in a study of a lesser-known pamphlet controversy of the 1670s that, judging by the number of participants in the debate, was very important to religious thought. It was a controversy over the interpretation of the Song of Songs.

John Owen and Thomas Watson on the Song of Songs

The controversy began in an attempt by a group of Anglican clergymen, including Simon Patrick, to claim back 'true religion', a phrase that was already the rallying cry of the Nonconformist constituency, who had appropriated the Reformed heritage of anti-Popery abandoned by Laudians in the 1630s.[18] In 1674 William Sherlock, a relatively unknown clergyman who was to become Master of the Temple and Dean of St. Paul's wrote *A Discourse*

Concerning the Knowledge of Jesus Christ, and our Union and Communion with him, the only work that we know for sure was part of this enterprise. R. F. Jones points out yet again that metaphor is made central to an attack on Nonconformity, and tries to link Sherlock with the scientists' drive for plain style: but Sherlock has nothing to do with the Royal Society, and his criticisms are focused on particular metaphors.[19] Attracta Anne Coppins points out that these metaphors are chosen less for any supposed stylistic deficiency than for their doctrinal implications: I want to go further, and expose what has been portrayed as a literary critical attack on stylistic excess as a politically-motivated dispute over religious doctrine.[20] Sherlock attacks several Nonconformist treatises, but I am going to focus on his treatment of two authors— Independent John Owen and Presbyterian Thomas Watson— along with treatises that they wrote in the same year, 1657.[21]

In 1657, of course, Owen and Watson had been respected establishment figures. Their treatises on the Song of Songs had been very much in the tradition of the Reformed commentaries described in chapter four of this book: as Arthur Jackson states of his 1658 *Annotations,*, 'When I first undertook this Work.... there was not, as I remember, any piece of this kind extant in English, save only the Geneva marginall notes.'[22] The years 1657 and 1658 had seen a kind of apotheosis of interest in the Song of Songs, particularly by Presbyterians who had seen political catastrophe a few years previously, and seemed intent on rescuing their reputation for godly ministry. As part of a study of the five 'poeticall' books of the Old Testatment—Job, Psalms, Proverbs, Ecclesiastes and the Song of Songs—both Edward Leigh and Arthur Jackson produced their own annotations. Educated under the famous Oxford Puritan William Pemble, Leigh had been a colonel in the Parliamentary army before becoming an MP; he was ejected and imprisoned at Pride's Purge. His commentary quotes from both the radical Puritan commentary of Brightman and the well-known Catholic sermons of St Bernard to produce a treatise that stresses the intimate union between Christ and the soul, particularly in a context of persecution. He points out that the formulation 'my sister, my spouse', which in the metaphorical scheme used to interpret the Song of Songs by both Catholics and Protestants refers to the believer, is used frequently in the book, because 'The nearest affinity is Spouse, and the nearest consanguinity Sister.'[23] Symptomatic of the Presbyterian predicament in the 1650s is the ambivalence towards authority: the watchmen of chapter five are godly ministers and magistrates, whereas in chapter three the watchmen are glossed as false teachers. Arthur Jackson had shared with Thomas Watson in the disaster for Presbyterians that was the 1651 plot to put Charles II on the throne, led by Christopher Love. Refusing to testify against Love, he was imprisoned with Watson in the Tower. Not surprisingly, Jackson sees the message of the Song of Songs as one of hidden privileged access to Christ; 'The drift of this song is prophetically to set forth the neere conjunction, and exceeding great love that is between Christ...and every faithfull soul.' The benefit of such a relationship to a church that is not politically in the ascendancy is seen in the gloss on chapter 1 verse 4 ('The King hath brought me into his chambers'): 'There he affords them, not only secret counsel, but also secret protection.'[24] This resort to a kind of love story in which Christ and the Soul are united against the world is expressed in the preface to Richard Turner's 1659 *The song of Solomon rendred in plain & familiar verse*:

> Behold! How *Love* in every vein doth run!
> How in each line a thread of Love is spun!
> ....How would this sweeten all
> The sharpest dispensations that befall;
> If by an eie of Faith thou couldest behold
> How tenderly thy Saviour doth enfold
> His arms, embracing thee? (sigs A3v–A4r).

The author of such observations might assume himself to be protected from criticism, but this was not to be the case a dozen or so years later. The content and tone of Owen and Watson's 1657 works would also appear to be uncontroversial, dealing with that most private of issues, the believer's relationship with Christ: John Owen's *Of Communion with God the Father, Sonne, and Holy Ghost, Each Person Distinctly; in Love, Grace, and Consolation* and Thomas Watson's *Christs Lovelinesse*.[25] The piety expressed there was of a kind that had become increasingly fashionable in the 1650s. Even as the political project that the godly revolution had become was failing, its proponents seemed to be looking ever inward for evidence that the Kingdom of God had truly come amongst them. John Owen resorted to the doctrine of the mystical marriage, which he linked with the union of the individual believer with Christ: this had been part of the Reformed heritage of the Church of England before the Civil War, expounded by the likes of John Preston and Richard Sibbes.[26]

In this treatise, however, Owen concentrates on communion with Christ, a rather less controversial concept than union. Nevertheless he points out that the communion he is advocating is dependent on union with Christ, which he has expounded elsewhere.[27] Certainly, in his 1654 treatise *The doctrine of the saints perseverance, explained and confirmed* Owen carefully explains what his concept of the union with Christ is: it is not a Personal Union, which he sees as doing violence both to the personality of Christ and the personality of the individual, but a Spiritual Union, achieved by the indwelling of the Holy Spirit. Such a union is not to be despised, because it is the same union as the man Christ had with God.[28] The most frequent illustration of this union in Scripture is earthly marriage: 'What the Apostle had spoken of the one, he would have understood of the other'. Owen selects the phrase 'one flesh', used of the married couple in Genesis 2:24, and used by the Apostle Paul in I Corinthians 6, and finds a metaphorical equivalent to describe the union between Christ and the soul: 'one spirit' (p. 196).

In the 1657 *Of Communion with God* the relationship offered with the Divine, based on this union, is represented as truly intimate: 'he presseth her hard to a closer union with him in the conjugall bond' (p. 61). The result of such union is ecstatic love to a Christ who is described in the rapturous terms of a human lover:

> *Lovely* in his person, *lovely* in his birth, and Incarnation, *lovely* in the whole course of his life, *lovely* in his Death, *Lovely* in his whole employ-ment, *lovely* in the glory and majesty, *lovely* in all these supplyes of Grace, *lovely* in all the tender Care Power and *wisedom*, *lovely* in all his *Ordinances*, *lovely* and *glorious* in the vengeance he taketh, *lovely* in the pardon he has purchased, *altogether lovely* (pp. 85–86).

After Thomas Watson, ejected minister of St. Stephen's, Walbrook, had been released from the Tower for his part in the Presbyterian Plot he seemed to preach a quietist piety dependent only on a sense of God's personal favour. His 1653 *The Art of Contentment* went into many editions during the seventeenth century. *Christ's Lovelinesse* was a kind of development from mere contentment into a mystical state of blissful contemplation based on the text of the Song of Songs, which Watson characterised as 'the purest allegories and metaphors' (p. 327). A prominent feature of both Owen's and Watson's volumes is the use of material from this Biblical book, that erotic poem which had for most of its history been celebrated as an account of the relationship between Christ and his Church. It is the metaphors suggested in this particular Biblical text, rather than the use of metaphorical discourse in general, which are Sherlock's target, and are at the heart of the political threat Anglicans of a Royalist politics perceived from Nonconformity.

Thomas Watson's treatment of the Song of Songs draws on the Fathers to produce a distillation of the Christian interpretative tradition which is at times alarmingly physical and even sensual in its description of spiritual bliss: 'This day I come a wooing for your love ... let Christ be as *a bundle of myrrhe*, always between your breasts' (p. 387). Incidentally, Simon Patrick's own 1685 version of The Song of Songs renders this verse, 'love Him above all things, and resolve never to let Him slip out of [your] minds', with the anx-ious comment; 'The bosome of all chaste Women is inaccessible to any hand, but that of their Husband.'[29] However, Watson has fully referenced his choice of language from Patristic commentaries on the Song of Songs, commentaries which are everywhere issued with the caveat that only the spiritually-minded will be able to correctly interpret this Biblical book of profound holiness. As if to implicitly distinguish between fit and unfit readers, their language often seems deliberately transgressive of contemporary bounds of decency. The rhetoric of the Song of Songs, which holds out a profound and mystical Christian experience of unity to the Elect, is thus implicitly divisive, but it is also explicitly so: union with Christ, in any particular author's view, entails separation from whatever his sect defines as 'the world'. Thus in the early part of the century the tropes of the mystical marriage had been employed in anti-Catholic pamphlets, and during the 1630s they had acquired a controversial edge in terms of English ecclesiastical politics. Benjamin King's 1640 treatise, *The Marriage of the Lambe,* highly coded in spiritual metaphor so as to escape Laudian censorship, is dedicated to Sir Thomas Barrington, who by his patronage of godly ministers shows himself to be a true spouse of Christ as opposed to 'the hypocrite and nominall Christian'.[30] To the initiated, the anti-Laudian message is clear. The continuing usefulness of such language in the anti-Royalist genres of Nonconformist martyrology, 'Eminent Lives' and 'Dying Speeches', is evident throughout the period after the Restoration.[31] The mystic experience of union with Christ of the eminent Nonconformist saint or martyr at the same time proved his favour with God, and the exclusion of his persecutors from any such intimacy with the Divine. Throughout his discourse, Watson uses the language of the Song of Songs to make similar distinctions between the truly elect and those whom he calls hypocrites; 'Tis little comfort for the soul to say, Christ is *altogether lovely*, unless it can also say, *My beloved is mine*'(p. 385). For Watson, in 1657, these spiritual reprobates were identified as the Independents, his political enemies, 'We shall grieve to see tolleration setting up its Masts and Top-sails, and multitudes sailing in this ship to Hell'(p. 393). Ironically, within a decade he would be working with those same reprobates, most eminent of whom was Dr. John Owen, now accepted with the Presbyterians into the true Bride of Christ, against a different enemy, the State-sponsored Church of England, in support of that very toleration which he had seen as heretical in 1657. Simon Patrick identified him as a virulent enemy of the Church of England: he accuses Owen of vices apparently incompatible with what Patrick sees as his self-indulgent spirituality, 'Covetousness, Oppression, Hard dealing, Unmercifulness, Malice, Revenge, Bitterness, Wrath, Implacableness.'[32]

The 1670s: the context of persecution

After the Restoration, and particularly after the 1662 ejection of Nonconformist ministers, the project to discern the true Elect acquired a new political urgency. The Restored Anglican church became official candidate for the true church, the Bride of Christ in England, and set out to show that all other claims were bogus, reinforcing its case with the oppressive measures of the Clarendon Code. In opposition to the persecution of the 1660s, Independent, Presbyterian and even Baptists found a new, united identity as the True Protestant church, the true Bride of Christ. The Song of Songs became imaginative quarry for preachers endeavouring to prove the tangible benefits of Nonconformist spirituality. Thus James Janeway, in *Heaven Upon Earth: Or, The Best Friend in the Worst of Times,* (published in the same year as Sprat's *History*), stressed knowing God 'by experiment', a word about to be annexed by scientific discourse, where it was to mean something rather different. Janeway seems to find in the lyrics of the Biblical Song of Songs a language for an intense experience that cannot otherwise be articulated:

> Those that are acquainted with a spiritual life know these things what they are and that they are the greatest realities in the world....They can tell you at such a time they were brought unto his Banquetting house and his Banner over them was Love: They can tell you at such time Christ came into his Garden to eat his pleasant Fruits; at such a time they heard the voice of their Beloved, saying *Open to me, my Sister, my Spouse, my Love, my Dove, my Undefiled* (p. 12).

This discourse acquired urgent political relevance in a decade which had seen 'persecution of Protestants by Protestants without parallel in seventeenth-century Europe': 215 out of the nearly 2000 ministers who had been deprived of their livings in the early 1660s had been imprisoned and 450 Quakers had died in prison.[33] Janeway, who had been in prison himself, offers this experience as the secret that sustained the Marian martyrs: 'Gods company is so refreshing, that it turns a prison into a palace; it brings joy and pleasure into a dungeon' (p.73). Finally, in a rhetoric echoing Thomas Watson's *Christs Loveliness* and to be repeated in various forms throughout this period, the metaphorical register suggested by the imagery of the Song of Songs is extended to that of contemporary romance as the preacher becomes a kind of marriage broker between Christ and the individual believer: 'Do you ever expect a better offer? Can you hope for a better, a richer match?'(p. 104)

   This rhetoric lays itself open to sceptical literary deconstruction, and it is perhaps the critical skill employed by Tory Anglicans which has commended their arguments to twentieth-century literary critics. A more historicised account, however, should take account of the fact that the exchange of pamphlets was taking place at the height of a severe persecution of Nonconformists. In the mid-70s Archbishop of Canterbury Gilbert Sheldon confidently endorsed legal harassment of Nonconformists by the State.[34] This fact should lend a more than literary significance to what looks like a difference over literary style. In 1669 Simon Patrick had criticised Watson's sermons: 'who is there that stuffs his Sermons with more ... little Sayings and Cadences of Sounds and Words, than T. W.'[35] Watson and Owen could no longer count on courteous treatment: in the late 1660s and early 1670s, they were radical opposition leaders. Owen was widely seen as the leader of the Nonconformists by 1670, and Watson's arrest in the same year had given rise to one of the most controversial Nonconformist trials in the Restoration.[36] The two men were also now on the same side, which had not been the case seventeen years before. The satirical treatment given by William Sherlock to Nonconformist commentary on the Song of Songs in *A discourse concerning the knowledge of Jesus*

Christ and our union and communion with him takes the form of ironic imitation of Thomas Watson's text.

> Who can forbear being smitten with so lovely a Person? Lovely as a Pillar of Cloud and fire, lovely as Noahs Ark, lovely as any Serpent, yea, as a brazen Serpent? But besides all these, Christ is resembled to a Rose, the Rose of Sharon, the Queen of flowers, and how lovely is this Rose. To a Vine, the noblest of Plants, and oh what lovely Clusters grow upon this Vine! ... to a Rock, and a River in a dry ground, and a rich treasure, and a beautiful Robe, and all these are lovely (and so should any thing have been, that came in his way at that time).[37]

Sherlock exposes the accumulation of hyperbole in both Watson's and Owen's texts as empty word association: 'Christ is Lovely, because he is rich and powerful, and he is powerful, because he is rich, and lovely, and Rich, because he is powerful and lovely' (p. 117). However, this attack is more profound than the rational man's distaste for emotionalism. Sherlock's literary critical point is that Nonconformist treatment of Biblical metaphor is incorrect, ascribing too much substantive meaning to a rhetorical strategy: 'He who would be an honest Reader of Books... ought carefully to distinguish between proper, and allusive, or metaphorical expressions.' Moreover, he identifies an illicit extension of Biblical metaphor: the methodology of Nonconformist preachers is to consider 'all the properties and qualifications of those things Christ is compared to, and applying all [these extra-Biblical properties], that will serve their turn, to Christ'. The result is, that Christ 'is what every man fancies him to be'. But as Nonconformists retorted, such application of metaphor in Biblical criticism has a perfectly respectable pedigree, in the hermeneutic and preaching practice of the pre-Civil War Church of England.[38]

Robert Ferguson's *The Interest of Reason in Religion*

Perhaps the most important response to Sherlock apart from Owen's own *Vindication*—at least the only one apart from Owen's which Sherlock felt it worth replying to—was the 1675 *The Interest of Reason in Religion,* by Owen's assistant, Robert Ferguson.[39] He had been one of the first to promote an alliance of ejected Presbyterians and Independents in the early 1660s, an initiative for which he spent time in prison. His treatise was dedicated to another City radical, Thomas Papillon, whom he thanked for various kindnesses: Papillon's father in law, the Cromwellian commander Broadnax, had been Ferguson's patron at Godmersham in Kent, from where he had been ejected in 1662. In the mid-1670s, when his correspondence was regularly monitored by the secret service, he ran a school for the sons of ex-Commonwealth's-men at his house in Clerkenwell Close, what Dryden called 'His College for a Nursery of Sects.'[40] Among his pupils were the sons of Lucy Hutchinson, Slingsby Bethel, and Henry Wilkinson, ex-Lady Margaret Professor of Divinity and John Owen's colleague in Interregnum Oxford.[41] Ferguson had already defended both John Owen and Andrew Marvell in print, and not surprisingly, he had a particularly acute understanding of the link between religion and politics.[42] He takes seriously the accusation of irrationality in Nonconformist discourse, and devotes the first book of his 656 page long treatise, *The Interest of Reason in Religion*, to it: the second book, however, concerns the correct interpretation of Scriptural metaphor. Some of his defences of Nonconformist practice have their origin in a kind of class politics, in opposition to Samuel Parker, who had scorned the practice of 'little and unlearned people'.[43] Many metaphorical phrases disliked by Tory Anglicans because of their physicality and vulgarity are in fact taken from Scripture itself: Ferguson supplies long lists of Biblical precedents for the phrases 'coming to Christ' and 'receiving of Christ' (p. 177). As George Herbert had done before him, Ferguson celebrates the fact that the Scripture itself is full of what Sherlock had derisively called '*Kitchin Metaphors*' and is therefore accessible to ordinary people (p. 327).[44] However, Ferguson also employs rather more sophisticated arguments.[45] He advocates a kind of roving application of the textual metaphors, renouncing intentionality as a guiding principle:

> There are many other things related to have fallen out then, which... though they neither were in the solemn Institution of God, nor yet in his Providential Ordination designed to prefigure anything referring to the kingdom of Christ, are yet meet to illustrate things and events now (p. 313).

This radical freedom of interpretation was of course particularly dangerous when applied to the text of the Song of Songs, which could not literally mean what it appeared to say, and which was therefore available as a prophetic key to contemporary events, as used by several radicals in the Civil War period: in his own commentary on the Song of Songs, first published in 1685, Simon Patrick eschewed this kind of hermeneutic with a shudder.[46] Part of this liberty, which Ferguson believes essential for the popular preacher as well as the Biblical interpreter, is use of the rhetorical technique of *amplificatio*, which had been so central to fashions of poetry earlier in the century:

> Wherever the resemblance of one thing to another is represented under a Metaphorick words or expression ... all the particulars which stand in Analogy with that expression ... ought to be included (p. 351).

It is this particular textual practice of using extended metaphor, common in pre-War Church of England practice but increasingly the province of the

Nonconformists, that created the main difficulty for Tory Anglicans when focusing on one particular group of metaphors. The trope of the mystical marriage included images drawn from the Song of Songs but articulated elsewhere in Scripture, as has been demonstrated earlier in this book.[47] It is the widespread extension of this metaphor into Nonconformist doctrine and spirituality that Sherlock declares 'An entire Scheme of a new Religion' (p. 75). Part of his quarrel is with Nonconformist interpretation of the marriage with Christ in terms of seventeenth-century marriage law and practice. As the title of his treatise suggests, Sherlock is most concerned about 'the union of persons' the doctrine implied. He grants, judiciously, that a wife is entitled by law to her husband's estate and 'all his excellences are hers': however, Nonconformists use this contemporary legal status as illustration of their doctrine of justification, stating that 'the *Personal virtues and qualities and perfection of the Husband should be settled upon his Wife, [the Church] for a jointure'.* Sherlock questions this: 'though the Husband be never so fair and comely, wise and vertuous, his Wife may be ugly and deformed, a Fool or a Harlot'(p. 285).

Similar illustrations of the doctrine of sanctification are also suspect: Sherlock attacked Nonconformist Thomas Shepard's suspicion of Arminian 'good works'. Shepherd encoded his criticism in a metaphor which is an extension of the mystical marriage trope:

> Foolish lovers, who when they are to wooe for the Lady, fall in love with the handmaid, that is only to lead them to her: so men fall in love with, and dote upon their own duties, and rest contented with the naked performance of them which are only Hand-maids to lead the Soul unto the Lord Jesus Christ.[48]

Sherlock commented, sarcastically, 'is not this the ready way to persuade people, that our love to Christ consists in something more refined and spiritual than obedience?'(p. 424). The frequent suggestion that the Christian faith be seen as a personal romance with Christ, shamelessly employed by earlier Anglicans, enraged Sherlock. Thomas Vincent in 1672 had urged a convention of Nonconformist women to deepen their personal commitment to Christ, in a sermon laced with references to contemporary ideas of 'Mr. Right' entitled *Christ the best Husband*. Sherlock had called this 'a piece of *fantastical Wit'* on the basis that the metaphor of the Bride should only be used to designate the whole Church (p. 144). This statement Ferguson demolished with an array of New Testament reference showing that St. Paul had also applied the doctrine of the mystical marriage to individual believers.[49] Sherlock was addressing a substantial issue here: the preaching strategy of offering Christ as a husband to individuals in a congregation was extremely popular in the 1670s. Edward Pearse's *The Best Match* was first published in 1673 for the price of 2s: it reached five editions by 1688 and became a seventeenth-century bestseller.[50] Introduced by the well-known

Devonshire Independent John Rowe, the treatise had as its epigraph 2 Corinthians 11:2, 'I have espoused you to one husband that I may present you as a chaste virgin to Christ', and the author's stated aim in his preface to the reader was 'to bring thee into, and build thee up in this union and communion with Christ'.[51] Pearse was placing himself in succession to John Preston and Richard Sibbes, but he had obviously read John Owen as well. He equated the mystical marriage with spiritual union between Christ and the believer (sig. B2r). In the move which was to irritate the likes of Sherlock so profoundly, he used verse 5 of the Song of Songs, 'I am blacke, but comely', to illustrate the fact that despite the inadequacy of the human being, the individual Christian receives everything he or she needs through the marriage with Christ (p.14). This encouraged Pearse to advertise the benefits of Christ as a husband in even more enthusiastic fashion than Thomas Vincent had done: the believer becomes united with 'Dignitie and Greatness', 'Riches and Treasures', 'a noble and generous Spirit', 'Wisdom and Knowledge', 'Beauty', 'Love', and of course, 'Immortality' (pp. 68–84). Such an evangelistic strategy was intended to be irresistible.

Sherlock responded to the powerful appeal of this rhetoric by mocking the doctrine of the mystical marriage of every true believer with Christ, implying that it was recommending a kind of polygamy (p.144). This approach laid him open to attack by Nonconformist critics. Not only was this doctrine demonstrably Biblical, and had been interpreted in this way for centuries; Sherlock's attack showed him to have engaged in the wrong kind of reading. Sherlock had allowed himself to imagine Jesus Christ in illicit sexual relationships with believers, even if only as something he himself condemned as false doctrine: this marked him out as an unspiritual reader. Thus Edward Polhill commented in pained fashion on Sherlock's use of the word 'smitten' that 'Mr Watson did not dream that his Discourses of Christs Loveliness should be traduced into carnal Expressions': and controversialist William Hickman, pointing out that Owen and Jacombe were more faithful to the historical Church of England than Sherlock, begged, 'let us conceive of things *spiritual spiritually*'.[52]

Sherlock's most vitriolic attack is reserved for the Calvinist doctrine of sanctification, which demands total dependence on Christ for actual righteousness. The corollary of this doctrine, that Christ is thereby responsible for the believer's behaviour, causes Sherlock some concern. Thomas Jacombe had celebrated this responsibility, using the trope of the mystical marriage, in terms of the contemporary legal status of a wife, ie. the Christian believer, as a *femme couvert*: 'A woman *under covert* is not liable to *an arrest* or *action* at Law, but all must fall upon her Husband'.[53] To this Sherlock replies in terms that by 1675 were probably unanswerable: 'it is true as to matter of Debt, but does not extend to Crimes: if a Woman kill her Child, or rob upon the High-way, I doubt her being under covert will not secure her from the Gallows' (p. 286). Christ is not responsible for a Christian's lawbreaking activities. 'Twas not ever thus, however: in a rather more Calvinist Church of England in the early 1630s George Herbert pronounced that a murderer could be saved from the gallows if he could persuade others that he was inspired by the Holy Spirit to do the crime.[54] Here, I would suggest, in the Antinomian tendencies of mainstream Reformed doctrine, is the essential reason for the Tory clergy's attack on metaphorical discourse, or on particular metaphors at least.[55] In his analysis of this controversy, Neil Keeble identifies at its root 'a debate about the nature of truth' centring on the claim of the Nonconformists to 'a more spiritual and intimate way of Communion with God'.[56] The physicality of the Nonconformist metaphors surrounding the doctrine of the person of Christ suggests the attractive possibility of a close personal relationship with the second person of the Trinity, as Joseph Glanville, member of the Royal Society, sneered in 1677:

> If you teach men to believe *Christs* Doctrine, to obey his Laws, to trust to his promises, and to conform to his Example; these shall be counted dull, dry and unedifying things, that no-ways affect, or move: but if you tell the people, that they must roll upon *Christ*, close with *Christ*, get into *Christ*, get a saving interest in the Lord *Christ*: O this is savoury, this is precious, this is spiritual teaching indeed.[57]

Intimacy with Christ was also, however, the political problem: this teaching held out to the believer the promise of an access to holiness that circumvented commonsense ideas of morality. It was this notion that Samuel Parker attacked as archetypal Enthusiasm in *A Discourse of Ecclesiastical Polity*. Thus at the start of his treatise, Sherlock announces his intention to weaken the power of the appeal of the person of Christ, and declares that the word 'Christ' often does not designate a person at all, but the mediatory office of the second person of the Trinity, or the Gospel, or even the Church itself (pp. 4–13). The problem for hierarchical Anglicans with the discourse of the Song of Songs, as interpreted within a long tradition of allegorical hermeneutic, was that it confirmed and encouraged the notion of an intimate personal relationship with Christ. As Benjamin King had declared in 1640, 'Christ will communicate … secrets to a beleeving soule espoused unto him, that hee will not communicate to a stranger.'[58] Such a doctrine, of blissful experience of Christ's love, linked with privileged communication of secret Divine knowledge, would be deeply sustaining for a radical community, even if the tropes were not already deeply implicated in Protestant martyrology: 'what was it that made the fiery faggots to these blessed witness of the truth to seeme as beds of Roses?' asks King of the Marian martyrs, assuming the obvious answer: espousal to Christ. The political consequences of such immediate access to the Divine by the individual believer are seen by some Restoration Anglicans as sectarianism and rebellion. As Sherlock claims, 'men … abuse themselves with a pretended devotion to our Saviour, while they contemn his laws' (p. 13).

Robert Ferguson recognises the political implications of Sherlock's problem with Nonconformist discourse. 'In removing all Immediate Union betwixt Believers and Christ' Ferguson suggests that Sherlock is Papist (p. 426) and associates him with Thomas Hobbes—grave charges indeed. If 'there is no infused Principle of Grace communicated to us from Christ as our life and Head by the efficacious operation of the Spirit' (p. 433), religion becomes an outward discipline, rather than an internal reality, an effective means of control for any governing party. Ferguson feels sure enough of his ground to quote Sherlock verbatim, counting on the self-evidently ridiculous nature of the argument to condemn the author out of his own mouth: 'Christ is (says he) *only styled our Head, because invested with Authority to Govern us by his Laws: and our Union with Him as such, consists only in an acknowledgement of his Authority, and in Subjection to his command... and by* our *Fellowship with Christ* which the Sacred Writers so Emphatically speak of, we are told there is only meet such a Political Union, as is betwixt a Prince and his Subjects, between Superiours, and Inferiors."[59] This is not a travesty of Sherlock's argument, which does claim that the union between Christ and believers is merely the political relationship in which King and subject are united. It is indeed the evasion of hierarchical government in Church and State in the more intimate union with God claimed by 'true Protestants' that motivates so much of Sherlock's prescriptions on interpreting Biblical metaphor.

The Song of Songs in the House of Lords

There were many other replies to Sherlock's treatise, besides Ferguson's: leading Nonconformists identified it as an attack on some of their most precious beliefs. John Collinges, author of one of the longest commentaries on the Song of Songs, was quick to perceive what Michael Winship has called the 'attempt at cultural marginalisation': 'Who sees not that there is a *New mess of Divinity* bringing into the world, which is not likely to be digested, nor received indeed, while the N. C. [Nonconformists] are in any reputation.'[60] Winship identifies such Anglican ideas about religious language and metaphor as the reason for the demise in eighteenth-century Massachusetts of the teaching of the mystical marriage, but in 1670s England Nonconformists were not prepared to give any ground to Anglican critics.[61] One swift and very funny response, *Anti-sozzo*, criticised by Anthony Wood as a crude Marvellian imitation, earned its author Vincent Alsop the pastorate of the large Westminster Presbyterian congregation, and the effective leadership of the Nonconformists in London.[62] Sherlock took up the pen in his own defence. In his 1675 *A defence and continuation of the discourse concerning the knowledge of Jesus Christ, and our union and communion with Him* he continued the attack on interpretation of the Song of Songs, going so far as to say the Biblical book was less than useful.

Allegories are of no use till they are expounded, and are of a very doubtful signification, when we want the true Key of Exposition; because they being a work of fancy and imagination, may by men of different fancies be expounded to very different and contrary purposes; which makes the Song of *Solomon* itself, though the most divine and spiritual thing that ever was penned under the Jewish Church, of much less use to us, than otherwise it might be.[63]

In the same year, *An Account of Mr Ferguson his Common-Place Book* was a collaboration of Sherlock and Joseph Glanville in which they identified various passages in *The Interest of Reason in Religion* copied rather closely from Sir Charles Wolseley, friend of Buckingham and Shaftesbury, with whom Ferguson was staying during the period in which his work was composed. Ferguson himself, however, never wrote another theological work. His pen was employed later in the 1670s in an explicitly political capacity, by that supreme political operator the Earl of Shaftesbury. His own list of the pamphlets for which he was responsible is preserved in Edinburgh, many of them crucial to the Whig cause during the Exclusion crisis: the 'Black Box' pamphlets, which tried to bolster the claims of the Duke of Monmouth to the English throne, and all three parts of that very effective pamphlet *No Protestant Plot*, written to encourage an *ignoramus* verdict in Shaftesbury's trial of November 1681. A rather more famous work had of course been written to encourage the opposite verdict on Shaftesbury: perhaps Dryden's relative failure in this attempt to do politics with literature accounts for his vicious attack on Ferguson in the second part of *Absalom and Achitophel*.[64]

The publication activities of Shaftesbury and Ferguson, 'Judas that pays the Treason-writers Fee', in Dryden's words, became so entwined that the authorship of several Exclusion pamphlets cannot be definitively assigned to one or the other. A similar closeness in thinking is, I think, discernible in a speech of Shaftesbury's from March 1679: of course, Ferguson may have been acting as Shaftesbury's speech-writer by this point. Significantly, his central metaphor is taken from the Song of Songs, an acknowledged source of material for antipopery; but merely to use this text in a speech about the state of the nation, after the controversies of the last few years, is to align himself categorically with Nonconformists. The hermeneutic used here confirms all Sherlock's worst suspicions about that party's interpretation of the Song of Songs. For a start, Shaftesbury assumes that the book may be used as a prophecy about the current Church, and is as definite as any preacher might be about his designation of the referent of the metaphor. The Spouse's little sisters are the weaker Protestant churches of France, Scotland and Ireland. In the metaphorical alternatives offered by the Song of Songs 8:9, they currently constitute doors to England for Popery, rather than the walls of protection that they should offer. In an audacious re-assigning of the metaphor, Shaftesbury later rechristens the 'two little sisters' as Popery and Slavery, pressing towards the doors to England: close relatives of Andrew Marvell's Popery and Arbitrary Government. He suggests that these doors should be boarded up, as the Song of Songs puts it: Shaftesbury's interpretation of this metaphor is that the Protestant churches in Scotland and Ireland should be supported against threats from the Catholic world. The rest of the speech, unencoded in Song of Songs diction, offers concrete measures for doing this, stating the perceived threat from Catholic France in clear non-metaphorical terms. This speech in fact caused a political storm, evoking an angry response from Lord Ossory who understood that his father's government of Ireland was under attack.[65]

Such a daring use of the Biblical rhetoric would have enraged the Tory Anglicans who heard Shaftesbury in the House of Lords. It exploits fully the freedom of Biblical interpretation asserted by Robert Ferguson: 'There are many other things related to have fallen out then, which ... are yet meet to illustrate things and events now.' The metaphorical discourse of the Song of Songs was of course particularly available to such a contemporary applica-tion. Shaftesbury uses it here to make a point about the rights of the people which the likes of Sherlock and Glanville had wished to forestall. To make matters worse, he claimed the authority of his own intimate relationship with God for the sentiments of this speech: 'I speak what I am commanded by the Dictates of the Spirit within me'. K.H.D. Haley declares that an effect of surprise was created by the very obscurity of the Biblical language: on the contrary, Shaftesbury's audience in March 1679 understood very well that his message had been emphasised and extended by the metaphors in which it was encoded. Moreover, a wider readership understood the impact of this speech. I first came across it amongst manuscripts at Stanton Harcourt, a location which suggests that the Nonconformist MP Philip Harcourt, who was briefly out of Parliament in 1679, received a manuscript copy from someone at Westminster who thought he should be aware of it. The BL manuscript copy of the speech is endorsed with the note that it would be available for printing and distribution in London and Norwich. Wing has no record of such printings—perhaps the speech was suppressed in England—but the speech was issued in The Hague in 1680, when the division between 'True Protestants' and the official Church of England had become even more marked, and their different ways of reading the Biblical text more established.[66] An anonymous pamphlet of 1681, attempting to reclaim the designation 'True Protestant' for Tory Anglicans, sets out *The Character of a True Protestant* in both political terms—'he dares not question his [king's] authority'—and literary critical: 'he can make a difference between *Types* and *Metaphors*, the one being in Persons, and the other in Words'. Someone else had taken on board the political significance of Sherlock's attempt to reduce the Persons of the Spouse and the Bridegroom to mere metaphors.

Shaftesbury's use of the text of the Song of Songs in the House of Lords shows that its political valency was well known in the 1670s. The policies with which it had been linked since the start of the century, international Protestantism and anti-Catholicism, are still part of its familiar frame of reference. Moreover, the claimed origin of the speech, in an intimate relationship with God by the indwelling of the Holy Spirit, asserts the Reformed interpretation of the Song of Songs, that it is about union and communion with God. The recent controversy over the meaning of the text, one that profoundly challenged these spiritual principles, has served by 1679 to highlight its significance in the context of a would-be absolutist regime. The significance of this speech by Shaftesbury in an Exclusion Parliament is to give the emerging Whig movement a Biblical justification for its claims for the importance of Protestantism in protecting the rights of the individual, an English buffer against Popery and Slavery. Rather than a demonstration that he was speaking by immediate inspiration of the Holy Spirit, as Shaftesbury asserted, the speech is a carefully-calculated attempt to harness some of the most important spiritual and political forces of the seventeenth century, symbolised in the text of the Song of Songs.

Epilogue: Benjamin Keach Rewriting the Bride

The discourse of the mystical marriage, which had started the century as characteristic of one influential group in the religious and political mainstream, had by the Restoration become the property of the radical wing of the Nonconformist constituency, as detailed in the last chapter. As political and religious disputes intensified in the second Restoration crisis of 1678–1682, often called the 'Exclusion' crisis, there was a further radicalisation of the use of the Song of Songs. The discourse of the mystical marriage was often treated by Baptists, themselves regarded as a radical and sometimes as a dangerous sect, as part of a popularising project that was part of Nonconformist propaganda in the 1670s and 1680s, in which the bestselling authors were Baptists John Bunyan and Benjamin Keach. As we shall see, the links established early in the Reformation between the discourses of the mystical marriage, anti-Catholicism and martyrology, are fully drawn upon in Keach's writing.

The bestseller allegories of Benjamin Keach, predecessors of the even better-selling *The Pilgrims Progress*, contain explicitly political material in which, as in the Song of Songs, each individual Christian reader is invited to take the role of chief protagonist. In *The Travels of True Godliness*, the eponymous character True Godliness is sent packing from the house of Riches as he is obviously some kind of revolutionary on behalf of the poor.[1] In its six pre-1688 editions *The Travels of True Godliness* contains a very partisan account of the Popish Plot (p. 73). In its post-1688 editions, the book mentions the Monmouth Rebellion, and the massive retaliation on West country Nonconformists thereafter:

> Divrs holy Persons were cut off by their [the enemies of True Godliness] bloody and traiterous Hands in the *West*; and also in the *chief City* of the Isle.[2]

The wider context for much of the allegory, then, is a violently unstable political situation, fitting well with the militant world that is seen as the context for the lover's happiness in the Song of Songs, for example in the second half of chapter 3. In some ways Baptist writing of the 1680s, taking place in the expectation or in the actual reign of an explicitly Catholic king, is well placed to exploit the political, anti-Catholic meanings that had been assigned over the course of the seventeenth century to the tropes of the Song of Songs.

As we saw in the last chapter, seventeenth-century Tory critics were very aware of the potentially revolutionary implications of Song of Songs discourse. Modern critics like Neil Keeble, however, tend to ignore the political dimension of Baptist writing, possibly because, as Derek Hirst judges, they posit a separate, distinct category of literary nonconformist, distinct from politics.[3] In the State Papers of the period, however, Baptists along with their patron the Duke of Buckingham figure large as a target for the Secret Service.[4] Baptist printers such as Francis Smith and Benjamin Harris produced huge numbers of anti-court tracts. The trials that followed the Monmouth rebellion saw many West Country Baptist congregations devastated for their involvement.[5] 'That truly apostolical man of God' Andrew Gifford, pastor of one of the Baptist congregations in Bristol, donated arms and money to Monmouth and invited him into the city: his grandson, also a pastor of a Baptist church in Bristol, composed a metrical version of the Song of Songs.[6]

Benjamin Keach and Biblical metaphors

John Dunton clearly considered himself as central to Whig culture after the Glorious Revolution, as opposed to Baptists, who had to work hard to change the extremist image generated by their radical roots. He was editor of *The Athenian Mercury,* and he dealt in what Keach felt to be a casual way with a correspondence about infant baptism in 1691: remedying the lack of seriousness, although perhaps misjudging tone of *The Athenian Mercury's* request for syllogisms, he supplied 27 of them in favour of infant baptism in 1692 and published his correspondence.[7] In Dunton's autobiography he leaves characterisation of Benjamin Keach until the very end of his list of authors, despite the money he made out of him as his publisher.

I next make room for a man of another character, and room must be made; for here comes Mr Keach, mounted on some Apocaplyptical Beast or other, with Babylon before him, and Zion behind him, and a hundred thousand Bulls and Bears and furious beasts of Prey, roaring, ramping, and bellowing at him... His Practical Books have met with a kind reception; and I believe his *War with the Devil* and *The Travels of True Godliness* (of which I printed ten thousand) will sell to the end of time.[8]

Dunton mocks Keach for his apocalyptic mentality, perhaps a justified criticism of an author who published in 1689 *Antichrist stormed, or, Mystery Babylon the great whore.* His obsession with allegorical Biblical figures, and the rather fierce landscape that he is portrayed as inhabiting, is seen to be rather out of date in the eighteenth century: there is clearly still a market for his kind of writing, but Dunton implies that it is a limited one. The mystical marriage had also been part of an apocalyptic and anti-Catholic discourse in the sixteenth century: but Keach charts a distinctively late-seventeenth century Nonconformist understanding of the trope in the two folio volumes of *Tropologia, or, A key to open Scripture metaphors.*[9] This appeared in 1681, co-authored by Thomas Delaune who wrote the first volume, and who was to die in Newgate in 1685: it was funded by subscription from most of the Nonconformist ministers in London. It triumphantly asserted distinctive Nonconformist literary critical methodology. As John Owen, Robert Ferguson and others had claimed, the rhetoric of the Scriptures as well as their message must be considered inspired: 'their Eloquence is to be esteemed the *best* and most elegant by the faithful, unless we suppose the God who immediately dictated them to his *Amanuensis*, spoke nonsense, and is inferior to his Creatures in that qualification'.[10]

The long list of Biblical metaphors with suggestions for their use includes, as 'the most pleasant *metaphor* of all', the metaphor of '*Espousals*'. The section on Christ as Bridegroom is the longest in the entire work and concludes with 'An Epithalamy on the Soul's Marriage with Christ'.[11] This treatment amply justifies the conclusion of George Scheper about seventeenth-century English Protestant versions of the trope: they tend to focus on details of the marriage contract.[12] It shamelessly suggests the use of contemporary marriage conventions to expound the mystical marriage metaphor, listing 33 ways in which Christ will behave like an earthly husband, and incidentally painting an interesting portrait of the seventeenth-century marriage. A prospective bridegroom will send letters to his beloved: so Christ sends those divine communications, 'the sweet Motions of his Spirit' (II, 100). A bridegroom settles a jointure on his bride: so Christ gives her eternal life as her inheritance. The bridegroom takes all his bride's debts and incurs the penalties himself: so does Christ take the penalty for his Bride's sins (II, 102). Continuing the theme of how the mystical marriage compensates for all earthy deficiencies, Keach also points out that the mystical marriage goes much further than earthly marriage: 'A Great and Mighty Prince will not set his heart upon or court a Leper, a Creature blind, deformed, full of running Sores and old Ulcers': Christ, however, will woo a sinner. 'If [an earthly bride] be hard-favoured, deformed, and ugly, so she must remain' whereas Christ bestows his beauty upon his spiritual Bride. 'A Princely Bridegroom provideth not the Wedding Garments for his Bride' whereas Christ 'is at all the charge of cloathing and adorning his Church' (II, 104). As we have seen, such a 'compensation culture' for Nonconformists was frowned upon by Anglicans, which discerned in this teaching a political subversiveness. Keach is in fact very aware of the political context for his volume, which is printed by the radical John Darby: '*England*, and particularly its famous *Metropolis*, is the very Butt of Antichristian Spite and Fury, because it is indeed thought to be the main Bulwark of the true Protestant Religion throughout the World' (II, sig. A2r).

The Bride in Baptist martyrology

Published in the same year, 1681, *Sion In Distress*, in the true tradition of martyrology, gives details of that 'Antichristian Spite and Fury', setting the poem firmly in the political context of the Popish Plot (sigs. A2r-v). To Nonconformists, who claimed the designation of True Protestants, the stage seemed set in the 1680s for a political scene in which the martyrdoms of the reign of Bloody Mary which had given rise to Foxe's *Acts and Monuments* could take place. *Sion in Distress* is not a martyrology as such – details of individual suffering could not be given until after the Glorious Revolution, and Keach did not even put his name to this first edition, although the second edition contained an elegy for Sir Edmund Berry Godfrey, the judge whose disputed death initiated the most virulent phase of the 'Popish Plot' controversy. However, to those who knew how to read the tropes of the mystical marriage in the context of martyrology, the message was clear. Sion is of course the True Protestant Church.This volume makes clear that the enemy within, which is also firmly on the side of the Whore of the Apocalypse, is not the Catholic church in the 1680s but the restored ceremonial and hierarchical Church of England.

> For some that *wish me well*, do yet ...
> Retain some *Romish Fragments,* which displeases
> The meek, the humble, self-denying *JESUS*. (p. 22)

The villain of the piece, who is of course the Rampant Whore, the Church of Rome, makes an appearance, and from then onwards the book takes on the character of Keach's favourite genre, apocalyptic allegory. The Marks of the Beast, so obvious in the Whore's countenance and behaviour, are then delineated, with heavy prose annotations which make clear the identification of the Beast with the Roman Catholic Church (pp.45–61). At last the Bridegroom hears the laments of the Bride, reappears, and there is a rapturous reunion. A rehearsal of the Whore's supposed crimes – the Powder-Treason, Modern Plot, and the Fire of London – continue in a trial scene so beloved of Baptist allegory. The righteous judge Justice calls witnesses of Popish massacres from across Europe, and sentences the Whore to a truly apocalyptic fate (pp. 113–15).

The sequel to *Sion in Distress, Distressed Sion Relieved*, issued when it was safe to do so after the Glorious Revolution in 1689, did function as a Nonconformist martyrology, giving details of individuals who had suffered during the executions in the 1680s in London and the West Country.[13] Keach clearly expected a repeat of the popularity of the first volume: he advertised himself on the front cover as the author of *Sion In Distress*. However, the mass readership rejected a rhetorical recreation of the scenes of execution in Keach's elegiac poetry, preferring what appeared to be the unmediated evidence of private documents from the pens of the martyrs in volumes compiled by John Tutchin like *The Western Martyrology or The Bloody Assizes*, which did sell well. Perhaps the believers in the narrative of the mystical marriage could not recognise the reign of the sober and distinctly non-fanatic William and Mary as the happy ending of *Sion in Distress* or the miracle Keach represents it as being on the front cover of *Distressed Sion Relieved*: 'the late Admirable and Stupendious Providence which hath wrought such a sudden and Wonderful Deliverance for this Nation, and Gods *Sion* therein'.[14]

The Bride as romantic heroine

Benjamin Keach's other major work featuring the Bride was a poem of 8,400 lines with pretensions to epic, *The Glorious Lover*, in which Keach moved away from sectarian rhetoric in a deliberate attempt to participate in a wider literary scene.[15] This too was an Exclusion Crisis publication of 1679, which reached another edition in 1685, and a further one in 1696. Keach is deliberately addressing himself to romance readers of both sexes – 'all you who amorous Stories gladly hear' – despite thundering with the conventional denouncement of romances as 'the poisoned froth of some infected brain'.[16] Nevertheless *The Glorious Lover* has the narrative structure of the romance familiar to readers of Keach from books like *War With the Devil* as well as *Sion in Distress*, charting the descent of Prince Jesus to Earth to woo his Bride. This is the narrative laid out in Francis Rous' *The Mysticall Marriage* fifty years before. The girl on the front cover is not Eve: the text spells out that she is alone in Paradise except for a divine Lover. She suffers Eve's fate of a fall which entails transportation to a 'strange land', although characteristically for Keach this is described in warlike terms as seduction by armed rebels, despite the snake on the front cover of *The Glorious Lover*. The 'creature' as she is called – she has suffered dreadful deformities—is not named until chapter 3, when it becomes clear that she represents the Soul, and at her first encounter with Christ she refuses him. This is the first of several attempts by Christ to woo the soul, one of which is distinctly recognisable from chapter 5 of the Song of Songs: as we know from seventeenth-century interpretations of that text, the Soul initially responds to Christ too late. Keach spends some time blaming the Soul for this (pp.118 –19) but it is not surprising that she did not recognise him; Christ is speaking just like the lover of Romance.

> I am a Person of no mean Degree
> Although my heart is set and fixt on thee. (p. 34)

There is much fierce opposition to this match, and many visits to Hell, before the consummation of the book: *Paradise Lost* is not far from the modern reader's mind, but perhaps the seventeenth-century reader was more aware of Dryden's *State of Innocence*, published two years before *The Glorious Lover* and a seventeenth-century bestseller like *War with the Devil* and *Sion in Distress*. Having dealt with the Devil in Book 1 Keach concentrates on what is really important for his readers in Book II: the mystical marriage. The bride is still not convinced about Christ being her suitor, which gives the Theologue the chance to spend chapter 3 talking about Christ's Loveliness, a chapter for which there is a great deal of material in the Song of Songs and elsewhere in the Bible. A further obstacle that has to be dealt with is the Bride's first husband, the allegorical Old Man of Romans 7, who appears as a character (p. 161). It is not until chapter 7, by which we have seen two more cabals in Hell, that a dart from the Holy Spirit finally overcomes the Soul's resistance (p. 185). The beneficial effects, for the Soul, are immediate and tangible:

> He doth transmit his beauty unto those
> Who are deform'd, as soon as e're they close
> With him in truth, in a contract of love,
> He all their homely features doth remove.
> Oh! he can make those lovely, very fair. (p. 178)

In chapter 8 Christ and the Soul go through a marriage ceremony, although it is unclear whether it is a marriage or a betrothal that takes place. The final line echoes the words of consummation in the Song of Songs, 'My well-belov'd is mine, and I am his.'

The Glorious Lover is the ultimate outcome of the domestication of the mystical marriage trope that takes place during the seventeenth century. Although the setting has the requisite allegorical furniture in apocalyptic mode, Keach's real concern is the love affair between Christ and the Soul. Sharon Achinstein calls Keach 'the great fabulist of romance genre as spiritual erotics' and although 'erotic' is the wrong word for this poem, 'romantic', in the sense of a love story, certainly is.[17] In effect he has supplied a story to go with a type, the image of Christ as Bridegroom: this is the end result of the technique he employs in *Tropologia*, where many extra-Biblical details and aspects of the marriage trope are elaborated. Many Nonconformist preachers have used this technique to good effect, as we have seen; but the transition from the experience of public sermon to private reading is dramatic. Like Thomas Vincent and other preachers throughout the century before him, Keach hopes that his words will persuade the reader to fall in love:

> *Read then, and learn to love truly by this.*
> *Until thy Soul can sing, (Raptur'd in Bliss)*
> My Well-beloved's mine, and I am his.[18]

The persuasive force of public oratory is replaced by the private power of narrative: emotions are mobilised by the story, which has all the imaginative appeal of the fictional romance. The reader's emotions may well become committed to the remorseless teleology of the happy ending, which he or she can provide by responding to Christ as his or her own personal Glorious Lover.

A vigorous appeal to the emotions had always been part of Reformed preaching. The encapsulation of the Gospel in terms of a divine romance had been available since the sermons of John Donne in the 1620s, and the pamphlets of Francis Rous in the 1630s. The 1635 emblem poems of Francis Quarles had popularised the importance of an emotional, and perhaps rapturous, response to the person of Christ. In the late-seventeenth century, the widening of literacy and the growth of denominations with a particular appeal to lower classes of society such as the Baptists led their authors to simplify their message in writing which Sharon Achinstein has described as offering 'an alternate set of literary values: openness, transparency, familiarity, and accessibility'.[19] Often, writers and preachers ventriloquized appeals from Christ to the individual human being, appeals which required the engagement of the emotions. Biblical precedent for the articulation of loving response to Christ was demonstrated at its most intense and sustained level in the book of the Song of Songs, or at least in the Nonconformist interpretation of it as the Divine Lover's courtship of the individual soul. This is why Nonconformist works return continually to the language of the Song of Songs: the nature of that text as poetry helps to explain the popularity of genres such as the verse allegory and the hymn. Dissenters were eventually to adopt the intellectual solution to the moral problem that the use of rhetoric posed put forward in Keach's *Tropologia*, that rhetorical figures should be Biblical in origin: in any case, this strategy that was already at work in the sermons and writings of Nonconformist preachers.

The reciprocated and passionate desire of the Song of Songs together with its traditional reading in the context of conflict and persecution seems to have sustained Nonconformist communities in what was also a decade of repression unprecedented even in the troubled years of the seventeenth century.[20] However, there is some evidence that the interpretation of the Song of Songs which had been hegemonic throughout the seventeenth century was to become the province of a narrower, more radical community in the next century. True, there are very few differences in the two sermons entitled identically *Christ the Best Husband*, in 1672 and 1740: George Whitefield adopted Thomas Vincent's sermon nearly seventy years later, proving that the relationship of Bride and Bridegroom in the Song of Songs could still be interpreted to describe the individual Christian's relationship with Christ. Even the cultural meanings of marriage are clearly very similar. However, Whitefield was a Calvinistic, anti-Catholic Methodist whose emotional preaching generated a good deal of opposition even from other Dissenters.[21] The change in Church of England interpretation from the start of the seventeenth century may be seen in the work of one of the few Restoration Anglicans to be interested in Biblical commentary, Simon Patrick. His paraphrase on the Song of Songs, with Annotations, published in 1685 and 1700, identified the Bride firmly as the whole Church rather than the individual soul. Although her words to her lover remained as erotic as they had been in Puritan paraphrase, this intimacy had no meaning for the individual Christian. Rather, Patrick practised a careful allegorical interpretation, often admitting that he was not sure what a particular utterance meant, and warning against those interpreters who 'strain too much' (p. 46). He tentatively suggests what the 'Myrrh and Spices' might be in 5:1: 'I have not adventured to be particular about specifying'.[22] His Annotations rarely mention the Roman Catholic Church and when they do, he is apologetic: identifying the sluggishness of the Bride in 5:3 as that of the Church after Constantine, he is careful to say that several Roman Catholic commentators think so too (p. 78). Characteristically for one who is in favour of authorities, the 'watchmen' in chapters 3 and 5 are entirely benign, and to be taken 'in a good sense'. (p. 81) The verse which Shaftesbury had interpreted so specifically and politically in 1678 in the House of Lords, Song of Songs 8:9, Patrick interprets entirely in moral terms, which he thinks 'the most simple Exposition of these words' and forbears 'to trouble the reader, with that vast variety....in Interpreters'(p. 141).

Perhaps Bishop Patrick differs most from previous interpretations when he insists, as he does for 4:7, 'Thou art all fair, my love' that these words 'are not to be applied to every particular person in the Church'(p.59). Anglican interpretation of the Song of Songs had changed a great deal since the English commentators of the start of the seventeenth century. The divine intoxication directed towards even the most humble 'particular person' is what had inspired political action and resistance to oppression since the Reformation. However, with the Monmouth rebellion – Sedgemoor was the last battle on English soil – the phase of religious warfare in English history had passed. That the Song of Songs, for the majority of the population, no longer was a significant factor in construction of the self or of the enemy, was partly a matter of a more stable politics in eighteenth-century England. Of course, it was partly a matter of textual interpretation too; but politics and textual interpretation are profoundly linked in the seventeenth century, as this book has shown.

Notes

Introduction

1. See Noam Flinker for Ranter use of the Song, *The Song of Songs in English Renaissance Literature* (Cambridge: D. S. Brewer, 2000), pp. 120–49: Nigel Smith discusses its use in the writing of Abiezer Coppe and other radicals, *Perfection Proclaimed: Language and Literature in English Radical Religion 1640–1660* (Oxford: Clarendon, 1989), pp. 57, 84, 112, 141, 158, 200, 262–3. Christopher Hill includes a brief survey of use of the Song of Songs in *The English Bible and the Seventeenth-Century Revolution* (Harmondsworth: Penguin, 1993), pp. 362–70.
2. Jeanne Shami, *John Donne and Conformity in Crisis in the Late Jacobean Pulpit* (Cambridge: D. S. Brewer, 2003), p. 16.
3. See Anthony Milton, *Catholic and Reformed: The Roman and Protestant Churches in English Protestant Thought, 1600–40* (Cambridge: CUP, 1995).
4. John Jekyll was written to by the four Bristol Nonconformist churches to ask for help under threat from the Lord Mayor of Bristol in 1675. See *The Records of a Church of Christ in Bristol, 1640–87* ed. Roger Hayden, Bristol Record Society's Publications XXVII (1974), p. 177 for the result.
5. J. Christopher King, *Origen on the Song of Songs as the Spirit of Scripture: The Bridegroom's Perfect Marriage-Song* (Oxford; Oxford University Press, 2005), p. 2.
6. I am grateful to Edward Ross for this reference: see http://gospelthemes.com/songcas.htm
7. Andre LaCocque and Paul Ricoeur, *Thinking Biblically: Exegetical and Hermeneutical Studies*, tr, David Pellauer (Chicago: University of Chicago Press, 1998), pp. 266–8.
8. John Barton, 'The Canonicity of the Song of Songs' in *Perspectives on the Song of Songs/Perspektiven der Höheliedauslegung* ed. Anselm C.Hagedorn (Berlin, Walter de Gruyter: 2005), pp. 1–7.
9. Stephen D. Moore, 'The Song of Songs in the History of Sexuality', *Church History* 69:2 (2000), pp. 329–48.
10. Ivy Schweitzer, *The Work of Self-Representation: Lyric Poetry in Colonial New England* (Chapel Hill: University of North Carolina Press, 1991), p. 87.
11. Shawn M. Krahmer, 'The Virile Bride of Bernard of Clairvaux', *Church History* 69 (2000), p. 311.
12. Tom Webster, '"Kiss me with the kisses of his mouth"; gender inversion and Canticles in godly spirituality' in *Sodomy in Early Modern Europe* ed. Tom Betteridge (Manchester; Manchester University Press, 2002), p. 159.
13. See Thomas Vincent, *Christ the best husband: or An invitation of young women unto Christ Delivered in a sermon to young women* (London, 1672): Edward Pearse, *The best match: or, The souls espousal to Christ* (London, 1673): Michael Harrison, *The best match, or, The believer's marriage with Christ* (London, 1691).
14. Richard Sibbes, *Bowels opened, or, A discovery of the neere and deere love, union and communion betwixt Christ and the Church, and consequently betwixt Him and every beleeving soule Delivered in divers sermons on the fourth fifth and sixt chapters of the Canticles* (London, 1639), p. 3. Schweitzer, *The Work of*

Self-Representation, p. 23, p. 179. See, for example, John Downame, *Lectures upon the foure first chapters of the prophecie of Hosea* (London, 1608), p. 272.

15. *The Life and Letters of John Winthrop*, ed. Robert C. Winthrop (Boston, 1869), I, p. 103 quoted in Schweitzer, *The Work of Self-Representation*, p. 5.

16. Webster, 'Kiss me with the kisses of his mouth', p. 150.

17. Krahmer, 'The Virile Bride', pp. 305, 316, 306.

18. Anne, Lady Southwell, *The Southwell-Sibthorpe Commonplace Book: Folger MS V.b.198*, ed. Jean Klene (Arizona: Renaissance English Text Society, 1997), p. 152.

19. F.W Dobbs-Allsopp finds many characteristics of Late Biblical Hebrew in the language of the Song of Songs (6th–4th century BC): see 'Late Linguistic Features in the Song of Songs' in *Perspectives*, ed. Hagedorn, pp. 26–77.

20. Marcia Falk, 'The *wasf*', *Love Lyrics from the Hebrew Bible: A Translation and Literary Study of the Song of Songs* (Sheffield: Almond Press, 1982), pp. 80–7: Athalya Brenner, '"Come Back, Come Back, the Shulammite": A Parody of the *wasf* Genre', *A Feminist Companion to the Song of Songs* ed. Athalya Brenner, (Sheffield: Sheffield Academic Press, 1993), pp. 234–57.

21. Origen, p. 268, *Perspectives*, ed. Hagedorn.

22. This is the opinion of André LaCocque, who believes that the text is actually a statement by a woman of resistance to religious and legal authority. LaCocque and Ricoeur, *Thinking Biblically*, pp. 236–63. See also J. William Whedbee, 'Paradox and Parody in the Song of Solomon: Towards a comic reading of the most sublime song', *A Feminist Companion to the Song of Songs* ed. Athalya Brenner, Sheffield: Sheffield Academic Press, 1993), pp. 266–78.

23. Joseph Stennett, *A version of Solomon's Song of Songs* (London, 1700), p. x.

24. Dudley Fenner, *The Song of Songs that is, the most excellent song which was Solomons, translated out of the Hebrue into Englishe meeter* (Middleburgh, 1587), sig. A8v.

25. Fenner, *The Song of Songs*, sig. A7v–A8r.

26. Théodore de Bèze, *Master Bezaes sermons upon the three chapters of the canticle of canticles tr, John Harmar* (Oxford, 1587), sig. ¶4r.

27. Stennett, *A version of Solomon's song*, p. iv.

28. George Wither, *The hymnes and songs of the Church diuided into two parts. The first part comprehends the canonicall hymnes, and such parcels of Holy Scripture as may properly be sung, with some other ancient songs and creeds. The second part consists of spirituall songs, appropriated to the severall times and occasions obserueable in the Church of England* (London, 1623), p. 32.

29. *Annotations upon all the books of the Old and New Testament* (London, 1657), sig.7G1r.

30. Samuel Woodford, *A paraphrase upon the Canticles* (London, 1679), p. 3. Compare George Herbert, 'Superliminare', the poem at the entrance to 'The Church'.

31. Downame, *Annotations*, sig. 7I3r.

32. Simon Patrick, *The Song of Solomon Paraphrased with Annotations* (London, 1700), p. 5, p. 16.

33. LaCocque and Ricoeur, *Thinking Biblically*, p. 270.

34. Charles M. Schulz, *Don't Hassle Me with Your Sighs, Chuck* (New York: Holt, Reinhart & Winston, 1976), p. 15.

35. Giovanni Diodati, *Pious and learned annotations upon the Holy Bible* (London, 1648), p. 441.

36. Fenner, *The Song of Songs*, sig. B7v.

37. James Durham, *Clavis cantici, or, An exposition of the Song of Solomon* (Edinburgh, 1668), p. 213.
38. Fenner, *The Song of Songs*, sig. A5r.
39. John Reeve, *Spiritual hymns upon Solomons song: or, Love in the right channel* (London, 1684), sig. A2r.
40. George Scheper, 'Reformation Attitudes Towards Allegory and the Song of Songs', *PMLA* 89 (1974), pp. 551–62.
41. Durham, *Clavis cantici*, p. 6.
42. J. Christopher King, *Origen on the Song Of Songs as the Spirit of Scripture: The Bridegroom's Perfect Marriage-Song* (Oxford: Oxford University Press, 2005), p. 72.
43. For a typological reading see the work commissioned by the Westminster Assembly, *Annotations upon all the books of the Old and New Testament* (London, 1645), sig. FFF1iiv.
44. See also John Collinges, *The intercourses of divine love betwixt Christ and the Church, or, The particular believing-soul* (London, 1676), sigs. A2v–A3r: he believes there to be types and metaphors in the text.
45. Durham, *Clavis cantici*, p. 8.
46. King, *Origen on the Song Of Songs as the Spirit of Scripture*, p. 57.
47. E. Ann Matter, *The Voice of the Beloved: The Song of Songs in Western Mediaeval Christianity* (Philadelphia: University of Pennsylvania Press, 1990), p. 3.
48. Antonio Brucioli, *A commentary upon the Canticle of Canticles* tr. Thomas James (London, 1598).
49. Matter, *The Voice of the Beloved*, p. 8.
50. Matter, *The Voice of the Beloved*, p. 125.
51. Max Engammare, *Qu'il me baise des baisiers de sa bouche: La Cantique des Cantiques à la Renaissance* (Geneva: Librarie Droz, 1993), pp. 147–77: p. 484.
52. Andre LaCocque and Paul Ricoeur, *Thinking Biblically*, p. 293.
53. Scheper, *Reformation Attitudes*, p. 555.
54. Elizabeth A. Clark, 'Origen, the Jews, and the Song of Songs: Allegory and Polemic in Christian Antiquity', *Perspectives on the Song of Songs*, p. 275.
55. Martin Luther, *Works*, ed. Jaroslav Pelikan (Concordia, St. Louis, 1972), XV, p. 200.
56. See Luther's political interpretation compared to Spenser's use of the trope in L. Johnson, 'Elizabeth, Bride and Queen; A Study of Spenser's April Eclogue and the Metaphors of English Protestantism', *Spenser Studies* II, eds P. Cullen and T. Roche (Pittsburgh: University of Pittsburgh Press, 1981), p. 79.
57. John Collinges, *The spouses hidden glory, and faithfull leaning upon her welbeloved* (London, 1647), p. 3.
58. Engammare, *Qu'il me baise*, p. 484.
59. Reeve, *Spiritual hymns upon Solomons song*, p. 1.
60. Flinker, *The Song of Songs*, pp. 120–49.
61. Thomas Beverley, *An exposition of the divinely prophetick Song of Songs which is Solomons* (London, 1687), sig. A2v.
62. See, for example, Thomas Watson, 'Christs Lovelinesse', attached to *The Saints Delight* (London, 1657); Matthew Poole, *Annotations upon the Holy Bible* (London, 1683).
63. Scheper, *Reformation Attitudes*, p. 557.
64. Théodore de Bèze, *Master Bezaes sermons upon the three chapters of the canticle of canticles wherein are handled the chiefest points of religion controversed and debated betweene us and the adversarie at this day, especially touching the true Iesus Christ and*

the true Church, and the certaine & infallible marks both of the one and of the other tr,
John Harmar (Oxford, 1587).

65. Matter, *The Voice of the Beloved*, p. 89.
66. John Bale, *The image of both Churches after the most wonderfull and heavenly Revelation of sainct Iohn the Evangelist, contayning a very fruitfull exposition or paraphrase upon the same* (London, 1670), sig. Aiiv.
67. John N. King, 'Bale, John (1495–1563)', *Oxford Dictionary of National Biography*, Oxford University Press, Sept 2004; online edn, Oct 2009. [http://www.oxforddnb.com/view/article/1175, accessed 16 March 2010]
68. John Bale, *The Second Part of the Image of Both Churches* (Antwerp, 1545?), p. 26.
69. Bale, *The Second Part*, sig. Civ.v, 110v. In the conclusion to the 1570 edition, Islam and Catholicism are also linked: 'by this they also differ, that Christ wold have all of love, Antichrist of tyrannous constraint, as evidently appeareth in Mahomete and the Pope', p. 143v.
70. John Foxe, *Christus triumphans comoedia apocalyptica autore Joanne Foxo; edita est olim Basileae, anno 1556 ; Nunc denuo edita*, ed. T.C. (London, 1672).
71. Charles H. Herford, *Studies in the Literary Relations of England and Germany in the Sixteenth Century* (Cambridge: Cambridge University Press, 1886), pp. 119–32.
72. See Chapter 2.
73. Marguerite, Queen of Navarre, *A godly medytacyon of the christen sowle, concerninge a loue towardes God and hys Christe, compyled in frenche by lady Margarete quene of Nauerre, and aptely translated into Englysh by the ryght vertuouse lady Elyzabeth doughter to our late souerayne Kynge Henri the. viij (1548)* p. 15.
74. Marguerite de Navarre, *A godly medytacyon of the christen sowle*, tr. Princess Elizabeth (London, 1548), p. 15.
75. Benjamin Keach, *The banquetting-house, or, A feast of fat things* (London, 1692), sig. A4r.
76. Miles Coverdale, *Goostly psalmes and spirituall songes drawen out of the holy Scripture, for the comforte and consolacyon of soch as love to reioyse in God and his Worde* (London, 1635?).
77. William Baldwin, *The canticles or balades of Salomon* (London, 1549), sig. A1v: see also Bartimaeus Andrewes, *Certaine verie worthie, godly and profitable sermons, upon the fifth chapter of the Songs of Solomon* (London, 1583), sig.7r.
78. Beverley, *An exposition*, sig. A1r.
79. Fenner, *The Song of Songs*, sig. A4r.
80. Fenner, *The Song of Songs*, sig. A3r.
81. Baldwin, *The canticles or balades of Salomon*, sig. Aiiiv.
82. Thomas Sternhold, *Certayne psalmes chosen out of the Psalter of David, and drawn into Englishe metre* (London, 1549), sig. Aiiir.
83. Philip Sidney, *An Apologie for poetrie* (London, 1595), p. 10.
84. Baldwin, *The canticles or balades of Salomon*, sig.Avr.
85. Flinker, *The Song of Songs in English Renaissance Literature*, pp. 34–6.
86. Baldwin, *The canticles or balades of Salomon*, sigs. Eviv–Eviir.
87. Flinker, *The Song of Songs in English Renaissance Literature*, pp. 54–6, spends some time on this poem explaining how its eroticism is gradually diffused.
88. Flinker describes this layout. *The Song of Songs in English Renaissance Literature*, pp. 32–3.
89. Samuel Woodford, *A paraphrase upon the Canticles* (London, 1679), p. 10.

90. Michael Drayton, *The Harmonie of the Church Containing, the Spirituall Songes and holy Hymnes, of godly men, Patriarkes and Prophetes: all, sweetly sounding, to the praise and glory of the highest* (London, 1591): *A Heavenly Harmonie of Spirituall Songes, and holy Himnes, of godly Men, Patriarkes, and Prophets* (London, 1610).

91. Francis Meres, *Palladis tamia Wits treasury being the second part of Wits common wealth* (London, 1598), p. 285b.

92. Gervase Markham, *The poem of poems. Or, Sions muse contayning the divine song of King Salomon, devided into eight eclogues* (London, 1596), sig. A4v.

93. John Calvin, *The institution of Christian religion, wrytten in Latine by maister Ihon Caluin, and translated into Englysh according to the authors last edition* (London, 1561), fol.51v.

94. See, for example, William Gearing, *The love-sick spouse, or, The substance of four sermons preached on Canticles 2.5.* (London, 1665).

95. Henry Finch, *An exposition of the Song of Solomon: called Canticles* (London, 1615), p. 3.

96. See Sharon Achinstein, 'Romance of the Spirit: Female Sexuality and Religious Desire in Early Modern England' *ELH* 69 (2002), pp. 413–38.

97. I have used the term 'mystical marriage' to describe the spiritual union with Christ that is often the referent of the marriage metaphor in seventeenth-century religious writing. Apart from 'holy wedlock', this phenomenon is referred to by seventeenth-century Puritans typically as 'spiritual marriage'. Francis Rous entitles his 1633 book (see ch. 2) *The Mysticall Marriage*, but I am aware that 'mystical marriage' is used in Catholic discourse to mean something rather different and much more hierarchical than the puritan phenomenon described here. See Poulain, Augustin. 'Mystical Marriage,' *The Catholic Encyclopedia*. Vol. 9. New York: Robert Appleton Company, 1910. 16 Mar. 2010 <http://www.newadvent.org/cathen/09703a.htm>. However, this is a phrase for a rather difficult spiritual phenomenon that I think will be familiar to my audience, and so I use it in this book.

1   Royal Brides and National Identity, 1603–25

1. Jeanne Shami, *John Donne and Conformity in Crisis in the Late Jacobean Pulpit* (Cambridge: D. S. Brewer, 2003), pp. 4–5.

2. Thomas Jackson, *Londons New-yeeres gift. Or The Uncouching of the foxe* (London, 1609), pp. 3b–5b.

3. Nicholas Tyacke, *Anti-Calvinists: The Rise of English Arminianism c. 1590–1640* (Oxford: OUP, 1987), p. 27.

4. C. W. Sutton, 'Jackson, Thomas (1570/71–1646)', rev. Margaret Sparks, *Oxford Dictionary of National Biography*, Oxford University Press, 2004; online edn, Jan. 2008 [http://www.oxforddnb.com/view/article/14552, accessed 16 Mar. 2010]

5. John King, *A sermon at Paules Crosse, on behalfe of Paules Church, March 26. 1620* (London, 1620), p. 48. Andrew Willet, *Ecclesia triumphans, that is, the joy of the English church* (London, 1603), pp. 64–5.

6. John Downame, *Lectures upon the foure first chapters of the prophecie of Hosea Wherein the text is exponded and cleered, and such profitable instructions observed, and applied, as naturally arise out of this holie Scripture, and are fit for these times* (London, 1608).

7. Downame, *Lectures*, p. 43, pp. 190–1.

8. Not that his Puritan credentials are not impeccable: another gloss on p. 275 reads 'The profane practice of Poets condemned'.

9. Michael McGiffert, 'God's Controversy with Jacobean England', *The American Historical Review*, 88 (1963), p. 1152.

10. Mary Morrissey, 'Elect nations and prophetic preaching: *types* and *examples* in the Paul's Cross Jeremiad' in Lori Anne Ferrell and Peter McCullough, eds, *The English Sermon Revised* (Manchester: Manchester University Press, 2000), pp. 43–58.

11. Durham, *Clavis cantici*, p. 8. Samuel Woodford sees the Bride as a type of the 'seed of Abraham': *A Paraphrase upon the Canticles*, p. 12.

12. John Owen, *The doctrine of the saints perseverance explained and confirmed* (London, 1654), pp. 193–4. See Chapter 6.

13. Richard A. McCabe, *Joseph Hall: a Study in Satire and Meditation* (Oxford, Clarendon Press, 1987), pp.8–9. Hall contributed prefatory verses to Donne's *An Anatomie of the World* (1611) and *The Second Anniversary* (1612). Several publications, including his huge *The Works of Joseph Hall*,went into multiple editions in the seventeenth century: Ian Green, *Print and Protestantism in Early Modern England* (Oxford, 2000), pp. 625–6. His paraphrase of The Song of Songs is bound with *Salomons divine arts, of 1. Ethickes, 2. Politickes, 3. Oeconomicks* (London, 1609).

14. See Bellany, Alistair. *The Politics of Court Scandal in Early Modern England: News Culture and the Overbury Affair, 1603–1660* (Cambridge: Cambridge University Press, 2002). For libels written on the nullification of Essex's marriage to Frances Howard, see 'Early Stuart Libels: an edition of poetry from manuscript sources'. Ed. Alastair Bellany and Andrew McRae. *Early Modern Literary Studies* Text Series I (2005). http://purl.oclc.org/emls/texts/libels/, section F.

15. Joseph Hall, *Salomons Song of Songs, Paraphrased* (London, 1609), p. 3.

16. George Abbot, *The reasons vvhich Doctour Hill hath brought, for the vpholding of papistry, which is falselie termed the Catholike religion: vnmasked and shewed to be very weake, and vpon examination most insufficient for that purpose* (London, 1604), pp. 12, 73, 235: Thomas Bell, *The anatomie of Popish tyranny* (London, 1603), p. 69: Andrew Willet, *A catholicon, that is, A generall preservative or remedie against the pseudocatholike religion* (London, 1602), pp. 11, 13, 18.

17. The evidence for Wriothesley's involvement with the circle around Prince Henry is his appearances at the Prince's spectacles: Roy Strong, *Henry, Prince of Wales, and England's Lost Renaissance* (Thomas and Hudson, 1986), p. 47.

18. *Calendar of State Papers Venetian*, p. 450.

19. Timothy Wilks describes this as operating through the head of the Prince's household, Sir Thomas Chaloner. Timothy Wilks, 'The Court Culture of Prince Henry and His Circle, 1603–1613', unpublished D.Phil thesis, University of Oxford, 1987, p. 4.

20. Strong, Henry, *Prince of Wales*, p. 14.

21. Leeds Barroll, *Anna of Denmark, Queen of England* (Philadelpia: University of Pennsylvania Press, 2001), pp. 121–2.

22. Strong, Henry, *Prince of Wales*, p. 141.

23. Ben Jonson, *The Workes of Benjamin Jonson* (London, 1616), pp. 970–2.

24. Fulke Greville, *The Life of the Renowned Sir Philip Sidney* (London, 1651), pp. 195–6.

25. Simon Adams, 'The Protestant Cause: religious alliance with the West European Calvinist communities as a political issue in England 1585–1630' , unpublished DPhil thesis, University of Oxford (1973), pp. 200–14.

26. *Calendar of State Papers Venetian*, p. 450.
27. George Wither, 'Obsequies for Prince Henry' in *Juvenilia* (London, 1633), pp. 303–4.
28. Henry Peacham, *The period of mourning Disposed into six visions. In memorie of the late prince. Together with nuptiall hymnes, in honour of this happy marriage betweene the great princes, Frederick Count Palatine of the Rhene, and the most excellent, and aboundant president of all virtue and goodnes Elizabeth onely daughter to our soveraigne, his Maiestie* (London, 1613), Sig. A3r.
29. George Webbe, *The bride royall, or The spirituall marriage betweene Christ and his Church Delivered by way of congratulation upon the happy and hopefull marriage betweene the two incomparable princes, the Palsegraue, and the Ladie Elizabeth* (London, 1613), p. 79. I owe reference to this sermon to Alice Eardley. His 'Hosead' is the first in a list of nine cited by McGiffert, 'Gods Controversy', p. 1170.
30. Andrew Willet, *A treatise of Salomons mariage or, a congratulation for the happie and hopefull mariage betweene the most illustrious and noble Prince Frederike the V. Count Palatine of Rhine, Elector of the Sacred Romane Empire, and Arch-Sewer, and in the vacancie thereof Vicar Generall: Duke of Bavaria, &c. Knight of the most noble order of the Garter. And the most gratious and excellent Princesse, the Ladie Elizabeth, sole daughter unto the High and Mighty Prince Iames, by the grace of God, King of great Britaine, France and Ireland* (London, 1613), p. 26.
31. Théodore de Bèze, *Master Bezaes sermons upon the three chapters of the canticle of canticles wherein are handled the chiefest points of religion controversed and debated betweene us and the adversarie at this day, especially touching the true Iesus Christ and the true Church, and the certaine & infallible marks both of the one and of the other* (Oxford, 1587), sig. ¶4r.
32. Willet, *Salomons marriage*, p. 49: Jonson, *Workes*, p. 974.
33. Joseph Hall, *Epistles,the second volume* (London, 1608), iii, 59–62.
34. *An Anatomie of the World (1611) The Second Anniversary (1612)*. McCabe, *Joseph Hall*, p. 9. Louis A. Knafla, 'More, Sir George (1553–1632)', *Oxford Dictionary of National Biography*, Oxford University Press, Sept. 2004; online edn, Jan. 2008 [http://www.oxforddnb.com/view/article/19177, accessed 11 Aug. 2008]
35. Wilks, 'The Court Culture of Prince Henry', p. 13.
36. Fulke Greville, *The Life of the Renowned Sir Philip Sidney* (London, 1651), p. 196.
37. George Gifford, *The Manner of Sir Philip Sidneyes Death*, ed. Bent Juel-Jensen, (Oxford, Bodleian Library, 1959).
38. Brett Usher, 'Gifford, George (1547/8–1600)', *Oxford Dictionary of National Biography*, Oxford University Press, 2004 [http://www.oxforddnb.com/view/article/10658, accessed 16 Mar. 2010]
39. Richard Sibbes, *Bowels opened, or, A discovery of the neere and deere love, union and communion betwixt Christ and the Church, and consequently betwixt Him and every beleeving soule Delivered in divers sermons on the fourth fifth and sixt chapters of the Canticles* (London, 1639), p. 147.
40. Prevenient grace is the Calvinist explanation for the divinely-granted but limited power whereby the totally depraved human being can respond to God: see John Boys, *The third part from S. Iohn Baptists nativitie to the last holy-day in the whole yeere dedicated vnto the right religious and resolute doctor, Matthew Sutcliffe, Deane of Exeter* (London, 1615), p. 125:.'He which is the father of mercies giveth us prevenient grace, subsequent grace, cooperant grace, grace before grace, and grace after grace, keeping us by his power thorough faith, and preserving us to his heavenly kingdome.'

41. Judith Stampfer, *John Donne and the Metaphysical Genre* (New York: Funk and Wagnals, 1970), p.258. Quoted in *The Variorum Edition of the Poetry of John Donne* gen. ed. Gary Stringer vol. 7, no. 1 'The Holy Sonnets' (Bloomington: Indiana UP, 2005), p. 222.

42. John Donne, *The divine poems*, ed. Helen Gardner (Oxford: Clarendon Press, 2000), p. 11.

43. Anthony Low, *The Reinvention of Love: Poetry, Politics and Culture from Sidney to Milton* (Cambridge: CUP, 1993), p. 81.

44. William Kerrigan, 'The Fearful Accomodation of John Donne' *English Literary Renaissance* 4 (1974), p. 352.

45. Richard Strier, 'John Donne Awry and Squint; the Holy Sonnets, 1608–1610', *Modern Philology* 86 (1989), p. 377.

46. Gene Edward Veith, *Reformation Spirituality: the Religion of George Herbert* (Associated University Presses, 1985), p. 121.

47. Robert Aylett, *The Song of Songs, which was Salomons metaphrased in English heroiks by way of dialogue. With certayne of the brides ornaments, viz. poeticall essayes upon a divine subiect. Whereunto is added a funerall elegie, consecrate to the memorie of that ever: honoured Lord, Iohn, late Bishop of London* (London, 1622), p. 13: Robert Aylett, *The brides ornaments viz. five meditations, morall and divine. 1. Knowledge, 2. zeale, 3. temperance, 4. bountie, 5. ioy* (London, 1625), p. 14.

48. Noam Flinker, *The Song of Songs in English Renaissance Literature* (Cambridge: D.S. Brewer, 2000), pp. 113–15.

49. Kenneth Fincham and Nicholas Tyacke denote Aylett a Calvinist on the basis of two statements which seem to favour election, and note with some puzzlement his poems of 1621 celebrating the consecration of a chapel in what would become Laudian style: *Altars Restored: the changing face of English Religious Worship, 1547–c1700* (Oxford: Oxford University Press, 2007), pp. 103–4. However, the residual use of such commonplaces as election in 1621 is hardly surprising: Aylett's non-Puritan tendencies are far more accurately traced in this analysis of his treatment of a Biblical text often intepreted by Calvinists more radical than Aylett.

50. See Edward Staunton, *Phinehas's zeal in execution of judgement. Or, A divine remedy for Englands misery. A sermon preached before the Right Honourable House of Lords in the Abby of Westminster, at their late solemne monethly fast, 30 Oct. 1644* (London, 1645).

51. Matthew Steggle, 'Aylett, Robert (*c.*1582–1655)', *Oxford Dictionary of National Biography*, Oxford University Press, 2004 [http://www.oxforddnb.com/view/article/932, accessed 16 March 2010]

52. See later in chapter 1: chapter 2.

53. Flinker, *The Song of Songs in English Renaissance Literature*, p. 103, p. 109.

54. *Master Bezaes sermons vpon the three chapters of the canticle of canticles*, sig. ¶4r.

55. Donne, *The divine poems*, ed. Gardner, p. 124. Other critics such as Frank Kermode in *The Poetry of John Donne* (Cambridge; CUP, 1968) and T.W. and R.J. Craik in *John Donne; Selected Poetry and Prose* (London: Methuen, 1986) follow this line.

56. George Potter and Evelyn Simpson eds, *The Sermons of John Donne*, (Berkeley: University of California Press, 1953–1962), III, p. 13.

57. Donne, *The Divine Poems*, ed. Gardner, p. 15.

58. See Stanley Stewart, *The Enclosed Garden: The Tradition and The Image in Seventeenth-Century Poetry* (Madison: University of Wisconsin Press, 1966), p. 21. Donne, *The divine poems*, ed. Gardner, p. 122.

59. Barbara Lewalski suggests that 'no-one but Donne would be witty enough to confuse the Bride with the Whore' *Protestant Poetics and the Seventeenth-Century English Religious Lyric* (Princeton, NJ: Princeton University Press, 1979), p. 274.

60. Donne, *The Divine Poems*, ed. Gardner, p. 123. Marotti agrees and suggests that the poem is meant for an intimate coterie: *John Donne, Coterie Poet* (Madison: University of Wisconsin Press, 1986), p. 283.

61. Catherine Gimelli Martin suggests that Donne is drawing on the story of Hosea, who married a prostitute at the command of God. See '"Unmeete Contraryes": The Reformed Subject and Religious Desire in John Donne's *Anniversaries* and *Holy Sonnets*' in *John Donne and the Protestant Reformation: New Perspectives*, ed. Mary Arshagouni Papazian (Detroit: Wayne State University Press, 2003), p. 214.

62. Wilks, 'The Court Culture of Prince Henry and His Circle', p. 22.

63. For the Synod of Dort, see Nicholas Tyacke, *Ant-Calvinists: The Rise of English Arminianism c. 1590–1640* (Oxford: Clarendon Press, 1987), pp. 87–106.

64. Shami, John Donne and Conformity in Crisis, p. 64.

65. James I, *A meditation upon the Lords prayer, written by the Kings Maiestie, for the benefit of all his subiects, especially of such as follow the court* (London, 1619), p. 14.

66. Milton, *Catholic and Reformed*, p. 507.

67. Thomas Cogswell, *The Blessed Revolution: English politics and the coming of war, 1621–4* (Cambridge: Cambridge UP, 1989), p. 18. Peter Lake and Nicholas Tyacke, 'The Ecclesiastical Policy of James I', *Journal of British History* 24 (1985), p. 198. See Jeanne Shami, *John Donne and Conformity in Crisis in the Late Jacobean Pulpit* (Cambridge: D. S. Brewer, 2003), pp. 41–4, for attempts to control sermons on Bohemia and the Spanish Match in this period.

68. 'The Ecclesiastical Policy of James I', p. 139.

69. *The Sermons of John Donne*, eds George Potter and Evelyn Simpson, X vols (Berkeley: University of California Press, 1953–1962) IV, pp. 178–209. Shami gives an account of this particular sermon, tracing the background to it and subsequent reactions: *John Donne and Conformity in Crisis*, pp. 102–38.

70. Nicholas Tyacke, *Anti-Calvinists: The Rise of English Arminianism c. 1590–1640* (Oxford; OUP, 1987), p. 104.

71. Shami, *John Donne and Conformity in Crisis*, p. 2.

72. Stephen Wright, 'Loe, William (d. 1645)', *Oxford Dictionary of National Biography*, Oxford University Press, 2004 [http://www.oxforddnb.com/view/article/16927, accessed 16 Mar. 2010]

73. William Loe, *The Mysterie of Mankind, made into a Manual, or The Protestants Portuize reduced into Explication Application, Invocation, tending to Illumination, Sanctification, Devotion* (London, 1619), sig. A7r.

74. William Loe, *Songs of Sion Set for the ioy of gods deere ones, who sitt here by the brookes of this worlds Babel, & weepe when they thinke on Hierusalem which is on highe* (Hamburg, 1620), p. 98.

75. Cogswell, *The Blessed Revolution*, p. 27.

76. See poem attributed to James I in 'Early Stuart Libels: an edition of poetry from manuscript sources', Ed. Alastair Bellany and Andrew McRae. *Early Modern Literary Studies* Text Series I (2005). http://purl.oclc.org/emls/texts/libels/ N0–Ni. Thomas Jackson, *Iudah must into captivitie Six sermons on Ierem. 7.16. Lately preached in the Cathedrall Church of Christ in Canterburie, and elsevvher* (London, 1622), sig. A3r.

77. Edmund Gosse, *The Life and Letters of John Donne*, 2 vols (London: Heinemann, 1899), II, 168, p. 161.

78. George Wither, *Juvenilia* (London, 1622), sig. Gg 7v, sig. Ff8r.

79. Milton, *Catholic and Reformed.* p. 58.
80. Peter Lake, 'The moderate and irenic case for religious war: Joseph Hall's *Via Media* in context' in Susan Amussen and Mark Kishlansky, eds, *Political culture and cultural politics in Early Modern England* (Manchester UP, 1995), p. 78.
81. Joseph Hall, *Contemplations, the sixth volume* (London, 1622), p. 264.
82. Peter McCullough, *Sermons at Court* (Cambridge: CUP, 1998), p. 206.
83. John Rawlinson, *Quadriga salutis* (London, 1625), sig. A2v.
84. Cogswell, *The Blessed Revolution*, pp. 6–8.
85. McCullough, *Sermons at Court*, p. 145, p. 208.
86. George Wither, *Britain's remembrancer* (London, 1628), p. 18.
87. Shami, *John Donne and Conformity in Crisis*, p. 1.
88. Ian Green, *Print and Protestantism in Early Modern England* (Oxford: OUP, 2000), p. 671.
89. George Wither, *The hymnes and songs of the Church divided into two parts. The first part comprehends the canonicall hymnes, and such parcels of Holy Scripture as may properly be sung, with some other ancient songs and creeds. The second part consists of spirituall songs, appropriated to the severall times and occasions observeable in the Church of England* (London, 1623), p. 54.
90. George Wither, *The schollers purgatory discovered in the Stationers common-wealth, and discribed in a discourse apologeticall, aswell for the publike advantage of the Church, the state & whole common-wealth of England, as for the remedy of private iniuryes* (London, 1624), p. 51.
91. Wither, *Hymnes and songs*, p. 32.
92. Nicholas Caussin, *The Holy Court*, tr. Thomas Hawkins (London, 1634), III, p. 149.
93. Stanley Stewart, *The Enclosed Garden* (Madison and. London: University of Wisconsin Press, 1966), p. 22.

2 *The Mysticall Marriage*, Martyrology and Arminianism, 1625–40

1. John Donne, *The Sermons of John Donne*, X vols, eds George R. Potter and Evelyn M. Simpson (Berkeley; University of California Press, 1957), VI, p. 280.
2. See Fulke Greville's *The life of the renowned Sr Philip Sidney. with the true interest of England as it then stood in relation to all forrain princes: and particularly for suppressing the power of Spain stated by him. His principall actions, counsels, designes, and death. Together with a short account of the maximes and policies used by Queen Elizabeth in her government.* (London, 1651). This had been circulating in manuscript: Fulke Greville had stopped working on it at the death of Prince Henry.
3. For instance, Donne 'relegates the issue of irresistibility to things indifferent', in 1617: 'challenges the Calvinist language of election and reprobation', Jeffrey Johnson, *The Theology of John Donne* (Cambridge: D. S.Brewer, 1999), p. 125, pp. 134–5. Shami, *John Donne and Conformity in Crisis*, p. 78.
4. Donne, *Sermons*, III, p. 252.
5. See Ivy Schweitzer, *The Work of Self-Representation: Lyric Poetry in Colonial New England* (Chapel Hill: University of North Carolina Press, 1991), p. 4.
6. Shami, *John Donne and Conformity in Crisis*, pp. 19–20.
7. McCullough, *Sermons at Court*, p. 7.
8. Milton, *Catholic and Reformed*, pp. 538–43.

9. Donne, *Sermons*, III, p. 248.
10. Donne, *Sermons*, V, p. 115.
11. Calvin, *The Institution of Christian Religion Translated into English according to the authors last edition* (London, 1561).
12. Donne, *Sermons*, VI, pp. 158–60.
13. Calvin, *The Institution of Christian Religion* (London, 1561), BK 3, ch. xv, iii, p. 194.
14. Donne, *Sermons*, VII, p. 409.
15. Donne, *Sermons*, X, p. 144, p. 171.
16. Ephesians 5:27.
17. Milton, *Catholic and Reformed*, p. 541.
18. Adams, 'The Protestant Cause', p. 22.
19. Richard Montagu, *Appello Caesarem A iust appeale from two vniust informers* (London, 1625), p. 55.
20. Tyacke, *Anti-Calvinists*, pp. 105–6.
21. Tyacke, *Anti-Calvinists*, p. 125. William Prynne, *The Perpetuitie of a Regenerate Man's Estate* (London, 1626).
22. Tyacke, *Anti-Calvinists*, p. 152.
23. *Proceedings in Parliament, 1625* eds Marija Jansson and William B. Bidwell (New Haven; Yale University Press, 1987), pp. 330–3.
24. This was not the last time such a technique was to be used. In 1642 someone printed a very short version of James' political opinions apparently collected by the long-dead but vehemently Calvinist Andrew Willet, in support of the Parliamentary cause: *King Iames his iudgement by way of counsell and advice to all his loving subjects extracted out of his own speeches / by Doctor Willet ; concerning politique government in England and Scotland* (London, 1642).
25. Colin Burrow, 'Rous, Francis (1580/81–1659)', *Oxford Dictionary of National Biography*, Oxford University Press, 2004.
26. The treatise takes as its target a 'wizard', friend of Montaigne and doctor of law Pierre Charron, who published *La Sagesse,* a volume arguing that philosophy is morally superior to religion, in 1601. Rous cites him as 'D. Char.'. *The diseases of the time, attended by their remedies* (London, 1622), p. 18. I owe this identification of him to Dr. Ingrid de Smet of Warwick University. Not surprisingly, the treatise is deeply anti-Catholic, although it also includes lengthy diatribes on drunkenness, the impersonation of women by boys on stage, and the dangers of rhetorical eloquence.
27. Francis Rous, *Oile of scorpions The miseries of these times turned into medicines and curing themselues.* (London, 1623), Table of Contents A8 +2, p. 34.
28. Tyacke, *Anti-Calvinists*, p. 138.
29. Francis Rous, *Testis veritatis the doctrine of King Iames our late soueraigne of famous memory, of the Church of England, of the Catholicke Church : plainely shewed to bee one in the points of pradestination, free-will, certaintie of salvation : with a discouery of the grounds naturall, politicke of Arminianisme* (London, 1626), pp. 86–7.
30. Wallace Notestein and Frances Helen Relf, eds, *Commons Debates for 1629* (Minneapolis: University of Minnesota Press, 1921), p. 12, p. 15, p. 267.
31. Francis Rous, *Catholick charitie complaining and maintaining, that Rome is uncharitable to sundry eminent parts of the Catholick Church, and especially to Protestants, and is therefore Uncatholick : and so, a Romish book, called Charitie mistaken, though undertaken by a second, is it selfe a mistaking* (London, 1641), pp. 1–2.
32. Rous, *Catholick charitie*, sig. A2r.
33. See Erica Longfellow, *Women and Religious Writing in Early Modern England* (Cambridge: Cambridge University Press, 2004), pp. 17–50.

34. Henoch Clapham, *Three partes of Salomon his Song of Songs, expounded* (London, 1603), pp. 179–80.
35. John R. Knott, *Discourses of Martyrdom in English Literature, 1563–1694* (Cambridge: CUP, 1993), p. 122.
36. See Numbers 13.
37. George Gifford, *Fifteene sermons, vpon the Song of Salomon* (London, 1598), pp. 15–16.
38. Donne, *Sermons*, V, p. 121.
39. Donne, *Sermons*, V, p. 115.
40. Donne, *Sermons*, V, p. 125.
41. Francis Rous, *Thule, or Vertues historie* (London, 1598), sig. D3r.
42. Antony Low, *The Reinvention of Love: Piety, Politics and Culture from Sidney to Milton* (Cambridge: Cambridge University Press, 1993), pp. 106–7.
43. Théodore de Bèze, *Master Bezaes sermons upon the three chapters of the canticle of canticles wherein are handled the chiefest points of religion controversed and debated betweene us and the aduersarie at this day, especially touching the true Iesus Christ and the true Church, and the certaine & infallible marks both of the one and of the other* tr, John Harmar (Oxford, 1587).
44. Nicholas Byfield, *The Signes or An essay concerning the assurance of Gods love, and mans salvation gathered out of the holy Scriptures* (London, 1614), pp. 14–19.
45. Thomas Gataker, *The ioy of the iust with the signes of such. A discourse tending to the comfort of the deiected and afflicted; and to the triall of sinceritie* (London, 1623), pp. 101–51.
46. Adam Harsnett, *A touch-stone of grace Discovering the differences betweene true and counterfeit grace: laying downe infallible evidences and markes of true grace: serving for the triall of a mans spirituall estate* (London, 1630), p. 170.
47. Donne, *Sermons*, II, p. 226.
48. Princeton University Library MS, Robert H. Taylor Collection RTC01 no. 62, fol. 34r.
49. Clement Cotton, *A complete concordance to the Bible of the last translation* (London, 1631).
50. Seven editions were printed 1613–1637. David Scott Kastan, 'Little Foxes' in Christopher Highley and John N. King,, eds, *John Foxe and his World* (Ashgate, 2002), p. 123. Ian Green includes it in his list of seventeenth-century 'bestsellers': *Pint ancd Protestantism*, p. 610.
51. Clement Cotton, *The mirror of martyrs in a short view lively expressing the force of their faith, the fervency of their love, the wisedome of their sayings, the patience of their suffrings, etc. : with their prayers and preparation for their last farewell : whereunto is added two godly letters written by M. Bradford, full of sweet consolation for such as are afflicted in conscience* (London, 1613), sig. A4v.
52. See Joseph Hall, *A plaine and familiar explication (by way of paraphrase) of all the hard texts of the whole divine Scripture of the Old and New Testament* (London 1633): *Select thoughts, one century. Also the breathings of the devout soul* (London, 1648).
53. Milton, *Catholic and Reformed*, p. 536.
54. Tom Webster, *Godly Clergy in Early Stuart England* (Cambridge: CUP, 1997), p. 91.
55. Mark E. Dever, *Richard Sibbes: Puritanism and Calvinism in late Elizabethan and early Stuart England* (Macon, Georgia: Mercer University Press, 2000).
56. Samuel Clarke, *A generall martyrologie containing a collection of all the greatest persecutions which have befallen the church of Christ from the creation to our present times : whereunto are added, The lives of sundry modern divines, famous in their generations*

for learning and piety, and most of them great sufferers in the cause of Christ (London, 1651), sig. A2v.

57. Mark E. Dever, 'Sibbes , Richard (1577?–1635)', *Oxford Dictionary of National Biography*, Oxford University Press, 2004.
58. For Sibbes on the Song of Songs, see Longfellow, *Women and Religious Writing*, pp. 41–7.
59. Richard Sibbes, *Bowels opened, or, A discovery of the neere and deere love, union and communion betwixt Christ and the Church, and consequently betwixt Him and every beleeving soule Delivered in divers sermons on the fourth fifth and sixt chapters of the Canticles*. (London, 1639), p. 4.
60. Mark. E. Dever, *Richard Sibbes: Puritanism and Calvinism in late Elizabethan and early Stuart England* (Macon, Georgia: Mercer University Press, 2000).
61. Samuel Clarke, *A martyrologic containing a collection of all the persecutions which have befallen the Church of England since the first plantation of the Gospel to the end of Queen Maries reign* (London, 1652), p. 149.
62. Webster, *Godly Clergy*, p. 165. This early evidence of the radicalism of Nye and Goodwin makes nonsense of Dever's claim that at the time Sibbes died he would not have known of their nonconformist tendencies.
63. John Calvin, *The Institution of Christian Religion* (London, 1561), fol. 51v.
64. Wilhelm Niesel, *Reformed Symbolics: a comparison of Catholicism, Orthodoxy, and Protestantism* tr. David Lewis (Edinburgh: Oliver and Boyd, 1962), p. 182.
65. See Chapter 6, below.
66. John Preston, *The golden scepter held forth to the humble with the Churches dignitie by her marriage. And the Churches dutie in her carriage. In three treatises. The former delivered in sundry sermons in Cambridge, for the weekely fasts, 1625. The two latter in Lincolnes Inne* (London, 1638). J. Fielding, 'Ball, Thomas (1590–1659)', *Oxford Dictionary of National Biography*, Oxford University Press, 2004.
67. Preston, 'The Churches Marriage', p. 17 (second sermon in *The golden sceptre*).
68. Webster, *Godly Clergy*, pp. 168–9. Princeton University Library, Robert H. Taylor Collection RTC01 no. 62, Elizabeth Isham's 'Booke of Remembrances', fol. 15r.
69. *The Diary of Samuel Rogers*, eds. Kenneth W. Shippps and Tom Webster (Woodbridge, Suffolk:Boydell Press, 2004), p. 141.
70. *The Diary of Samuel Rogers*, pp. xvi–xviii.
71. For Richard Rogers' diary, see *Two Puritan Diaries* ed. Marshall M. Knappen (Chicago, 1653).
72. Adams, 'The Protestant Cause', pp. 439–46.
73. Jacqueline Eales, 'Vere, Mary, Lady Vere (1581–1671)', *Oxford Dictionary of National Biography*, Oxford University Press, 2004.
74. Shami, *John Donne and Conformity in Crisis*, p. 18.
75. Henry Burton, *For God, and the King. The summe of two sermons preached on the fifth of November last in St. Matthewes Friday-streete. 1636* (Amsterdam, 1636), sig. A2v.
76. *The Diary of Samuel Rogers*, p. 23.
77. Kenneth Gibson, 'Burton, Henry (bap. 1578, d. 1647/8)', *Oxford Dictionary of National Biography*, Oxford University Press, 2004.
78. *Letters of the Rev Samuel Rutherford*, pp. 34–5.
79. J. Fielding, 'Ball, Thomas (1590–1659)', *Oxford Dictionary of National Biography*, Oxford University Press, 2004.
80. Webster, *Godly Clergy*, p. 87.

81. John Bastwick, *The Letany of John Bastwick, Doctor of Phisicke, being now full of devotion, as well in respect of the common calamities of plague and pestilence; as also of his owne patticular miserie : lying at this instant in Limbo Patrum. Set downe in two letters to Mr. Aquila Wykes, keeper of the Gatehouse, his good angell* (London, 1637).

82. Knott, *Discourses of Martyrdom*, pp. 134–47.

83. See the illegally published accounts of the regicides' last days in prison: *The speeches and prayers of Major General Harison, Octob. 13. Mr. John Carew, Octob. 15. Mr. Justice Cooke, Mr. Hugh Peters, Octob. 16. Mr. Tho. Scott, Mr. Gregory Clement, Col. Adrian Scroop, Col. John Jones, Octob. 17. Col. Daniel Axtell, & Col. Fran. Hacker, Oct. 19 the times of their death. Together with severall occasionall speeches and passages in their imprisonment till they came to the place of execution.* (1660) and subsequent variants. The accounts of those executed after the Monmouth Rebellion show the same kind of piety: *The dying speeches, letters, and prayers, &c. of those eminent Protestants who suffered in the vvest of England, (and elsewhere,) under the cruel sentence of the late Lord Chancellour, then Lord Chief Justice Jefferys with an account of their undaunted courage at the barr, and afterwards; and the most remarkable circumstances that attended their execution. Never before published.* (London, 1689) and other variants.

84. John Bastwick, *A breife relation of certaine speciall, and most materiall passages, and speeches in the Starre-Chamber* (Amsterdam, 1638), p. 24.

85. *The Diary of Samuel Rogers*, p. 108.

86. Henry Burton, *A narration of the life of Mr. Henry Burton* (London, 1643), pp. 40, 42–3.

87. John Ley, *A patterne of pietie. Or The religious life and death of that grave and gracious matron, Mrs. Jane Ratcliffe widow and citizen of Chester* (London, 1640). Peter Lake, 'Feminine Piety and Personal Potency: the Emancipation of Mrs. Jane Ratcliffe', *The Seventeenth Century* no. 2 (1987) pp. 143–65. Clarke also included in his volume a Life of Margaret Duck, wife of the persecutor of Daniel Rogers and Samuel Rutherford Arthur Duck: her Puritan godliness in the face of the Arminian activism of her husband, member of the Court of High Commission in the 1630s, was clearly a cause for triumph.

88. Byfield, *The signes*, sig. A7r.

89. Samuel Clarke, *A collection of the lives of ten eminent divines famous in their generations for learning, prudence, piety, and painfulness in the work of the ministry : whereunto is added the life of Gustavus Ericson, King of Sueden, who first reformed religion in that kingdome, and of some other eminent Christians* (London, 1662), p. 417.

90. Webster, *Godly Clergy*, p. 82.

91. Webster, *Godly Clergy*, p. 27.

92. Isabel. M. Calder, *Activities of the Puritan faction of the Church of England 1625–1633* (London: SPCK, 1957), xii–xxiv.

93. J. Fielding, 'Ball, Thomas (1590–1659)', *Oxford Dictionary of National Biography*, Oxford University Press, 2004.

94. Richard Sibbes, *The saints cordialls delivered in sundry sermons at Graies-Inne, and in the citie of London. Whereunto is now added, The saints safety in evill times, preached in Cambridge upon speciall occasions* (1637), p. 206, p. 208.

95. Richard Sibbes, *The Brides Longing for her Bride-Groomes second comming. A Sermon preached at the funerall of the right Worshipfull, Sir Thomas Crew, Knight, Sergeant at Law to his Majestie* (Banbury, 1638), pp. 120–1.

96. Anthony Milton, 'Censorship and Religious Orthodoxy in Early Stuart England', *Historical Journal* (1998), pp. 625–51.

97. Cornelius Burgess, *Two sermons preached to the Honorable House of Commons assembled in Parliament at their publique fast, Novem. 17, 1640 by Cornelius Burges ... and Stephen Marshall* (London, 1641), pp. 67, 61.

98. Francis Cornwell, *King Jesus is the beleevers prince, priest, and law-giver, in things appertaining to the conscience* (London, 1645), sig, A3r.

3   Emblematic Marriage at the 1630s Court

1. 'I am black, but comely'(AV). Gilbert Foliat, *Expositio in Canticum Canticorum* (London, 1638), p. 62. NB: verse divisions pre-Reformation begin after what was later designated as verse 2, leaving what is currently verse one of the book – 'The Song of Songs, which is Solomons' 1:1 (AV) – as part of the title. See Richard A. Norris, *The Song of Songs Interpreted by Early Christian and Medieval Commentators*, p. 1, p. 43.

2. Prynne suggested that, like Mary Tudor, Laud suppressed annotated Bibles 'for feare that the Notes in them should over-much instruct the people in the knowledge of the Scriptures', William Prynne, *Canterburies Doome* (London, 1646), p. 181. (mispaginated: actually 183).

3. For Laudian censorship, see Peter McCullough, 'Making Dead Men Speak: Laudianism, Print and the Works of Lancelot Andrewes 1626–1642', *The Historical Journal* no. 41 (1998): Anthony Milton, *Catholic and Reformed: The Roman and Protestant Churches in English Protestant Thought 1600–1640* (Cambridge, Cambridge University Press, 1995), p. 535, p. 71.

4. See Malcom Smuts, 'Religion, European Politics and Henrietta Maria's Circle 1625–41' in *Henrietta Maria; Piety, Politics, Patronage* ed. Erin Griffey (Aldershot, England: Ashgate, 2008), pp. 13–36.

5. Jessica Bell, 'TheThree Marys: The Virgin: Marie de Medicis:and Henrietta Maria', *Henrietta Maria*, pp. 91–2.

6. Malcom Smuts, 'Religion, European Politics and Henrietta Maria's Circle 1625–41', pp. 19–20, p. 23, p. 26.

7. Nicholas Caussin was a leading practitioner of emblem theory among the Jesuits. His comprehensive 1631 work, *De Symbolica Aegyptiorum Sapientia*, began with the tiny Egyptian lexicon of emblems in the ancient work of Horapollo, continued with major Christian iconologies, and finished with the 1626 *Theologia Symbolica* of Sandaeus.

8. Nicholas Caussin, *The holy court in three tomes. written in French by Nicolas Caussin, S.I. Translated into English by Sr. T.H. and dedicated to the Queene of Great Brittaine* (Rouen, 1634), sig. A5r.

9. Danielle Clarke, 'The Iconography of the Blush: Marian Literature of the 1630s' in Kate Chedgzoy, Melanie Hansen and Suzanne Trill (eds.), *Voicing Women: Gender and Sexuality in Early Modern Writing* Keele University Press (Paperback edition Edinburgh University Press, 1998), p. 115.

10. J. E. Secker, 'Henry Hawkins, S. J. 1577–1646: a recusant writer and translator of the early seventeenth century', *Recusant History* 11 (1971–2), p. 239. Veevers, *Images of Love and Religion*, p. 98.

11. Michael Bath gives a list of sources for *Partheneia Sacra*: see *Speaking Pictures: English Emblem Books and Renaissance Culture* (London: Longman, 1994), p. 234.

12. Erica Veevers, *Images of Love and Religion: Queen Henrietta Maria and Court Entertainment* (Cambridge: CUP, 1989), p. 124.
13. Henry Hawkins, *Partheneia Sacra 1633*, ed. Karl Josef Höltgen (Aldershot; Scolar Press, 1993), p. 7.
14. Veevers, *Images of Love and Religion*, p. 92.
15. Veevers, *Images of Love and Religion*, p. 122.
16. Bath, *Speaking Pictures*, p. 237.
17. Veevers, *Images of Love and Religion*, p. 94.
18. Secker, 'Henry Hawkins', p. 248.
19. Bath, *Speaking Pictures*, pp. 247–8.
20. Danielle Clarke, 'The Iconography of the Blush: Marian Literature of the 1630s', p. 117.
21. *Thinking Biblically: Exegetical and Hermeneutical Studies*, André Lacocque and Paul Ricoeur (Chicago: Chicago University Press, 1998), p. 272.
22. Gordon Williams, *Dictionary of Sexual Language and Imagery in Shakespearean and Stuart literature* (New Jersey: Athlone Press, 1997) does not have an entry for 'lily', and given that the rest of a substantial dictionary is filled with terms less familiar to a modern eye as having a sexual referent I think it can be taken for granted that 'lily' retains its associations with chastity in the early modern period.
23. Bath, *Speaking Pictures*, p. 47.
24. Bath, *Speaking Pictures*, p. 45.
25. Bath, *Speaking Pictures*, p. 234.
26. Nicholas Caussin, *De Symbolica Aegyptorum* sig. *8r. 'Emblema licet cum isto aenigmatum genere in ratione symboli conveniat, differt tamen, quod rem sublatis aenigmatum velis purius liquidiusque proponet. Est enim proprie symbolum aliquod ingeniosum, suave, et moratum, ex pictura et lemmate constans, quo aliqua gravior sententia indicari lolet'.
27. George Wither, *A Collection of Emblemes* (London, 1635), sig. A2r.
28. Andrew Willet, *Sacrorum emblematum centuria una* (London, 1592), sig. A3r.
29. Robert Wilcher, *The Writing of Royalism 1628–1660* (Cambridge: CUP, 2001), p. 256.
30. Ian Green, *Print and Protestantism in Early Modern England* (Oxford, 2000), pp. 394–5: Diarmaid McCulloch, *Reformation: Europe's House Divided, 1490–1700* (London: Penguin, 2004), pp. 558–63.
31. J.D.Loach, 'The influence of the Counter-Reformation Defence of Images on the Contemporary Concept of Emblem' in Peter. M. Daly and John Manning, eds, *Aspects of Renaissance and Baroque Symbol Theory 1500–1700* (New York: AMS Press, c1999), p. 155.
32. Francis Quarles, *Emblemes* (London, 1635), sig, A3v.
33. Francis Quarles, *Sions sonets. Sung by Solomon the King, and periphras'd by Fra. Quarles* (London, 1625) sig. A4r.
34. Ernst B. Gilman, *Iconoclasm and Poetry in the English Reformation: Down Went Dagon* (Chicago; University of Chicago Press, 1986), p. 95.
35. Herman Hugo, *Pia Desideria 1624*, ed. and intr. Hester Black (Scolar Press: 1971). Otto Van Veen's *Amorum Emblemata* (1608) was converted in 1615 into *Amoris Divini Emblemati*. Hugo's work is based on this volume.
36. Karl Josef Höltgen, 'Francis Quarles' *Emblemes and Hieroglyphikes*; Some Historical and Critical Perspectives' in Ayers L. Bagley, Edward M. Griffin and Austin J. Mclean (eds) *The Telling Image: Explorations in the Emblem* (New York; AMS, 1996), p. 8.

37. Quarles, *Emblemes*, pp. 125–6.
38. J.D.Loach, 'The influence of the Counter-Reformation Defence of Images on the Contemporary Concept of Emblem', p. 155.
39. Gilman, *Iconoclasm and Poetry*, p. 102.
40. Quarles, *Emblemes*, p. 216.
41. Gilman, *Iconoclasm and Poetry*, p. 101.
42. Gilman, *Iconoclasm and Poetry*, p. 95.
43. Gilman, *Iconoclasm and Poetry*, pp. 103–12.
44. Henry Finch, *An exposition of the Song of Solomon: called Canticles* (London, 1615), sig. A3v–A4r.
45. Höltgen, 'Francies Quarles' *Emblemes and Hieroglyphikes'*, p. 8. Michael Bath wants to see Quarles as a Royalist and 'middle-of-the-road Anglican' (*Speaking Pictures*, p. 200). As the last chapter made clear, it is very difficult to be anything of the sort in the 1630s.
46. Bath, *Speaking Pictures*, p. 33, p. 165.
47. Wilcher, *The Writing of Royalism*, p. 256.
48. I owe this reference to Alice Eardley. Elizabeth Isham clearly bought this volume in 1635, although her sister preferred the verse of Wither: Princeton University Library MS, Robert H. Taylor Collection RTC01 no.62, f.29v.
49. Veevers, *Images of Love and Religion*, p. 124.
50. D. J. Gordon, 'Poet and architect; the intellectual setting of the quarrel between Ben Jonson and Inigo Jones' in D. J. Gordon and Stephen Orgel, eds, *The Renaissance Imagination* (Berkeley; University of California Press, 1975), pp. 79–81.
51. Hawkins, *Partheneia Sacra*, pp. 114–15.
52. Veevers, *Images of Love and Religion*, p. 122.
53. Kevin Sharpe, *Criticism and Compliment* (Cambridge; CUP, 1987), p. 143, p. 287.
54. Wither, *A Collection of Emblemes*, sig. *4r.
55. Gordon, 'Poet and Architect', p. 98.
56. Joanne Altieri, 'Responses to a Waning Mythology in Carew's Poetry', *Studies in English Literature, 1500–1900*, 26, no. 1 (1986 Winter): p. 112.
57. Thomas Carew, *Poems, with a maske* (London, 1651), p. 176.
58. Sharpe, *Criticism and Compliment*, pp. 23–7.
59. Joanne Altieri, 'Carew's Momus: A Caroline Response to Platonic Politics', *Journal of English and Germanic Philology* 88, no. 3 (1989 July): p. 338.
60. The Song of Songs, 1:5.
61. Altieri, 'Carew's Momus', p. 342.
62. Sarah Poynting, 'A Critical Edition of Walter *Montagu's The Shepherd's Paradise*, Acts 1–3', unpublished D Phil thesis, University of Oxford, 1999, pp. 100–101.
63. Sharpe, *Criticism and Compliment*, p. 193.
64. Sharpe, *Criticism and Compliment*, pp. 280–1.
65. Martin Butler, *Theatre and Crisis 1632–1642* (Cambridge: CUP, 1984), p. 28.
66. Sharpe, *Criticism and Compliment*, p. 252.
67. Karen Britland, *Drama at the Courts of Queen Henrietta Maria* (Cambridge: CUP, 2006), p. 171.
68. *A Book of masques: in honour of Allardyce Nicoll*, ed. Terence Spencer (Cambridge: Cambridge University Press, 1980), p. 340. I owe this reference to Sarah Poynting.
69. *CSPD 1639–40*, pp. 301–2.

70. Martin Butler, 'Politics and the Masque: *Salmacida Spolia*', *Literature and the English Civil War*, eds Thomas Healy and Jonathan Sawday (Cambridge: Cambridge University Press, 1990), p. 59.
71. G. E. Bentley, *The Elizabethan and Caroline Stage* (Oxford: Clarendon, 1956), III, pp. 213–14.
72. Wayne H. Phelps, 'The second Night of Davenant's *Salmacida Spolia*', *Notes and Queries* 26 (1979), pp. 512–13.
73. Butler, 'Politics and the Masque', p. 64.
74. Richard McCoy, *The Rites of Knighthood: The Literature and Politics of Elizabethan Chivalry* (Berkeley: University of California Press, 1989), p. 6.
75. Fletcher's plays were performed 14 times at the Caroline court, Shakespeare's 3, between 1621–5: see Karen Britland, *Queen Henrietta Maria's Theatrical Patronage* in Erin Griffey (ed.) *Henrietta Maria; Piety, Politics, Patronage* (Ashgate, 2008), p. 64.
76. John Fletcher, *The Royal Shakespeare Company Production of The Tamer Tamed*, ed. Gordon Macmullan (London; Nick Hern Books, 2003), p. xiii.
77. John Fletcher, 'The Womans prize or The Tamer tamed', in *Comedies and tragedies written by Francis Beaumont and Iohn Fletcher* (London, 1647), p. 123.
78. David Norbrook, 'The Reformation of the Masque' in ed. David Lindley, *The Court Masque* (Manchester: MUP, 1984), p. 102.
79. 'To my Cousin (C.R.) marrying my Lady (A.)', in Thomas Carew, *Poems* (London, 1640), p. 89.
80. Carew, *Poems*, p. 136.
81. Paula Johnson, 'Carew's "A Rapture": The Dynamics of Fantasy' *Studies in English Literature, 1500–1900*, Vol. 16, No. 1, The English Renaissance (Winter, 1976), p. 147. A. F. Allison tantalisingly suggests that Crashaw used Carew's 'The Rapture' for expressions of union in his own devotional poem very reminiscent of the Song of Songs: see 'Some Influences in Crashaw's Poem 'On a Prayer Booke Sent to Mrs. M. R.', *The Review of English Studies*, Vol. 23, No. 89 (Jan. 1947), p. 41.
82. Kevin Sharpe tries to redeem the poem from the accusation that it is 'an incitement to social sexual licence' by arguing that the garden, which is figured as Elyzium, is removed from society and in fact a political as well as a personal paradise where all kinds of ideal conditions prevail. The objection I would raise to this is that sexually-adventurous aristocrats are represented at the start of the poem as being able to enter the garden through the legs of the giant, Honour, whenever they feel like it. Sharpe, *Criticism and Compliment*, pp. 118–19.
83. The issue of whether the death of Charles I is debated in this poem is debated in the introduction to the poem in Nigel Smith, ed., *The Poems of Andrew Marvell* (London; Longman, 2003), pp. 66–7.
84. *The Poems of Andrew Marvell*, pp. 70–1. Karina Williamson in 'Marvell's The Nymph Complaining for the Death of Her Fawn: a Reply', *Modern Philology*, 51 (1954) pp. 268–71, insists on the Song of Songs references.
85. Karina Williamson points out that the choice of the word 'nymph' with its associations of chastity aligns Marvell's heroine with 'the undefiled Bride of Christ': "A Reply", p. 270.
86. See Robin Skelton, 'Rowland Watkins and Andrew Marvell', *Notes and Queries* N. S. 203 (1958), pp. 531–32.
87. Rowland Watkyns, *Flamma Sine Fumo, or Poems without fictions* (1662), p. 105.

88. Alan Rudrum, 'Watkyns, Rowland (*c.* 1614–1664)', *Oxford Dictionary of National Biography*, Oxford University Press, 2004 [http://www.oxforddnb.com/view/article/70939, accessed 16 Mar. 2010]
89. Clarke, 'The Iconography of the Blush', p. 117.
90. Graham Parry makes this point as part of a case for a generally Royalist interpretation of the poem. See 'What is the nymph complaining about?', *Critical Survey* 5 (1993), pp. 244–51.
91. The Song of Songs, 2:16.
92. Richard Lovelace, *Lucasta posthume poems of Richard Lovelace, Esq* (London, 1659).

4   From Annotations to Commentary: New Spectacles on the Song of Songs

1. See Ian Green, *Print and Protestantism in Early Modern England* (Oxford: OUP, 2000), pp. 130, 671.
2. Thomas Wilson, *A Christian dictionarie Opening the signification of the chiefe words dispersed generally through Holy Scriptures of the Old and New Testament, tending to increase Christian knowledge. Whereunto is annexed, a perticular dictionary for the Revelation of S. Iohn. For the Canticles or Song of Salomon. For the Epistle to the Hebrues* (London, 1612), p. 173.
3. Robert Young, ed., *Untying the Text: A Post-Structuralist Reader* (London: Routledge, 1981), p. 58.
4. *Proceedings, principally in The County of Kent in connection with the Parliaments called in 1640, and Especially with The Committee of Religion appointed in that year*, ed. Rev. Lambert B. Larking, Camden Society 80, 1862, p. 80. I am grateful to Jacqueline Eales for directing me to this reference.
5. William Laud, *The Works of the most reverend father in God William Laud* eds. James Bliss and William Scott, VII vols. (Oxford: 1847–60) IV, p. 263.
6. Clement Cotton, *A complete concordance of the Bible of the last translation* (London, 1631), sig. A5v, sig. A6r. Cotton had produced his first concordance, of the New Testament, from the Geneva Bible translation in 1622: in 1627 his concordance to the Old Testament was from the Authorised Version: and the 1631 concordance updated the 1622 volume to the Authorised Version. See Green, *Print and Protestantism*, p. 125.
7. Despite being an inferior production, the King James version had become dominant because of the monopoly owned by the King's Printer, Robert Barker: Norton comments 'in fair competition it would probably have lost, but its supporters had foul means at their disposal'. David Norton, *A History of the Bible as Literature* 2 vols, (CUP, 1993), I, pp. 212–13.
8. William Barlow, *The Summe and Substance of the Conference* (London, 1605), p. 47.
9. Michael Sparke, *Scintilla, or, A light broken into darke warehouses with observations upon the monopolists of seaven severall patents, and two charters* (London, 1641), p. 3.
10. William Laud, *Works* (Oxford, 1834), IV, 262, cited in Norton, *A History of the Bible as Literature*, p. 213.
11. William Prynne, *Canterburies doome, or, The first part of a compleat history of the commitment, charge, tryall, condemnation, execution of William Laud, late Arch-bishop of Canterbury* (London, 1646), p. 181 (mispaginated: actually 183).

12. *The Holy Bible containing the Old Testament and the New: newly translated out of the originall tongues and with the former translations diligently compared and revised by His Majesties speciall commandment, with most profitable annotations upon all the hard places and other things of great importance* (Amsterdam, 1642), p. 516.
13. Edmund Calamy, *An Abridgement of the Life of Mr Richard Baxter* (London, 1702), p. 86.
14. See front cover of Sir John Birkenhead, *The Assembly-man* (London, 1681).
15. Meric Casaubon, John Downame, Daniel Featley, William Gataker, William Gouge, John Ley, Francis Pemberton, John Reading, Edward Reynolds, and Francis Taylor, *Annotations upon all the books of the Old and New Testament*, (London, 1645), sig. B3r.
16. John Calvin, *The Institution of Christian Religion* (London, 1634), I, 6 (p. 17).
17. *Annotations*, sig. B3r-v.
18. *Annotations*, sig. B3v–B4r.
19. *Annotations*, sig. ¶r.
20. Green, *Print and Protestantism*, p. 614.
21. John Diodati, *Pious Annotations*, (London, 1643), sig. b1r.
22. Matthew Poole, *Annotations upon the Holy Bible. wherein the sacred text is inserted, and various readings annex'd, together with parallel scriptures, the more difficult terms in each verse are explained, seeming contradictions reconciled, questions and doubts resolved, and the whole text opened / by the late reverend and learned divine Mr. Matthew Poole*, sig. A4r.
23. The works to be discussed are: Meric Casaubon *et al.*, *Annotations upon all the books of the Old and New Testament* (London, 1645); *The Bible translated according to the Ebrew and Greeke, and conferred with the best translations in divers languages; with most profitable annotations upon all the hard places, and other things of great importance* (London; Robert Barker, 1614); Giovanni Diodati, *Pious Annotations* (London, 1643); Theodore Haak (trans,) *The Dutch annotations upon the whole Bible* (London, 1657). The practice of these commentaries is not to paginate the volume, but to delineate the text merely by Biblical chapter and verse: I have followed this practice.
24. Green, *Print and Protestantism*, p. 120.
25. Anthony à Wood, *Athenae Oxonienses,* ed. P. Bliss, 4 vols (London, 1813–20), III, p. 1085.
26. *Annotations upon all the books of the Old and New Testament* (London, 1645), sig. FFF1iiv.
27. E. Ann Matter, *The Voice of My Beloved: The Song of Songs in Western Mediaeval Christianity* (Philadelphia: University of Pennsylvania Press, 1990), p. 28.
28. John Barton, 'The Canonicity of the Song of Songs' in *Perspectives on the Song of Songs/ Perspektiven der Hoheliedauslegung* ed. Anselm C. Hagedorn (Berlin, Walter de Gruyter: 2005), p. 5.
29. Bible, King James. Canticles (Song of Solomon), from The holy Bible, King James version .Electronic Text Center, University of Virginia Library; http://etext. virginia.edu/toc/modeng/public/KjvCant.html
30. See Stanley Stewart, *The Enclosed Garden: The Tradition and The Image in Seventeenth-Century Poetry* (Madison: University of Wisconsin Press, 1966), pp. 60–2.
31. Theodore de Bèze, *Master Bezaes sermons upon the three chapters of the canticle of canticles wherein are handled the chiefest points of religion controversed and debated betweene us and the adversarie at this day, especially touching the true Iesus Christ and*

the true Church, and the certaine & infallible marks both of the one and of the other, tr. *John Harmar* (Oxford, 1587), p. 56.

32. Princeton University Library MS, Robert H. Taylor Collection RTC01 no. 62, fol. 30v.

33. Rous, *The Mysticall Marriage*, p. 171.

34. Matter, *The Voice of My Beloved*, p. 56.

35. Bible, King James. Canticles (Song of Solomon), from The holy Bible, King James version .Electronic Text Center, University of Virginia Library; http://etext. virginia.edu/toc/modeng/public/KjvCant.html

36. Grotius, Hugo, *Annotata ad Vetus Testamentum* (Paris, 1644), p. 544.

37. Joseph Symonds, *The case and cure of a deserted soule, or, A treatise concerning the nature, kindes, degrees, symptomes, causes, cure of, and mistakes about spirituall desertions* (London, 1639).

38. John Calvin, *The Institution of the Christian Religion* (London, 1561), I, p. 46b.

39. Calvin, *Institution*, II, p. 24b.

40. Gifford, 'The Manner of Sir Philip Sidneyes Death', sig. B6r.

41. George Herbert, *The Works of George Herbert*, ed. F. E. Hutchinson (Oxford: Clarendon Press, 1945), p. 316.

42. Edward Reynolds, *A Treatise of the Passions and Faculties of the Soule of Man* (London, 1640), p. 18.

43. François de Sales, *An Introduction to the Devoute Life* (Douai, 1613), p. 170.

44. Samuel Petto, *The voice of the Spirit. Or, An essay towards a discoverie of the witnessings of the spirit* (London, 1654), p. 97.

45. Thomas Wilson, *A complete Christian dictionary* (London, 1655), p. 1154.

46. Matter, *The Voice of My Beloved*, p. 14.

47. Simon Patrick, *A Friendly Debate between a Conformist and a Non-conformist* (London, 1669), pp. 58–63.

48. Baxter insists on the distinction, which was clearly becoming blurred in the later seventeenth century. Calamy, *An Abridgement of the Life of Mr Richard Baxter*, p. 86.

49. Sir John Birkenhead, *The Assembly-Man; Written in the Year !647* (London 1663), p. 7.

50. *Annotations* (1645), Bodleian Library shelfmark 101 c. 196 (ii), flyleaf. Anthony a Wood, *Athenae Oxoniensis*, ed Philip Bliss (London, 1813), vol. 111, 1083. Wood attributes this opinion to Matthew Poole and those who completed Poole's commentary, but I have not been able to locate it.

51. Patrick, *A Friendly Debate*, p. 215.

52. Henry Ainsworth, *Solomon's Song of Songs in English Metre with Annotations* (London, 1623), sig A2ʳ.

53. Everett Emerson Twayne, *John Cotton* (Boston, 1990), p. 138.

54. Cotton had used the word 'Congregationalist' to differentiate his churches from others using the label 'Independent', such as Baptist congregations. Twayne, *John Cotton*, pp. 48–51.

55. John Cotton, *A brief exposition with practical observations upon the whole book of Canticles never before printed* (London, 1655), sig.A6r.

56. Thomas Brightman, *A commentary on the Canticles or the Song of Salomon wherein the text is analised, the native signification of the words declared, the allegories explained, and the order of the times whereunto they relate observed* (London, 1644), sig. A3r–v.

57. For this lack of closure in the context of spiritual journals see Tom Webster, 'Writing to Redundancy: Approaches to Spiritual Journals and Early Modern Spirituality', *Historical Journal* 39 (1996), p. 55.

58. Nathanael Homes, 'A Commentary Literal and Historical, or Mystical and Spiritual, on the whole book of Canticles' in *The works of Dr. Nathanael Homes* (London, 1652).

59. Nathanael Homes, *A sermon, preached before the Right Honourable, Thomas Foote, Lord Maior, and the right worshipfull the aldermen, sheriffs, and severall companies of the City of London. Upon the generall day of thanksgiving, October the 8. 1650. at Christ-Church, London* (London, 1650).

60. Edmund Hall, *Manus testium movens: or, A Presbyteriall glosse upon many of those obscure prophetick texts in Canticles, Isay, Jeremiah, Ezekiel, Daniel, Habakkuk, Zachary, Matthew, Romans, and the Revelations: which point at the great day of the witnesses rising; Antichrists ruine, and the Jews conversion, neare about this time. Wherein Dr. Homes, with the rest of the independent antichristian time-servers are clearly confuted, and out of their own writings condemned: and against them proved, that the present usurpers in England are that antichristian party who have slain the witnesses, and shall reign but three yeers and an half, which time is almost at an end* (London, 1651).

61. Martin Luther, *Lectures on the Song of Solomon*, tr. Jaroslav Pelican (St Louis: Concordia Publishing, 1959), pp. 192, 196.

62. Joshua Sprigg, *Solace for saints in the saddest times from the consideration of the happy temperature and lovely composure of all times and providences as to Gods glory and their good : held forth in a brief discourse on the first words of the Canticles* (London, 1648): Hanserd Knollys, *An exposition of the first chapter of the Song of Solomon. Wherein the text is analysed, the allegories are explained, and the hidden mysteries are unveiled, according to the proportion of faith. : With spiritual meditations upon every verse* (London, 1656).

63. Thomas Wilson, *A complete Christian dictionary wherein the significations and several acceptations of all the words mentioned in the Holy Scriptures of the Old and New-Testament are fully opened, expressed, explained : also, very many ambiguous speeches, hard and difficult phrases therein contained, are plainly interpreted, cleered, and expounded : with a particular dictionary for the [brace] Canticles, or Song of solomon, Epistle to the Hebrews, Revelation of St. John* (London, 1655), p. 1064.

64. Noam Flinker, *The Song of Songs in English Renaissance Literature: Kisses of Their Mouths* (Cambridge: D.S. Brewer, 2000), pp.124–5, p. 133.

65. Nigel Smith (ed.), *A Collection of Ranter Writings from the 17th century* (London: Junction Books, 1983), p. 181.

66. Luther, *Lectures on the Song of Solomon*, p. 194.

67. Hall, *Manus testium movens*, sig. A2v.

68. Wilson, *Christian Dictionary* (enlarged 6th edition, 1655), sig. a2r.

69. *Annotations* (1645), sigs. B3r–v.

70. Diodati, *Pious Annotations* (1648) sig. A3v.

71. Green, *Print and Protestantism*, p. 118.

72. Grotius, *Annotata ad Vetus Testamentum* (Paris, 1644), p. 544.

73. Matthew Poole, *Synopsis criticorum aliorumque S. Scripturae interpretum*, 6 vols (London, 1669), II, p. 1969.

74. Thomas Beverley, *An exposition of the divinely prophetick Song of Songs which is Solomons* (London, 1687), sigsA2v., A3r, A4v.

75. Simon Patrick, *A Friendly Debate between a Conformist and a Non-conformist* (London, 1669), p. 42.
76. Simon Patrick, *A paraphrase upon the books of Ecclesiastes and the Song of Solomon with arguments to each chapter, and annotations thereupon* (London, 1685), sig. A4r.
77. Norton, *The Bible as Literature*, I, p. 214.
78. The early modern success of this commentary is charted in Green, *Print and Protestantism*, p. 119.
79. Matthew Henry, *An Exposition of the Five Poetical Books of the Old Testament* (London, 1711): Thomas Wright, ed. *A Selection of Latin Stories, from Manuscripts of the Thirteenth and Fourteenth Centuries: A Contribution to the History of Fiction During the Middle Ages* (London, The Percy Society, 1842), p. 203.

5   The Seventeenth-century Woman Writer and the Bride

1. *The Monument of Matrones* ed. Thomas Bentley (London, 1582), sig. B2v.
2. *The Monument of Matrones*, sig. B1r.
3. *The Monument of Matrones*, sig. B4r.
4. *The Monument of Matrones*, sig. A1v.
5. Sharon Achinstein, 'Romance of the Spirit: Female Sexuality and Religious Desire in Early Modern England' ELH 69 (2002), p. 417.
6. *The Monument of Matrones*, sig. B1r.
7. See Sylvia Brown, *Women's Writing in Stuart England* (Thrupp, Gloucestershire: Sutton, 1999) for an annotated edition of three such 'Mother's Legacies'.
8. Wendy Wall, *The Imprint of Gender: Authorship and Publication in the English Renaissance* (Ithaca: Cornell University Press, 1993), pp. 283–96.
9. Diane Purkiss, 'Producing the voice, consuming the body; women prophets of the seventeenth century' in eds Isobel Grundy and Susan Wiseman, *Women, Writing, History 1640–1740* (London: B.T. Batsford, 1992), p. 140. See Richard Lovelace's opinion on the woman poet: 'Now as her self a Poem she doth dresse,/And curls a Line as she would so a tresse;/Powders a Sonnet as she does her hair/Then prostitutes them both to publick Aire.' *Poems* (1657), p. 200. For male reaction to even a sober religious treatise written by a woman, see F.W. van Heertum, *A Critical Edition of Joseph Swetnam's The Arraignment of Lewd, Idle, Froward and Inconstant Women* (Nijmegen: The Cicero Press, 1981), pp. 87–8.
10. I have written elsewhere on the perceived danger in the early seventeenth century of self-indulgence for women in an emotionally difficult situation. See '"A Heart terrifying Sorrow": the deaths of children in women's manuscript writing', in *Representations of Childhood Death* eds. Gillian Avery and Kimberley Reynolds (Basingstoke: Macmillan, 2000), pp. 65–86.
11. Elizabeth Jocelin, *The mothers legacie, to her unborne childe* (London, 1624), sigs. a3r–v.
12. See Elizabeth Clarke, 'The Character of a non-Laudian Country Parson', *RES* (2003), p. 483.
13. Richard L.Greaves, 'Foundation Builders: The Role of Women in Early English Nonconformity': Charmarie Jenkins Blaisdell, 'Women in the Lutheran and Calvinist movements' both in *Triumph Over Silence: Women in Protestant History* ed. Richard L. Greaves (Westport, Connecticut: Greenwood Press, 1985), p. 77, p. 33.

14. Elizabeth Isham, 'Booke of Rememberance', Princeton University Library MS, Robert H. Taylor Collection RTC01 no.62; see fol. 11v where she legitimises her mother's sentiments using those of David: fol. 18r where she talks about her own feelings and compares them to David's: fols 5r–5v where she uses David as an example of expressing emotion in eloquent rhetoric.

15. Achinstein, 'Romance of the Spirit', p. 434.

16. One rare exception to this apparent ignorance of other women's writing is Elizabeth Ashburnham's manuscript treatment of Mary Sidney's *A Discourse of Life and Death* (1592). See Margaret Hannay, 'Elizabeth Ashburnham Richardson's Meditation on the Countess of Pembroke's *Discourse*' in *English Manuscript Studies*, 8 (2000), 114–28. Sylvia Brown argues that Elizabeth Jocelin had read Dorothy Leigh's *The Mother's Blessing* (1616). See Sylvia Brown (ed.) *Women's Writing in Stuart England: the mothers' legacies of Dorothy Leigh, Elizabeth Jocelin and Elizabeth Richardson* (Stroud: Sutton, 1999), p. 98.

17. Ed. Jean Klene, *The Southwell-Sibthorpe Commonplace Book* (MRTS, 1997), p. 72.

18. Jane Stevenson in 'Female Authority and Authorization Strategies in Early Modern Europe' argues that the Bride in the Song of Songs is an important figure for early modern women writers, but she is talking about a European culture of learned Humanist women which did not flourish in mid-seventeenth century England. See *This Double Voice; Gendered Writing in Early Modern England* ed. Danielle Clarke and Elizabeth Clarke (Macmillan, 2000), p. 23.

19. Benjamin Keach, *Troposchemalogia, tropes and figures, or, A treatise of the metaphors, allegories, and express similitudes, &c., contained in the Bible of the Old and New Testament* (London, 1682) sigs. A3r–v.

20. See Theodore de Bèze, *Master Bezaes sermons upon the three chapters of the canticle of canticles* tr. John Harmar (Oxford, 1587), sig. ¶4r.

21. Henry Finch, *An exposition of the Song of Solomon: called Canticles Together with profitable obseruations, collected out of the same* (London, 1615) p. 96.

22. William Gouge, *Of Domesticall Duties* (London, 1622), sig.¶4v.

23. Keith Thomas, 'Women and the Civil War Sects', *Past and Present* 13 (1958) pp. 42–62.

24. Sylvia Brown, 'The Approbation of Elizabeth Jocelin', *English Manuscript Studies* 9 (2000), pp. 137–8.

25. Longfellow, *Women and Religious Writing*, pp. 59–91; Sharon Cadman Seelig, '"To All Vertuous Ladies in Generall": Aemilia Lanyer's Community of Strong Women', in eds Summers, Claude J. and Pebworth, Ted-Larry, *Literary Circles and Cultural Communities in Renaissance England* (Columbia, MO: University of Missouri Press, 2000), pp. 44–58.

26. Susanne Woods, ed., *The Poems of Aemilia Lanyer: Salve Deus Rex Judaeorum* (Oxford: OUP, 1993), p. 107.

27. *The Poems of Aemilia Lanyer*, p. 101.

28. For Anne Southwell, see Victoria Burke, 'Medium and Meaning in the Manuscripts of Anne, Lady Southwell', in G. Justice and N. Tinker (eds), *Women's Writing and the Circulation of Ideas: Manuscript Publication in England, 1550–1800* (Cambridge University Press, 2002), pp. 94–120. Longfellow, *Women and Religious Writing*, pp. 92–121: Erica Longfellow, 'Lady Anne Southwell's Indictment of Adam', Victoria Burke and Jonathan Gibson (eds), *Early Modern Women's Manuscript Writing: Selected Papers of the Trinity-Trent Colloquium*, (Ashgate, 2004). Danielle Clarke, *The Politics of Early Modern Women's Writing* (Harlow: Longman, 2001) pp. 10–11.

29. *The Southwell-Sibthorpe Commonplace Book*, p. 152.

30. *The Southwell-Sibthorpe Commonplace Book*, p. 113.
31. See Elizabeth Clarke, 'Anne Southwell: Coteries and Culture' in *The Intellectual Culture of Puritan Women, 1558–1680*, eds Johanna Harris and Elizabeth Scott-Baumann (Basingstoke Palgrave, 2010), pp. 57–70.
32. See Elizabeth Clarke, 'The legacy of mothers and others; women's theological writing, 1640–1660' in *Religion in Revolutionary England*, eds Christopher Durston and Judith Maltby (Manchester: MUP, 2006), pp. 78–81.
33. Mary Pope, *A Treatise of Magistracy* (London, 1647), sig. C2r.
34. Phyllis Mack, *Visionary Women: Ecstatic Prophecy in Seventeenth-Century England* (Berkeley: University of California Press, 1992) p. 96.
35. Pope, A Treatise of Magistracy, sig. C3r, p. 125.
36. Judging by her last two publications, this included Pope. On 24 January 1649 Mrs. Edwards, the book-binder's widow, published Pope's last rebuke to the Army, based on the text of a previous publication a month before, *Heare, heare, heare, heare, a word or message from heaven*. The title page of the pamphlet shows a supreme faith in the effectiveness of the printed prophetic word: *Read this book imediately, and observe what God would have you doe; and doe it; and so you shall be freed suddainly out of this your bondage, through the power of God*.
37. *A message from God, by a dumb woman to his Highness the Lord Protector. Together with a word of advice to the Commons of England and Wales, for the electing of a Parliament. By Elinor Channel. Published according to her desire, by Arise Evans* (London, 1653). Sue Wiseman suggests he was giving Channel's prophecy a Royalist interpretation: 'Unsilent instruments and the devil's cushions: authority in seventeenth-century women's prophetic discourse' in *New Feminist Discourses: Critical Essays on Theories and Texts*, ed. Isobel Armstrong (London: Routledge, 1992), p. 177.
38. Mary Cary, *The little horns doom & downfall: or A scripture-prophesie of King James, and King Charles, and of this present Parliament, unfolded* (London, 1651).
39. Wiseman, 'Unsilent instruments', p. 184.
40. Hilary Hinds, *God's Englishwomen: Seventeenth-century radical sectarian writing and feminist criticism* (Manchester: MUP, 1996), 21.
41. Mary Pocock, *The Mystery of the Deity in the Humanity* (London, 1649), pp. 1–16.
42. Thodore de Bèze, *Master Bezaes sermons upon the three chapters of the canticle of canticles* tr. *John Harmar* (Oxford, 1587), sigs. ¶4r–¶¶2v, p. 3.
43. See Longfellow, *Women and Religious Writing*, pp. 149–79.
44. Anna Trapnel, *A Legacy for Saints* (London, 1654), p. 3.
45. Wiseman, 'Unsilent Instruments', pp. 187–9.
46. Purkiss, 'Producing the voice, consuming the body', p. 157. Jane Lead, *A Fountain of Gardens* (London, 1696), p. 71.
47. Purkiss, 'Producing the voice, consuming the body', p. 141.
48. This volume is catalogued as 'Poetical addresses or discourses delivered to a gathering of 'Companions' in 1657 and 1658.' James Holstun treats this volume in *Ehud's Dagger: Class Struggle in the English Revolution* (London: Verso, 2000), pp. 298–300.
49. James Holstun identifies these enemies as Thomas Venner on the radical left and John Simpson on the right, in collaboration with Cromwell. *Ehud's Dagger* p. 299.
50. Diane Purkiss notes that both Anna Trapnel and Sarah Wight use food imagery from the Song of Songs: 'Producing the voice, consuming the body', p. 147.

51. Sidney Gottlieb rehearses the various religious positions she has been ascribed in An Collins, *Divine Songs and Meditacions* ed. Sidney Gottlieb, (Tempe Arizona: MRTS, 1996), pp. xvii–xviii. See p. 65 for evidence of my assessment of her politico-religious attitudes.
52. Collins, *Divine Songs and Meditacions*, p. 32.
53. Collins, *Divine Songs and Meditacions*, p. 65.
54. Collins, *Divine Songs and Meditacions*, pp. 55–6.
55. See chapter 2: *The Sermons of John Donne*, X vols, eds George R. Potter and Evelyn M. Simpson (Berkeley; University of California Press, 1957), III, p. 252. *John Cotton, A brief exposition of the whole book of Canticles, or Song of Solomon* (London, 1642), p. 209.
56. Peter Stallybrass, 'Patriarchal Territories: The Body Enclosed' in Margaret W. Ferguson, Maureen Quilligan and Nancy J. Vickers, eds, *Rewriting the Renaissance: The Discourse of Sexual Difference in Early Modern Europe* (Chicago: University of Chicago Press, 1986), pp. 123–42.
57. See Longfellow, *Women and Religious Writing*, pp. 123–48.
58. 'Eliza', *Eliza's Babes;Or, The Virgin's Offering (1652)* ed. Liam Semler (London: Associated University Press, 2001), p. 83.
59. 'Eliza', *Eliza's Babes*, pp. 77–8.
60. Achinstein, 'Romance of the Spirit', p. 417.
61. See Elizabeth Delaval's mid-seventeenth century diary, Bodleian MS Rawl D 78 for an example of women's deployment of romantic language in a secular context: she was an avid reader of romances and employed that discourse in recounting her own love affairs.
62. Thomas Watson, *The saints delight. To which is annexed a treatise of meditation. and Christs Loveliness* (London, 1657); John Owen, *Of Communion with God: The Father, Sonne and Holy Ghost, Each Person Distinctly; or, The Saints' Fellowship with the Father, Sonne and Holy Ghost, Unfolded,* (Oxford, 1657).
63. Tom Webster, 'Writing to Redundancy: Approaches to Spiritual Journals and Early Modern Spirituality' *Historical Journal* 39 (1996), p. 37.
64. Isaac Ambrose, *Media: the middle things, in reference to the first and last things: or, The means, duties, ordinances, both secret, private and publike, for continuance and increase of a godly life, once begun, till we come to Heaven. Wherein are discovered many blessed medium's or duties, in their right method, manner and proceedings; that so a Christian (the spirit of Christ assisting) may walk on in the holy path, which leads from his new birth to everlasting life* (London, 1650), pp. 164–5, p. 170, p. 150.
65. Ibid., p. 39.
66. Edmund Calamy, *The Godly Mans Ark* (1657) which prints his funeral sermon for Elizabeth Moore, and adds 'Mrs. Elizabeth Moores Evidences for Heaven Collected by her self'. Ian Green identifies this as one of the bestsellers of the seventeenth century: *Print and Protestantism in Early Modern England* (Oxford: OUP, 2000), appendix 1.
67. See Samuel Clarke, *A collection of the lives of ten eminent divines famous in their generations for learning, prudence, piety, and painfulness in the work of the ministry : whereunto is added the life of Gustavus Ericson, King of Sueden, who first reformed religion in that kingdome, and of some other eminent Christians* (London, 1662), pp. 433, 513. One of the women he treats is Jane Ratcliffe, and he reprints her 1640 funeral sermon, which contained extracts from her journal. See Peter Lake, 'Feminine Piety and Personal Potency: The "Emancipation" of Mrs. Jane Ratcliffe', *The Seventeenth Century 2* (1987), pp. 143–65.

68. For a more detailed treatment of women's manuscript journals in a political con-
    text see Elizabeth Clarke, 'Beyond Microhistory: the use of women's manuscripts
    in a widening political arena' in ed. James Daybell, *Women and Politics in Early
    Modern England, 1450–1700* (Aldershot: Ashgate, 2004), pp. 211–27.
69. On 7 September 1666 she went to Beadle: see BL MS Add 27, 358, fol. 3r.
70. BL MS Add 27,358, fol.17v.
71. See, for example, BL MS Add 27, 351, fol. 32v, fol. 141r.
72. Centre for Kentish Studies, Maidstone MS U1015 F 27, [p. 60] (MS unpaginated:
    this is my own pagination).
73. Dr. Williams Library MS 24.49 fol. 26v.
74. Julia Palmer, *The 'Centuries' of Julia Palmer*, eds V. Burke and E. Clarke (Nottingham;
    Trent Editions, 2001), p. 217.
75. Palmer, *The Centuries*, p. 254.
76. Green, *Protestantism and Print*, p. 415.
77. Philip Stubbes, *A Christal Glasse for Christian Women* (London, 1592), sig. A4r.
78. Centre for Kentish Studies, Maidstone MS U1015 F 27, [p. 59].
79. Palmer, *The Centuries*, p. 307.
80. Victoria Burke, 'A Note on the Text', *The Centuries of Julia Palmer* p. xxiv.
81. Elizabeth Clarke, 'Introduction', *The Centuries of Julia Palmer* pp. vii–xi.
82. *The Christian Life and Death of Mistris Katherin Brettergh* (London, 1612),
    sig. C3v.
83. Ed. David George Mullan, *Women's Life Writing in Early Modern Scotland: Writing
    the Evangelical Self, c. 1670–1730* (Ashgate, 2003).
84. Ed. David George Mullan, *Women's Life Writing in Early Modern Scotland: Writing
    the Evangelical Self, c. 1670–1730* (Ashgate, 2003) p. 12. National Library of
    Scotland MS Adv. 34.6.22 is a seventeenth-century copy of the memoirs of
    Marion Veitch.
85. Mullan, *Women's Life Writing*, p. 15.
86. Cheshire and Chester Archives, MS D/Basten/8, (Sarah Savage's diary, 1686–87),
    Bodleian MS Eng. misc.e.331 (copy of diary of Sarah Savage, 1714–23). The Henry
    Papers in Dr. Williams Library Add. MSS. 45534–45538 contain copied extracts
    from the journals of Sarah Savage and her sisters. See Crawford, P., 'Katherine and
    Philip Henry and their children: a case study in family ideology'. *Transactions of
    the Historical Study of Lancashire and Cheshire,* 134 (1984), pp. 39–74.
87. Dr. William's Library MS 24.49, fol. 19v.
88. Mullan, *Women's Life Writing*, p. 242 (ftn.). James Durham, *Clavis Cantici: or, an
    exposition of the Song of Solomon* (Edinburgh, 1668), p. 132. John Owen wrote a
    preface to the English edition in 1669.
89. Mullan, *Women's Life Writing*, p. 18.
90. Mentioned in Suzanne Trill, 'Early Modern Women's Writing in the Edinburgh
    Archive, c. 1550–1740: a Preliminary Checklist', *Women and the Feminine in
    Medieval and Early Modern Scottish Writing*, eds Sarah Dunnigan, C. Marie Harker,
    Evelyn Newlyn (Palgrave, 2004), p. 223.
91. Piers Wauchope, 'Mackay, Hugh (*d.* 1692)', *Oxford Dictionary of National Biography*,
    Oxford University Press, Sept 2004; online edn, May 2006 [http://www.oxforddnb.
    com/view/article/17557, accessed 16 Mar. 2010]
92. National Library of Scotland, MS Wodrow Qu. xxvii, fol. 8v. I owe this refer-
    ence to Dr. Victoria Burke, and Dr. Faith Eales has helped me with the research.
    The precise date of this MS is unknown, although it appears to be after the birth

of her first child in 1657, and probably before the murder of her two brothers by Mary Sinclair's husband in 1668.

93. Julia Palmer, *The Centuries of Julia Palmer,* eds. E. Clarke and V. Burke (Nottingham: Trent Editions, 2000) pp. 57, 72.

94. See Elizabeth Clarke, '"A heart terrifying Sorrow": the Deaths of Children in Seventeenth-Century Women's Manuscript Journals' in Gillian Avery and Kimberley Reynolds, eds, *Representations of Childhood Death* (Basingstoke: Macmillan, 2000), p. 154.

95. Mary Rich, *Memoir of Lady Warwick, also her Diary, from 1666–72* (London, 1847), p. 219, quoted in in Ramona Wray, 'Constructing the Past: the Diametric Lives of Mary Rich' in *Betraying Ourselves* eds. Henk Dragstra, Sheila Otway, Helen Wilcox (Basingstoke, Macmillan, 2000), p. 154. For her regret at reading romances in her youth, see Rich, *Diary,* pp. 129, 221, 259.

96. University of Yale, Beineke Library, MS Osborn b 221, pp. 19–20. Elizabeth Turner also imagines God taking away her husband, 'to try if under the losse of my chief outward delight I should not more delight myselfe in the Lord' Centre for Kentish Studies, Maidstone MS U1015 F 27 [p. 44].

97. Achinstein, *Literature and Dissent in the Age of Milton* (Cambridge: CUP, 2003), p. 193.

98. Smith, Jude, *A misticall deuise of the spirituall and godly loue betwene Christ the spouse, and the church or congregation* (London, 1575).

99. Sarah Ross, '"Give me thy hairt and I desyre no more": the Song of Songs, Petrarchism and Elizabeth Melville's puritan poetics' in *The Intellectual Culture of Puritan Women, 1558–1680* edited by Johanna Harris and Elizabeth Scott-Baumann (Palgrave Macmillan, 2010), pp. 96–107.

100. Mullan, *Women's Life Writing in Early Modern Scotland,* pp. 146–7.

101. Elizabeth Isham, 'Booke of Rememberance', fol. 30r.

102. Elizabeth Isham, 'Booke of Rememberance', fols 26r–26v.

103. Rich, *Diary,* p. 262, quoted in Ramona Wray, 'Constructing the Past: the Diametric Lives of Mary Rich' in *Betraying Ourselves* eds. Henk Dragstra, Sheila Otway, Helen Wilcox (Basingstoke: Macmillan, 2000), p. 161.

104. Ramona Wray, 'Constructing the Past: the Diametric Lives of Mary Rich' in *Betraying Ourselves* eds. Henk Dragstra, Sheila Otway, Helen Wilcox (Basingstoke: Macmillan, 2000), p. 162.

105. Mary Ann Schofield, '"Women's Speaking Justified": the Feminine Quaker Voice, 1662–1797', *Tulsa Studies in Women's Literature* 6 (1987) p. 67.

106. Elizabeth Stirredge, *Strength in weakness manifest: in the life, various trials, and Christian testimony of that faithful servant and handmaid of the Lord, Elizabeth Stirredge* (London, 1711), p. 53.

107. Wray, '[Re]Constructing the Past', p. 151. Wray is probably more accurate in assigning Rich's spiritual journal to the genre of the exemplary life, the kind of text that Mary Rich certainly read and found congenial. I have argued elsewhere that the spiritual journal is often an exemplary life in the making: see 'Beyond Microhistory; the use of women's manuscripts in a widening political arena' in ed. James Daybell, *Women and Politics in Early Modern England* (Palgrave, 2004), p. 210.

108. Michael Mascuch, *Origins of the Individualist Self: Autobiography and Self-Identity in England, 1591–1791* (Cambridge: Polity Press, 1997), p. 19. I am grateful to Kate Evans for directing me to this extremely useful volume.

109. Roland Greene, 'Anne Lock's *Meditation:* Invention versus Dilation and the Founding of Puritan Poetics' in eds Amy Boesky and Mary Thomas Crane, *Form and Reform in Renaissance England; Essays in honour of Barbara Kiefer Lewalski* (University of Delaware Press, 2000), p. 158, p. 165.

110. Erica Longfellow has shown the verbal parallels between Isham's manuscript and the 1631 translation of Augustine's Confessions by William Watts; '"Take unto ye words": Elizabeth Isham's "Book of Rememberance" and Puritan Cultural Forms' in *The Intellectual Culture of Puritan Women*, eds Johanna Harris and Elizabeth Scott-Baumann (Basingstoke: Palgrave Macmillan, 2010), pp. 122–34.

111. Northampton Record Office IL 3365 section 26 (1638): 'I began my confessions which was my Chiefest worke for this yere'.

112. Elizabeth Isham, 'Booke of Rememberance', Princeton University Library, Robert H. Taylor Collection RTC 01 no. 62. The quotation is a marginal note on the left side of f. 33v.

113. Elizabeth Isham, 'Booke of Rememberance' fol. 14v where she disagrees with Mr. Dod on his harsh views on playing cards:fol.15r when she considers the general adulation he inspires and disagrees with this.

114. Augustine, *Saint Augustines confessions translated*, tr. William Watts (London, 1631), p. 30 Augustine is wrestling with the idea that godly parents beat him when he was younger in spite of his prayers.

115. Augustine, *Confessions,* pp. 590–8.

116. Augustine, *Confessions,* pp. 159–63: Isham, 'Booke of Rememberance' fols 19r–v, fols. 30r–31r.

117. Mary Rich, *Autobiography of Mary, Countess of Warwick* ed. T. Crofton Croker (London, The Percy Society; 1848), p. vii.

118. Rich, *Autobiography*, p. 14.

119. Rich, *Autobiography*, p. 24.

120. Rich, *Autobiography*, p. 33.

121. Rich, *Autobiography*, p. 34.

122. Humfrey Ellis, *Pseudochristus: or, A true and faithful relation of the grand impostures, horrid blasphemies, abominable practises gross deceits; lately spread abroad and acted in the county of Southampton, by William Frankelin and Mary Gadbury, and their companions. The one most blasphemously professing and asserting himself to be the Christ, the Messiah, the Son of God who dyed and was crucified at Jerusalem for the sins of the people of God. The other as wickedly professing and asserting her self to be the Spouse of Christ, called, the Lady Mary, the Queen, and Bride, and Lambs Wife* (London, 1650), p. 8.

123. *A vindication of Anne Wentworth*, pp. 4–5.

124. Hanserd Knollys, *An exposition of the first chapter of the Song of Solomon* (London, 1656), pp. 24, 16.

125. I owe much of the information on Jane Lead to personal communication from Julie Hirst, who has written a book on her. *Jane Lead: Visionary England in the Seventeenth Century* (Aldershot: Ashgate, 2006).

126. Jane Lead, *A Fountain of Gardens,* (London, 1697), I, 66–71.

127. Bodleian MS Rawl 1262, p. 433.

128. *Calendar of State Papers Domestic 1677–8* (Hereford, 1911), p. 478. Copies of Anne Wentworth's publications were also sent to Arlington.

129. Ibid., p. 279.

130. Jane Lead, *A Fountain of Gardens* (London, 1696), II, p. 520.

131. Personal information from Manfred Brod.

132. Rachel Speght, *A Mouzell for Melastomous* (London, 1617), pp. 16–17.

133. Lancelot Andrewes, *Selected Sermons and Lectures,* ed. Peter McCullough (Oxford: OUP, 2005), p. 100.
134. Augustine, 'Enarrationes in psalmos' 56: 11; *Patrologia Latina* vol. 36 (1861), col. 0668.
135. Lucy Hutchinson, *Order and Disorder,* ed. David Norbrook (Oxford: Blackwell, 2001), p. 47.
136. Eds. Jill Seal Millman and Gillian Wright, *Early Modern Women's Manuscript Poetry* (Manchester: MUP 2005), p. 62.
137. See *Debating Gender in Early Modern England 1500–1700,* eds Christina Malcolmson and Mihoto Suzuki (Basingstoke: Palgrave, 2000).
138. See Achinstein, 'Romance of the Spirit', p. 420.
139. This pamphlet is attached to *The saints testimony finishing through sufferings: or, The proceedings of the court against the servants of Jesus, who were called before them to be tryed at the late assizes (or sessions) held in Banbury in the county of Oxon, the 26 day of the seventh moneth, 1655. Also a relation of Margret Vivers, going to the steeple-house in Banbury, after he assize (or sessions) as aforesaid: and a testimony against false prophets, and false doctrine* (London, 1655).
140. Catherine Belsey, *The Subject of Tragedy: Identity and Difference in Renaissance Drama* (London: Methuen, 1985), p. 219.
141. Judith Kegan Gardiner, 'Margaret Fell Fox and Feminist Literary History: A 'Mother in Israel' calls to the Jews' in *The Emergence of Quaker Writing: Dissenting Literature in Seventeenth-Century England,* eds Thomas N. Corns and David Loewenstein (Portland, Oregon: Frank Cass, 1995), pp. 42–56.
142. Elaine Hobby points out that 'brief defenses of women prophesying often appear in the midst of Quaker women's writings' and warns against a blanket judgement of Quakers, who came from a variety of different backgrounds and congregations. See 'Handmaids of the Lord and Mothers in Israel: Early Vindications of Quaker Women's Prophecy' in *The Emergence of Quaker Writing: Dissenting Literature in Seventeenth-Century England,* eds Thomas N. Corns and David Loewenstein (Portland, Oregon: Frank Cass, 1995), pp. 88–98.
143. The gender equality assumed within the Quaker movement and particularly for Quaker publications is not so marked after 1673 when the Second Morning Meeting was set up to consider whether manuscripts were suitable for publication. Scrutiny of the Minutes of that meeting in Friends House Library suggest that the standard which women's manuscripts had to reach was rather higher than that of men, and a high proportion of women's writing offered to the Meeting was rejected.
144. Stubbes, *A Christal Glasse,* sig. A2r.
145. Mullan, *Women's Life Writing,* p. 13.

6   Politics, Metaphor and the Song of Songs in the 1670s

1. It was the work of R.F. Jones that gave rise to this belief: R.F. Jones, *The Seventeenth Century: Studies in the History of English Thought and Literature form Bacon to Pope* (Stanford, 1965). Originally published 1951.
2. N.H. Keeble, *The Literary Culture of Nonconformity in Later Seventeenth-Century England* (Athens: University of Georgia Press, 1987), p. 249.
3. Brian Vickers, 'The Royal Society and English Prose Style – a Reassessment' in Brian Vickers and Nancy S. Striever, *Rhetoric and the Pursuit of Truth:Language Change in the Seventeenth and Eighteenth Centuries* (William Andrewes Clark Memorial Library, 1985), p. 9.

4. Nicholas van Maltzahn, 'The First Reception of *Paradise Lost*, 1667', *Review of English Studies*, 47 (1996), pp. 479–99.

5. Nancy Armstrong and Leonard Tennenhouse, *The Imaginary Puritan: Literature, Intellectual Labor and the Origins of Personal Life* (Berkeley: University of California Press, 1992).

6. Roger L'Estrange, *The Holy Cheat, proving, from the Undeniable Practices and Positions of the Presbyterians, that the Design of that Party, is to enslave both King and People under the Masque of Religion* (1662), p. 98. This volume was reprinted in 1682, with the admission by L'Estrange that the original book was in fact printed in 1661 – the work was postdated to make it look more of a novelty.

7. I have used the term 'Tory Anglicans' to describe those who were politically engaged against Nonconformists in the Restoration. John Coffey uses the term 'conservative Anglicans'. Obviously not all Anglicans are included in this terminology. Senior churchmen like Stillingfleet and Tillotson had contacts with Dissenters and worked for their political benefit.

8. Vickers and Striever, *Rhetoric and the Pursuit of Truth*, p. 9.

9. Michael Heyd, *'Be Sober and Reasonable': The Critique of Enthusiasm in the Enlightenment* (New York: E.J. Brill, 1995), pp. 144–63.

10. In her extended critique of R. F. Jones, Anne Attracta Coppins exposes the weakness of Joseph Glanville's attempt to prove the benign influence of the Royal Society on preachers in the Church of England: he simply cannot find enough clergymen's names with which to prove his point. Attracta Anne Coppins, 'Religious Enthusiasm from Robert Browne to George Fox: A Study of its meaning and the reaction against it in the seventeenth century', unpublished D. Phil thesis, University of Oxford, 1983, pp. 207–12.

11. Derek Hirst, '"Making all religion ridiculous". Of Culture High and Low: the Polemics of Toleration, 1667–1673', *Renaissance Forum* vol. 1 no. I (March, 1996).

12. Samuel Parker, *A Discourse of Ecclesiastical Polity* (London, 1670), p. 75.

13. John Owen, *Truth and innocence vindicated in a survey of a discourse concerning ecclesiastical polity, and the authority of the civil magistrate over the consciences of subjects in matters of religion* (London, 1669), pp. 18–20.

14. See Roger Pooley, 'Language and Loyalty; Plain Style at the Restoration', *Literature and History* 6 (1980), p. 11.

15. John Owen, *Truth and Innocence Vindicated* (London, 1669), p. 20.

16. Simon Patrick, *A Friendly Dialogue between a Conformist and a Non-Conformist* (London, 1669), p. 42.

17. John Coffey, *Persecution and Toleration in Protestant England 1558–1689* (Longman, 2000), p. 170.

18. Patrick, *Works*, IX (1859), pp., 454, 457.

19. Jones, *The Seventeenth Century*, p. 115.

20. Coppins, 'Religious Enthusiasm from Robert Browne to George Fox', p. 250.

21. See Longfellow, *Women and Religious Writing*, pp. 50–8.

22. Arthur Jackson, *Annotations upon the five books immediately following the historicall part of the Old Testament (commonly called the five doctrinall or poeticall books) to wit, the book of Iob, the Psalms, the Proverbs, Ecclesiastes, and the Song of Solomon* (London, 1658), sig. *4r.

23. Edward Leigh, *Annotations on five poetical books of the Old Testament (viz.) Job, Psalmes, Proverbs, Ecclesiastes, and Canticles* (London, 1657), p. 177.

24. Arthur Jackson, *Annotations upon the five books immediately following the historicall part of the Old Testament (commonly called the five doctrinall or poeticall books) to*

wit, the book of Iob, the Psalms, the Proverbs, Ecclesiastes, and the Song of Solomon (London, 1658), p. 119, p. 123.

25. Thomas Watson's 'Christ's Lovelinesse' was attached to the end of *The saints delight* (London, 1657).

26. See chapter 2.

27. John Owen, *Of communion with God the Father, Sonne, and Holy Ghost, each person distinctly in love, grace, and consolation, or, The saints fellowship with the Father, Sonne, and Holy Ghost* (London, 1657), p. 5.

28. John Owen, *The doctrine of the saints perseverance, explained and confirmed, or, The certain permanency of their 1. acceptation with God & 2. sanctification from God manifested & proved from the 1. eternal principles 2. effectuall causes 3. externall meanes thereof* (London, 1654), pp. 193–5.

29. Simon Patrick, *The Song of Solomon Paraphrased with Annotations* (London, 1700), p. 5, p. 16.

30. Benjamin King, *The Marriage of the Lambe or a Treatise concerning the spirituall espousing of Christ, to a believing Soule, wherein the subject is fully handled in the nature of it, in the effects, priviledgs, symptomes, with the comforst that arise to a beleever from this relation* (London, 1640).

31. Samuel Clarke, *The Lives of Ten Eminent Divines* (1662). Clearly written as a response to hostility to Presbyterianism, this volume went into many editons in the rest of the century.

32. Patrick, *A Friendly Dialogue*, p. 197.

33. John Coffey, *Persecution and Toleration in Protestant England 1558–1689* (Longman, 2000), p. 170.

34. Coffey, *Persecution and Toleration*, p. 178.

35. Patrick, *A Friendly Debate*, p. 197.

36. See Elizabeth R. Clarke, 'Jekyll, John (1611–1690)', *Oxford Dictionary of National Biography*, Oxford University Press, Sept 2004; online edn, Oct. 2008 [http://www.oxforddnb.com/view/article/67136, accessed 14 Mar. 2010]

37. William Sherlock, *A discourse concerning the knowledge of Jesus Christ and our union and communion with him* (London, 1674), p. 115.

38. Robert Ferguson, *The interest of reason in religion with the import & use of scripture-metaphors, and the nature of the union betwixt Christ & believers : (with reflections on several late writings, especially Mr. Sherlocks Discourse concerning the knowledg of Jesus Christ, &c.) modestly enquired into and stated* (London, 1675), pp. 422–3.

39. Other answers to Sherlock were Henry Hickman's *Speculem Sherlockianum* (1674); Samuel Rolle's *Prodromus* (1674); Vincent Alsop's *Anti-sozzo* (1675); Edward Polhill's *An Answer to the Discourse of Mr William Sherlock* (1675); Joseph Glanville joined with Sherlock to attack Ferguson in *An Account of Mr. Ferguson his Common-Place Book in Two Letters* (1675).

40. *The Works of John Dryden II: Poems 1681–4* (Berkeley: University of Califoria Press, 1972) p. 71.

41. See letters to Robert Ferguson from the mothers of two of his pupils in 1674, Lucy Hutchinson and Vere Wilkinson. CSPD 1673–5, p. 231, p. 325.

42. See 'To the Reader' in Ferguson's *A Sober Enquiry into he Nature, Measure, and Principle of Moral Virtue, Its distinction from Gospel-Holiness* (London, 1673).

43. Parker, *Discourse of Ecclesiastical Politie*, p. xx.

44. He points out that many of Sherlock's examples of illicit interpretation of metaphor in Nonconformist discourse are in fact taken directly from Scripture, such as Thomas Watson's interpretation of the significance of the brazen serpent lifted up

before the children of Israel in the wilderness; St Paul, long before Watson, had seen in this incident a type of the crucifixion of Christ. (p. 112).

45. He points out the Eastern context for the composition of Scriptural texts, suggesting that symbolism and typology are deeply embedded in Eastern culture and writing (pp. 318–19). He suggests that the straightforward articulation of the mysteries of the Gospel is inadequate to communicate its Divine truth fully without the use of metaphor (p. 334): likewise, in preaching, 'the things themselves are not capable of being declared in *Logical* and *Metaphysical* terms' (p. 279). However, slightly inconsistently, he rejoices that for every metaphorical expression in the Bible, there is elsewhere a declaration of the same truth 'in proper Words' (p. 353). Likewise, there is a tension between the measures he recommends as good practice for interpreting and using Scripture metaphor (pp. 334–53) and the glee with which he points out that Jesus himself was not always scrupulous in his own literary critical practice of the Old Testament (p. 314).

46. See chapter 4. Simon Patrick, *The Song of Solomon Paraphrased*, p. 24.

47. See particularly chapter 2.

48. Thomas Shepard, *The sincere convert, discovering the paucitie of true beleevers: and the great difficultie of saving conversion. Newly corrected and amended* (London, 1647), p. 197.

49. Robert Ferguson, *The Interest of Reason in Religion* (1675), p. 384.

50. Green, *Print and Protestantism*, p. 646.

51. Edward Pearse, *The Best Match, or, The souls espousal to Christ opened and improved* (London, 1673), sig. A2r. I owe this reference to Mary Deane.

52. Edward Polhill, *An Answer to the Discourse of Mr William Sherlock* (1675) p. 133: Henry Hickman, *Speculem Sherlockianum, or, a looking-Glass in which the Admirers of Mr Sherlock may behold the Man* (1674), pp. 67, 68.

53. Thomas Jacombe, *Several sermons preach'd on the whole eighth chapter of the Epistle to the Romans* (London, 1672), p. 85.

54. George Herbert, *The Works of George Herbert* (Oxford, 1945), p. 316 (Note to Valdesso's 62 Consideration).

55. See Patrick, *A Friendly Debate*, p. 47.

56. Keeble, *The Literary Culture of Nonconformity*, pp. 247–8.

57. Joseph Glanville, *Essay Concerning Preaching* (London, 1677), p. 26.

58. King, *The Marriage of the Lambe*, p. 46.

59. Ferguson, *The Interest of Reason in Religion*, p. 451.

60. John Collinges, *A reasonable account why some pious, nonconforming ministers in England judge it sinful for them to perform their ministerial acts, in publick, solemn prayer by the prescribed forms of others* (London, 1679), sig. A5r, quoted in Michael P. Winship, '"Behold the Bridegroom Cometh": Marital Imagery in Massachusetts Preaching, 1630–1730', Early American Literature 27 (1992), pp. 176–7.

61. Winship, '"Behold the Bridegroom Cometh"', p. 171.

62. William Lamont, 'Alsop, Vincent (*bap.* 1630, *d.* 1703)', *Oxford Dictionary of National Biography*, Oxford University Press, 2004 [http://www.oxforddnb.com/view/article/424, accessed 14 Mar. 2010]

63. William Sherlock, *A defence and continuation of the discourse concerning the knowledge of Jesus Christ, and our union and communion with Him* (London, 1675), p. 169.

64. K.H.D. Haley, *The First Earl of Shaftesbury* (Oxford: Clarendon Press, 1968), p. 670.

65. Haley, *The First Earl of Shaftesbury*, p. 511, 570.

66. Anthony Ashley Cooper, Earl of Shaftesbury, *Two Speeches made in the House of Peers, the one November 20th 1675, the other November 1678, by a Protestant Peer of the Realm of England* (The Hague, 1680). I have not yet been able to ascertain whether the misdating of this speech is significant.

Epilogue: Benjamin Keach Rewriting the Bride

1. Benjamin Keach, *The Travels of True Godliness* (London, 1684), p. 20.
2. Benjamin Keach, *The Travels of True Godliness* (London, 1763), p. 91.
3. Derek Hirst, 'Samuel Parker, Andrew Marvell, and political culture 1667–73'. *In Writing and Political Engagement in Seventeenth-Century England* eds. Derek Hirst and Richard Strier (Cambridge: CUP 1999), p. 145.
4. James Harris' reports are in CSPD 1682, pp. 356–8, 494–6.
5. W. T. Whitley, *A History of British Baptists* (London, 1932), p. 149.
6. Joseph Ivimey, *The Principal Events of the History of the Protestant Dissenters from the Revolution in 1688 until 1760* (London, 1823), III, 595; Andrew Gifford, *A dissertation on the Song of Solomon: with the original text, divided according to the metre; and a poetical version* (London, 1751).
7. Benjamin Keach, *Pedo-baptism disproved being an answer to two printed papers (put forth by some gentlemen called the Athenian Society, who pretend to answer all questions sent to them of what nature soever) called the Athenian Mercury, one put forth November 14, the other November 28, 1691 : in which papers they pretend to answer eight queries about the lawfulness of infant-baptism : likewise divers queries sent to them about the true subjects of baptism, &c.* (London, 1691): *An appendix to the answer unto two Athenian Mercuries concerning pedo-baptism containing twenty seven syllogistical arguments proving infant-baptism a mere humane tradition : the gentlmen called the Athenian Society desiring in the last of the said Mercuries to have syllogism* (London, 1692).
8. John Dunton, *The Life and Errors,* (London, 1818), p. 177.
9. Nigel Smith, *Literature and Revolution in England 1640–1660* (New Haven and London: Yale University Press, 1994) p. 27.
10. Benjamin Keach and Thomas Delaune, *Tropologia, or, A key to open Scripture metaphors*, II vols (London, 1681), I, sig.A3r.
11. Keach, *Tropologia*, II, pp. 97–107.
12. Scheper, 'Reformation Attitudes Towards Allegory and the Song of Songs', p. 559.
13. Clarke, '"The Glorious Lover": Baptist Literature of the 1680s and the Bride of Christ', *Baptist Quarterly* 43, 2010, pp. 452–72.
14. Benjamin Keach, Distressed Sion *RELIEVED, OR, The Garment of Praise for the Spirit of Heaviness. Wherein are Discovered the Grand Causes of the Churches Trouble and Misery under the late Dismal Dispensation. With a Compleat History of, and Lamentation for those Renowned Worthies that fell in England by Popilh Rage and Cruelty, from the Year 1680 to 1688. Together with an Account of the late Admirable and Stupendious Providence which hath wrought such a sudden and Wonderful Deliverance for this Nation, and Gods Sion therein. Humbly Dedicated to their Present Majesties. By Benjamin Keach, Author of a Book called, Sion in Distress, or the Groans of the True Protestant Church* (London, 1689).
15. Walker, *The Excellent Benjamin Keach*, p. 168.
16. Benjamin Keach, *The Glorious Lover*, 3rd ed (1685) A2v.

17. Achinstein, *Literature and Dissent*, p. 198.
18. Keach, *The Glorious Lover*, sig. A3v.
19. Achinstein, *Literature and Dissent*, p. 221.
20. John Coffey charts the massive persecution of Dissenters between 1681 and 1686, when 3,800 Londoners were tried for attending conventicles. John Coffey, *Persecution and Toleration in Protestant England 1558–1689* (London: Longman, 2000), p. 173.
21. Boyd Stanley Schlenther, 'Whitefield, George (1714–1770)', *Oxford Dictionary of National Biography*, Oxford University Press, Sept 2004; online edn, May 2009 [http://www.oxforddnb.com/view/article/29281, accessed 13 March 2010]
22. Simon Patrick, *A paraphrase upon the books of Ecclesiastes and the Song of Solomon* (London, 1700), p. 75.

Bibliography

Primary

Manuscripts

Beineke Library, Yale University, MS Osborn b 221 (Copy of Elizabeth Jekyll's spiritual diary).

Bodleian MS Eng. misc.e.331 (copy of Sarah Savage's diary, 1714–23).

Bodleian MS Rawl D 1262 (Ann Bathurst's Meditations and Visions).

Bodleian MS Rawl D 78 (Elizabeth Delaval's Meditations and Prayers).

British Library Add MS 27,358 (Collections out of Mary Rich's papers).

Centre for Kentish Studies, Maidstone MS U1015 F 27 (Elizabeth Turner's spiritual journal).

Cheshire and Chester Archives, MS D/Basten/8,(Sarah Savage's diary, 1686–87).

Dr. William's Library MS 24.49 (Ollive Cooper's Meditations, prayers, hymns and a diary).

National Library of Scotland MS Adv. 34.6.22 (copy of the memoirs of Marion Veitch).

National Library of Scotland MS Wodrow qu. Xxvii, fols 9r–29v (Poems by Barbara Mackay (c 1657) incl. paraphrase of Song of Songs).

Northampton Record Office IL 3365 (Elizabeth Isham's diary, 1608–54).

Princeton University Library, Robert H. Taylor Collection RTC 01 no. 62 (Elizabeth Isham, 'Booke of Rememberance').

Printed books

'Eliza', *Eliza's Babes; Or, The Virgin's Offering (1652)* ed. Liam Semler (London: Associated University Press, 2001).

Ainsworth, Henry, *Solomon's Song of songs In English metre: with annotations and references to other Scriptures, for the easier understanding of it* (Amsterdam, 1623).

Alsop, Vincent, *Anti-sozzo, sive, Sherlocismus enervatus in vindication of some great truths opposed, and opposition to some great errors maintained by Mr. William Sherlock* (London, 1675).

Andrewes, Bartimaeus, *Certaine verie worthie, godly and profitable sermons, upon the fifth chapter of the Songs of Solomon* (London, 1583).

Andrewes, Lancelot, *Selected Sermons and Lectures,* ed. Peter McCullough (Oxford: OUP, 2005).

Anon, *Poems on affairs of state, from the reign of K. James the First, to this present year 1703. Written by the greatest wits of the age* 2 vols (London, 1703).

Anon, *The Christian Life and Death of Mistris Katherin Brettergh* (London, 1612).

Aylett, Robert, *The brides ornaments viz. five meditations, morall and divine. 1. Knowledge, 2. zeale, 3. temperance, 4. bountie, 5. ioy* (London, 1625).

Aylett, Robert, *The Song of Songs, which was Salomons metaphrased in English heroiks by way of dialogue. With certayne of the brides ornaments, viz. poeticall essayes upon a divine subiect. Whereunto is added a funerall elegie, consecrate to the memorie of that ever honoured Lord, Iohn, late Bishop of London* (London, 1622).

Baldwin, William, *The canticles or balades of Salomon* (London, 1549).

Bale, John, *The image of both Churches after the most wonderfull and heavenly Revelation of sainct Iohn the Evangelist, contayning a very fruitfull exposition or paraphrase upon the same* (London, 1670).

Bale, John, *The Second Part of the Image of Both Churches* (Antwerp, 1545?).

Barlow, William, *The summe and substance of the conference which, it pleased his excellent maiestie to have with the lords bishops, and other of his cleargie, (at which the most of the lordes of the councell were present) in his maiesties privie-chamber, at Hampton Court. Ianuary 14. 1603* (London, 1605).

Barrow, Henry, *A plaine refutation of M. G. Giffardes reprochful booke, intituled a short treatise against the Donatists of England Wherein is discovered the forgery of the whole ministrie, the confusion, false worship, and antichristian disorder of these parish assemblies, called the Church of England. Here also is prefixed a summe of the causes of our separation* (London, 1591).

Barton, William, *Hallelujah. Or certain hymns, composed out of Scripture, to celebrate some special and publick occasions. By W.B. M.A. … Upon occasion of those two glorious and most remarkable appearances of God for them, at Dunbar and Worcester: both upon that memorable day Septemb. 3. 1650. 1651* (London, 1651).

Barton, William, *Psalms and hymns composed and fitted for the present occasion of publick thanks-giving, October 24, 1651* (London, 1651).

Barton, William, *Six centuries of select hymns and spiritual songs collected out of the Holy Bible together with a catechism, the canticles, and a catalogue of vertuous women* (London, 1688).

Barton, William, *The choice and flower of the old Psalms* (London 1645).

Bastwick, John, *The Letany of John Bastwick, Doctor of Phisicke, being now full of devotion, as well in respect of the common calamities of plague and pestilence; as also of his owne patticular miserie : lying at this instant in Limbo Patrum. Set downe in two letters to Mr. Aquila Wykes, keeper of the Gatehouse, his good angell* (London, 1637).

Beverley, Thomas, *An exposition of the divinely prophetick Song of Songs which is Solomons beginning with the reign of David and Solomon, ending in the glorious kingdom of our Lord, adjusted to the expositor's line of time, and illustrating it, and composed into verse* (London, 1687).

Bèze, Théodore de, *Master Bezaes sermons upon the three chapters of the canticle of canticles wherein are handled the chiefest points of religion controversed and debated betweene us and the adversarie at this day, especially touching the true Iesus Christ and the true Church, and the certaine & infallible marks both of the one and of the other* (Oxford, 1587).

Birkenhead, John, *The Assembly-man* (London, 1681).

Brightman, Thomas, *A commentary on the Canticles or the Song of Salomon wherein the text is analised, the native signification of the words declared, the allegories explained, and the order of the times whereunto they relate observed* (London, 1644).

Burgess, Cornelius, and Stephen Marshall, *Two sermons preached to the Honorable House of Commons assembled in Parliament at their publique fast, Novem. 17, 1640* (London, 1641).

Burton, Henry, *For God, and the King. The summe of two sermons preached on the fifth of November last in St. Matthewes Friday-streete. 1636* (Amsterdam, 1636).

Burton, Henry, *A narration of the life of Mr. Henry Burton* (London, 1643).

Byfield, Nicholas, *The Signes or An essay concerning the assurance of Gods love, and mans salvation gathered out of the holy Scriptures* (London, 1614).

Calamy, Edmund (1600–1666), *The Godly Mans Ark* (1657).

Calamy, Edmund (1671–1732), *An Abridgement of the Life of Mr Richard Baxter* (London, 1702).

Calvin, John, *The Institution of Christian Religion Translated into English according to the authours last edition* (London, 1561).

Calvin, John, *The Institution of the Christian Religion Translated into English according to the authours last edition. With sundry tables to finde the principall matters intreated of in this booke. And also the declaration of places of Scripture therein expounded. By Thomas Norton. Whereunto there are newly added in the margine of the booke, notes containing in briefe the substance of the matter handled in each section* (London, 1634).

Carew, Thomas, *Poems* (London, 1640).

Cary, Mary, *The little horns doom & downfall: or A scripture-prophesie of King James, and King Charles, and of this present Parliament, unfolded* (London, 1651).

Casaubon, Meric, Downame, John, Featley, Daniel, Gataker, William, Gouge, William, Ley, John, Pemberton, Francis, Reading, John, Reynolds, Edward, and Francis Taylor, *Annotations upon all the books of the Old and New Testament* (London, 1645).

Casaubon, Meric, Downame, John, Featley, Daniel, Gataker, William, Gouge, William, Ley, John, Reading, John, Reynolds, Edward, and Francis Taylor *Annotations upon all the books of the Old and New Testament this third, above the first and second, edition so enlarged, as they make an entire commentary on the sacred scripture: the like never before published in English* (London, 1657).

Caussin, Nicholas, *De Symbolica Aegyptorum Sapientia, in qua Symbola, Parabola, Historiae, Selecta,* quae *ad omnem Emblematum, Aenigmatum, Hieroglyphicorum cognitionem praestant* (Cologne, 1631).

Caussin, Nicholas, *The holy court in three tomes. written in French by Nicolas Caussin, S.I. Translated into English by Sr. T.H. and dedicated to the Queene of Great Brittaine* (Rouen, 1634).

Channel, Elinor, *A message from God, by a dumb woman to his Highness the Lord Protector. Together with a word of advice to the Commons of England and Wales, for the electing of a Parliament. By Elinor Channel. Published according to her desire, by Arise Evans* (London, 1653).

Clapham, Henoch, *Three partes of Salomon his Song of Songs, expounded* (London, 1603).

Clarke, Samuel, *A collection of the lives of ten eminent divines famous in their generations for learning, prudence, piety, and painfulness in the work of the ministry : whereunto is added the life of Gustavus Ericson, King of Sueden, who first reformed religion in that kingdome, and of some other eminent Christians* (London, 1662).

Clarke, Samuel, *A generall martyrologie containing a collection of all the greatest persecutions which have befallen the church of Christ from the creation to our present times : whereunto are added, The lives of sundry modern divines, famous in their generations for learning and piety, and most of them great sufferers in the cause of Christ* (London, 1651).

Clarke, Samuel, *A martyrologic containing a collection of all the persecutions which have befallen the Church of England since the first plantation of the Gospel to the end of Queen Maries reign* (London, 1652).

Coad, John, *A Memorandum of the Wonderful Providences of God to a poor unworthy Creature, during the time of the duke of Monmouth's Rebellion and to the Revolution in 1688* (London, 1849).

Collins, An, *Divine Songs and Meditacions* ed. Sidney Gottlieb, (Tempe Arizona: MRTS, 1996).

Cornwell, Francis, *King Jesus is the beleevers prince, priest, and law-giver, in things appertaining to the conscience* (London, 1645).

Cotton, Clement, *A complete concordance of the Bible of the last translation* (London 1631).

Cotton, Clement, *The mirror of martyrs in a short view lively expressing the force of their faith, the fervency of their love, the wisedome of their sayings, the patience of their suffrings, etc. : with their prayers and preparation for their last farewell : whereunto is added two godly letters written by M. Bradford, full of sweet consolation for such as are afflicted in conscience* (London, 1613).

Cotton, John, *A brief exposition of the whole book of Canticles, or Song of Solomon lively describing the estate of the church in all the ages thereof, both Jewish and Christian, to this day* (London, 1642).

Cotton, John, *A conference Mr. John Cotton held at Boston with the elders of New-England 1. concerning gracious conditions in the soule before faith, 2. evidencing against stinted forms of prayer and praise: together with the difference between the Christian and antichristian church* (London, 1646).

Cotton, John, *A practical commentary, or, An exposition with observations, reasons, and uses upon the First epistle generall of John* (London, 1656).

Coverdale, Miles, *Goostly psalmes and spirituall songes drawen out of the holy Scripture, for the comforte and consolacyon of soch as love to reioyse in God and his Worde* (London, 1535).

Crosby, Thomas, *The history of the English Baptists, from the Reformation to the beginning of the reign of George I*, 4 vols (London, 1738–40).

de Bèze, Théodore, *Master Bezaes sermons upon the three chapters of the canticle of canticles wherein are handled the chiefest points of religion controversed and debated betweene us and the adversarie at this day, especially touching the true Iesus Christ and the true Church, and the certaine & infallible marks both of the one and of the other* tr, John Harmar (Oxford, 1587).

Diodati, Giovanni, *Pious and learned annotations upon the Holy Bible also a methodicall analysis upon severall book of the Old and New Testament, setting down the chiefe heads contain'd therein : a worke not before this extant in English* (London, 1648).

Diodati, Giovanni, *Pious annotations upon the Holy Bible expounding the difficult places thereof learnedly, and plainly: with other things of great importance. By the reverend, learned and godly divine, Mr. Iohn Diodati, minister of the gospell; and now living in Geneva. It is ordered this 11. of Ianuury, 1642, by the committee of the House of Commons in Parliament, concerning printing, that this exposition of the book of the Old and new Testament, be printed by Nicholas Fussel, stationer* (London, 1643).

Donne, John, *The divine poems*, ed. Helen Gardner (Oxford: Clarendon Press, 2000).

Donne, John, *The Sermons of John Donne*, eds. George Potter and Evelyn Simpson, X vols. (Berkeley: University of California Press, 1953–62).

Downame, John, *Lectures upon the foure first chapters of the prophecie of Hosea Wherein the text is expounded and cleered, and such profitable instructions observed, and applied, as naturally arise out of this holie Scripture, and re fit for these times* (London, 1608).

Drayton, Michael, *A Heavenly Harmonie of Spirituall Songes, and holy Himnes, of godly Men, Patriarkes, and Prophets* (London. 1610).

Drayton, Michael, *The Harmonie of the Church Containing, the Spirituall Songes and holy Hymnes, of godly men, Patriarkes and Prophetes: all, sweetly sounding, to the praise and glory of the highest* (London, 1591).

Dryden, John, *The Works of John Dryden II: Poems 1681–4* (Berkeley: University of Califoria Press, 1972).

Durham, James, *Clavis cantici, or, An exposition of the Song of Solomon* (Edinburgh, 1668).

Ellis, Humfrey, *Pseudochristus: or, A true and faithful relation of the grand impostures, horrid blasphemies, abominable practises gross deceits; lately spread abroad and acted in the county of Southampton, by William Frankelin and Mary Gadbury, and their companions. The one most blasphemously professing and asserting himself to be the Christ, the Messiah, the Son of God who dyed and was crucified at Jerusalem for the sins of the people of God. The other as wickedly professing and asserting her self to be the Spouse of Christ, called, the Lady Mary, the Queen, and Bride, and Lambs Wife* (London, 1650).

Fenner, Dudley, *The Song of Songs that is, the most excellent song which was Solomons, translated out of the Hebrue into Englishe meeter* (Middleburgh, 1587).

Ferguson, Robert, *The interest of reason in religion with the import & use of scripture-metaphors, and the nature of the union betwixt Christ & believers : (with reflections on several late writings, especially Mr. Sherlocks Discourse concerning the knowledg of Jesus Christ, &c.) modestly enquired into and stated* (London, 1675).

Finch, Henry, *An exposition of the Song of Solomon: called Canticles* (London, 1615).

Fletcher, John, 'The Womans prize or The Tamer tamed', in *Comedies and tragedies written by Francis Beaumont and Iohn Fletcher* (London, 1647).

Fletcher, John, *The Royal Shakespeare Company Production of The Tamer Tamed*, ed. Gordon Macmullan (London; Nick Hern Books, 2003).

Foliat, Gilbert, *Expositio in Canticum Canticorum* (London, 1638).

Foxe, John, *Christus triumphans comoedia apocalyptica autore Joanne Foxo ; edita est olim Basileae, anno 1556 ; Nunc denuo edita*, ed. T.C. (London, 1672).

Gataker, Thomas, *The ioy of the iust with the signes of such. A discourse tending to the comfort of the deiected and afflicted; and to the triall of sinceritie* (London, 1623).

Gearing, William, *The love-sick spouse, or, The substance of four sermons preached on Canticles 2.5.* (London,1665).

Geddes, William, *The Saints Recreation, Third Part, Upon the Estate of Grace* (Edinburgh, 1683).

Gifford, George, *A short treatise against the Donatists of England, whome we call Brownists* (London, 1590).

Gifford, George, *Fifteene sermons, vpon the Song of Salomon* (London, 1598).

Glanville, Joseph, *An Account of Mr. Ferguson his Common-Place Book in Two Letters* (London, 1675).

Gosse, Edmund, *The Life and Letters of John Donne*, 2 vols (London: Heinemann, 1899).

Gouge, William, *Of Domesticall Duties* (London, 1622).

Grantham, Thomas, *Christianismus primitivus, or, The ancient Christian religion, in its nature, certainty, excellency, and beauty, (internal and external) particularly considered, asserted, and vindicated from the many abuses which have invaded that sacred profession, by humane innovation, or pretended revelation* (London, 1678).

Greville, Fulke, *The life of the renowned Sr Philip Sidney. with the true interest of England as it then stood in relation to all forrain princes: and particularly for suppressing the power of Spain stated by him. His principall actions, counsels, designes, and death. Together with a short account of the maximes and policies used by Queen Elizabeth in her government.* (London, 1651).

Grotius, Hugo, *Annotata ad Vetus Testamentum* (Paris, 1644).

Haak, Theodore, *The Dutch annotations upon the whole Bible* (London, 1657).

Hall, Edmund, *Manus testium movens: or, A Presbyteriall glosse upon many of those obscure prophetick texts in Canticles, Isay, Jeremiah, Ezekiel, Daniel, Habakkuk, Zachary, Matthew, Romans, and the Revelations: which point at the great day of the witnesses rising; Antichrists ruine, and the Jews conversion, neare about this time. Wherein Dr. Homes, with the rest of the independent antichristian time-servers are clearly confuted, and out of their own writings condemned: and against them proved, that the present usurpers in England are that antichristian party who have slain the witnesses, and shall reign but three yeers and an half, which time is almost at an end* (London, 1651).

Hall, Joseph, *Contemplations, the sixth volume* (London, 1622).

Hall, Joseph, *Epistles, the second volume* (London, 1608).

Hall, Joseph, *Salomons diuine arts, of 1. Ethickes, 2. Politickes, 3. Oeconomicks* (London, 1609).

Harsnett, Adam, *A touch-stone of grace Discovering the differences betweene true and coun-terfeit grace: laying downe infallible evidences and markes of true grace: serving for the triall of a mans spirituall estate* (London, 1630).

Hawkins, Henry, *Partheneia Sacra 1633*, ed. Karl Josef Höltgen (Aldershot; Scolar Press, 1993).

Henry, Matthew, *An Exposition of the Five Poetical Books of the Old Testament* (London, 1711).

Herbert, George, *The Works of George Herbert*, ed. F. E. Hutchinson (Oxford: Clarendon Press, 1945).

Hickman, Henry, *Speculem Sherlockianum or, A looking-glass in which the admirers of Mr. Sherlock may behold the man, as to his accuracy, judgement, orthodoxy by an obedient son of the Church of England* (London, 1674).

Hildersham, Arthur, *The canticles, or Song of Solomon paraphrased and explained by divers others texts of Scriptures, very useful , as also the same, together with the two songs of Moses, and the song of Deborah, collected into meeter* (London, 1672).

Homes, Nathanael, *The works of Dr. Nathanael Homes* (London, 1652).

Hoskins, John, *Directions for Speech and Style by John Hoskins* ed. Hoyt H. Hudson (Princeton; Princeton UP, 1935).

Hugo, Herman, *Pia Desideria 1624*, ed. and intr. Hester Black (Scolar Press: 1971).

Jackson, Arthur, *Annotations upon the five books immediately following the historicall part of the Old Testament (commonly called the five doctrinall or poeticall books) to wit, the book of Iob, the Psalms, the Proverbs, Ecclesiastes, and the Song of Solomon* (London, 1658).

Jackson, Thomas, *Londons New-yeeres gift. Or The Uncouching of the foxe* (London, 1609.

Jacombe, Thomas, *Several sermons preach'd on the whole eighth chapter of the Epistle to the Romans* (London, 1672).

James I, *A meditation upon the Lords prayer, written by the Kings Maiestie, for the benefit of all his subiects, especially of such as follow the court* (London, 1619).

Janeway, James, *Heaven Upon Earth: Or, The Best Friend in the Worst of Times* (London, 1667).

Jocelin, Elizabeth, *The mothers legacie, to her unborne childe* (London, 1624).

Jonson, Ben, *The Workes of Benjamin Jonson* (London, 1616).

Keach, Benjamin and Thomas Delaune, *Tropologia, or, A key to open Scripture metaphors*, II vols (London, 1681).

Keach, Benjamin, *Distressed Sion relieved, or, The garment of praise for the spirit of heaviness wherein are discovered the grand causes of the churches trouble and misery under the late dismal dispensation : with a compleat history of, and lamentation for those renowned worthies that fell in England by popish rage and cruelty, from the year 1680 to 1688* (London, 1689).

Keach, Benjamin, *The banquetting-house, or, A feast of fat things* (London,1692).

Keach, Benjamin, *The Glorious Lover*, 3rd edn (1685).

Keach, Benjamin, *The Travels of True Godliness* (London, 1684).

Keach, Benjamin, *War with the devil: or, The young mans conflict with the powers of dark-ness in a dialogue* (London: 1675).

Keach, Elias, *A banquetting-house full of spiritual delights: or, Hymns and spiritual songs on several occasions* (London, 1696).

King, Benjamin, *The Marriage of the Lambe or a Treatise concerning the spirituall espousing of Christ, to a believing Soule, wherein the subject is fully handled in the nature of it, in the effects, priviledgs, symptomes, with the comforst that arise to a beleever from this rela-tion* (London, 1640).

Knollys, Hanserd, *An exposition of the first chapter of the Song of Solomon. Wherein the text is analysed, the allegories are explained, and the hidden mysteries are unveiled, according to the proportion of faith. : With spiritual meditations upon every verse* (London, 1656).

L'Estrange, Roger, *The Holy Cheat, proving, from the Undeniable Practices and Positions of the Presbyterians, that the Design of that Party, is to enslave both King and People under the Masque of Religion* (1662).

Lanyer, Aemilia, *The Poems of Aemilia Lanyer: Salve Deus Rex Judaeorum*, ed. Susanne Woods (Oxford: OUP, 1993).

Larking, Lambert B., ed., *Proceedings, principally in The County of Kent in connection with the Parliaments called in 1640, and Especially with The Committee of Religion appointed in that year* Camden Society 80 (1862).

Laud, William, *The Works of the most reverend father in God William Laud* eds. James Bliss and William Scott, VII vols (Oxford: 1847–60).

Lead, Jane, *A Fountain of Gardens* (London, 1697).

Leigh, Edward, *Annotations on five poetical books of the Old Testament (viz.) Job, Psalmes, Proverbs, Ecclesiastes, and Canticles* (London, 1657).

Ley, John, *A patterne of pietie. Or The religious life and death of that grave and gracious matron, Mrs. Jane Ratcliffe widow and citizen of Chester* (London , 1640).

Loe, William, *Songs of Sion Set for the ioy of gods deere ones, who sitt here by the brookes of this worlds Babel, & weepe when they thinke on Hierusalem which is on highe* (Hamburg, 1620).

Loe, William, *The Mysterie of Mankind, made into a Manual, or The Protestants Portuize reduced into Explication Application, Invocation, tending to Illumination, Sanctification, Devotion* (London, 1619).

Lovelace, Richard, *Lucasta: posthume poems of Richard Lovelace, Esq* (London, 1659).

Luther, Martin, *Lectures on the Song of Solomon*, tr. Jaroslav Pelican (St. Louis: Concordia Publishing, 1959).

Markham, Gervase, *The poem of poems. Or, Sions muse contayning the divine song of King Salomon, devided into eight eclogues* (London, 1596).

Marlow, Isaac, *Prelimited forms of praising God, vocally sung by all the church together, proved to be no gospel ordinance* London 1691).

Marlowe, Isaac, *Some short observations made on a book newly published by Mr. Benjamin Keach intituled, The breach repaired in God's worship, &c. wherein is contained a pretended answer to Isaac Marlow's Brief discourse concerning singing in the publick worship of God* (London, 1691).

Marvell, Andrew, *The Poems of Andrew Marvell* ed. N. Smith (London; Longman, 2003).

Matthews, A. J., ed., *Calamy Revised* (Oxford: Clarendon, 1934).

Meres, Francis, *Palladis tamia Wits treasury being the second part of Wits common wealth* (London, 1598).

Montagu, Richard, *Appello Caesarem A iust appeale from two uniust informers* (London, 1625).

Owen, John, *Of communion with God the Father, Sonne, and Holy Ghost, each person distinctly in love, grace, and consolation, or, The saints fellowship with the Father, Sonne, and Holy Ghost* (London, 1657).

Owen, John, *The doctrine of the saints perseverance explained and confirmed* (London, 1654).

Owen, John, *Truth and Innocence Vindicated* (1671).

Palmer, Julia, *The 'Centuries' of Julia Palmer*, eds. V. Burke and E. Clarke (Nottingham; Trent Editions, 2001).

Parker, Samuel, *A Discourse of Ecclesiastical Polity* (1670).

Patrick, Simon, *A Friendly Debate between a Conformist and a Non-conformist* (London, 1669).

Patrick, Simon, *A paraphrase upon the books of Ecclesiastes and the Song of Solomon with arguments to each chapter, and annotations thereupon* (London, 1685).

Patrick, Simon, *The Song of Solomon Paraphrased with Annotations* (London, 1700).

Peacham, Henry, *The period of mourning Disposed into sixe visions. In memorie of the late prince. Together with nuptiall hymnes, in honour of this happy marriage betweene the great princes, Frederick Count Palatine of the Rhene, and the most excellent, and abound-ant president of all virtue and goodnes Elizabeth onely daughter to our soveraigne, his Maiestie* (London, 1613).

Pearse, Edward, *The Best Match, or, The souls espousal to Christ opened and improved* (London, 1673).

Petto, Samuel, *The voice of the Spirit. Or, An essay towards a discoverie of the witnessings of the spirit* (London, 1654).

Pocock, Mary, *The Mystery of the Deity in the Humanity* (London, 1649).

Polhill, Edward, *An Answer to the Discourse of Mr William Sherlock* (London, 1675).

Poole, Matthew, *Synopsis criticorum aliorumque S. Scripturae interpretum*, 6 vols (London, 1669).

Pope, Mary, *A Treatise of Magistracy* (London, 1647).

Preston, John, *The golden scepter held forth to the humble with the Churches dignitie by her marriage. And the Churches dutie in her carriage. In three treatises. The former delivered in sundry sermons in Cambridge, for the weekely fasts, 1625. The two latter in Lincolnes Inne* (London, 1638).

Prynne, William, *Canterburies doome, or, The first part of a compleat history of the com-mitment, charge, tryall, condemnation, execution of William Laud, late Arch-bishop of Canterbury* (London, 1646).

Quarles, Francis, *Emblemes* (London, 1635).

Quarles, Francis, *Sions sonets. Sung by Solomon the King, and periphras'd by Fra. Quarles* (London,1625).

Rawlinson, John, *Quadriga salutis* (London, 1625).

Reeve, John, *Hymnes and spiritual songs extracted from Scripture* (London, 1682).

Reeve, John, *Spiritual hymns upon Solomons song: or, Love in the right channel* (London, 1684).

Reeve, John, *Spiritual hymns upon Solomons song: or, Love in the right channel* (London, 1684).

Reynolds, Edward, *A Treatise of the Passions and Faculties of the Soule of Man* (London, 1640).

Rogers, Richard and Samuel Ward, *Two Puritan Diaries* Knappen, Marshall M., ed. (Chicago, 1653).

Rogers, Samuel, *The Diary of Samuel Rogers*, eds. Kenneth W. Shipps and Tom Webster (Woodbridge, Suffolk: Boydell Press, 2004).

Rolle, Samuel, *Prodromus, or The character of Mr. Sherlock's book: called A discourse of the knowledg of Jesus Christ In which, the evil spirit, and design, of that book is discovered, and several errours therein, confuted. Written to Mr. Sh. himself* (London, 1674).

Rous, Francis, *Catholick charitie complaining and maintaining, that Rome is uncharitable to sundry eminent parts of the Catholick Church, and especially to Protestants, and is therefore Uncatholick : and so, a Romish book, called Charitie mistaken, though under-taken by a second, is it selfe a mistaking* (London, 1641).

Rous, Francis, *Oile of scorpions The miseries of these times turned into medicines and curing themselves* (London, 1623).

Rous, Francis, *Testis veritatis the doctrine of King Iames our late soveraigne of famous memory, of the Church of England, of the Catholicke Church : plainely shewed to bee one in the points of pradestination, free-will, certaintie of salvation : with a discovery of the grounds naturall, politicke of Arminianisme* (London, 1626).

Rous, Francis, *The diseases of the time, attended by their remedies* (London, 1622).

Rous, Francis, *The mysticall marriage Experimentall discoveries of the heavenly marriage betweene a soule and her saviour* (London, 1631).

Rous, Francis, *Thule, or Vertues historie* (London, 1598).

Rutherford, Samuel, *Letters of the Rev. Samuel Rutherford*, ed. A. A. Bonar (Edinburgh, 1658).

Sales, François de, *An Introduction to the Devoute Life* (Douai, 1613).

Sales, François de, *Select thoughts, one century. Also the breathings of the devout soul* (London, 1648).

Shaftesbury, Anthony Ashley Cooper, Earl of *Two Speeches made in the House of Peers, the one November 20th 1675, the other November 1678, by a Protestant Peer of the Realm of England* (The Hague, 1680).

Shepard, Thomas, *The sincere convert, discovering the paucitie of true beleevers: and the great difficultie of saving conversion. Newly corrected and amended* (London, 1647).

Sherlock, William, *A discourse concerning the knowledge of Jesus Christ and our union and communion with* him (London, 1674).

Sibbes, Richard, *Bowels opened, or, A discovery of the neere and deere love, union and communion betwixt Christ and the Church, and consequently betwixt Him and every beleeving soule Delivered in divers sermons on the fourth fifth and sixt chapters of the Canticles* (London, 1639).

Sibbes, Richard, *The Brides Longing for her Bride-Groomes second comming. A Sermon preached at the funerall of the right Worshipfull, Sir Thomas Crew, Knight, Sergeant at Law to his Majestie* (Banbury, 1638).

Sibbes, Richard, *The saints cordialls delivered in sundry sermons at Graies-Inne, and in the citie of London. Whereunto is now added, The saints safety in evill times, preached in Cambridge upon speciall occasions* (1637).

Singer-Rowe, Elizabeth, *Devout Exercises of the Heart*, ed. Issac Watts (London, 1738).

Southwell, Anne, *The Southwell-Sibthorpe Commonplace Book* ed. Jean Klene (Tempe, Arizona: MRTS, 1997).

Sparke, Michael, *Scintilla, or, A light broken into darke warehouses with observations upon the monopolists of seaven severall patents, and two charters* (London, 1641).

Speght, Rachel, *A Mouzell for Melastomous* (London, 1617).

Sprat, Thomas, *The history of the Royal-Society of London for the improving of natural knowledge* (London, 1667).

Sprigg, Joshua, *Solace for saints in the saddest times from the consideration of the happy temperature and lovely composure of all times and providences as to Gods glory and their good : held forth in a brief discourse on the first words of the Canticles* (London, 1648).

Staunton, Edward, *Phinehas's zeal in execution of judgement. Or, A divine remedy for Englands misery. A sermon preached before the Right Honourable House of Lords in the Abby of Westminster, at their late solemne monethly fast, October 30. 1644* (London, 1645).

Stennett, Joseph, *A version of Solomon's Song of Songs* (London, 1700).

Stennett, Joseph, *An Answer to Mr. David Russen's book, entitul'd Fundamentals without a Foundation, or a True Picture of the Anabaptists* (London, 1704).

Sternhold, Thomas. *Certayne psalmes chosen out of the Psalter of David, and drawn into Englishe metre* (London, 1549).

Stirredge, Elizabeth, *Strength in weakness manifest: in the life, various trials, and Christian testimony of that faithful servant and handmaid of the Lord, Elizabeth Stirredge* (London, 1711).

Stubbes, Philip, *A Christal Glasse for Christian Women* (London, 1592).

Symonds, Joseph, *The case and cure of a deserted soule, or, A treatise concerning the nature, kindes, degrees, symptomes, causes, cure of, and mistakes about spirituall desertions* (London, 1639).

Trapnel, Anna, *A Legacy for Saints* (London, 1654).

Turner, Richard, *The song of Solomon rendred in plain & familiar verse* (London, 1659).

Vincent, Thomas, *Christ the best Husband* (London, 1672).

Vivers, Margaret, *The saints testimony finishing through sufferings: or, The proceedings of the court against the servants of Jesus, who were called before them to be tryed at the late assizes (or sessions) held in Banbury in the county of Oxon, the 26 day of the seventh moneth, 1655. Also a relation of Margret Vivers, going to the steeple-house in Banbury, after the assize (or sessions) as aforesaid: and a testimony against false prophets, and false doctrine* (London, 1655).

Watson, Thomas, *The saints delight* (London, 1657).

Webbe, George, *The bride royall, or The spirituall marriage betweene Christ and his Church Delivered by way of congratulation upon the happy and hopefull marriage betweene the two incomparable princes, the Palsegraue, and the Ladie Elizabeth* (London, 1613).

Wentworth, Anne, *A Vindication of Anne Wentworth* (London, 1677).

Wentworth, Anne, *The revelation of Jesus Christ just as he spake it in verses at several times, and sometimes in prose, unto his faithful servant Anne Wentworth, who suffereth for his name* (London, 1679).

Whitefield, George, *Christ the best husband: or an earnest invitation to young women to come and see Christ. A sermon preached to a society of young women, in Fetter-lane* (London, 1740).

Wild, Robert, *Dr. Wild's humble thanks for His Majesties gracious declaration for liberty of conscience, March 15, 1672* (London, 1672).

Willet, Andrew ? *King Iames his iudgement by way of counsell and advice to all his loving subjects extracted out of his own speeches by Doctor Willet ; concerning politique government in England and Scotland* (London, 1642).

Willet, Andrew, *A treatise of Salomons mariage or, a congratulation for the happie and hopefull mariage betweene the most illustrious and noble Prince Frederike the V. Count Palatine of Rhine, Elector of the Sacred Romane Empire, and Arch-Sewer, and in the vacancie thereof Vicar Generall: Duke of Bavaria, &c. Knight of the most noble order of the Garter. And the most gratious and excellent Princesse, the Ladie Elizabeth, sole daughter unto the High and Mighty Prince Iames, by the grace of God, King of great Britaine, France and Ireland* (London, 1613).

Willet, Andrew, *Sacrorum emblematum centuria una* (London, 1592).

Wilson, Thomas, *A Christian dictionarie Opening the signification of the chiefe words dispersed generally through Holy Scriptures of the Old and New Testament, tending to increase Christian knowledge. Whereunto is annexed, a perticular dictionary for the Revelation of S. Iohn. For the Canticles or Song of Salomon. For the Epistle to the Hebrues* (London, 1612).

Wilson, Thomas, *A complete Christian dictionary* (London, 1655) continued by John Bagwell.

Wilson, Walter, *History and antiquities of Dissenting churches and meeting houses in London, Westminster and Southwark*, IV vols (London 1808).

Winthrop, John, *The Life and Letters of John Winthrop*, ed. Robert C. Winthrop (Boston, 1869).

Wither, George, *A Collection of Emblemes* (London, 1635).

Wither, George, *Britain's remembrancer*, (London, 1628).

Wither, George, *Juvenilia* (London, 1633).

Wither, George, *Speculum speculativum, or, A considering-glasse being an inspection into the present and late sad condition of these nations : with some cautional expressions made thereupon* (London, 1660).

Wither, George, *The hymnes and songs of the Church diuided into two parts. The first part comprehends the canonicall hymnes, and such parcels of Holy Scripture as may properly be sung, with some other ancient songs and creeds. The second part consists of spirituall songs, appropriated to the severall times and occasions observeable in the Church of England* (London, 1623).

Wither, George, *The schollers purgatory discovered in the Stationers common-wealth, and discribed in a discourse apologeticall, aswell for the publike advantage of the Church, the state & whole common-wealth of England, as for the remedy of private iniuryes* (London, 1624).

Wood, Anthony à, *Athenae Oxonienses*, ed. P. Bliss, 4 vols. (London, 1813–20).

Woodford, Samuel, *A paraphrase upon the Canticles* (London, 1679).

Secondary

Achinstein, S. (2002) 'Romance of the Spirit: Female Sexuality and Religious Desire in Early Modern England', *ELH*, 69, 413–38.

Achinstein, S. (2003) *Literature and Dissent in Milton's England* (Cambridge: Cambridge University Press, 2003).

Adams, S. (1973) 'The Protestant Cause: Religious Alliance with the West European Calvinist Communities as a Political Issue in England 1585–1630', unpublished DPhil thesis, University of Oxford.

Adolph, A.R.J.S. (2004) 'Hawkins, Sir Thomas (*bap.* 1575, *d.* 1640?)', *Oxford Dictionary of National Biography*, (Oxford: Oxford University Press).

Aitken, D. (1991–2) '*The Glorious Lover*: An Analogue of *Paradise Lost*?', *Baptist Quarterly*, 34, 132–5.

Altieri, J. (1986) 'Responses to a Waning Mythology in Carew's Poetry', *Studies in English Literature, 1500–1900*, 26, 107–24.

Altieri, J. (1989) 'Carew's Momus: A Caroline Response to Platonic Politics', *Journal of English and Germanic Philology*, 88, 332–43.

Appleby, D.J. (2007) *Black Bartholomew's Day: Preaching, Polemic and Restoration Nonconformity* (Manchester: Manchester University Press).

Armstrong N.and Tennenhouse, L. (1992) *The Imaginary Puritan: Literature, Intellectual Labor and the Origins of Personal Life* (Berkeley: University of California Press).

Bagley, A.L.; Griffin, E.M. and Mclean, A.J. (eds) (1996) *The Telling Image: Explorations in the Emblem* (New York: AMS).

Barroll, L. (2002) *Anna of Denmark, Queen of England* (Philadelphia: University of Pennsylvania Press).

Barton, J. (2005) 'The Canonicity of the Song of Songs' in A.C. Hagedorn (ed.), *Perspectives on the Song of Songs/ Perspektiven der Hoheliedauslegung* (Berlin: Walter de Gruyter), 1–7.

Bath, M. (1994) *Speaking Pictures: English Emblem Books and Renaissance Culture* (London: Longman).

Bellany, A. (2002) *The Politics of Court Scandal in Early Modern England: News Culture and the Overbury Affair, 1603–1660* (Cambridge: Cambridge University Press).

Bellany A. And McRae A, (eds) (2005) 'Early Stuart Libels: An Edition of Poetry from Manuscript Sources', eds. Alastair Bellany and Andrew McRae. *Early Modern Literary Studies* Text Series I. http://purl.oclc.org/emls/texts/libels/.

Bentley, G.E. (1956) *The Elizabethan and Caroline Stage* (Oxford: Clarendon).

Brenner, A. (1993) '"Come Back, Come Back, the Shulammite": A Parody of the *wasf* Genre' in A. Brenner (ed.), *A Feminist Companion to the Song of Songs* (Sheffield: Sheffield Academic Press), 234–57.

Britland, K. (2008) *Queen Henrietta Maria's Theatrical Patronage* in E. Griffey (ed.), *Henrietta Maria; Piety, Politics, Patronage* (Aldershot: Ashgate).

Brown, S. (2000) 'The Approbation of Elizabeth Jocelin', *English Manuscript Studies 1100–1800*, 9.

Burke, V. (2002) 'Medium and Meaning in the Manuscripts of Anne, Lady Southwell' in G.L. Justice and N. Tinker (eds), *Women's Writing and the Circulation of Ideas: Manuscript Publication in England, 1500–1800* (Cambridge: Cambridge University Press), 94–120.

Burrow, C. (2004) 'Rous, Francis (1580/81–1659)', *Oxford Dictionary of National Biography*, Oxford University Press; online edn, Jan 2008 [http://www.oxforddnb.com/view/article/24171, accessed 17 March 2010].

Butler, M. (1990) 'Politics and the Masque: *Salmacida Spolia*' in T. Healy and J. Sawday (eds), *Literature and the English Civil War* (Cambridge: Cambridge University Press), 55–74.

Cambers, A. (2007) 'Reading, the Godly and Self Writing in England, circa 1580–1720', *Journal of British Studies*, 2007, 796–825.

Chedgzoy, K., Hansen, M. and Trill, S. (eds) (1998) *Voicing Women: Gender and Sexuality in Early Modern Writing* (Keele: Keele University Press; pbk edn Edinburgh: Edinburgh University Press).

Clark, E.A. (2005) 'Origen, the Jews, and the Song of Songs: Allegory and Polemic in Christian Antiquity' in A.C. Hagedorn (ed.), *Perspectives on the Song of Songs/ Perspektiven der Hoheliedauslegung* (Berlin: Walter de Gruyter), 274–93.

Clarke, D. (1998) 'The Iconography of the Blush: Marian Literature of the 1630s' in K. Chedgzoy, M. Hansen and S. Trill (eds), *Voicing Women: Gender and Sexuality in Early Modern Writing* (Keele: Keele University Press; paperback edition Edinburgh: Edinburgh University Press), 111–28.

Clarke, D. (2001) *The Politics of Early Modern Women's Writing* (London: Longman).

Clarke, D and Clarke, E. (eds) (2000) *This Double Voice; Gendered Writing in Early Modern England,* eds Danielle Clarke and Elizabeth Clarke (Basingstoke: Macmillan).

Clarke, E (2006) 'Re-reading the Exclusion Crisis', *The Seventeenth Century*, 21, 141–59.

Clarke, E. (2000) '"A heart terrifying Sorrow": the Deaths of Children in Seventeenth-Century Women's Manuscript Journals' in K. Reynolds, ed., *Representations of Childhood Death* (Basingstoke: Macmillan), 65–86.

Clarke, E. (2003) 'Beyond Microhistory: The Use of Women's Manuscripts in a Widening Political Arena' in J. Daybell (ed.), *Women and Politics in Early Modern England, 1450–1700* (Aldershot: Ashgate), 211–27.

Clarke, E. (2003) 'The Character of a non-Laudian Country Parson', *RES*, 2003, 479–96.

Clarke, E. (2006) 'The Legacy of Mothers and Others; Women's Theological Writing, 1640–1660" in *Religion in Revolutionary England,* eds C. Durston and J. Maltby (Manchester: Manchester University Press).

Clarke, E. (2010) 'Anne Southwell: Coteries and Culture' in *The Intellectual Culture of Puritan Women, 1558–1680,* eds Johanna Harris and Elizabeth Scott-Baumann (Basingstoke: Palgrave Macmillan).

Cogswell, T, (1989) *The Blessed Revolution: English Politics and the Coming of War, 1621–4* (Cambridge: Cambridge University Press).

Coffey, J. (2000) *Persecution and Toleration in Protestant England 1558–1689* (London: Longman).

Coppins, A. A. (1983) 'Religious Enthusiasm from Robert Browne to George Fox: A Study of Its Meaning and the Reaction Against It in the Seventeenth Century', unpublished DPhil thesis, University of Oxford.

Corns, T. N, and Loewenstein, D. (eds) (1995) *The Emergence of Quaker Writing: Dissenting Literature in Seventeenth-Century England* (Portland, Oregon: Frank Cass).

Crawford, P. (1984) 'Katherine and Philip Henry and Their Children: A Case Study in Family Ideology', *Transactions of the Historical Study of Lancashire and Cheshire,* 134, 39–74.

Daly, P.M., and Manning, J. (eds) (c.1999) *Aspects of Renaissance and Baroque Symbol Theory 1500–1700* (New York: AMS Press).

Dever, M.E. (2000) *Richard Sibbes: Puritanism and Calvinism in late Elizabethan and early Stuart England* (Macon, Georgia: Mercer University Press).

Dever, M. E. (2004) 'Sibbes , Richard (1577?–1635)', *Oxford Dictionary of National Biography,* Oxford University Press; online edn, May 2007 [http://www.oxforddnb.com/view/article/25498, accessed 12 Mar. 2010].

Dobbs-Allsopp, F. W. (2005) 'Late Linguistic Features in the Song of Songs' in A.C. Hagedorn (ed.), *Perspectives on the Song of Songs/ Perspektiven der Hoheliedauslegung* (Berlin: Walter de Gruyter), 26–77.

Emerson E. H. (1990), *John Cotton* (Twayne: Boston).

Engammare, M. (1993) *Qu'il me baise des baisiers de sa bouche: La Cantique des Cantiques à la Renaissance* (Geneva: Libraire Droz).

Exum, J.C. (2005) *Song of Songs: A Commentary (*Louisville: Westminster John Knox).

Falk, M. (1982) 'The *wasf* in M. Falk (ed.), *Love Lyrics from the Hebrew Bible: A Translation and Literary Study of the Song of Songs* (Sheffield: Almond Press), 80–7.

Ferrell, L.A., and McCullough, P. (eds) (2000) *The English Sermon Revised* (Manchester: Manchester University Press).

Fielding, J. (2004) 'Ball, Thomas (1590–1659)', *Oxford Dictionary of National Biography,* Oxford University Press; online edn, Jan. 2008 [http://www.oxforddnb.com/view/article/1223, accessed 12 Mar. 2010].

Fincham, K. and Tyacke, N. (2007) *Altars Restored: the changing face of English Religious Worship, 1547–c1700* (Oxford: Oxford University Press).

Flinker, N, *The Song of Songs in English Renaissance Literature* (Cambridge: D. S. Brewer, 2000).

Gardiner, J.K. (1995) 'Margaret Fell Fox and Feminist Literary History: A 'Mother in Israel' calls to the Jews' in T.N. Corns and D. Loewenstein (eds), *The Emergence of Quaker Writing: Dissenting Literature in Seventeenth-Century England* (Portland, Oregon: Frank Cass), 42–56.

Gibson, K. (2004) 'Burton, Henry (*bap.* 1578, *d.* 1647/8)', *Oxford Dictionary of National Biography,* Oxford University Press; online edn, Jan. 2008 [http://www.oxforddnb.com/view/article/4129, accessed 12 Mar. 2010].

Gilman, E.B. (1986) *Iconoclasm and Poetry in the English Reformation: Down Went Dagon* (Chicago: University of Chicago Press).

Gimelli Martin, C. (2003)'"Unmeete Contraryes": 'The Reformed Subject and Religious Desire in John Donne's *Anniversaries* and *Holy Sonnets'* in *John Donne and the Protestant Reformation: New Perspectives*, ed. Mary Arshagouni Papazian (Detroit: Wayne State University Press).

Gordon, D. J. (1975) 'Poet and architect; the intellectual setting of the quarrel between Ben Jonson and Inigo Jones' in D. J. Gordon and S. Orgel (eds) *The Renaissance Imagination* (Berkeley; University of California Press) 77–101.

Green, I. (2000) *Print and Protestantism in Early Modern England* (Oxford: Oxford University Press, 2000).

Greene, R. (2000) 'Anne Lock's *Meditation:* Invention versus Dilation and the Founding of Puritan Poetics' in A.Boesky and M.T. Crane (eds), *Form and Reform in Renaissance England; Essays in honour of Barbara Kiefer Lewalski* (Newark: University of Delaware Press), 153–70.

Grundy, I. and Wiseman, S. (eds) (1992) *Women, Writing, History 1640–1740* (London: B.T. Batsford).

Hagedorn, A.C. (ed.) (2005) *Perspectives on the Song of Songs/ Perspektiven der Hoheliedauslegung* (Berlin: Walter de Gruyter).

Haley, K. H. D. (1968) *The First Earl of Shaftesbury* (Oxford: Clarendon Press).

Hannay, M. (2000) 'Elizabeth Ashburnham Richardson's Meditation on the Countess of Pembroke's *Discourse'* in *English Manuscript Studies, 1100–1800*, 8.

Heyd, M. (1995) *'Be Sober and Reasonable': The Critique of Enthusiasm in the Enlightenment* (New York: E.J. Brill).

Hill, C. (1993) *The English Bible and the Seventeenth-Century Revolution* (Harmondsworth: Penguin).

Hirst, D. (1996) ''Making all religion ridiculous'. Of Culture High and Low: the Polemics of Toleration, 1667–1673', *Renaissance Forum* vol. 1, no I.

Hirst, D. (1999) 'Samuel Parker, Andrew Marvell, and political culture 1667–73', in *Writing and Political Engagement in Seventeenth-Century England*, eds D. Hirst and R. Strier (Cambridge: Cambridge University Press).

Hirst, J. (2006) *Jane Lead: Visionary England in the Seventeenth Century* (Aldershot: Ashgate).

Hobby, E. (1995) 'Handmaids of the Lord and Mothers in Israel: Early Vindications of Quaker Women's Prophecy' in T.N. Corns and D. Loewenstein (eds), *The Emergence of Quaker Writing: Dissenting Literature in Seventeenth-Century England*, (Portland, Oregon: Frank Cass), 88–98.

Höltgen, K.J. (1996) '"Francis Quarles" *Emblemes and Hieroglyphikes*; Some Historical and Critical Perspectives' in A. L. Bagley, E. M. Griffin and A. J. Mclean (eds), *The Telling Image: Explorations in the Emblem* (New York; AMS), 1–28.

Johnson, L. (1981)'Elizabeth, Bride and Queen; A Study of Spenser's April Eclogue and the Metaphors of English Protestantism', *Spenser Studies* II, eds P.Cullen and T. Roche (Pittsburgh: University of Pittsburgh Press).

Johnson, J. (1999) *The Theology of John Donne* (Cambridge: D. S. Brewer).

Johnson, P. (1976) 'Carew's "A Rapture": The Dynamics of Fantasy', *Studies in English Literature, 1500–1900*, 16, 145–55.

Johnston, W. (2005) 'The Patience of the Saints, the Apocalypse, and Moderate Nonconformity', *Historical Journal*, 48, 351–8.

Jones, R. F. (1965) *The Seventeenth Century: Studies in the History of English Thought and Literature form Bacon to Pope* (Stanford: Stanford University Press).

Keeble, N. H. (1987) *The Literary Culture of Nonconformity in Later Seventeenth-Century England* (Athens: University of Georgia Press).

Kerrigan, W. (1974) 'The Fearful Accommodations of John Donne', *English Literary Renaissance*, 4, 337–63.

King, J. C. (2005) *Origen on the Song of Songs as the Spirit of Scripture: The Bridegroom's Perfect Marriage-Song* (Oxford; Oxford University Press).

King, J. N. (2004) 'Bale, John (1495–1563)', *Oxford Dictionary of National Biography*, Oxford University Press, Sept 2004; online edn, Oct. 2009. [http://www.oxforddnb.com/view/article/1175, accessed 16 Mar. 2010].

Knappen, M. M. Ed., (1933) *Two Elizabethan Puritan Diaries by Richard Rogers and Samuel Ward* (Chicago: The American Society for Church History).

Krahmer, S.M. (2002) 'The Virile Bride of Bernard of Clairvaux', *Church History*, 69, 304–27.

LaCocque, A and Ricoeur, P, (1998) *Thinking Biblically: Exegetical and Hermeneutical Studies*, tr, David Pellauer (Chicago: University of Chicago Press), pp. 266–8.

Lake, P. (1987) 'Feminine Piety and Personal Potency: the Emancipation of Mrs. Jane Ratcliffe', *The Seventeenth Century*, 2, 143–65.

Lake, P (1995) 'The Moderate and Irenic Case for Religious War: Joseph Hall's *Via Media* in Context' in Susan Amussen and Mark Kishlansky eds, *Political Culture and Cultural Politics in Early Modern England* (Manchester: Manchester University Press).

Lake, P. and Tyacke, N. (1985) "The Ecclesiastical Policy of James I", *Journal of British History*, 24, 169–207.

Lamont, W. (2004) 'Alsop, Vincent (*bap.* 1630, *d.* 1703)', *Oxford Dictionary of National Biography*, Oxford University Press [http://www.oxforddnb.com/view/article/424, accessed 14 Mar. 2010].

Lewalski, B.K. (1979) *Protestant Poetics and the Seventeenth-Century English Religious Lyric* (Princeton, NJ: Princeton University Press).

Loach, J.D. (1999) 'The Influence of the Counter-Reformation Defence of Images on the Contemporary Culture of Emblems' in P.M. Daly and J. Manning (eds), *Aspects of Renaissance and Baroque Symbol Theory 1500–1700* (New York: AMS), 155–200.

Longfellow, E. (2004) 'Lady Anne Southwell's Indictment of Adam' in V. Burke and J. Gibson,(eds), *Early Modern Women's Manuscript Writing: Selected Papers from the Trinity—Trent Colloquium* (Aldershot: Ashgate), 111–33.

Longfellow, E. (2004) *Women and Religious Writing in Early Modern England* (Cambridge: CUP).

Low, A. (1993) *The Reinvention of Love: Poetry, Politics and Culture from Sidney to Milton* (Cambridge: CUP).

McCabe, R. A. (1987) *Joseph Hall: A Study in Satire and Meditation* (Oxford: Clarendon Press).

Malcolmson, C and Suzuki, M. (eds) (2000) *Debating Gender in Early Modern England 1500–1700* (Basingstoke: Palgrave).

Marotti, A. (1986) *John Donne, Coterie Poet* (Madison: University of Wisconsin Press).

Mascuch, M. (1997) *Origins of the Individualist Self: Autobiography and Self-Identity in England, 1591–1791* (Stanford: Stanford University Press).

Masson, M. (1976) 'The Typology of the Female as a Model for the Regenerate: Puritan Preaching, 1690–1750', *Signs*, 2, 304–15.

Matter, E. A. (1990) *The Voice of the Beloved: The Song of Songs in Western Mediaeval Christianity* (Philadelphia: University of Pennsylvania Press).

McCoy, R. (1989) *The Rites of Knighthood: The Literature and Politics of Elizabethan Chivalry* (Berkeley: University of California Press).

McCullough, P. (1986) 'Making Dead Men Speak: Laudianism, Print and the Works of Lancelot Andrewes 1626–1642', *The Historical Journal*, 41, 401–24.

McGiffert, M. (1963) 'God's Controversy with Jacobean England', *The American Historical Review*, 88, 1151–74.

Millman J. S. and Wright, G. (eds) (2005) *Early Modern Women's Manuscript Poetry* (Manchester: MUP).

Milton, A. (1995) *Catholic and Reformed: The Roman and Protestant Churches in English Protestant Thought, 1600–1640* (Cambridge: Cambridge University Press).

Monaghan, F. (1932) 'Benjamin Harrs: Printer, Bookseller and The First American Journalist', *The Colophon*, 12, unfoliated.

Moore, S.D. (2000) 'The Song of Songs in the History of Sexuality', *Church History*, 69:2, 329–48.

Morgan, E. (1966) *The Puritan Family: Religon and Domestic Relations in Seventeenth-Century New England* (Westport, Conn.: Greenwood Press).

Morrissey, M. (2000) 'Elect Nations and Prophetic Preaching: *Types* and *Examples* in the Paul's Cross Jeremiad' in L.A. Ferrell and P. McCullough (eds), *The English Sermon Revised* (Manchester: Manchester University Press), 43–58.

Mullan, D.G. (2003) *Women's Life Writing in Early Modern Scotland: Writing the Evangelical Self, c. 1670–1730* (Aldershot: Ashgate).

Niesel, W. (1962) *Reformed Symbolics: A Comparison of Catholicism, Orthodoxy, and Protestantism* tr. David Lewis (Edinburgh: Oliver and Boyd).

Norbrook, D. (1984) 'The Reformation of the Masque' in D. Lindley (ed.), *The Court Masque* (Manchester: Manchester University Press), 94–109.

Norris, R. A. Jr. (trans. and ed.) (2003) *The Song of Songs Interpreted by Early Christian and Medieval Commentators* (Gand Rapids, Michigan: William B. Eerdmans).

Norton, D. (1993) *A History of the Bible as Literature* (Cambridge: Cambridge University Press).

Parry, G. (1993) 'What Is the Nymph Complaining About?', *Critical Survey*, 5, 244–51.

Phelps, W. H. (1979) 'The Second Night of Davenant's *Salmacida Spolia*', *Notes and Queries*, 26, 512–13.

Phillipson, N. and Skinner, Q. (eds) *Political Discourse in Early Modern Britain*, (Cambridge: Cambridge University Press), 208–31.

Pocock, J.G.A. (1997) 'Enthusiasm: The Antiself of Enlightenment', *HLQ*, 60, 7–28.

Pooley, R. (1980) 'Language and Loyalty; Plain Style at the Restoration', *Literature and History*, 6, 3–18.

Porterfield, A. (1980) *Feminine Spirituality in America* (Philadelphia: Temple University Press).

Poynting, S. (1999) 'A Critical Edition of Walter Montagu's *The Shepherd's Paradise*, Acts 1–3', unpublished DPhil. thesis, University of Oxford.

Purkiss, D. (1992) 'Producing the Voice, Consuming the Body; Women Prophets of the Seventeenth Century' in I. Grundy and S. Wiseman (eds), *Women, Writing, History 1640–1740* (London: B.T.Batsford), 139–58.

Ross, S. (2010) '"Give me thy hairt and I desyre no more": the Song of Songs, Petrarchism and Elizabeth Melville's puritan poetics' in *The Intellectual Culture of Puritan Women, 1558–1680*, eds J. Harris and E.Scott-Baumann (Basingstoke: Palgrave Macmillan).

Rudrum, A. (2004) 'Watkyns, Rowland (c.1614–1664)', *Oxford Dictionary of National Biography* (Oxford: Oxford University Press), [http://www.oxforddnb.com/view/article/70939, accessed 16 Mar. 2010].

Scheper, G.L. (1974) 'Reformation Attitudes Towards Allegory and the Song of Songs', *PMLA*, 89, 551–62.

Schofield, M.A. (1987) '"Women's Speaking Justified": the Feminine Quaker Voice, 1662–1797', *Tulsa Studies in Women's Literature*, 6, 61–77.

Schweitzer, I. (1991) *The Work of Self-Representation: Lyric Poetry in Colonial New England* (Chapel Hill: University of North Carolina Press).

Schlenther, B. S. (2004) 'Whitefield, George (1714–1770)', *Oxford Dictionary of National Biography*(Oxford: OUP); online edn, May 2009 [http://www.oxforddnb.com/view/article/29281, accessed 13 Mar. 2010].

Scott Kastan, D. (2002) 'Little Foxes' in C. Highley and J. N. King,, eds *John Foxe and his World* (Farnham, Surrey: Ashgate).

Secker, J.E. (1971–2) 'Henry Hawkins, S. J. 1577–1646: A Recusant Writer and Translator of the Early Seventeenth Century', *Recusant History*, 11, 237–52.

Seelig,S.C. (2000) '"To All Vertuous Ladies in Generall": Aemilia Lanyer's Community of Strong Women', in eds. Summers, C. J. and Pebworth, T., *Literary Circles and Cultural Communities in Renaissance England* (Columbia, MO: University of Missouri Press).

Shami, J. (2003) *John Donne and Conformity in Crisis in the Late Jacobean Pulpit* (Cambridge: D. W. Brewer).

Sharpe, K. (1987) *Criticism and Compliment: The Politics of Literature in the England of Charles I* (Cambridge; Cambridge University Press).

Silcox, M.V. (c.1999) 'The Device in Puttenham', in P. M. Daly and J. Manning (eds), *Aspects of Renaissance and Baroque Symbol Theory 1500–1700* (New York: AMS Press).

Skelton, R. (1958) 'Rowland Watkins and Andrew Marvell', *Notes and Queries*, N. S. 203, 531–2.

Smith, N. (ed.) (1983) *A Collection of Ranter Writings from the 17*th Century (London: Junction Books).

Smith, N. (1989) *Perfection Proclaimed: Language and Literature in English Radical Religion 1640–1660* (Oxford: Clarendon).

Smith, N., (1994) *Literature and Revolution in England 1640*–1660 (New Haven and London: Yale University Press).

Smith, N., ed., (2003) *The Poems of Andrew Marvell* (London; Longman).

Smuts, M. (2008) 'Religion, European Politics and Henrietta Maria's Circle 1625–41' in E. Griffey (ed, *Henrietta Maria; Piety, Politics, Patronage* (Aldershot, England: Ashgate), 13–36.

Stallybrass, P. (1986) 'Patriarchal Territories: The Body Enclosed', in M.W. Ferguson, M. Quilligan and N. J. Vickers (eds), *Rewriting the Renaissance: The Discourse of Sexual Difference in Early Modern Europe* (Chicago: University of Chicago Press), 123–42.

Stampfer, J. (1970) *John Donne and the Metaphysical Genre* (New York: Funk and Wagnals).

Steggle, M. (2004) 'Aylett, Robert (c.1582–1655)', *Oxford Dictionary of National Biography* (Oxford: OUP) [http://www.oxforddnb.com/view/article/932, accessed 16 Mar. 2010].

Stewart, S. (1966) *The Enclosed Garden: The Tradition and the Image in Seventeenth-Century Poetry* (Madison: University of Wisconsin Press).

Strier, R. (1989) 'John Donne Awry and Squint: The "Holy Sonnets", 1608–1610', *Modern Philology*, 86, 4, 357–84.

Stringer, G. (gen. ed.) (2005) *The Variorum Edition of the Poetry of John Donne* , 7, 1 'The Holy Sonnets' (Bloomington: Indiana University Press).

Strong, R. (1986) *Henry, Prince of Wales, and England's Lost Renaissance* (Thomas and Hudson).

Sutton, C. W. (2004) 'Jackson, Thomas (1570/71–1646)', rev. Margaret Sparks, *Oxford Dictionary of National Biography*, Oxford University Press. online edn, Jan. 2008 [http://www.oxforddnb.com/view/article/14552, accessed 16 Mar. 2010].

Thomas, K. (1958) 'Women and the Civil War Sects', *Past and Present*, 13, 42–62.

Trill, S. (2004) 'Early Modern Women's Writing in the Edinburgh Archive, c. 1550–1740: A Preliminary Checklist', *Women and the Feminine in Medieval and Early Modern Scottish Writing* in S. Dunnigan, C. M. Harker, E. Newlyn, eds (New York: Palgrave Macmillan), 210–26.

Tyacke, N. (1987) *Anti-Calvinists: The Rise of English Arminianism c. 1590–1640* (Oxford: Clarendon Press).

Tyacke, N. (2001) *Aspects of English Protestantism c. 1530–1700* (Manchester: Manchester University Press).

Usher, B. (2004) 'Gifford, George (1547/8–1600)', *Oxford Dictionary of National Biography*, Oxford University PresS [http://www.oxforddnb.com/view/article/10658, accessed 16 Mar. 2010].

van Maltzahn, N. (1996) 'The First Reception of *Paradise Lost*, 1667', *Review o f English Studies*, 477–99.

Veith,G. E. (1985) *Reformation Spirituality: the Religion of George Herbert* (Cranbury, NJ: Associated University Presses).

Veevers, E.(1989) *Images of Love and Religion: Queen Henrietta Maria and Court Entertainment* (Cambridge: CUP).

Vickers, B. (1985) 'The Royal Society and English Prose Style – a Reassessment' in B.Vickers and N. S. Striever eds, *Rhetoric and the Pursuit of Truth: Language Change in the Seventeenth and Eighteenth Centuries* (William Andrewes Clark Memorial Library).

Wall,W. (1993) *The Imprint of Gender: Authorship and Publication in the English Renaissance* (Ithaca: Cornell University Press).

Wallace, D. (1978) 'George Gifford, Puritan Propaganda and Popular Religion in Elizabethan England', *Sixteenth Century Journal*, 9, 1, 27–49.

Wauchope, P. (2004) 'Mackay, Hugh (*d.* 1692)', *Oxford Dictionary of National Biography (Oxford:* OUP); online edn, May 2006 [http://www.oxforddnb.com/view/article/17557, accessed 16 Mar. 2010].

Webster, T. (1996) 'Writing to Redundancy: Approaches to Spiritual Journals and Early Modern Spirituality', *Historical Journal*, 39, 33–56.

Webster, T. (1997) *Godly Clergy in Early Stuart England: The Caroline Puritan Movement c. 1620–43* (Cambridge: Cambridge University Press).

Webster, T. and Shipps, K.W. (eds) (2004) *The Diary of Samuel Rogers* (Woodbridge, Suffolk:Boydell Press).

Wells, R.H. (2000) '"Manhood and chevalrie": *Coriolanus*, Prince Henry, and the Chivalric Revival', *Review of English Studies*, 51, 395–422.

Whedbee, J.W. (1993) 'Paradox and Parody in the Song of Solomon: Towards a Comic Reading of the Most Sublime Song' in A. Brenner (ed.,) *A Feminist Companion to the Song of Songs* (Sheffield: Sheffield Academic Press), 266–278.

Wilcher, R. (2001) *The Writing of Royalism 1628–1660* (Cambridge: Cambridge University Press).

Wilks, T. (1987) 'The Court Culture of Prince Henry and His Circle, 1603–1613', unpublished DPhil thesis, University of Oxford.

Williams, G. (1997) *Dictionary of sexual language and imagery in Shakespearean and Stuart literature* (New Jersey: Athlone Press).

Williamson, K. (1954) 'Marvell's The Nymph Complaining for the Death of Her Fawn: a Reply', *Modern Philology*, 51, 268–71.

Winship, M.P. (1992) "Behold the Bridegroom Cometh": Marital Imagery in Massachusetts Preaching, 1630–1730', *Early American Literature*, 27, 170–84.

Wiseman, S. (1992) 'Unsilent Instruments and the Devil's Cushions: Authority in Seventeenth-century Women's Prophetic Discourse' in I. Armstrong (ed.), *New Feminist Discourses: Critical Essays on Theories and Texts* (London: Routledge), 176–96.

Wiseman, S. (2006) *Constancy and Virtue: Women, Writing and Politics in Seventeenth-Century England* (Oxford: Oxford University Press).

Wray, R. (2000) 'Constructing the Past: the Diametric Lives of Mary Rich' in H. Dragstra, S. Otway, H. Wilcox (eds), *Betraying Ourselves* (Basingstoke: Macmillan), 148–65.

Wray, R. (2004) *Women Writers of the Seventeenth Century* (Tavistock, Devon: Northcote House).

Wright, S. (2004)'Loe, William (*d.* 1645)', *Oxford Dictionary of National Biography* (Oxford: Oxford University Press) [http://www.oxforddnb.com/view/article/16927, accessed 16 Mar. 2010].

Wright, T. (ed.) (1842) *A Selection of Latin Stories, from Manuscripts of the Thirteenth and Fourteenth Centuries: A Contribution to the History of Fiction During the Middle Ages* (London, The Percy Society).

Index